COVID-19 and Islamic Social Finance

It is said that the COVID-19 pandemic has turned back the poverty clock. As such, there is a need to have social mechanisms put in place to provide relief to those who are affected in this regard. Islamic social finance consists of tools and institutions that could be used to alleviate poverty. This book explores the impact of COVID-19 on Islamic finance to better understand the effectiveness of Islamic social finance in helping those who have been affected by poverty overnight due to the halt in all major economic activities in the context of the pandemic.

Since the struggle against poverty in each country will be different, the book attempts to shed light on the experiences of different countries by presenting successful models of Islamic social finance. The book first looks at poverty and COVID-19 before delving into the role of Islamic social financial institutions and how they have risen against COVID-19. The book concludes by examining the impact of COVID-19 on Islamic microfinance.

This book is the first of its kind on the subject of COVID-19, and it intends to bridge the gap in the literature.

M. Kabir Hassan is Professor of Finance in the Department of Economics and Finance in the University of New Orleans, Louisiana. He currently holds three endowed Chairs – Hibernia Professor of Economics and Finance, Hancock Whitney Chair Professor in Business, and Bank One Professor in Business – in the University of New Orleans. Professor Hassan is the winner of the 2016 Islamic Development Bank (IDB) Prize in Islamic Banking and Finance. Professor Hassan received his BA in Economics and Mathematics from Gustavus Adolphus College, Minnesota, and MA in Economics and PhD in Finance from the University of Nebraska–Lincoln, Nebraska.

Aishath Muneeza is Associate Professor at the International Centre for Education in Islamic Finance (INCEIF), Malaysia. She is the first female Deputy Minister of the Ministry of Islamic Affairs and was the Deputy Minister of the Ministry of Finance and Treasury of the Republic of Maldives. She is considered as the founder of Islamic finance in the Maldives. Her contribution to Islamic finance includes structuring of the corporate *sukuks*, sovereign private *sukuk* of the country including the Islamic treasury instruments, designing the first

Islamic microfinance scheme, and establishing and heading the Maldives Hajj Corporation, the Tabung Haji of Maldives.

Adel M. Sarea is Associate Professor of Accounting and Economics at Ahlia University, Kingdom of Bahrain. He obtained a PhD in Economics and *Muamalat* Administration (Accounting) from the Islamic Science University of Malaysia in 2011. He joined Ahlia University in September 2011 and has been Director of the Ahlia MBA program since 2013. Dr Sarea is the winner of the Emerald Literati Award 2014 for Excellence (best paper). In 2015, he was appointed as a recognized PhD supervisor by Brunel University London, UK.

Islamic Business and Finance Series

Series Editor: Ishaq Bhatti

There is an increasing need for western politicians, financiers, bankers, and indeed the western business community in general to have access to high-quality and authoritative texts on Islamic finance and business practices. Drawing on expertise from across the Islamic world, this new series will provide carefully chosen and focused monographs and collections, each authored/edited by an expert in their respective field all over the world.

The series will be pitched at a level to appeal to middle and senior management in both the western and the Islamic business communities. For the manager with a western background, the series will provide detailed and up-to-date briefings on important topics; for the academics, postgraduates, business communities, and managers with western and Islamic backgrounds, the series will provide a guide to best practice in business in Islamic communities around the world, including Muslim minorities in the west and majorities in the rest of the world.

The Evolution of Interest and Debt
From Middle Ages to Modern Times
Edited by Murat Ustaoğlu and Ahmet İncekara

Growth of Islamic Banking in Indonesia
Theory and Practice
Sigit Pramono and Yasushi Suzuki

Islamic Monetary Economics
Finance and Banking in Contemporary Muslim Economies
Edited by Taha Eğri and Zeyneb Hafsa Orhan

COVID-19 and Islamic Social Finance
Edited by M. Kabir Hassan, Aishath Muneeza, and Adel M. Sarea

For more information about this series, please visit: www.routledge.com/Islamic-Business-and-Finance-Series/book-series/ISLAMICFINANCE

COVID-19 and Islamic Social Finance

Edited by
M. Kabir Hassan, Aishath Muneeza,
and Adel M. Sarea

Routledge
Taylor & Francis Group
LONDON AND NEW YORK

First published in English 2021
by Routledge
2 Park Square, Milton Park, Abingdon, Oxon OX14 4RN

and by Routledge
605 Third Avenue, New York, NY 10017

Routledge is an imprint of the Taylor & Francis Group, an informa business

British Library Cataloguing-in-Publication Data
A catalogue record for this book is available from the British Library

Library of Congress Cataloging-in-Publication Data
A catalog record has been requested for this book

ISBN 13: 978-0-367-63994-5 (pbk)
ISBN 13: 978-0-367-63993-8 (hbk)
ISBN 13: 978-1-003-12171-8 (ebk)

DOI: 10.4324/9781003121718

Typeset in Galliard
by Deanta Global Publishing Services, Chennai, India

Contents

List of illustrations x
List of contributors xii
Foreword xx

Introduction 1
M. KABIR HASSAN, AISHATH MUNEEZA, AND ADEL M. SAREA

PART I
Poverty and COVID-19 7

1 **Impact of COVID-19 on Islamic social finance** 9
M. KABIR HASSAN, AISHATH MUNEEZA, AND ADEL M. SAREA

2 **Financial capacity indicators and risk exposure among different income groups: influence of COVID-19** 24
MONSURAT AYOJIMI SALAMI AND ADEL M. SAREA

3 **Financial inclusion and risk exposure among different income groups: the impact of COVID-19 pandemic** 40
MONSURAT AYOJIMI SALAMI, ADEL M. SAREA, AND M. KABIR HASSAN

4 **Iran and COVID-19: an alternative crisis management system based on bottom-up Islamic social finance and faith-based civic engagement** 58
NAJMODDIN YAZDI, ALI MARVI, AND ALI MALEKI

5 **Impact of COVID-19 on sustainable development: a way forward** 76
NUSRAT JAFRIN, MUHAMMAD MEHEDI MASUD, AND ABU NASER MOHAMMAD SAIF

PART II
Innovation in Islamic social finance to fight against COVID-19 89

6 **Islamic FinTech: the digital transformation bringing sustainability to Islamic finance** 91
MOHAMMAD ATIF, M. KABIR HASSAN, MUSTAFA RAZA RABBANI, AND SHAHNAWAZ KHAN

7 **Artificial intelligence and Natural language processing (NLP) based FinTech model of *Zakat* for poverty alleviation and sustainable development for Muslims in India** 104
MUSTAFA RAZA RABBANI, M. KABIR HASSAN, SHAHNAWAZ KHAN, AND MAHMOOD ASAD MOH'D ALI

8 **Online monetary donations to mitigate the impacts of the COVID-19 crisis: evidence from Kuwait** 115
SAEED AWADH BIN-NASHWAN

9 **Adapting the Al Rajhi *waqf* model to mitigate the impact of COVID-19 on the *ummah*: a lesson to Muslim philanthropists** 133
UMAR HABIBU UMAR

10 **Funding the refugee crisis in Turkey: a case for social impact *sukuk*** 148
ZIYAAD MAHOMED, IBRAHIM MUSA UNAL, AND SHAMSHER MOHAMAD

PART III
Impact of COVID-19 on Islamic microfinance 165

11 **COVID-19 pandemic: the Islamic social capital perspective in *Baitul Maal Wat Tamwil* institutions movement in Indonesia** 167
RAHMAWATI AND FITRI RINALDI

12 **Unlocking Islamic social finance to assist micro small medium enterprises in Brunei Darussalam** 185
KHAIRUL HIDAYATULLAH BASIR AND MOHD HAIRUL AZRIN BESAR

13 The role of Islamic microfinance in eradicating the impact of COVID-19 on socio-economic wellbeing in Nigeria **199**
ABDULLATEEF ABDULQADIR MAIKABARA, ROMZIE ROSMAN, AND HABEEBULLAH ZAKARIYAH

14 Islamic social finance during economic uncertainty: special roles of *Ar-Rahnu* **214**
NOR FADILAH BAHARI, MUSTAFA MOHD HANEFAH, AND ZURINA SHAFII

15 Profit-loss sharing principle: the strategic answer of solidarity in Islamic finance **225**
AMIRA KADDOUR, BADRI NARAYANAN GOPALAKRISHNAN, MOHAMED BECHIR BELAID, AND MOHAMMAD NURUNNABI

Index 239

Illustrations

Figures

2.1 Conceptual framework of financial capacity indicators and associated risk across four income groups 27
5.1 Post-COVID-19 pandemic new business model 77
7.1 *Zakat* distribution system 111
10.1 Social impact *sukuk* structure for refugee camp construction 157

Tables

2.1 Descriptive statistics of income groups 28
2.2 Financial capacity indicators across different income groups 29
2.3 Type of risk assessed 31
2.4 Summary of the income groups' vulnerability to different risk 32
2.5 Spearman's correlation for financial capacity indicators 33
2.6 Analysis of variance (ANOVA) result of financial capacity indicators across different income groups 35
2.7 Tukey post hoc test 36
3.1 Descriptive statistics of income groups 43
3.2 Financial inclusion strategy 44
3.3 Summary of financial inclusion strategy and their associated groups 45
3.4 Financial inclusion policy 46
3.5 Access to finance 47
3.6 Specific targeted group for financial inclusion 48
3.7 Type of risk assessed 49
3.8 Test of homogeneity of variance 49
3.9 Pearson's correlation matrix result 51
3.10 T-test result for Financial Inclusion Indicator 52
3.11 Tukey post hoc test 52

7.1 *Zakat* distribution issues and solution 110
8.1 Measurement model assessment 124
8.2 Discriminant validity 125
8.3 Structural model assessment 126
13.1 Demographic distributions 204
13.2 Descriptive statistics (frequency, percentage (%), mean and standard deviation) 207
14.1 *Ar-Rahnu* operators 216
14.2 Pillars of *ar-rahn* 218

Contributors

Abdullateef Abdulqadir Maikabara is an MSc graduate of Islamic banking and finance at the IIUM Institute of Islamic Banking and Finance (IIiBF), International Islamic University Malaysia (IIUM). He obtained his LLB (Hons) in Islamic law from Al-Azhar University in Cairo, Egypt, in 2017. He is a co-founder and teacher at the Islamic Knowledge Foundation. His research interests are in the area of Islamic law, Islamic banking and finance, and Islamic social finance. He has co-authored **Chapter 13**.

Abu Naser Mohammad Saif is serving as Assistant Professor in the Department of Management Information Systems at the University of Dhaka, Bangladesh. Mr Saif has published high-quality research articles in top peer-reviewed journals like *Information Development* (SAGE Publications) and *Cogent Business & Management* (Taylor & Francis). He presented research papers in different international conferences held in Malaysia, Thailand, Sri Lanka, and India. Currently, he is working as a reviewer of a Taylor & Francis journal. His research interests include innovation and entrepreneurship, human resource information systems, sustainable development, technology acceptance models for industry-specific studies, and supply chain management. He has co-authored **Chapter 5**.

Ali Marvi is Director of Governance and Policy Think Tank (GPTT), a unit of the Sharif Policy Research Institute (SPRI). SPRI is affiliated with the Sharif University of Technology (SUT), Iran. He is also Assistant Professor of Economics at Allame Tabataba'i University, Iran. He received his PhD in Economics from Bocconi University, Italy. His main areas of research are Islamic economics, taxation, and international economics. He teaches topics such as international trade, international finance, Islamic economics, contract theory, mechanism design, and industrial organization. He has co-authored **Chapter 4**.

Ali Maleki is Director and Assistant Professor of Science and Technology Policy at Sharif Policy Research Institute, Sharif University of Technology, Iran. He received his PhD in Science and Technology Studies from the University of Edinburgh, UK. He also has been a visiting researcher at Science Policy

Research Unit (SPRU), University of Sussex, Brighton, UK. He has worked on national and sectoral innovation systems and technology policy in resources-based developing countries. He authored several reports and presented articles in international conferences. He teaches topics such as systems of innovation, the economics of innovation, and industrial policy and policy analysis at several universities. He has co-authored **Chapter 4**.

Amira Kaddour is Associate Professor at the Higher School of Sciences and Advanced Technologies, Carthage University, Wisconsin. Since September 2008, she has taught at Tunisian universities on different subjects linked to socio-economic sciences. She received her PhD in Finance from Manouba University, Tunisia; she also has professional certificates in FinTech. Her research interests span behavioural finance, FinTech, and green finance. Her main domain of interest is FinTech and green finance, mainly through an Environmental, Social, and Corporate Governance (ESG) approach. She has contributed to the steering committee of several conferences and projects, focusing on inclusive economy and outlooks of green and digital transition. She has contributed to different projects on the efficient implementation of Sustainable Development Goals and the UN agenda for road safety 2020–2030. She has co-authored **Chapter 15**.

Badri Narayanan Gopalakrishnan is a Senior Economist with the School of Environmental and Forestry Sciences, University of Washington, Seattle. He has also been a consultant to the UN, World Bank, McKinsey, and several governments, etc. His areas of research include economic modelling, international trade, development, agriculture, industry, energy, environment, technology, and labour. He has published over 100 peer-reviewed articles and five books and presented his work in 30 countries across the world. He has co-authored **Chapter 15**.

Fitri Rinaldi is a PhD student in Universitas Pertahanan Indonesia. He is a lecturer in the Professional Education of Accounting. His areas of research interest include taxation, governmental accounting, and accounting for small and medium enterprises. He is involved in government projects on the establishment of the Public Service Agency at the Ministry of Cooperatives and the Ministry of Finance. He has co-authored **Chapter 11**.

Habeebullah Zakariyah is Assistant Professor at the IIUM Institute of Islamic Banking and Finance, International Islamic University Malaysia, specializing in Islamic Law and Transactions, 'Muamalat'. He graduated with an LLB (Hons) in Shariah and Law from Omdurman Islamic University, Sudan. He was awarded an MA of Arts and PhD in Islamic Jurisprudence (Islamic Finance) from the IIUM. His research interests include Islamic finance, Contemporary issues in Islamic Law and Islamic social finance. He has co-authored **Chapter 13**.

Ibrahim Musa Unal is currently a Qatar HBKU Islamic finance PhD student. He has experience in accounting and finance for the banking sector. He completed his MSc degree at the International Centre for Education in Islamic

Finance (INCEIF), Malaysia. Ibrahim specializes in Islamic social finance. He also has experience as a mentor and research assistant in Istanbul and Kuala Lumpur and is currently living in Doha, Qatar. He has co-authored **Chapter 10**.

Mahmood Asad Moh'd Ali is currently working as Assistant Professor in the College of Business Administration, University of Bahrain. He received his PhD in Business Management (HR) from Philippine Christian University, Philippines. He has around 20 years of teaching and administrative experience. He has served at various administrative positions at the University of Bahrain including Director of Administration and Logistics at Bahrain Teachers College and served as the Director of Co-ordination and Follow-up Department. He has co-authored **Chapter 5**.

Mohamed Bechir Belaid is a senior banker with more than ten years of experience between the teaching and banking sectors. As Assistant Professor he lectured on several courses such as accounting, international financial management, Islamic finance principles, Islamic accounting, and Islamic bank governance. He holds professional certificates from recognized international institutions such as the Islamic Finance Certificate in Education and Training from the CIBAFI, a Training of Trainers certificate from the International Training Council England, and Islamic finance principles certificate from the Kuwait International Bank. He is also the author of articles and publications about Islamic finance in international journals and is a frequent speaker in different seminars and training sessions for both academics and professionals. He was recently nominated as a Master Trainer by the Accounting and Auditing Organization for Islamic Financial Institutions (AAOIFI). He has co-authored **Chapter 15**.

Mohammad Nurunnabi, PhD, CMA, SFHEA, FRSA, FAIA (Acad), CMBE, is the Aide to the Rector on Research and Internationalization, and Chair of the Department of Accounting at Prince Sultan University, Saudi Arabia. He is Academic Visitor (Senior Member) of St Antony's College, University of Oxford, UK. He holds a PhD with an outright pass (no corrections) from the University of Edinburgh, UK. He is a Senior Fellow of the Higher Education Academy (SFHEA), UK, a Chartered Management Accountant (CMA), an Academic Fellow of the Association of International Accountants (FAIA-Acad), and Fellow of the Royal Society of Arts (FRSA). His most recent book is *The Role of the State and Accounting Transparency* (Routledge: London and New York). He currently serves as Editor-in-Chief of *PSU Research Review: An International Journal*, Emerald, and is Senior Associate Editor of the *Journal of the Knowledge Economy*, Springer (Scopus Indexed). He has co-authored **Chapter 15**.

Mohammad Atif is currently Assistant Professor at the Department of Commerce and Business Studies, Jamia Millia Islamia (JMI), New Delhi, India. Prior to joining JMI in 2016, he served at the Central University of Himachal Pradesh,

Dharamshala, Himachal Pradesh, India, for four years. He has more than seven years of teaching experience. He received his PhD from JMI in finance after completing his MCom from the same university. He teaches statistics, finance, and econometrics to undergraduate and postgraduate students. His research interests include applied econometrics and financial markets, especially derivatives, asset pricing, and behavioural finance. He has co-authored **Chapter 6**.

Mohd Hairul Azrin Besar is a faculty member in the School of Business and Economics, University of Brunei Darussalam, Brunei, with an interest in the fields of accounting, governance, and Islamic finance. He has been involved in the Islamic banking industry in Brunei Darussalam, specifically in *Shariah* governance and auditing since the year 2000 and is currently an alternate member in the *Shariah* Financial Supervisory Board (SFSB). He has published works and presented papers in several conferences in the area of governance, Islamic banking and finance, *takaful*, and financial reporting. He is also part of the editorial team for the *Journal of Islamic Accounting and Business Research* (JIABR). Azrin graduated with first-class honours as a BA of Accounting, holds an MBA specializing in Islamic banking and finance from the International Islamic University Malaysia, and was awarded a PhD in Accounting and Finance from the University of Glasgow, UK. He has co-authored **Chapter 12**.

Monsurat Ayojimi Salami is postdoctoral research fellow at the IIUM Institute of Islamic Banking and Finance (IIiBF), Malaysia. She is certified in quantitative risk management (CQRM). She has successfully trained groups of participants in professional examination of real options. In addition, she has published a series of academic papers in journals indexed in Scopus and Web of Science (WoS) such as the *Journal of Advances in Management Research*, *Pertanika Journal of Social Science and Humanities*, *Journal of Asian Business and Economic Studies*, and *Journal of Capital Markets Studies*. She is an academic journal reviewer for some journals in Emerald Publishing. She has co-authored **Chapters 2** and **3**.

Khairul Hidayatullah Basir is Assistant Lecturer at the Faculty of Islamic Economics and Finance, University Islam Sultan Sharif Ali, Brunei. His research interest lies in socio-economic development, particularly in the areas of agriculture and resource economics, youth unemployment and entrepreneurship, and Islamic social finance. He has presented papers at conferences in Australia, Brunei, Malaysia, Philippines, Indonesia, and Thailand. To date, he has successfully published two books and written a number of journal articles and book chapters. He has acted as an ad-hoc peer reviewer for Scopus indexed journals. Khairul completed his undergraduate studies at the University of Brunei Darussalam, where he earned a BA (Hons) in Economics and minored in Islamic Banking and Finance. He holds an MA degree in Development Studies from the University of Melbourne, Australia, and went to the University of Oxford, UK, for the Global Mobility Program where he was awarded a Global Mobility Grant for the University of Melbourne. He has co-authored **Chapter 12**.

Muhammad Mehedi Masud is Senior Lecturer in the Department of Development Studies, Faculty of Economics and Administration, University of Malaya. He has published books, book chapters, and more than 40 scientific papers in internationally refereed journals. His research interests are development economics, the environment and sustainable development, environmental impact assessment, ecotourism development, climate change adaptation and mitigation, community development, livelihoods, poverty, and social mobility. He has received several awards such as the Academic Excellence Award (2014), Excellence Award (2015), and Bangladeshi Students Night Award (2016) from the University of Malaya. He has co-authored **Chapter 5**.

Mustafa Mohd Hanefah is Professor of Accounting, *Shariah* Governance, Islamic Accounting and Reporting, and Taxation at the Faculty of Economics and Muamalat, University Sains Islam Malaysia (USIM). He was the first Deputy Vice-Chancellor (Research and Innovation) USIM (2010–2016) and was the Dean of the Faculty of Economics and Muamalat (2007–2010). Professor Dato' Mustafa was a Visiting Professor at the Economic Research Centre, Nagoya University, Japan, from 15 April 2011 to 15 June 2011, and Aoyama Gakuin University, Tokyo, Japan, from 1 to 15 February 2016. He and his team initiated the first *Shariah* audit training (SAT) program in Malaysia in 2015. He is a Fellow and Treasurer of Akademi Profesor Malaysia and member of the Chartered Tax Institute of Malaysia (CTIM). He has co-authored **Chapter 14**.

Mustafa Raza Rabbani is currently serving as Assistant Professor at the Department of Finance and Accounting, Kingdom University, Bahrain. He holds a PhD in Banking and Financial Services from the prestigious Jamia Millia Islamia, New Delhi, India. His areas of specialization are financial technology (FinTech), artificial intelligence and its application in Islamic economics, blockchain, cryptocurrency, and ethical issues in FinTech application. He is working to develop a 'blueprint' of the Islamic financial system using FinTech and the first principle approach. He has also co-founded a publishing company and served as a managing director and has been associated with Jamia Millia Islamia, Saudi Electronic University, and IMS Unison University as Assistant Professor, course coordinator, and program coordinator. He has co-authored **Chapters 6** and **7**.

Najmoddin Yazdi is a researcher at the Sharif Policy Research Institute (SPRI), affiliated with the Sharif University of Technology (SUT), Iran. He is also a PhD candidate of Science and Technology Policy at the Iran University of Science and Technology (IUST). He holds an MBA from the University of Tehran, Iran, and BSc in Mechanical Engineering from the Amirkabir University of Technology, Iran. His research interests are Islamic studies, public policy, public procurement of innovation (PPI), research governance and evaluation, and knowledge production processes. He has co-authored **Chapter 4**.

Nor Fadilah Bahari is Lecturer at the Department of Accounting and Finance, Faculty of Management and Muamalah, Kolej Universiti Islam Antarabangsa Selangor (KUIS), Malaysia. She received her BA in Banking (Hons) in 2006, and her MA in Science Banking in 2009 from the University Utara Malaysia (UUM). Currently, she is pursuing a PhD degree in Economics and Muamalat Administration at the University Sains Islam Malaysia (USIM), specializing in Islamic finance. Her area of expertise is in the field of Islamic finance, and she is actively involved in a research project and writing academic articles related to Islamic finance, Islamic banking, and Islamic social finance. She has co-authored **Chapter 14**.

Nusrat Jafrin is Assistant Professor at the Department of Population Sciences, Faculty of Social Sciences, University of Dhaka, Bangladesh. Since joining, she has been involved as a core member of national-level research projects related to demographics with the department in collaboration with the United Nations Population Fund (UNFPA), Bangladesh. Her research interests are economic demography, development economics, sustainable development, poverty and inequality, population, and environment. Currently, she is doing a PhD in the field of demographic dividends and sustainable development at the Department of Development Studies, Faculty of Economics and Administration, University of Malaya, Malaysia. She has co-authored **Chapter 5**.

Rahmawati is Lecturer at the Department of Accounting, Faculty of Economics and Business, Islamic State University Syarif Hidayatullah Jakarta, Indonesia. Her areas of research interest are Islamic accounting, financial accounting and reporting, Islamic cooperative governance, internal auditing, and finance in Islamic cooperatives. She has co-authored **Chapter 11**.

Romzie Rosman is Associate Professor at the International Islamic University Malaysia (IIUM), specializing in Islamic banking and finance. He graduated with a BA (Hons) in Accounting and Finance from Lancaster University, UK, in 2000. He was awarded an MA degree in Business Administration (Islamic banking and finance) in 2005 and a PhD (Islamic banking and finance) in 2012 from the IIUM. He has published his research in several refereed journals, such as the *Journal of Economic Cooperation and Development*, *Pacific-Basin Finance Journal*, and *Journal of Islamic Accounting and Business Research*. His research interests include Islamic finance and Islamic social finance. He has co-authored **Chapter 13**.

Saeed Awadh Bin-Nashwan is Assistant Professor at the Faculty of Administrative Sciences, Seiyun University, Seiyun, Yemen. He holds a PhD in Accounting from Tunku Puteri Intan Safinaz School of Accountancy, University Utara

Malaysia, Sintok, Malaysia. His research interests are in the fields of Islamic accounting, taxation, and social work. Bin-Nashwan has published many articles in indexed international journals as well as presented others at some of prominent international conferences. He has authored **Chapter 8**.

Shahnawaz Khan is serving as Secretary General of the Scientific Research Council and Assistant Professor in the Department of Information Technology, University College of Bahrain. He received his PhD in Computer Science from the Indian Institute of Technology (Banaras Hindu University), Varanasi, India. His areas of specialization are machine learning, natural language processing, blockchain, and FinTech. He has co-founded two IT companies, served as chief technical officer (CTO), and has been associated with IIT (BHU), Saudi Electronic University (SEU), and Galgotias University (GU) as lecturer, course coordinator, and program coordinator. He has co-authored **Chapters 6** and **7**.

Shamsher Mohamad holds a PhD in Finance from the University of Glasgow, UK. Prior to the International Centre for Education in Islamic Finance (INCEIF), he taught finance courses at both undergraduate and graduate level at the University Putra Malaysia (UPM). He served UPM for 30 years starting as a tutor in the same faculty in 1980. In 2012, he joined INCEIF as Professor in Finance and Accounting. His areas of interest are accounting and finance. He has co-authored **Chapter 10**.

Umar Habibu Umar started his academic career as a pioneer of Yusuf Maitama Sule (Formerly Northwest) University Kano, Kano, Nigeria, established in 2013. He is based at the Department of Accounting in the university and a member of the Institute of Chartered Accountants of Nigeria. Umar's major area of research is Islamic accounting, banking, and finance. Specifically, *waqf* is one of the aspects on which he has a number of publications. He was among the few scholars selected across the globe who presented papers at the international research workshop entitled 'Revival of Waqf for Socio-economic Developments', jointly organized by the Islamic Research and Training Institute (IRTI) Jeddah, Islamic Bank Bangladesh Limited (IBBL), and the Centre for Zakat Management (CZM), Bangladesh held at the Hotel Pan Pacific Sonargaon, Dhaka Bangladesh, from 4 to 5 November 2017. He has authored **Chapter 9**.

Ziyaad Mahomed is *Shariah* Adviser to numerous Islamic financial institutions in Africa and Asia. He presently serves as Associate Dean and Director of E-Learning and Executive Education and Assistant Professor and Head of Social Finance at the International Centre for Education in Islamic Finance, Malaysia (INCEIF). He specializes in *Shariah*, social finance, FinTech, and Islamic capital markets. Dr Ziyaad Mahomed holds a PhD in Islamic Finance from Malaysia (INCEIF), BA (Hons) Business (Finance) from Anglia Ruskin University, UK, and an MBA from MANCOSA, South Africa. He is also a Chartered Islamic Finance Practitioner and Certificate in Islamic Law holder from INCEIF and University of KwaZulu-Natal, South Africa, respectively. He studied the Islamic sciences with specialization in *Fiqh Mu'amalat* from scholars in South Africa, Egypt, and Jordan. He has co-authored **Chapter 10**.

Zurina Shafii is Lecturer in the Faculty of Economics and *Muamalat*, University Sains Islam Malaysia (USIM) and a Research Fellow in the Islamic Finance and Wealth Management Institute (IFWMI), a research centre of excellence in USIM. She holds an Accounting degree from University Teknologi Mara (UiTM), Malaysia, and an MA degree and PhD in Islamic Finance from Durham University, UK. She holds a professional accounting qualification, ACCA, and is a Certified Islamic Financial Planner. Her research interests are *Shariah* audit, Islamic financial institution accounting and reporting, Islamic financial planning, and Halal compliance procedures. She has co-authored **Chapter 14**.

Foreword

It is an honour for me to write this foreword to the first book published on the impact of COVID-19 on Islamic social finance. Islamic social finance is an area that needs research attention. The pandemic has reminded us the importance of Islamic social financial institutions and tools to alleviate poverty and assist low income families. This is a very timely book coinciding with the paradox struggle faced by humanity to fight against poverty using all available resources. I am confident that the chapters found in this book will renew our hope to find solutions to the issues we are facing today.

COVID-19 is a pandemic that has forced governments all over the world to take different measures like lockdown, border control and physical distancing to save human race from extinction. The most common measure taken in this regard is lock down measure and it is said that the economic and financial effect caused by the lockdown measure is irrecoverable in a near future. This is because, the lockdown measure restricts human movement to any place such as work or school or any place of public gatherings for social purpose including congregation prayers. This led to contraction of economy where the inability in opening the businesses led to liquidity issues which eventually led to laying-off workers to reduce operational cost and some businesses had to close down fully as they had no way to continue the business during the pandemic lock down. The statistics on this are recorded and the analysis of this data shows one thing common in all parts of the world: that is the world poverty clock has turned back.

The rationale for having Islamic social finance institutions and instruments is to provide social justice, harmony and equity among all members of the society. Islamic social finance institutions and instruments include untapped but powerful institutions and instruments that can close the widening gap between rich and poor in societies. These institutions and instruments include *zakat* (alms), *sadaqat* and *infaq* (voluntary charity), *waqf* (Islamic endowment), *takaful* (social insurance), microfinance, *qard* (interest-free loans). History proves that if the full potential of these Islamic social finance institutions and instruments are unlocked, poverty can be eliminated in the societies. For instance, in the era of Caliph Umar ibn Abdel Aziz, it was said that there was none who volunteered to receive zakat money. One of the reasons for this could be due to implementation of a full-fledge successful Islamic economic system where social justice is achieved through implementation of policies that assist all classes in the society to increase their economic productivity in a self-sufficient manner.

Today, it is certain that we cannot merely just say that poverty is the result of a state of mind. More work need to be done in implementing various types of Islamic social finance institutions and tools. I am happy to note that the three parts found in this book are comprehensive to cover not only the impact of COVID-19 on Islamic social finance, but the innovation in Islamic social finance to fight against COVID-19 and impact of COVID-19 on Islamic microfinance has been included. Through this book, practitioners, academicians and students all over the world would have the opportunity to understand the impact of COVID-19 on Islamic social finance and will comprehend its socio-economic impact on societies. Definitely, the way forward in implementation of Islamic social finance is via innovation, technology and customization.

Professor Dato' Dr Mohd Azmi Omar
President & Chief Executive Officer
International Centre for Education in
Islamic Finance (INCEIF)
Kuala Lumpur, Malaysia

Introduction

M. Kabir Hassan, Aishath Muneeza, and Adel M. Sarea

Islamic social finance is a branch of Islamic finance. COVID-19 is a global crisis that was first perceived to be a mere health crisis that has eventually led to a human crisis, and the end of it is yet unknown. In the midst of this unprecedented event, it is imperative to understand the effect of COVID-19 on Islamic finance. The sustainable development of Islamic finance is also at stake, just like conventional finance and as such, understanding the future of Islamic finance has become imperative. Islamic finance has not only been considered as a mode of commercial financing, where the only motive is to make a profit. Islamic finance has a specific branch dealing with social finance where the motive is not to make a profit but to provide social justice to society by providing financing options that are affordable and suitable for the underprivileged population who might not be able to access formal financial institutions as they are not financially eligible or physically unable due to geographical barriers.

One of the major effects of COVID-19 that is undeniable is the increase in poverty in the world. Poverty is like a pandemic that spreads invisibly, and those who are affected by it live a hard life where they have no idea on how to come out of it unless financial relief is provided to them so they can think beyond the basic necessities and find innovative means to sustain their livelihood without relying on the mercy of others. Islamic social finance instruments such as *zakat* (alms), *sadaqat* (charity), and *waqf* (endowment) are there to provide a helping hand to those in need without incurring debt. The classical, physical way of dealing with these instruments is not enough, and COVID-19 has made the world realize that an innovative means to help people in need must be adopted in a socially and physically distant and a cheap and efficient manner. This is a major challenge for Islamic social finance to face and as such innovative ways need to be thought of and implemented for the sake of the sustainable development of Islamic finance in this area and to assist those that need help the most in this critical time of the pandemic.

Even during pre-pandemic times, a number of innovative ways to link FinTech to Islamic finance have emerged, but there was no collective effort made towards this as there was all the time in the world to experiment with these methods and go slow. As a result, FinTech in Islamic social finance was not a priority and when COVID-19 hit, suddenly, more than ever, the need for this became more evident as physically going from one place to another became life-threatening and as such, alternatives to the physical way of dealing with social finance, including Islamic social finance, became a priority. Innovative ways were required, and there was a need to review the existing successful models adopted in different parts of the world such as the successful case studies of implementing Islamic microfinance where the default rate is nil or low. Not only this, but soon it was realized that the disbursement of aid or relief was not the only issue facing humankind, but the need to find ways to replenish the funds used for this purpose was also realized as giving would only will dry out the existing avenues if there was no sustainable means to access those funds in the community.

In the midst of COVID-19, there is a pressing need to publish a book with research on imperative areas of Islamic social finance. The papers that are compiled in this book can be broadly classified into three parts: the first part deals with poverty and COVID-19, the second part deals with innovation in Islamic social finance to combat COVID-19, and the final part deals with the impact of COVID-19 on Islamic microfinance. All of the chapters in this book cover various aspects of Islamic social finance by highlighting the impact of COVID-19 on them. Each of these chapters is contributed by researchers in the field who even at the time of pandemic took the initiative to enlighten stakeholders on important areas of Islamic social finance that ought to be considered for the sustainable development of Islamic finance at a global level.

In Chapter 1, 'Impact of COVID-19 on Islamic social finance', M. Kabir Hassan, Aishath Muneeza, and Adel M. Sarea provide an overview of the impact of COVID-19 on Islamic social finance by studying its impact on different components of Islamic social finance. They argue that COVID-19 is an opportunity for Islamic social finance provided that innovation is utilized to overcome the challenges faced, and there are case studies ready to prove this that are discussed in the chapter. They believe that the future of Islamic social finance is in combining it with Islamic commercial finance in the hope that Islamic social finance could be developed in a sustainable manner. They anticipate that the findings of this research would assist policy-makers and Islamic financial institutions focus on the development of Islamic social finance by merging it with Islamic commercial financial institutions where under one roof, all kinds of customers could be given service without excluding anyone.

In Chapter 2, 'Financial capacity indicators and risk exposure among different income groups: influence of COVID-19', Monsurat Ayojimi Salamia and Adel M. Sarea examine financial capacity as well as risk exposure among different income groups. They argue that financial capacity is highly essential, especially during this period of COVID-19 where essential items are only required for sustainability. As such, they examine the statistical difference in the mean score of financial capacity indicators across different income groups. They reveal that the most adversely affected group in this regard is the low-income group, and there should be customized financial capacity indicators developed to specifically deal with this group to provide them with relief.

In Chapter 3, 'Financial inclusion and risk exposure among different income groups – the impact of COVID-19 pandemic', Monsurat Ayojimi Salamia, Adel M. Sarea, and M. Kabir Hassan argue that it is the low-income group that faces more financial challenge than any other group as they are the financially excluded group. As such, they propose that the financial inclusion strategy adopted for each income group should be unique. In this study, to quantify the approaches of financial inclusion adopted in different income groups in different countries, data from 121 countries are used.

In Chapter 4, 'Iran and COVID-19: an alternative crisis management system based on bottom-up Islamic social finance and faith-based civic engagement', Najmoddin Yazdi, Ali Marvi, and Ali Maleki illustrate how the COVID-19 pandemic can bring Islamic societies much learning in terms of crisis management and revitalization of their faith-based and Islamic assets. They conceptualize the case of Iran to draw upon its impressive citizen-centred collaborative crisis management with Islamic leadership and bottom-up Islamic social finance at its core. They show that in this proposed model, with the directing role of leadership and discourse on the Islamic concepts of *Jihad*, *infaq*, holy defence, and martyrdom, the community was mobilized far from mere social financing, but also by civic engagement and faith-driven participation.

In Chapter 5, 'Impact of COVID-19 on sustainable development: a way forward', Nusrat Jafrin, Muhammad Mehedi Masud, and Abu Naser Mohammad Saif discuss the effects of COVID-19 on the economy, society, and environment based on secondary data. They argue that since the world has already entered a recession and global GDP growth is expected to decrease from 3.2% to 5.2% due to this pandemic, making the situation far worse than the 2008–2009 global financial crisis, and since the rate of domestic violence – physical, emotional, and sexual – continues to increase at an alarming rate in addition to the economic, social, and environmental degradation around the world, the world will face major challenges in achieving sustainable development. As such, to overcome the pandemic, they propose that the whole world should work together as individualistic and social efforts are essential in protecting the earth from a global outbreak.

In Chapter 6, 'Islamic FinTech – the digital transformation bringing sustainability to Islamic finance', Mohammad Atif, M. Kabir Hassan, Mustafa Raza Rabbani, and Shahnawaz Khan illustrate the importance of being innovative via Islamic FinTech for the sustainable development of Islamic finance. They explore the effective use of different types of technology to achieve this. They argue that the utilization of FinTech in Islamic finance is the required tonic to regroup and attract more customers, increase efficiency, reduce costs, and provide more attractive and innovative products and services and they believe that this will enable Islamic financial institutions to become more competitive without compromising profits or ethical values. They propose a five-step strategy ('IslamicFintech4SD Gearbox') to achieve sustainable development through Islamic FinTech.

In Chapter 7, 'Artificial intelligence and natural language processing (NLP) based FinTech model of *Zakat* for poverty alleviation and sustainable development for Muslims in India', Mustafa Raza Rabbani, M. Kabir Hassan, , Shahnawaz

Khan, and Mahmood Asad Moh'd Ali argue that *zakat* could be used to fight against COVID-19 where the life of those with low income can be uplifted, and an artificial intelligence-based model is proposed for this purpose. With industry 4.0 and with the rise of FinTech, it is believed that even *zakat* should be improved with technology to make it more effective.

In Chapter 8, 'Online monetary donation to mitigate the impacts of the COVID-19 crisis – evidence from Kuwait', Saeed Awadh Bin-Nashwan argues that charitable projects, internet technology features, and religiosity are significant motivators that influence attitudes toward online donations related to the COVID-19 response. The results presented in this chapter could provide insight into and empirical evidence for governments, non-profit organizations, charities, and communities to focus attention on appropriate proactive policies to boost online fundraising campaigns for those affected by epidemic diseases.

In Chapter 9, 'Adapting Al Rajhi *waqf* model to mitigate the impact of COVID-19 on *ummah*: a lesson to other Muslim philanthropists', Umar Habibu Umar argues that Al Rajhi Waqf Model is suitable for Muslim philanthropists to adapt to mitigate the impact of COVID-19 on Muslim *Ummah*. The author believes that if Muslim philanthropists across the globe adapted this model, the social and economic crises caused by COVID-19 would be minimized.

In Chapter 10, 'Funding the refugee crisis in Turkey: a case for social impact *sukuk*', Ziyaad Mahomed, Ibrahim Musa Unal, and Shamsher Mohamad observe that funding refugee camps has become a significant financial responsibility for host countries and the Turkish government spent more than US$40 billion on Syrian refugees since 2011, around 5% of the Turkish GDP. Mahomed et al. propose the application of a structured social impact *sukuk* (SIS) as a sustainable solution to reduce the financial pressure of refugees on Turkey. They believe that this will not only protect the Turkish people from undue foreign political influence but also develop the Turkish Islamic capital market sector for future funding.

In Chapter 11, 'COVID-19 pandemic: the Islamic social capital perspective *in Baitul Maal Wat Tamwil* institutions (BMTIs) movement in Indonesia', Rahmawati and Fitri Rinaldi illustrate how Islamic social finance could be strengthened via Islamic social capital through networking, spirituality, norms, and trust activities of BMTI, which is a suitable model to be adopted in other countries too. Rahmawati and Rinaldi argue that understanding Islamic social capital will shape the character of social relationships.

In Chapter 12, 'Unlocking Islamic social finance to help micro small medium enterprises in Brunei Darussalam', Khairul Hidayatullah Basir and Mohd Hairul Azrin Besar observe that many businesses around the world, particularly, MSMEs have been greatly impacted by the COVID-19 outbreak and Brunei Darussalam is no exception to this. This chapter looks at how Islamic social finance tools based on philanthropy, such as *zakat* (obligatory charity), *sadaqah* (voluntary charity), and *waqf* (endowment) can be leveraged to address the MSMEs' financing issues in Brunei.

In Chapter 13, 'The role of Islamic microfinance in eradicating the impact of COVID-19 on socio-economic wellbeing in Nigeria', Abdullateef Abdulqadi Maikabara, Romzie Rosman, and Habeebullah Zakariyah assess the role of Islamic microfinance as a viable instrument in eradicating the impact of COVID-19 on social wellbeing in Nigeria as they believe that the incidence of the coronavirus pandemic has a significant impact on every economic and social segment, especially the wellbeing of the people as most workers have unprecedentedly lost their job and ordinary people are unable to access basic amenities. They argue that Islamic microfinance has the potential to effectively eradicate the impact of COVID-19 on the socio-economic wellbeing of the country.

In Chapter 14, 'Islamic social finance during economic uncertainty: the special role of *Ar-Rahnu*', Nor Fadilah Baharia, Mustafa Mohd Hanefahb, and Zurina Shafii shows how *Ar-Rahnu* or Islamic pawnbroking introduced in Malaysia have helped those whose income was adversely affected due to COVID-19 to overcome their personal liquidity challenges. In this chapter, they shed light on the historical development of *Ar-Rahnu*, the legality of *Ar-Rahnu* financing according to the *Quran* and *Hadith*, and compare it with its conventional counterparts by highlighting the role of *Ar-Rahnu* during the pandemic.

In Chapter 15, 'Profit-loss sharing principle: the strategic answer of solidarity in Islamic finance', Amira Kaddour, Badri Narayanan Gopalakrishnan, Mohamed Bechir Belaid, and Mohammad Nurunnabi show the significance of having the principle of profit and loss sharing being applied to Islamic finance as the COVID-19 crisis has prompted a call for solidarity from all economic stakeholders. An inclusive and integrated crisis management response must offer quick and efficient support in order to enhance recovery, particularly given the prolonged nature of this crisis, with some potentially permanent impacts on how the global economy operates. Kaddour et al. believe that investments in the greater good of society in terms of rebuilding the economy and redistribution of wealth and income are other aspects that are important in this post-COVID era and they believe that efficient adoption of this principle will be a new pillar of development for the Islamic finance market.

Part I

Poverty and COVID-19

1 Impact of COVID-19 on Islamic social finance

M. Kabir Hassan, Aishath Muneeza, and Adel M. Sarea

1.1 Introduction

COVID-19 is considered by some as a 'black swan event', which is a pandemic that is unpredictable, unprepared for, and totally spontaneous (Gubler, 2020). This pandemic is different from four other recent pandemics the world has witnessed within the last 25 years (Gubler, 2020) as its impact has created not only a health crisis, but has led to an economic as well as human crisis brought due to a halt in all major economic activities in the world. The impact of COVID-19 on the sudden increase of poverty is uncontainable.

By 12 March 2020, the World Health Organization (WHO) declared COVID-19 a pandemic, as, since December 2019, the disease had been spreading worldwide, putting the world population at risk. Simultaneously, the number of unemployed increased turning back the poverty clock (Kharas & Hamei, 2020). This is because as Sumner et al. (2020; p.2) state: 'global poverty could increase for the first time since 1990 and, depending on the poverty line, such increase could represent a reversal of approximately a decade in the world's progress in reducing poverty'. They also observe that in some regions, the poverty levels could be what they were exactly 30 years ago (Sumner et al., 2020) ruining the progress that has been achieved by the world so far in this regard. According to the International Labour Organization (ILO), the continuous decline in working hours globally due to COVID-19 means that 1.6 billion workers in the informal economy, which is nearly half of the global workforce, are at immediate risk of losing their livelihood (ILO, 2020).

It is estimated that there are 12 countries in the world where poverty levels will increase to more than 1 million people due to the pandemic and these countries are India, Nigeria, Indonesia, Bangladesh, Congo-Kinshasa, Philippines, Ethiopia, Brazil, Afghanistan, Sudan, and Zimbabwe (Kharas & Hamei, 2020). It is observed that except for Brazil, which is in the South American continent, the rest of the countries are located in the Asian and African continents. The impact of the pandemic on poverty includes the contraction of per capita household income or consumption, where it is predicted that the minimum international poverty earning of USD 1.90 per day for the low poverty level will decrease by 5%, while the medium poverty level, which is USD 3.20 per day, will decrease by 10%, and the high poverty level, which is USD 5.50 per day, will decrease by 20% posing a real challenge to eliminating poverty by 2030, which is one of the United Nation's Sustainable Development Goals (Sumner et al., 2020).

The ILO Director-General Guy Ryder states: 'for millions of workers, no income means no food, no security and no future. [...] As the pandemic and the jobs crisis evolve, the need to protect the most vulnerable becomes even more urgent'. As such, to protect the most vulnerable at this time of human crisis, governments of different countries have also been formulating different policies such as stimulus packages and debt relief measures to ease their situations (ILO, 2020). As an immediate measure, the only way to help those affected in this regard is to provide cash payments or basic necessities in-kind. Therefore, many countries of the world have engaged in doing so via fiscal policies. For example, it is reported that in Afghanistan, with the support of the World Bank, humanitarian agencies, and other partners, the government has developed relief packages to provide food security to the most vulnerable households by cash transfer programmes and if transferring cash is not possible, in-kind assistance is provided; on 29 April 2020, the government started a programme to provide bread to about 2.5 million low-income families in Kabul (IMF, 2020). There are also some countries like Algeria where exports of several products, including food, medical, and hygiene items are banned (IMF, 2020) to have enough of these available to the local communities during the pandemic. Countries like Argentina has even banned exports of these essentials while at the same time controlling the price of food and medical supplies (IMF, 2020).

1.2 Islamic social finance

Islamic social finance is a branch of Islamic finance that offers not-for-profit products and services. The objectives of Islamic social finance are to achieve social justice via the redistribution of wealth. Islamic social finance has also been dubbed as 'Islamic social safety nets', and this is also considered as the charitable sector (Mohammed & Feddad, 2020). From *Maqasid al-Shariah* or the objectives of Islamic law perspective, it is mandatory for people to help each other and protect one another from hardship to achieve success in this world and the hereafter. The tools and institutions of Islamic finance include *zakat*, which is a compulsory payment paid every year by those who are eligible for the benefit of those who are stated in Quran, 9:60; *sadaqat* or *infaq* is a non-compulsory payment given to assist the poor and needy to seek the pleasure of Allah (SW); *waqf* like *sadaqat* is also a voluntarily made contribution, but unlike *sadaqat* is a permanent contribution of one's wealth whether cash or in-kind to seek the pleasure of Allah (SW) for a social purpose; *takaful* is a concept based on mutual assistance or *Ta'awun* and donation or *Tabarru'* where a joint guarantee is provided by a group of people who agree to participate with each other, known as contributors, by contributing an amount of money as a donation to help each other with damages caused due to unfortunate events to any participant in the group by helping them use the donation; and microfinance is providing finance to those who are poor to finance via non-profitable means interest-free loans (*qard hasan*) or profitable means such as *mudharabah* or *musharakah*. This list of tools and institutions of Islamic social finance is not exhaustive as it is still developing, and today, retail *sukuk* could also be seen as an Islamic social finance tool. In this regard, Rehman (2020) observed that Sustainable Development Goals (SDGs)-linked *sukuk* could be a vital source of long-term capital for governments and companies to fight the pandemic. In this pandemic, Islamic social finance tools and institutions have been considered as a way to provide relief to populations in poverty. Furthermore, a 'pandemic *sukuk*' could also be issued to overcome the financial challenges faced by the low-income groups due to the pandemic (Aassouli, 2020). The other instruments include *qard* (interest-free loan) and *Kafalah* (guarantee) as well (Zain & Ali, 2017).

1.2.1 Zakat

The administration of *zakat* in different parts of the world is different as some countries have centralized systems of collection while other countries have a decentralized system. The size of the *zakat* fund depends on the collection method, and the procedures and mechanisms followed to make the collection effective, such as instead of physically queuing to pay it or requiring one's physical presence to pay it via cash or cheque, there is the option to pay it online or via mobile applications using Unstructured Supplementary Service Data (USSD) code. It is estimated by the Islamic Development Bank that each year, between USD 230 and USD 560 billion *zakat* is given worldwide (Modéer, 2018). The potential of the *zakat* fund and the actual amount received differ greatly, which may be due to the inability of the *zakat* administration bodies to successfully convince and reach the potential *zakat* payers to pay the *zakat* due in a timely manner. For instance, the *zakat* administrative body of Indonesia, BAZNAS, states that the potential *zakat* in Indonesia is valued at around 286 trillion rupiah per year, but the actual collection was 9.5 trillion rupiah ($577.3 million) in 2019 (Winosa, 2020). The discrepancy in this regard shows that there is a need to work towards an effective system for *zakat* administration. *Zakat* is viewed as a sustainable source of funds compared to other Islamic social funds as it is compulsory and needs to be collected every year. Zakat is also disbursed to its recipients in a yearly manner and one of its categories include the poor and needy. There are two types of *zakat*, which are *zakat al maal* and *zakat al fitr*. *Zakat al maal* is known as *zakat* on wealth whereby one will have to pay from income, business, savings, gold and silver, shares, livestock, and crops if the person fulfilled the condition to pay it. There are two main conditions to pay this type of *zakat*: they are *nisab* which is the minimum amount of wealth and *hawl* which is minimum period of wealth retention (1 lunar year). *Zakat al fitr* is paid starting the month of Ramadhan before *Eid al Fitr* by every adult Muslim who has food in excess of their own needs. They are supposed to pay a minimum of two *qadahs* (an old measure equalling just over two kilograms) of flour, wheat, barley, or rice from each person in a household.

In this pandemic, *zakat* has been viewed as a means to assist the poor and needy. The fundamental benefit of *zakat* is that it is something that is spent on the poor without expecting any return as it is their right from the wealth of the rich. Therefore, *zakat* funds established all over the world have become an effective and efficient way to help the poor and needy who need immediate financial assistance for survival. This is the main reason why Rehman (2020), the senior adviser on Islamic finance of the United Nations Development Programme has stated that emergency support in the short term could be given using *zakat*. To make a *zakat* system effective, *zakat* could be integrated with technology like blockchain and artificial intelligence, and this process has been ongoing. It has been reported that Muslims living in the UK have been hit hard by the pandemic, and during this Ramadhan, *zakat* has become a source of their strength (Naseem, 2020). With the pandemic, the number of debtors among the poor and needy are also increasing and to save them from a debt crisis, *zakat* could be an effective tool. One of the recipients of *zakat* stated in the Quran is debtors, and as such, the debts of those who are needy could be paid off using *zakat* money provided that they fulfil the required conditions imposed by *shariah* rules. The World Zakat Forum (WZF) has called for the united action of *zakat* institutions worldwide to fight against the pandemic (World Zakat Forum, 2020). In Abu Dhabi, it was reported that the *zakat* fund had provided 86.3 million dinars in aid to 5,109 eligible families since the beginning of 2020, and with 2,764 families affected by the coronavirus crisis, 93.3% of them are eligible for *zakat* (Emirati News, 2020). During this pandemic, the request to receive *zakat* is made online through a website and via mobile phones (Emirati News, 2020). In Malaysia, it was announced that Tenaga Nasional Berhad (TNB) disbursed *zakat* money amounting to RM4.325 million to 21,000 people comprising the poor, senior citizens, people with disabilities, orphans, and those from the bottom 40% of household income (B40), groups facing financial constraints during the movement control order (MCO) period (Bernama, 2020). Due to the pandemic, the number of *zakat* recipients has increased as well due to widespread poverty. In this regard, for instance, in Selangor, one of the states of Malaysia, it was reported that the pandemic had made 10,000 more families in Selangor *zakat* recipients (Aiman, 2020). Furthermore, due to switching to the online collection of *zakat al fitr* due to the pandemic, *zakat* collection has become much more effective as the number of people paying it and the amount collected has increased. For instance, it was reported that in Selangor, there was a 400% jump in the online collection of *zakat* and up to 15 May, they collected RM8 million online from about 224,000 people compared with RM1.6 million from 41,000 people in 2019 (Aiman, 2020). Not only this, but *zakat* was distributed earlier due to COVID-19 as many were in need of assistance (Wahab, 2020) and as such, *fatwas* have been issued to bring the payment of *zakat* forward as well to ensure that enough funds are there to give to those affected and in need assistance due to pandemic. Also in this regard, Dr Yusuf Al-Qaradawi's commented that paying *zakat* at a higher rate was a commendable act (Ahmad, 2020) in the hope that there would be an increase in collection this year to help the poor created by the pandemic.

To assist those unable to pay *zakat* online, *zakat* payment methods such as drive-through payment and house-to-house collection was also made available during the pandemic to increase the number of *zakat* collections (Ahmad, 2020). There is also hope that proper use of the *zakat* fund can even create jobs. In this regard, President of Minhaj-ul-Quran International Dr Hussain Mohi-ud-Din Qadri has claimed that Pakistan can create at least 10.5 million employment opportunities within five years with the meaningful use of *zakat* funds. He said:

> By changing the non-transparent *zakat* distribution system and giving away the funds as loan in the form of merchandise through Small and Medium Enterprise Authority (SMEDA) to the needy people may work wonders and offer employment to over 10.5 million jobless people within a span of five years.
>
> (*The News*, 2020)

The United Nations High Commissioner for Refugees (UNHCR) has also established a refugee *zakat* fund, and according to their 2020 Annual Impact Brief report, during the first year of its incorporation, it provided support to 1,025,014 beneficiaries in eight countries by 'zakat-compliant cash and in-kind distribution activities, including hard-to-reach areas' where they follow a 100% *zakat* distribution policy which follows the *fatwa* or *shariah* opinion given in this regard and have helped to address basic needs such as shelter, food, education, and healthcare, as well as debt repayment (UNHCR, 2020b). It was also observed that the UNHCR's refugee *zakat* fund helped women in particular who face cultural and legal barriers in childcare and job-related issues by stopping child labour and pulling children out of school as a last resort for survival when faced with difficulty in life to fulfil basic necessities (UNHCR, 2020b). In the year 2019, the UNHCR received and distributed $43.165 million as *zakat* and $222,907 as *sadaqat* (UNHCR, 2020b). It is a common practice among Muslims to pay *zakat* in excess of the mandatory amount obliged to pay, and as such, any amount in excess to the compulsory *zakat* amount would be considered as *sadaqat* or *infaq*. It was also stated that *zakat* funds received by the UNHCR covered 12% of its total expenditure in cash and in-kind assistance extended to needy and vulnerable refugees (UNHCR, 2020b). In the pandemic crisis, the UNHCR has called for the payment of *zakat* to help those affected by the pandemic (UNHCR, 2020a).

1.2.2 Sadaqat

There were many *sadaqat* or *infaq* electronic platforms introduced to help the needy and poor. *Sadaqat* can be given in monetary and non-monetary forms. Since it is not obligatory, the marketing tools used are important to mobilizing such funds. Prior to the pandemic, *sadaqat* was physically given by many, especially during the holy month of Ramadhan while going or coming from mosque or via mosque donations funds. Salih (1999) also observes that donors prefer to make their *sadaqat* directly to private individuals, low-income families, or private charities. However, due to the ban on gatherings to pray at mosques and movement controls, the traditional way of giving *sadaqat* for many have been transformed to online platforms. This is the "new normal" not only for *sadaqat* but for all other types of donations given including compulsory *zakat* and voluntary cash *waqf* as well. *Sadaqat* is a powerful tool that is used to fight poverty as it provides a mechanism from which to obtain funds, whether large or small amounts, from those who are able to donate to those who need it. This mechanism creates a win-win situation for the donor as well as the recipient as the donor gets the satisfaction of helping a person in need while the recipient gets the opportunity to fulfil his/her basic necessities. Numerous charity funds have been initiated to fight COVID-19, not only for poverty alleviation but many other purposes as well such as World Health Organization's COVID-19 Solidarity Response Fund (World Health Organization, 2020).

Due to the pandemic, traditional methods of raising money have become impossible. As such, raising money has been switched to online platforms using social media as well. For instance, in the UAE, Facebook groups have been formed for this purpose and the most famous groups for this purpose include the 'Stop and Help' initiative where if anyone cannot afford essentials, anonymous help could be provided; the 'UAE Fusion Socialites' initiative is where 19,658 group members are encouraged to donate groceries and these are delivered to the homes of needy; the 'In This Together' initiative connects people who need help with those who can help; 'Freecycle Abu Dhabi and Dubai' is an initiative where members of the group are encouraged to set aside time to clear out their closets and storage and specifically donate any of their items to those most in need, and during Ramadhan, the group created a special initiative known as 'The Grocery Gift' where e-gift cards are used to connect donors with families in need; and the 'Surviving Hijab' initiative fostered a massive community encouraging women all over the world and giving 700,000 members support on how to stay strong, while wearing the hijab (Zaki, 2020). In Oman, it is reported that due to the economic hardship created by the pandemic, around 7,000 applicants registered within a period of a month and a half with Dar Al Atta'a Association, which is an inclusive charity association that caters for the needy in Oman (Asif, 2020).

1.2.3 Waqf

Waqf is another Islamic social financial institution that has the potential to alleviate poverty. Rehman (2020) states that for long-term resilience against COVID-19 poverty, *waqf* is an important tool. There are two types of *waqf*: immovable (land) and movable (cash) *waqf*. Movable or cash *waqf* is a recent innovation while traditionally immovable *waqf* has been used successfully in Muslim civilizations. For example, during the time of the Ottoman Empire *waqf* was a successful source of finance for the health sector, education sector, and welfare of the general public and the revenue received from *waqf* contributions was over one-third of the Ottoman state's total revenue (Kuran, 2001). The person who gives *waqf* is the *waqf* founder, and they appoint a private manager to manage it, and if *waqf* is regulated by the country, there is a regulator to supervise it. Dr Firas Raad, country manager for Malaysia, East Asia, and the Pacific, and the World Bank Group believe that *waqf* is in line with the World Bank's twin goal to eliminate extreme poverty and promote sustainable shared prosperity (The World Bank Group et al., 2019).

As such, *waqf* can play a vital role in eliminating poverty created by COVID-19. Anyone who wants to help can donate assets or cash for this purpose by transferring ownership to a *waqf* management institution, and subsequently, the *waqf* management institution as the trustee will manage the *waqf* in the best interest of society. *Waqf* has been used in this pandemic crisis to assist as well. For instance, in India, it has been reported that various *waqf* boards across the country have contributed Rs 51 crore to the prime minister's and chief minister's relief funds for the pandemic to help various religious, social, and educational organizations; they have been distributing food and other essential commodities among the needy (*The Rahuma Daily*, 2020). In this pandemic, experts have urged innovation of the 'long term socially driven waqf sukuk' (*Gulf Daily News*, 2020). To stop the spread of the pandemic and its impact on society, the UAE and the General Authority of Islamic Affairs and Endowments has inaugurated a campaign to support *waqf* in healthcare services to establish new endowment investments (MENAFN, 2020). One of the most critical challenges facing the development of *waqf* is mismanagement, and it is observed that digital finance could enhance the efficiency of the collection and distribution of cash *waqf* (Ramasamy, 2020). Currently, UNDP Indonesia is working with Badan Wakaf Indonesia (BWI), the Indonesian *waqf* board, to innovate a digital *waqf* platform to create awareness of *waqf* by promoting trust and confidence in the *waqf* administration system and, considering the increase in the youth population of Indonesia, technology-based *waqf* crowdfunding is also considered as an innovative way to attract the attention of "tech-savvy youth" (Pickup et al., 2018).

1.2.4 Takaful

Takaful has also been used as a tool of Islamic social finance. Social guarantee schemes provided to the poor and needy helps eliminate poverty, and in the pandemic, assistance via these schemes has been extended. For example, the 'Takaful and Karma' scheme in Egypt is a scheme that provides a social guarantee for Egyptians living below the poverty line (Kaldas, 2020) and it has been extended to support those who have been affected adversely in the pandemic (IMF, 2020). In Malaysia, mySalam is a national health protection scheme initiative started by the government. The aim of this scheme is to provide 8 million ringgit worth of free *takaful* protection to eligible individuals with the intention of helping the poor and needy to overcome their financial difficulties. The unexpected events covered in this scheme include critical illness. During this pandemic, *takaful* health coverage is provided for 3.8 million Bantuan Sara Hidup (BSH) and Bantuan Prihatin Nasional (BPN) who are currently insured under this scheme (*Malay Mail*, 2020). It is also reported that this scheme will be expanded to include some 8 million of those who do not receive BSH with an annual income of less than RM 100,000, aged between 18 and 65 years (*Malay Mail*, 2020). Via social *takaful* schemes, the objectives of Islamic social finance can be achieved.

1.2.5 Islamic microfinance

Different modes of innovative financing (charity and non-charity) are provided to the needy and poor via Islamic microfinance institutions. During this pandemic, the poor and needy can escape from poverty through Islamic microfinance institutions. Even in conventional microfinance, some countries such as the Republic of Cabo Verde (IMF, 2020) have started providing interest-free loan schemes to assist the needy and poor during the pandemic. Furthermore, to provide relief to those who took financing facilities from microfinance institutions and who are unable to pay their debts owing to the financial institutions due to economic hardship created by COVID-19, debt moratoriums are being provided. For instance, in Ivory Coast, a framework has been set up to allow microfinance institutions to accommodate demands from customers with COVID-19-related repayment difficulties to set the parameters to enable the customer to postpone their debt obligations for a three-month without classifying the postponed debts as non-performing (IMF, 2020). For Islamic financing facilities the amount agreed in the original financing facility will not be varied even if the payment duration is changed as any amount charged in excess to what has been initially agreed by the customer and the Islamic financial institution will be deemed as *riba* which is prohibited in Islam. As for Islamic microfinance, in Pakistan, the Akhuwat and Dunya Foundation launched the Akhuwat–Dunya interest-free emergency loan through which they have already assisted more than 5,000 families and anticipate reaching out to more daily and monthly wagers who have been severely affected during the pandemic lockdown. The objective of this scheme is to provide a loan to buy food and medicine, to pay children's education fee, rent, and utility bills (Akhuwat, 2020). The progress of pandemic relief by Akhuwat includes distributing 82,539 bags of rations; financial assistance provided for 4,377 families with Rs 11.6 million; 18 hospitals funded; and Rs 42 million given as interest-free emergency loans, that is a total of 5,098 loans (Akhuwat, 2020). Technology could be used to improve microfinance services and institutions. The challenge in this regard is for consumers who are poor and might not have access to technology, and as a result, disbursements need to be done in a remote manner like home delivery. The microfinance model used in each country is unique. In Indonesia, there are two types of institutions offering Islamic finance: via Islamic cooperatives and Baitul Maal wat Tamwil (BMT) where the former is not allowed to collect *zakat* while the latter is allowed to collect *zakat* (Pickup et al., 2018). BMT is owned by the community and collects deposits from its members. It provides financing facilities for members and it includes two organs: *baitul mal* and *baitul tamweel* (Pickup et al., 2018). The *baitul mal* organ collects and disburses *zakat*, *sadaqat*, and *infaq* to those in need while the *baitul tamweel* organ collects funds from the public for profit providing savings and investment benefits

(Pickup et al., 2018). In this pandemic, BMT has been providing financial relief to those affected by providing relief assistance as *qard* or interest-free loans and by providing leeway to the existing *mudharabah* agreements made between the customers (Ucu, 2020).

1.3 Scope for innovation in Islamic social finance

It is evident from the above discussion that Islamic social finance has the strength to eliminate poverty during this pandemic. There is no doubt that even Islamic social finance has adapted to the "new normal" created by COVID-19. Already there is evidence to show the success of Islamic social finance tools and institutions. However, in this regard, no one uniform model or mechanism could be adopted or replicated. As such, the experience of using different tools and institutions adopted in different parts of the world need to be studied to understand how such a tool or an institution can be adopted or replicated in other parts of the world via local customization. COVID-19 has provided the opportunity to prove the resilience of Islamic finance and for Islamic social finance to emerge as a separate branch of Islamic finance. The progress of Islamic social finance at this time of crisis indicates that in future, Islamic social finance could be fused with Islamic commercial finance to achieve value-based intermediation (VBI).

The VBI strategy (BNM/RH/DP 034–2) was launched by Bank Negara Malaysia in 2018 to focus on the adoption of relevant practices, offerings, and conduct that generate a positive and sustainable impact on the economy, community, and environment, consistent with the shareholders' sustainable returns and long-term interests. VBI benefits the financial industry as adopting it will lead to greater innovation, enhanced efficiency, and an effective ecosystem; the customer/community benefits as it improves the standard of living, and it is fair and transparent in dealings; the government benefits as it realigns business focus with the national agenda; and the regulator contributes to the strengthening of financial stability via adoption of it (Bank Negara Malaysia, 2018). The envisioned future financial landscape of VBI includes achieving long-term and wider objectives considering profit, people, and the planet and measuring performance considering both financial and non-financial aspects (Bank Negara Malaysia, 2018). VBI strategy has not just influenced Islamic commercial finance to merge with Islamic social finance, but the sustainable and responsible investment (SRI) *sukuk* framework issued by the Securities Commission Malaysia in 2014 has also made Islamic social finance an important component to be considered in the *sukuk* market (Securities Commission Malaysia, 2014).

The trend to use *sukuk* to achieve the goals of Islamic social finance has been gaining momentum. For instance, the government of Indonesia has issued retail *sukuk* at low prices to support financial inclusion, and it is also planning to issue a *waqf*-based *sukuk* where development of *waqf* land is a project from which the return will be used for the development of microfinance (Pickup et al., 2018). With the assistance of UNDP Indonesia, the first global sovereign green *sukuk* was issued in 2018, and in 2019, a global sovereign green *sukuk* of USD 2 billion was also issued (Bahuet, 2018; Gorbiano, 2019). Green *sukuk* was first pioneered in Malaysia by Tadau Energy Sdn Bhd in 2018 under the SRI *sukuk* framework of the Securities Commission of Malaysia where RM 250 million was used to finance the construction of large scale solar (LSS) photovoltaic power plants in Kudat, Sabah, with a tenure of 2–16 years (Ali, 2018). As Dr Yusuf Al-Qaradawi has said, preservation and conservation of the environment is also an objective of *shariah*, and via instruments like green *sukuk*, this objective can be achieved. *Sukuk* Ihsan, issued by Khazanah Nasional Berhad in 2015, is Malaysia's first SRI *sukuk* and was exclusively opened to institutional investors and on 8 August 2017; Khazanah Nasional Berhad issued the second tranche of *Sukuk* Ihsan with a retail portion (Khazanah Nasional Berhad, 2018).

For the sustainable development of Islamic social finance, it is imperative to eliminate the challenges facing its development. The challenges facing the development of Islamic social finance include not having a proper framework that is uniform across the globe on tools and institutions of Islamic social finance; refusal on the part of some Muslims to pay *zakat* resulting in the full potential of *zakat* not being achieved; corruption makes it impossible to have an effective and transparent system of Islamic social finance, and this causes people to lose confidence in the system; due to the decentralization of fund collection, different countries have different levels of collection; lack of skills to invest funds results in the poor performance of the asset; and lack of comprehensive records of the poor and needy, and issues in updating the list in real-time (Zain & Ali, 2017). It is important in this regard for standard-setting bodies and regulatory authorities of Islamic finance to join hands and formulate *shariah* standards and rules that can be applied to Islamic social finance, specifying the scope of each and every instrument, tool, and institution to be used to achieve social harmony without breaching *shariah* rules, emphasizing not only the substantive aspects of law such as contracts but the procedural aspects of the law too. This would harmonize the practice of it in the world.

It is predicted that the future of Islamic social finance would be linked with technology. The demand for Islamic social finance is ever-growing. However, the fear lies in the supply side as to whether the supply of different types of Islamic social finance instruments/institutions/tools could be increased in a sustainable manner. This can only be possible via a transparent system that could boost the confidence of contributors. In this regard, for instance, it was announced that Global Sadaqah, in collaboration with SINEGY and LuxTag, can now accept cryptocurrency donations on their platform for *zakat* and *waqf* (*FinTech News Malaysia*, 2020) and it was announced in 2019 that a pilot project would be initiated based on 'ZakatTech', where blockchain will be used to track the movement of *zakat* money from the point of collection to disbursement with transparency (Aziz, 2019). In 2018, BAZNAS, Indonesia introduced 'Zaki' a *zakat* chatbot to facilitate *zakat* transactions in a digital way (Nabila, 2018). Likewise, in 2018 it was announced that an Islamic social financing app that leverages blockchain technology was to be launched. When users turn it on, they are given two options to choose between *sadaqat* or *zakat*, and if they opt for *zakat*, the app will ask the *mazhab* their preference and the project to which they want to donate money, and then, the donor can check out by paying the money via a secure gateway (Noordin, 2018). Furthermore, it is essential to note that technology should be used for *zakat* distribution. If money is transferred, instead of giving physical cash, online transfer should be possible. However, when assistance is given in-kind, the issue of how distribution can occur arises. Rice ATMs are an innovation in this regard, where without human intervention, rice could be distributed to the needy (Muneeza, 2019). *Waqf* is also linked to technology regarding administrative enhancement and to boost public confidence and increase the supply side of it. For instance, the second fully-fledged Islamic bank of Malaysia, Bank Muamalat, introduced in 2016, a debit card named 'Aisya' where for every retail transaction conducted, it will give 20% of the interchange fee to *waqf* (Bank Muamalat, 2016). Finterra is a technology-based firm formed in 2017 providing blockchain-based Islamic applications that address global issues. They have introduced WAQFChain and Ensany Sadaqah Chain to revive the Islamic social-economic system in the digital era of industry 4.0 using blockchain technology (Finterra, n.d.). The myWakaf initiative is also a digital platform created exclusively for the development of the supply of *waqf* and includes some Islamic banks of Malaysia such as Affin Islamic Bank Berhad, Bank Islam Malaysia Berhad, Bank Muamalat Malaysia Berhad, Bank Rakyat, Maybank Islamic Berhad, and RHB Islamic Malaysia Berhad (myWakaf, n.d.), proving that the future champions of Islamic social finance could be the Islamic commercial banks. There is also a trend to link *sukuk* with blockchain as well. In 2019, the world witnessed the world's smallest and the first blockchain-based *sukuk*, which is a private placement *sukuk al-mudaraba* for BMT Bina Ummah, Indonesia used to expand Indonesian microfinance, where USD 50,000 was raised (Blossom, 2019).

1.4 Conclusion

There is no doubt that Islamic social finance plays an important role in reflecting the humanitarian nature of Islamic finance as it has practically proved that it can bridge the gap in humanitarian funding and that its full potential has yet to be unlocked. In this regard, Ulrika Modéer, the UN assistant secretary-general and director of the Bureau of External Relations and Advocacy of UNDP, states that *zakat*, *sadaqat*, and *waqf* have 'a significant potential to address marginalization and vulnerability, when directed towards locally driven programmes promoting social and economic inclusion' (Modéer, 2018). Before Islamic social finance was acknowledged as part of Islamic finance, its tools and institutions were considered a personal Muslim matter used only for personal or domestic purposes. This classical mindset found in Muslim societies has been changed now due to the awareness and acknowledgement created over the past few years in fighting poverty and the usefulness of Islamic social finance tools and institutions has been realised through experience.It is anticipated that this crisis will unlock the full potential of Islamic social finance and will assist Islamic finance recalibrate towards achieving the highest level of *Maqasid al-Shariah*.

References

Aassouli, D. (2020). Islamic Finance and Prospects for Weathering COVID-19. Retrieved from https://intpolicydigest.org/2020/05/13/islamic-finance-and-prospects-for-weathering-covid-19/.

Ahmad, S. (2020, 21 April). Covid-19: Zakat collection should be done online. *New Straits Times*. Retrieved from https://www.nst.com.my/news/nation/2020/04/586206/covid-19-zakat-collection-should-be-done-online.

Aiman, A. (2020). Virus Impact Sees 10,000 More Families in Selangor Becoming Zakat Recipients. Retrieved from https://www.freemalaysiatoday.com/category/nation/2020/05/22/virus-impact-sees-10000-more-families-in-selangor-becoming-zakat-recipients/.

Akhuwat. (2020). COVID-19. Retrieved from https://akhuwat.org.pk/.

Ali, M. M. (2018, 17 March). Malaysi's green sukuk. *New Straits Times*. Retrieved from https://www.nst.com.my/opinion/columnists/2018/03/346085/malaysias-green-sukuk.

Asif, M. (2020). COVID-19: 7,000 register with Oman's Dar Al Atta'a for help. *Zawya*. Retrieved from https://www.zawya.com/mena/en/economy/story/COVID19_7000_register_with_Omans_Dar_Al_Attaa_for_help-SNG_174777790/.

Aziz, A. (2019, 21 August). ZakatTech Blockchain to track zakat collection. *The Malaysian Reserve*. Retrieved from https://themalaysianreserve.com/2019/08/21/zakattech-blockchain-to-track-zakat-collection/.

Bahuet, C. (2018). Indonesia's green sukuk. UNDP. Retrieved from https://www.undp.org/content/undp/en/home/blog/2018/Indonesias-green-sukuk.html.

Bank Muamalat. (2016). Press Release: Bank Muamalat Launches the Aisya Debit Card-I. Retrieved from https://www.muamalat.com.my/downloads/media-room/press/2016/PR-BANK_MUAMALAT_Debit_Card_Launch_2016.pdf.

Bank Negara Malaysia. (2018). Value-based Intermediation: Strengthening the Roles and Impact of Islamic Finance. Retrieved from https://www.bnm.gov.my/index.php?ch=57&pg=137&ac=612&bb=file.

Bernama. (2020, 23 May). TNB distributes RM4.3m zakat aid during Ramadan. *The Edge Markets*. Retrieved from https://www.theedgemarkets.com/article/tnb-distributes-rm43m-zakat-aid-during-ramadan.

Blossom. (2019). Wor's First Primary Sukuk Issuance on Blockchain Closes. Retrieved from https://blossomfinance.com/press/world-s-first-primary-sukuk-issuance-on-blockchain-closes

Emirati News. (2020, 24 May). Zakat Fund Provides $86.282 Million in Aid to More than 5,000 Eligible Families since the Beginning of 2020. Retrieved from https://emirati.news/zakat-fund-provides-86-282-million-in-aid-to-more-than-5-000-eligible-families-since-the-beginning-of-2020.

Fintech News Malaysia. (2020, 11 May). Global Sadaqah to Enable Zakat and Waqf Payments Using Bitcoin. Retrieved from https://fintechnews.my/23658/blockchain/globalsadaqah-to-enable-zakat-and-waqf-payments-in-bitcoin/.

Finterra. (n.d.). The Company. Retrieved from https://finterra.org/about-us/.

Gubler, D. J. (2020). Covid-19 is No 'Black Swan' and This Crisis Shows Pandemic Prevention Must be Part of Government Policy the World Over. Retrieved from https://www.scmp.com/comment/opinion/article/3082788/covid-19-no-black-swan-and-crisis-shows-pandemic-prevention-must-be.

Gorbiano, M. I. (2019, 18 February). Indonesia issues US$ 2b global green, regular sukuk. *The Jakarta Post*. Retrieved from https://www.thejakartapost.com/news/2019/02/18/indonesia-issues-us-2-27b-global-green-sukuk.html.

ILO (International Labour Organization). (2020). Press Release: ILO: As Job Losses Escalate, Nearly Half of Global Workforce at Risk of Losing Livelihoods. Retrieved from https://www.ilo.org/global/about-the-ilo/newsroom/news/WCMS_743036/lang--en/index.htm.

IMF (International Monetary Fund). (2020). Policy Responses to COVID-19: Policy Tracker. Retrieved from https://www.imf.org/en/Topics/imf-and-covid19/Policy-Responses-to-COVID-19#M.

Kaldas, T. (2020). The Pandemic Should Spur New Reforms in Egypt, Bloomberg. Retrieved from https://au.finance.yahoo.com/news/pandemic-spur-reforms-egypt-040036700.html.

Kharas, H. & Hamei, K. (2020). Turning back the Poverty Clock: How Will COVID-19 Impact the World's Poorest People? Retrieved from https://www.brookings.edu/blog/future-development/2020/05/06/turning-back-the-poverty-clock-how-will-covid-19-impact-the-worlds-poorest-people/.

Khazanah Nasional Berhad. (2018). Sukuk Ihsan: Sustainable and Responsible Investment Sukuk. Retrieved from https://www.khazanah.com.my/About-Khazanah/Our-Case-Studies/Khazanah-360/Sukuk-Ihsan-Sustainable-and-Responsible-Investme.

Kuran, T. (2001). The provision of public goods under Islamic law: Origins, impact, and limitations of the waqf system. *Law & Society Review*, *35*(4), 841–898.

Malay Mail. (2020, 26 April). 3.8 Million BSH Recipients Protected under MySalam Scheme to Date. Retrieved from https://www.malaymail.com/news/malaysia/2020/04/26/rm3.8m-of-bsh-recipients-protected-under-mysalam-scheme-to-date/1860426.

Middle East North Africa Financial Network (MENAFN). (2020). UAE-General Authority of Islamic Affairs and Endowments Launches Campaign to Support Waqf in Healthcare Services. Retrieved from https://menafn.com/1100121345/UAE-General-Authority-of-Islamic-Affairs-and-Endowments-launches-campaign-to-support-Waqf-in-Healthcare-Services.

Modéer, U. (2018). Unlocking Islamic Social Finance to Help Communities Address Vulnerability and Inequality. Retrieved from https://www.undp.org/content/undp/en/home/news-centre/speeches/2018/Unlocking_Islamic_Social_Finance_to_Help_Communities_Address_Vulnerability_and_Inequality.html.

Mohammed, A., & Feddad, L. (2020). Mitigating the Impact of Covid-19 through Islamic Social Safety Nets. Retrieved from https://blogs.irti.org/mitigating-the-impact-of-covid-19-through-islamic-social-safety-nets/.

Muneeza, A. (2019). Rice ATMs: Technology based innovations for enhancement of zakat. *IF Hub*. Retrieved from https://ikr.inceif.org/viewer/simple_document.php?subfolder=81/64/58/&doc=816458528850720873260317903835634000008&bitsid=19c07bc0-dde1-44d7-a0a2-acaa13d79fb4&uid=.

myWakaf. (n.d.). About Us. Retrieved from https://www.mywakaf.com.my/about-us/.

Nabila, M. (2018). Baznas Rilis Chatbot Zakat Virtual Zaki. Retrieved from https://dailysocial.id/post/baznas-chatbot-zakat-virtual-zaki.

Naseem, I. (2020). Patience, Sacrifice and Zakat: An Islamic Response to Coronavirus. Retrieved from https://www.aljazeera.com/indepth/opinion/patience-sacrifice-zakat-islamic-response-coronavirus-200414132512318.html.

Noordin, K. A. (2018). Islamic finance: Using blockchain to improve transparency of zakat process. *The Edge Markets*. Retrieved from https://www.theedgemarkets.com/article/islamic-finance-using-blockchain-improve-transparency-zakat-process.

Pickup, F., Beik, I. S., & Buana, G. K. (2018). The Potential of Zakat and Other Forms of Islamic Finance to Achieve the SDGs in Indonesia. *UNDP & BAZNAS*. Retrieved from https://www.undp.org/content/dam/indonesia/2018/Doc/INS-Unlocking%20the%20Potential%20of%20Zakat%20and%20Other%20Forms%20of%20Islamic%20Finance%20to%20Achieve%20SDGs%20in%20Indonesia.pdf.

Ramasamy, M. (2020). Digitalisation Can Solve Problems in Administering Waqf, Says Muhajid. Retrieved from https://www.freemalaysiatoday.com/category/nation/2019/07/12/digitalisation-can-solve-problems-in-administering-waqf-says-muhajid/.

Rehman, A. A. (2020). Islamic finance takes on COVID-19. *UNDP*. Retrieved from https://www.undp.org/content/undp/en/home/blog/2020/islamic-finance-takes-on-covid-19.html.

Salih, S. A. (1999). The challenges of poverty alleviation in IDB member countries. *Islamic Development Bank*. Retrieved from https://www.isdb.org/sites/default/files/media/documents/2018-12/OP2_Chalanges_Proverty_IDB_MCs.pdf.

Securities Commission Malaysia. (2014). SC Introduces Sustainable and Responsible Investment Sukuk Framework. Retrieved from https://www.sc.com.my/resources/media-releases-and-announcements/sc-introduces-sustainable-and-responsible-investment-sukuk-framework.

Sumner, A., Hoy, C., & Ortiz-Juarez, E. (2020). Estimates of the impact of COVID-19 on global poverty. WIDER Working Paper 2020/43. Retrieved from https://www.wider.unu.edu/sites/default/files/Publications/Working-paper/PDF/wp2020-43.pdf.

The News. (2020, 15 May). Meaningful Use of Zakat Funds Could Create 10m Jobs in Pakistan. Retrieved from https://www.thenews.com.pk/print/658862-meaningful-use-of-zakat-funds-could-create-10m-jobs-in-pakistan.

The Rahuma Daily. (2020, 10 May). Various Waqf Boards across the Country Have Contributed Rs 51 Crore to Fight COVID-19: Union Minister Mukhtar Abbas Naqvi. Retrieved from https://www.therahnuma.com/various-waqf-boards-across-the-country-have-contributed-rs-51-crore-to-fight-covid-19-union-minister-mukhtar-abbas-naqvi/.

The World Bank Group, INCEIF, and ISRA. (2019). Report on Maximizing Social Impact through Waqf Solutions. Retrieved from https://www.inceif.org/2019/07/12/the-world-bank-inceif-isra-waqf-report-maximizing-social-impact-through-waqf-solutions/.

Ucu, K. R. (2020). Keuangan Sosial Islam Melawan Dampak Covid-19. Retrieved from https://translate.google.com/translate?hl=en&sl=id&u=https://republika.co.id/berita/q7xqm5282/keuangan-sosial-islam-melawan-dampak-covid19&prev=search.

UNHCR. (2020a). Over 1 Million Zakat Beneficiaries through the Refugee Zakat Fund: UNHCR Reveals, Urging Continued Islamic Philanthropy Contributions

Amid COVID-19 Emergency. Retrieved from https://www.prnewswire.com/ae/news-releases/over-1-million-zakat-beneficiaries-through-the-refugee-zakat-fund-unhcr-reveals-urging-continued-islamic-philanthropy-contributions-amid-covid-19-emergency-301043814.html.

UNHCR. (2020b). Refugee Zakat Fund: Islamic Philanthropy 2020 Annual Impact Brief. Retrieved from https://zakat.unhcr.org/wp-content/uploads/2020/04/IP-English-Impact-Brief-Final.pdf.

Wahab, F. (2020, 5 May). RM13mil in zakat paid out. *The Star*. Retrieved from https://www.thestar.com.my/metro/metro-news/2020/05/05/rm13mil-in-zakat-paid-out.

Winosa, Y. (2020). Time to mobilise zakat, retail sukuk for Indonesia's COVID-hit MSMEs: KNEKS official. Salaam Gateway. Retrieved from https://salaamgateway.com/story/time-to-mobilise-zakat-retail-sukuk-for-indonesias-covid-hit-msmes-kneks-official.

World Health Organization. (2020). COVID-19 Solidarity Response Fund: Help WHO Fight against COVID-19. Retrieved from https://www.who.int/emergencies/diseases/novel-coronavirus-2019/donate.

World Zakat Forum. (2020). Press Release: WZF Calls for United Action Oof Zakat Institutions Worldwide to Fight against COVID-19 Pandemic. Retrieved from http://www.worldzakatforum.org/images/download/WZF_CALLS_FOR_UNITED_ACTION_OF_ZAKAT_INSTITUTIONS_WORLDWIDE_TO_FIGHT_AGAINTS_COVID-19_PANDEMIC.pdf.

Gulf Daily News. (2020, 21 May). Social Waqf sukuk urged for Islamic finance industry. *Gulf Daily News*. Retrieved from https://www.zawya.com/mena/en/business/story/Social_Waqf_sukuk_urged_for_Islamic_finance_industry-SNG_175058973/.

Zain, N. R. M., & Ali, E. R. A. E. (2017). An analysis on Islamic social finance for protection and preservation of Maqāṣid al-Sharī'ah. *Journal of Islamic Finance* (Special Issue), 133–141.

Zaki, Y. (2020, 21 April). COVID-19: UAE residents start their good deeds way ahead of the Ramadan this year. *The Gulf News*. Retrieved from https://gulfnews.com/going-out/covid-19-uae-residents-start-their-good-deeds-way-ahead-of-the-ramadan-this-year-1.1587469697580.

2 Financial capacity indicators and risk exposure among different income groups

Influence of COVID-19

Monsurat Ayojimi Salami and Adel M. Sarea

2.1 Introduction

Financial capacity is an essential aspect of human life as it is defined as individual autonomy in day-to-day life (Marson et al., 2000; Moye and Marson, 2007; Sousa et al., 2014) and it is more relevant to older adults and associated with ageing (Gerstenecker et al., 2018). Similarly, a study by Marson et al. (2016) further argued that financial capacity issues always arise in older adults with cognitive decline and dementia. As a result, financial capacity is different from performance skills (such as counting of currency) as it involves a judgement skill (to optimize financial interest) and values to guide personal financial choices (Marson et al., 2016). Melton et al. (1987) argued that financial capacity is vital in assessing individual functional ability in the community.

However, Jackson and Hafemeister (2012) and Lichtenberg (2016) argued the limitations of such earlier studies on financial capacity. Jackson and Hafemeister (2012) reveal that studies on financial capacity did not focus on real-world financial exploitation but rather focused on older people with Alzheimer's disease. In the same vein, Lichtenberg (2016) argued in support of the clear link between financial capacity, Alzheimer's disease, and financial explorations, but they remain disconnected in actual practice. As a result, this study is neither assessing financial capacity from a psychological perspective nor medical viewpoint but rather examining financial capacity from social context with the opportunities provided by different authorities in 121 countries to enhance the financial capacity of their citizens. Therefore, income groups are used as a proxy to identify countries and types of financial capacity provision made to enhance the decisions made by those countries on income groups. Similarly, 194 countries agreed with the United Nations on changing the world for the better through 17 sustainable development goals (SDG) designed to cater for the less privileged, especially those living below USD$2 per day. In waiting for a promising future that might enhance the financial capacity of the majority of the global population, the COVID-19 pandemic turned back the poverty clock. Despite that 17 of the SDGs show some promising outcomes, these were not attained until the COVID-19 pandemic hit. This has drastically changed the financial lifestyle of the global economy, including that of the ageing generation. The situation is even worse as grandparents that provide childcare services have been discouraged from doing so due to the increase in mortality of older generations; they cannot provide childcare as they must also maintain social distancing. It has also been predicted that the effects of the COVID-19 pandemic shock are likely to outlast the actual pandemic (Alon et al., 2020).

As a result, this study aims to examine the effectiveness of the financial capacity indicators employed across 121 countries and to identify the income groups that are really benefiting from the established social protection system. This study is currently essential because of two contradicting events, while the world is looking forward to seeing positive outcomes of the 17 SDGs, the COVID-19 pandemic that started as a health crisis became an economic crisis. The result of this study shows that the mean difference in the majority of the financial capacity indicators and the associated risks are not significantly different across the four different income groups. The results further reveal that the high-income group is in favour of government supervision of financial capacity. Therefore, this study argues against using similar financial capacity indicators for different income groups.

The rest of this paper is structured as follows: section two focusses on the literature review, section three discusses the data and methodology, section four explains the findings, and section five is the conclusion of this study.

2.2 Literature review

Despite that financial capacity plays a critical role that is applicable in everyday life, there are few empirical studies on this (Marson, 2016). Over three decades ranging from 1970 until 1999, there are no conceptual studies relating to financial capacity from clinical or legal points of view (Marson, 2016). In addition, it is also argued that there is no specific instruments developed to test the financial capacity which is general to all jurisdictions (Sousa et al., 2014). There is also no specific instrument that has been developed to assess financial capacity in Portugal in the context of forensic mental health assessments (Sousa et al., 2015); as a result, the financial capacity instrument remains a serious concern. Even until now, empirical studies on financial capacity from social sciences remain scarce. Similarly, Wood and Lichtenberg (2017) reveal that financial capacity is an important component for clinical conceptual models on financial exploitation. Pachana et al. (2014) argued from the clinical point of view that anxiety predicts financial capacity performance. However, clinical judgement alone cannot provide reliable results unless it is supported by objective data (Braun et al., 2009).

Marson et al. (2016) assessed financial capacity from a clinical perspective and traced older adult vulnerability and diminishing financial capacity to a decline in cognitive function, which is associated with both normal cognitive ageing and cognitive disorders of ageing. Lu et al. (2019) examined financial capacity from the perspective of non-profit organizations and concluded that diversification has a slightly negative effect on financial capacity. Blanchard and Eberle (2013) suggested assessing the financial capacity of an organization through revenue sufficiency, creditworthiness, fiscal management, and controls.

From the studies cited here, it can be inferred that financial capacity studies from the social sciences are very limited therefore there is a disconnect between findings on financial capacity and conditions in the real world remain un-addressed.

2.3 Methodology

Data for conducting a study on financial capacity and associated risks across different income groups through responsible finance were obtained from the World Bank database. The financial capacity indicators as identified in the data obtained are in six groups, namely lending facility, creating awareness, monitoring and evaluation, educational curriculum, educational level, and government supervision on financial capacity. The risks associated with the income group to attain efficient financial capacity are classified into operational risk, customer risk, and other risks. The World Bank database provided financial capacity information on 121 countries, and they are classified under four income groups, namely, the low-income group, lower-middle-income group, upper-middle-income group, and high-income group. For this study, the income groups are dependent variables, while financial capacity indicators and associated risk are independent variables.

We first investigate the frequency summary of the dependent variable, followed by a descriptive summary of the independent variables. Statistical significance in the mean difference across different income groups is examined using analysis of variance (ANOVA) followed by a post hoc test to identify the income group in which the mean difference is statistically significant. ANOVA (F-statistics) is used to determine the overall significance of the explanatory variable on the dependent variable (Naicker, 2017). Marson et al. (2010) adopted ANOVA in their financial capacity study. Noting that financial capacity studies are mostly common among medical and psychological sectors than other sectors, there is no specific methodology to be employed, only that the method should be able to address the objective of the study. This implies there is no specific modelling technique to quantify financial capacity among people (Sousa et al., 2014). Therefore, Peisah and Shulman (2012) argue that instruments for assessing financial capacity are available in abundance.

Since the objective of this study is to investigate whether the financial capacity indicators adopted across different income groups provide opportunities for the less privileged population to make individual financial decisions, two broad hypotheses were developed followed by sub-hypotheses for empirical testing (Figure 2.1).

H_1. Financial capacity indicators significantly favour low-income groups as part of the strategy to improve the financial capacity of the less privileged population.

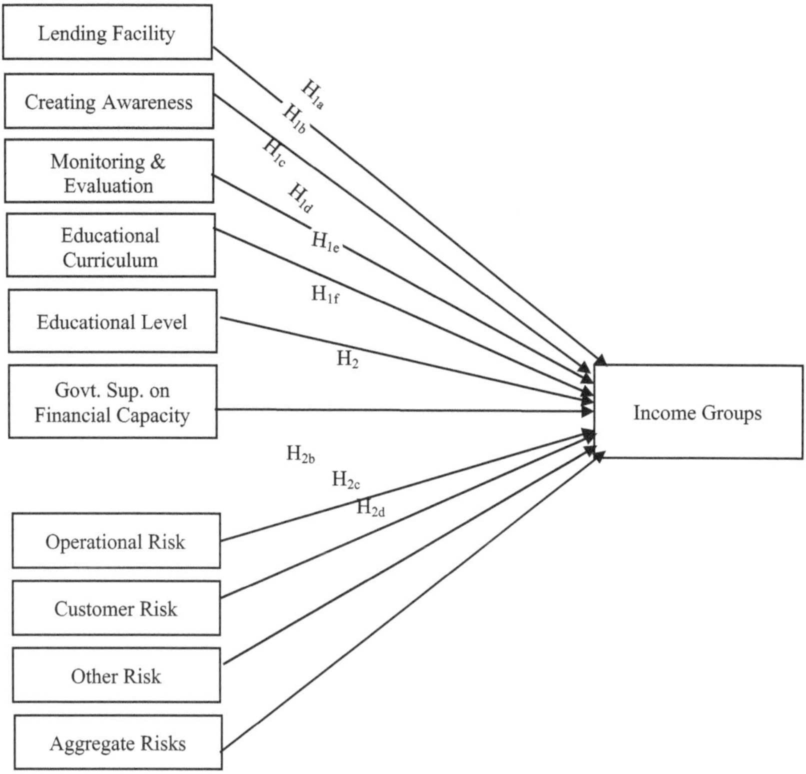

Figure 2.1 Conceptual framework of financial capacity indicators and associated risk across four income groups. Source: Author's own

Since financial capacity indicators comprise six different indicators, therefore sub-hypotheses are developed as follows:

H_{1a}. The lending facility positively and significantly favours the low-income group as part of the strategy to improve the financial capacity of the less privileged population.

H_{1b}. Creating awareness is positively significant and related to the low-income group as part of the strategy to improve the financial capacity of the less privileged population.

H_{1c}. Monitoring and evaluation positively and significantly favours the low-income group as part of the strategy to improve the financial capacity of the less privileged population.

H_{1d}. The educational curriculum positively and significantly favours the low-income group as part of the strategy to improve the financial capacity of the less privileged population.

H_{1e}. The educational level positively but significantly favours the low-income group as part of the strategy to improve the financial capacity of the less privileged population.

H_{1f}. Government supervision of financial capacity positively and significantly favours the low-income group as part of the strategy to improve the financial capacity of the less privileged population.

H_{2}. The risk associated with financial capacity indicators negatively and significantly favour low-income groups as part of the strategy to improve the financial capacity of the less privileged population.

H_{2a}. Operational risk negatively but significantly favours the low-income group as part of the strategy to improve the financial capacity of the less privileged population.

H_{2b}. Customer risk negatively but significantly favours the low-income group as part of the strategy to improve the financial capacity of the less privileged population.

H_{2c}. Other risks negatively but significantly favour the low-income group as part of the strategy to improve the financial capacity of the less privileged population.

H_{2d}. Aggregate risk negatively but significantly favours the low-income group as part of the strategy to improve the financial capacity of the less privileged population.

2.4 Empirical results

2.4.1 Descriptive summary and ANOVA result

Table 2.1 reports a summary of the four income groups classification used in the present study with relative frequency (%). Country data obtained from the World Bank database are categorized according to their income classification. The smallest number of participants came from the low-income group which constituted 9.1% (11) while the highest number of participants came from the high-income group which constituted 32.3% (39). The lower-middle-income and upper-middle-income groups' participation rates were 28.1% (34) and 30.6% (37), respectively.

Table 2.2 below reveals the mean and standard deviation of the different income groups in relation to the financial capacity indicators. For lending facility,

Table 2.1 Descriptive statistics of income groups

Income Group	*Frequency*	*Percentage*
Low income	11	9.1%
Lower-middle income	34	28.1%
Upper-middle income	37	30.6%
High income	39	32.2%

Source: Author's own

Table 2.2 Financial capacity indicators across different income groups

Financial Capacity Indicators	*Income Groups*	*Mean*	*SD*
Lending facility	Low income	1.3636	0.5045
	Lower-middle income	1.3824	0.4933
	Upper-middle income	1.3784	0.4917
	High income	1.5135	0.5067
Creating awareness	Low income	1.3636	0.5045
	Lower-middle income	1.2941	0.4625
	Upper-middle income	1.2162	0.4173
	High income	1.1351	0.3466
Monitoring and evaluation	Low income	1.1818	1.1678
	Lower-middle income	1.3529	1.2180
	Upper-middle income	1.3889	1.1283
	High income	1.5405	1.0953
Educational curriculum	Low income	1.0000	0.0000
	Lower-middle income	0.9706	0.1715
	Upper-middle income	1.0000	0.0000
	High income	0.9744	0.1601
Education level	Low income	1.2727	1.7939
	Lower-middle income	1.9412	1.4759
	Upper-middle income	2.1944	1.5084
	High income	2.2703	1.6440
Government supervision of financial capacity	Low income	0.8182	0.8739
	Lower-middle income	1.2647	1.0534
	Upper-middle income	1.5135	1.2388
	High income	1.8718	1.2393

Note: SD, standard deviation. Source: Author's own

the high-income group has the mean (mean = 1.5135, standard deviation (SD) = 0.5067), this is followed by the lower-middle-income group (mean = 1.3824, SD = 0.4933), and then the low-income group (mean = 1.3636, SD = 0.5045). These statistics indicate that the high-income group provides better lending facilities for citizens followed by the lower-middle-income group countries, low-income group countries provide the least lending facilities for their citizens. This provides some justification for the attitude of the low-income groups relying on others to create credit relief facilities such as cooperative societies, microfinancing, crowdfunding, and much more.

On creating an awareness indicator, the mean score of low-income-group countries is the highest (mean = 1.3636, SD = 0.5045) followed by the lower-middle-income-group countries (mean = 1.2941, SD = 0.4625), while the mean score of high-income-group countries is the lowest (mean = 1.1351, SD = 0.3466). On the one hand, with the fact that low-income groups borrow among themselves, they are more likely to increase the number of their group-lending participants by creating more awareness about the benefit of joining such groups. On the other hand, high-income groups have opportunities to use lending facilities provided by their authority; therefore, there is less concern regarding awareness creation.

The educational curriculum indicator shows that the mean score for the low-income group (mean = 1.0000, SD = 0.0000) and the upper-middle-income group (mean = 1.0000, SD = 0.0000) are the highest while the high-income group (mean = 0.9744, SD = 0.1601) and lower-middle-income group (mean = 0.9706, SD = 0.1715) have a lower mean score.

For the educational level indicator, the mean score for the high-income group is the highest (mean = 2.2703, SD = 1.6440), followed by upper-middle-income group (mean = 2.1944, SD = 1.5084), and the low-income group (mean = 1.2727, SD = 1.7939) has the lowest mean score. This implies that high-income groups are highly educated about financial capacity followed by the upper-middle-income group, and the group least educated about financial capacity is the low-income group. This finding is justifiable by identifying financial capacity education as a gap needing to be filled in the low-income group. This finding is partially consistent with Xu and Zia (2012), who reported that policymakers from both developed and developing countries are increasing their spending on financial education programmes.

On government supervision of the financial capacity indicator, the mean score for the high-income group is mean = 1.8718, SD = 1.2393, while the mean score for the low-income group is mean = 0.8182, SD = 0.8937, the lowest among the groups. This result supports the finding on the lending facility, i.e., once the lending facility is made available for the high-income group, there is a need for the government to provide supervision of those facilities and the income group that is benefiting from the facility. Similarly, the low-income group scores the lowest mean for some financial capacity indicators such as lending facility and government supervision on financial capacity.

In summary, four out of six financial capital indicators, namely the lending facility, monitoring and evaluation, educational level, and government supervision on financial capacity, support the high-income group while the educational curriculum and creating awareness support the low-income group. This implies that high-income-group countries provide more supportive financial capacity indicators to their citizens, while low-income-group countries are not paying sufficient attention to their citizens' financial capacity. The conclusion supports the findings by Xu and Zia (2012) that provision of financial education is considered part of consumer protection in high-income countries while such provision is limited in low-income countries.

Table 2.3 reports the associated risk of different income groups in relation to the financial capacity indicators. Regarding the lending facility indicator, the low-income group is more vulnerable to operational and other risks with a mean of 1.4444 and SD of 0.5271, while the low-income group is the least vulnerable to customer risk (mean = 1.0000, SD = 0.7071). However, the upper-middle-income group is the least vulnerable to operational risk (mean = 1.2500, SD = 0.5501) and other risk (mean = 1.2000, SD = 0.6156) while the high-income group is the most vulnerable to customer risk (mean = 1.3333, SD = 0.6172).

Table 2.3 Type of risk assessed

Financial Capacity Ind.	*Income Groups*	*Operational Risk*		*Customer Risk*		*Other Risk*	
		Mean	*SD*	*Mean*	*SD*	*Mean*	*SD*
Lending facility	Low income	1.4444	0.5271	1.0000	0.7071	1.4444	0.5271
	Lower middle	1.2667	0.6397	1.2000	0.6644	1.2667	0.6915
	Upper middle	1.2500	0.5501	1.0500	0.7592	1.2000	0.6156
	High income	1.2667	0.5936	1.3333	0.6172	1.2667	0.5936
Creating awareness	Low income	1.4444	0.5271	1.0000	0.7071	1.4444	0.5271
	Lower middle	1.1333	0.5714	1.1000	0.6074	1.1000	0.6074
	Upper middle	1.2500	0.5501	1.0000	0.7255	1.2000	0.6156
	High income	1.0000	0.3780	1.0000	0.3780	1.0000	0.3780
Monitoring and evaluation	Low income	1.2000	1.2293	0.8000	1.1353	1.2000	1.2293
	Lower middle	1.1563	1.2472	1.1563	1.2472	1.1563	1.2472
	Upper middle	1.0385	1.0763	0.9231	1.1287	1.0000	1.0955
	High income	1.1111	1.3235	1.1667	1.2948	1.0000	1.2367
Educational curriculum	Low income	1.0000	0.0000	0.7778	0.4410	1.0000	0.0000
	Lower middle	0.8667	0.3458	0.8333	0.3791	0.8333	0.3791
	Upper middle	0.9500	0.2236	0.7500	0.4443	0.9000	0.3078
	High income	0.8750	0.3416	0.8750	0.3416	0.8750	0.3416
Education level	Low income	1.2727	1.7939	0.8182	1.3280	1.2727	1.7939
	Lower middle	1.7419	1.5699	1.8387	1.6145	1.8710	1.5219
	Upper middle	1.6957	1.7172	1.3913	1.6443	1.6522	1.7480
	High income	1.6000	1.7592	1.6000	1.7592	1.4500	1.7614
Government supervision of financial capacity	Low income	0.8182	0.8739	0.5455	0.8202	0.8182	0.8739
	Lower middle	1.0625	1.0758	1.0938	1.0583	1.0938	1.0583
	Upper middle	1.1200	1.3013	1.0400	1.2741	1.1600	1.3128
	High Income	1.3889	1.4200	1.4444	1.3815	1.3333	1.4142

Note: SD, standard deviation. Source: Author's own

Regarding the creating awareness indicator, the vulnerability of the low-income group to operational and other risks (mean = 1.4444, SD = 0.5271) is the highest while the vulnerability of the high-income group is the lowest for operational and other risks (mean = 1.0000, SD = 0.3780). The lower-middle-income group is most vulnerable to customer risk (mean = 1.1000, SD = 0.6074).

The low-income group is consistently more vulnerable to operational and other risks for monitoring and evaluation and educational curriculum indicators while it is the least vulnerable to operational and other risks under educational level and financial capacity government supervisor indicators. Contrarily, the lower-middle-income group is the most vulnerable to operational, customer, and other risks under the educational level indicator but least vulnerable to risk under the educational curriculum indicator. The high-income group is the most vulnerable to both operational and other risks under government supervision of the financial capacity indicator.

After we identified the income groups that are vulnerable to different types of risk, Table 2.4 reveals the summary of the associated risk of each income group based on each financial capacity indicator. Table 2.4 explicitly shows that the low-income group is more vulnerable to operational and other risks for the majority of the financial capacity indicators while the high-income group is most vulnerable to customer risk than any other income group. This implies that the most vulnerable income group as identified by financial capacity indicators is the low-income group. The finding consistently argues that the low-income group is at a disadvantage regarding the financial capacity indicators adopted in most of the countries globally and highly vulnerable to operational and other risks.

Prior to identifying the significance of the mean difference across different income groups, we examined the correlation among the financial capacity indicators, and the result is presented in Table 2.5.

Table 2.4 Summary of the income groups' vulnerability to different risk

Financial Capacity Indicators	*Operational Risk*	*Customer Risk*	*Other Risk*
Lending facility	Low-income group	High-income group	Low-income group
Creating awareness	Low-income group	Lower-middle-income group	Low-income group
Monitoring and evaluation	Low-income group	High-income group	Low-income group
Educational curriculum	Low-income group	High-income group	Low-income group
Educational level	Lower-middle-income group	Lower-middle-income group	Lower-middle-income group
Government supervision of financial capacity	High-income group	High-income group	High-income group

Source: Author's own

Table 2.5 Spearman's correlation for financial capacity indicators

	Lending Facility	*Creating Awareness*	*Monitoring and Evaluation*	*Educational Curriculum*	*Education Level*	*Fin. Cap. Govt.*
Lending facility	1					
Creating awareness	0.155^{c} [10] (0.090)	1				
Monitoring and evaluation	0.613^{a} [3] (0.0000)	0.234^{b} [8] (0.0100)	1			
Educational curriculum	–0.154^{c} [11] (0.0900)	0.070 (0.4460)	0.072 (0.4340)	1		
Educational level	0.365^{a} [6] (0.0000)	0.260^{b} [7] (0.0040)	0.545^{a} [5] (0.0000)	0.040 (0.6630)	1	
Government supervision of financial capacity	0 562^{a} [4] (0.0000)	0.192^{b} [9] (0.0350)	0.631^{a} [1] (0.0000)	–0.119 (0.188)	0.625^{a} [2] (0.0000)	1

Source: Author's own
^{a}1% significance level
^{b}5% significance level
^{c}10% significance level indicate 1%.
Significant correlations (r) are ranked in the parentheses [].

Table 2.5 presents the correlation matrix of the six financial capacity indicators using Spearman's rank correlation coefficient. The majority of the financial capacity indicators are significantly correlated, except in a few cases, as indicated in Table 2.5, where they are statistically insignificant. Noticeable strong positive relationships are established, as indicated by the correlation coefficients of the variables. The correlation between lending facility and creating awareness is $r = 0.613$, $p = 0.000$, between monitoring and evaluation and financial capacity support is $r = 0.631$, $p = 0.000$, between education level and financial capacity support is $r = 0.625$, $p = 0.0000$, between financial capacity support and monitoring and evaluation is $r = 0.562$, $p = 0.0000$, and monitoring and evaluation and educational level is $r = 0.545$, $p = 0.0000$. The correlation coefficients among the financial capacity indicators are within the threshold range since the Variance Inflation Factors (VIFs) of all the variables are less than 10, which implies no evidence of multi-collinearity.

Having shown most of the financial capacity indicators are significantly correlated without evidence of multi-collinearity, the most strongly significantly correlated positive relationship is between monitoring and evaluation and government supervision of financial capacity ($r = 0.631$), while the least significantly correlated negative relationship is between the lending facility and educational curriculum ($r = -0.154$). This concludes that monitoring and evaluation is positively correlated with government supervision of financial capacity while the lending facility provided by most governments is negatively correlated with the quality of knowledge acquired across income groups as measured by the educational curriculum.

We then proceed with examining the significance of the mean differences using one-way analysis of ANOVA. ANOVA is used to examine whether there are statistically significant mean variations between groups (Al-shammari, 2005; Shimizu et al., 2012). The ANOVA results for mean differences across the income groups in relation to associated financial capacity indicators are presented in Table 2.6 at a 95% level of significance.

Table 2.6 presents the findings on the significance of the mean difference in financial capacity indicators across the income groups. The result shows that mean of different groups are relatively similar. This is because the *p*-value of most of the financial capacity indicators and all associated risks are greater than 0.05. Although a series of noticeable mean differences were examined, the majority of the mean difference in financial capacity indicators and associated risks are not statistically significant across the different income groups (p-value > 0.05). This shows that the value of the calculated F-statistics is less than the value of the critical statistics (Al-shammari, 2005). Interestingly, despite the different financial capacity indicators adopted across 121 countries for the income groups, there is no significant difference except for the indicator for government supervision of financial capacity ($F = 3.0610$, $p < 0.0310$). However the f-statistics and *p*-values for the lending facility are $F = 0.6330$, $p > 0.5950$, creating awareness are ($F = 1.2810$, $p > 0.2840$), monitoring and evaluation ($F = 0.3340$, $p > 0.8010$), educational curriculum ($F = 0.4320$, $p > 0.7310$),

Table 2.6 Analysis of variance (ANOVA) result of financial capacity indicators across different income groups

Financial Capacity Indicators	*Sum of Squares*	*df*	*Mean Square*	*F*	*Significant Level*	*Remark*
Lending facility	0.471	3	0.1570	0.6330	0.5950	Insignificant
Creating awareness	0.675	3	0.2250	1.2810	0.2840	Insignificant
Monitoring and evaluation	1.3290	3	0.4430	0.3340	0.8010	Insignificant
Educational curriculum	0.0220	3	0.0070	0.4320	0.7310	Insignificant
Education level	9.5840	3	3.1950	1.2960	0.2790	Insignificant
Government supervision of financial capacity	12.3920	3	4.1310	3.0610	0.0310	Significant
Operational risk	0.0790	3	0.0260	0.4010	0.7520	Insignificant
Consumer risk	0.3480	3	0.1160	0.8380	0.4780	Insignificant
Other risk	0.1380	3	0.0460	0.5190	0.6710	Insignificant
Aggregate risk	0.4940	3	0.1650	0.4160	0.7420	Insignificant

Source: Author's own

Note: df, degree of freedom. The degree of freedom between groups = 3, and degree of freedom within groups = 117, therefore F(3,115).

education level (F = 1.2960, $p > 0.2790$), operational risk (F = 0.4010, $p > 0.7520$), customer risk (F = 08380, $p > 0.4780$), other risk (F = 0.5190, p > 0.6710), and aggregate risk (F = 0.4160, $p > 0.7420$). These findings reveal that there is no sufficient empirical evidence to conclude significant differences between most of the financial capacity indicators concerning different income groups. Thus, H_{1a}, H_{1b}, H_{1c}, H_{1d}, H_{1e}, H_{2a}, H_{2b}, H_{2c}, and H_{2d} are rejected. This finding is consistent with the finding by Ju et al. (2005), whereby only one construct is statistically significant while all other constructs are statistically insignificant. Elayan et al. (2003) reported as insignificant the mean variation for all the constructs used in their study.

Unfortunately, the result of the study implies that those in the low-income group who are living on less than $2 per day, which constitutes the majority of the world population, attract less attention to their terrible situation. We then proceed with the post hoc test to identify the direction of the significant mean variation among the income groups under study. The result of the post hoc test will reveal the particular income group favoured by government supervision.

Table 2.7 reports the post hoc test results. The findings indicate that there is a statistically significant mean difference between the high-income and low-income groups on the indicator for government supervision of financial capacity. The finding shows that the high-income group has been favoured against the low-income group. This implies that governments are more interested in the financial capacity of the high-income group as they have more accessibility to lending facilities than the low-income group.

Table 2.7 Tukey post hoc test

Financial Capacity Indicator	*Income Group*	*Income Group*	*Mean Difference*	*Significant Level*
Government supervision of financial capacity	High	Low	1.0536	0.044

Source: Author's own

2.4.2 *Impact of the COVID-19 pandemic on inefficient financial capacity indicators*

This study concludes that available financial capacity indicators provided by several authorities across 121countries fail to address grassroots problems even when the economy is relatively stable. This is because the indicators for assessing financial capacity across different income groups show no significant variation. Unfortunately, several economies are currently performing poorly and this poses more challenges for the less privileged population, especially during the COVID-19 pandemic. For example, no less than 4000 companies stopped operating in Malaysia alone, and the situation is even worse in some other nations. In developed economies such as the United States of America, millions of jobs have been lost as reported in February 2020 (Baker et al., 2020) and the situation is becoming worse now than that recorded in February 2020. It is obvious that the extensive spread of the COVID-19 pandemic has become catastrophic to the global economy (Sarker, 2020), which has resulted in a global economic downturn (Alon et al., 2020). This might further widen the inequality gap and make the feasibility of financial capacity of the less privileged population difficult to attain in the near future.

Since the available financial capacity indicators across 121 countries are not structured in favour of the most affected populations, even during a stable economy, the COVID-19 pandemic might have reduced the probability of giving adequate attention to the struggle of the less privileged as most of the rich economies are currently struggling with pandemic shock. Global trade as well as GDP are reported to be in a sharp decline in the first six months of 2020 (Congressional Research Service, 2020) and have continued to decline in the third quarter of the year 2020. This is because any form of mass gathering, such as protest, may trigger a new wave of the COVID-19 pandemic. Malaysia is expecting a third COVID-19 wave due to political protests. Obviously, the global economy is experiencing a high level of uncertainty due COVID-19 pandemic, therefore increasing unemployment rates and uncertainty about future direction would widen the margin between the rich and the poor further.l. The COVID-19 pandemic would have a negative impact on the economies of developing countries (Jackson et al., 2020). Therefore, emerging and developing economies are at serious risk, especially after the COVID-19 pandemic.

2.5 Conclusion

This study examined financial capacity indicators and the risk associated with each across different income groups. The findings show that most of the financial capacity indicators provided by the authorities in 121 countries are not in favour of low-income groups. This is because there is no statistically significant mean difference across the different income groups except for government supervision of financial capacity indicators, and it is even in favour of high-income groups at the expense of low-income groups. Despite the continuous promotion of the 17 SDGs prior to the occurrence of the COVID-19 pandemic, but has been affected by pandemic shocks. COVID-19 has brought significant drawbacks towards achieving the 17 SDGs in the near future. This is because several trillions of dollars have been borrowed globally to combat the COVID-19 pandemic.

The COVID-19 pandemic should have been a great lesson, especially to emerging and developing economies, to restructure most of the unworkable systems and develop a unique approach that is appropriate to the local values and culture to improve the financial capacity of their citizens rather than replicating the financial capacity indicators of developed economies.

References

Alon, T. M., Doepke, M., Olmstead-Rumsey, J., & Tertilt, M. (2020). *The Impact of Covid-19 on Gender Equality, NBER Series.* Retrieved from https://ideas.repec.org/p/bon/boncrc/crctr224_2020_163.html.

Al-shammari, M. (2005). Assessing the learning experience in a business process re-engineering (BPR) course at the University of Bahrain technology and innovation management. *Business Process Management Journal, 11*(1), 47–62. DOI: 10.1108/14637150510578728.

Baker, S. R., Bloom, N., Davis, S. J., & Terry, S. J. (2020). *Covid-Induced Economic Uncertainty.* Retrieved from https://www.nber.org/papers/w26983.

Blanchard, C. S., & Eberle, W. D. (2013). Technical, managerial, and financial capacity among small water systems. *American Water Works Association, 105*(5), 229–235. doi: 10.5942/jawwa.2013.105.0045.

Braun, M., Gurrera, R. J., Karel, M. J., Armesto, J. C., & Moye, J. (2009). Are clinicians ever biased on their judgements of the capacity of older adults to make medical decisions? *Generations, 33*, 78–91.

Congressional Research Service. (2020). Global economic effects of COVID-19. *Congressional Research Service.* Retrieved from https://fas.org/sgp/crs/row/R46270.pdf.

Elayan, F. A., Lau, J. S. C., & Meyer, T. O. (2003). Executive incentive compensation schemes and their impact on corporate performance: Evidence from New Zealand since compensation disclosure requirements became effective. *Studies in Economics and Finance, 21*(1), 54–92.

Gerstenecker, A., Triebel, K., Eakin, A., Martin, R., & Marson, D.(2018). Exploring the factor structure of financial capacity in cognitively normal and impaired older adults. *Clinical Gerontologist, 41*(1), 33–41. doi: 10.1080/07317115.2017.1387211.

Jackson, S. L., & Hafemeister, T. L. (2012). APS investigation across four types of elder maltreatment. *Journal of Adult Protection*, *14*, 82–92. doi: 10.1108/14668201211217530.

Ju, T. L., Chen, S. H., Li, C. Y., & Lee, T. S. (2005). A strategic contingency model for technology alliance. *Industrial Management and Data Systems*, *105*(5), 623–644. doi: 10.1108/02635570510599995.

Lichtenberg, P. A. (2016). Financial exploitation, financial capacity, and Alzheimer's disease. *American Psychological Association*, *71*(4), 312–320.

Lu, J., Lin, W., & Wang, Q. (2019). Does a more diversified revenue structure lead to greater financial capacity and less vulnerability in nonprofit organizations ? A bibliometric and meta-analysis. *International Journal of Voluntary and Nonprofit Organizations*, *30*(3), 1–17. doi: 10.1007/s11266-019-00093-9.

Marson, D. (2016). Conceptual models and guidelines for clinical assessment of financial capacity. *Clinical Neuropsychology*, *1969*, 1–13. doi: 10.1093/arclin/acw052.

Marson, D. C., Sawrie, S. M., Snyder, S., McInturff, B., Stalvey, T., Boothe, A., Aldridge, T., Chatterjee, A., & Harrell, L. E. (2000). Assessing financial capacity in patients with Alzheimer disease: A conceptual model and a prototype instrument. *Archives of Neurology*, *57*, 877–884. doi:10.1001/archneur.57.6.877.

Marson, D. C., Martin, R. C., Wadley, V., Griffith, H. R., Snyder, S. Goode, P. S., Kinney, F. C., Nicholas, A. P., Steele, T., Anderson, B., Zamrini, E., Raman, R., Bartolucci, A., & Harrel, L. E. (2010). Clinical interview assessment of financial capacity in older adults with mild cognitive impairment and Alzheimer's disease. *NIH Public Access*, *57*(5), 806–814. doi: 10.1111/j.1532-5415.2009.02202.x.Clinical.

Marson, D. C., Sawrie, S. M., Snyder, S., McInturff, B., Stalvey, T., Boothe, A., Aldridge, T., Chatterjee, A., & Harrell, L. E. (2016) Financial decision-making and capacity in older adults. In *Handbook of the Psychology of Aging*. K.W. Schaie & S.L. Willis (Eds), 8th edition. London: Elsevier.

Melton, G. B., Petrila, J., Poythress, N., and Slobogin, C., Otto, R. K., Mossman, D., & Condie, L. O. (1987). *Psychological Evaluations for the Courts*. New York: Guilford Press.

Moye, J., & Marson, D. C. (2007). Assessment of decision-making capacity in older adults: An emerging area of practice and research. *The Journals of Gerontology Series B: Psychological Sciences and Social Sciences*, *62*(1), 3–11.

Naicker, M. (2017). The impact of the deferred tax adjustment on the economic value added (EVA) measure. *Investment Management and Financial Innovations*, *14*(3), 227–242. doi: 10.21511/imfi.14(3-1).2017.07.

Pachana, N. A., Byrne, G., Wilson, J., Tilse, C., Pinsker, D. M., Massavelli, B., Vearncombe, K. J., & Mitchell, L. K. (2014). Predictors of financial capacity performance in older adults using the financial competence assessment inventory. *International Psychogeriatrics*, *26*(6), 921–927.

Peisah, C., & Shulman, K. I. (2012). Testamentary capacity. In G. J. Demakis (ed.), *Civil Capacities in Clinical Neuropsychology: Research Findings and Practical Applications* (pp. 95–120). Oxford, UK: Oxford University Press.

Sarker, P. K. (2020). COVID crisis: Fiscal, monetary and macro-financial policy responses. *SSRN Electronic Journal*, *27*(3)1–8.

Shimizu, T., Won Park, Y., & Hong, P. (2012). Project managers for risk management: Case for Japan. *Benchmarking: An International Journal*, *19*(4/5), 532–547. doi: 10.1108/14635771211257990.

Sousa, L. B., Simões, M. R., Firmino, H., & Peisa, C. (2014). Financial and testamentary capacity evaluations: Procedures and assessment instruments underneath a functional approach. *International Psychogeriatrics*, *26*(2), 217–228. doi: 10.1017/S1041610213001828.

Sousa, L.B., Villar, M. Firmino, H., & Simões, M. R. (2015). Financial capacity assessment instrument (IACFin): Development and qualitative study using focus groups. *Psychiatry, Psychology and Law*, *22*(4), 571–585. doi: 10.1080/13218719.2014.960038.

Wood, S., & Lichtenberg, P. A. (2017). Financial capacity and financial exploitation of older adults : Research findings, policy recommendations and clinical implications. *Clinical Gerontologist*, *40*(1), 3–13. doi: 10.1080/07317115.2016.1203382.

Xu, L., & Zia, B. (2012). Financial literacy around the world: An overview of the evidence with practical suggestions for the way forward. World Bank Policy Research Working Paper No. 6107 , Retrieved from https://papers.ssrn.com/sol3/papers.cfm?abstract_id=2094887.

3 Financial inclusion and risk exposure among different income groups

The impact of COVID-19 pandemic

Monsurat Ayojimi Salami, Adel M. Sarea, and M. Kabir Hassan

3.1 Introduction

In 2009, no less than three billion of the world population lacked access to formal financial services (Chibba, 2009) such as bank accounts, credit, as well as insurance, and much more. Financial inclusion has been recognized globally and especially in Africa since 2000 (Ain et al., 2020; Nizam et al., 2020). As part of efforts to reduce poverty and narrow inequality gaps, several individuals and organizations have donated generously to financial inclusion programmes (Chibba, 2009), which has given rise to the development of several foundations aiming to alleviate poverty. However, when the global COVID-19 pandemic emerged, even developed countries were hit hard, and currently, it is the topmost challenge facing the global economy. Therefore, the ability to abide by the global standard operating procedure (SOP) for combating the COVID-19 pandemic is of less priority in developing countries as poverty is their topmost challenge. As a result, the International Monetary Fund (IMF) and World Bank advised giving developing countries sufficient cash injections to ease the impact of the COVID-19 pandemic, as they have no safety net to stop them from falling into deeper poverty (OXFAM, 2020).

With current conflicting priorities between developing countries and the rest of the world, examining financial inclusion in the context of the COVID-19 pandemic is currently essential. Financial inclusion is a means to tackle poverty by reducing inequality (Omar & Inaba, 2020) and addressing millennium development goals (Chibba, 2009). Through this, the financially excluded population is expected to reduce drastically. However, the COVID-19 pandemic is currently a pressing global issue with the potential to increase the poverty level and further widen inequality gaps globally. This is because most financial inclusion aids are from wealthy economies and most of those countries are facing economic challenges. About 52 donor countries were reported to have contributed about USD $82 billion, while low-income and lower-middle-income countries need an additional USD$ 2.4 trillion yearly for sustainable development goals (SDGs) (OXFAM, 2019). Although studies have established the potential of financial inclusion to reduce poverty (Ghosh & Sahu, 2020; Melubo & Musau, 2020) and even promote pro poor growth which are national policies to stimulate economic growth for the benefit of poor people (Waghmare, 2020), this has led to several meetings and conferences to find a breakthrough for the poverty issue through financial inclusion (Chibba, 2009; Fowowe, 2020). As a result, a series of conferences were held in developed countries in 2007 on financial inclusion including the global conference titled "Next Generation Access to Finance: Gaining Scale and Reducing Costs with Technology and Credit Scoring" held in Washington, DC, in September 2007, and "Making Finance Work for the Poor" held in the UK (Chibba, 2009; Nicole, 2008). Financial inclusion is a means of promoting resilience and at the same time preventing poverty traps (Fowowe, 2020). Still, there is no significant improvement in the poverty level of the billions of low-income families. However, Kenya has made a significant difference as about 82.9% of the population in financially inclusive (Arthur et al., 2020; Melubo & Musau, 2020). The question here is how efficient and effective are those strategies and policies on financial inclusion if financial inclusion introduced in the last two decades does not work efficiently?

As a result, the current study aims to firstly, examine and quantify different financial inclusion indicators commonly employed at the country level across different income groups. Secondly, the study will investigate the income group that is most vulnerable to risk. Thirdly, this study will explore and identify the targeted income group for financial inclusion across 121 countries. Fourthly, this study will make recommendations to policymakers based on the empirical findings of this study.

Briefly, the findings of this study are that few financial inclusion indicator variables are statistically significant, and they show that country-level financial inclusion is in favour of the lower-middle-income group than any other income groups examined. To be more precise, the national financial inclusion strategy seems to be broad enough to accommodate both low-income, low-middle-income, and upper-middle-income groups. The general financial inclusion strategy favours mainly the middle-income groups, while the microfinance strategy seems to have been designed for the lower-middle-income group. Similarly, financial inclusion policy indicators such as the requirement policy and priority lending policy tend to favour the lower-middle-income group.

3.2 Literature review

Chibba (2009) references the 2008 global financial crisis as well as the food and energy crisis to stress the importance of financial inclusion for developing countries. Sarma (2008) developed an index for financial inclusion, having argued that financial inclusion research is facing a lack of comprehensive studies. Similarly, Ghosh and Sahu (2020) developed an index for comparing the degree of financial inclusion achievement of 26 Asian countries between 2013 and 2017 using a weighted arithmetic mean and concluded a significant difference between the income groups. In addition, Fauzan et al. (2020) developed a financial inclusion index of 33 provinces in Indonesia and concluded that poverty negatively and significantly affects financial inclusion.

Fowowe (2020) conducted a study on the effect of financial inclusion on household agricultural productivity in Nigeria and concluded that financial inclusion enhances agricultural productivity in Nigeria. Prasetiyani and Vikaliana (2020) revealed that the national vision for financial inclusion in Indonesia is to develop a financial system that would be accessible to all levels of society through which economic growth would be encouraged, and income redistributed to alleviate poverty. Mengesha et al. (2020) conducted a study on the relationship between the education level and financial literacy of households in the Jimma zone of Ethiopia using Analysis of Variance (ANOVA). They concluded that there is a positive and significant mean difference across different education levels.

Brahim and Kamalu (2020) examined the financial inclusion of 30 samples of Islamic banks in Organisation of Islamic Cooperation (OIC) member countries using panel analysis for the data from 2013 to 2018 using a system generalized method of moments (system GMM), panel cointegration, and panel causality test to establish that Islamic banks significantly affect the level of financial inclusion in OIC countries. However, Brahim and Kamalu's (2020) findings committed an overstating error by including the result of the coefficient of interaction with the marginal effect of interaction. To avoid understating or overstating the interpretation of interaction model, both the coefficient of interaction and marginal effect need to be statistically significant and reported (Kingsley et al., 2017).

In making a comparison between developed and developing countries, Rodrigue and Roger (2020) narrow the main causes of inequality of access to finance and banking sectors. Rodrigue and Roger (2020) established a direct relationship between financial inclusion and remittances using GMM for panel data of 47 countries in Sub-Saharan Africa for the period from 2004 to 2014. The authors reveal that regular remittance to the poor may enable the bank sector to grant credit to low-income people to start an economic activity. Similarly, Arthur et al. (2020) also reveal a positive and statistically significant relationship between remittances to Kenya and financial inclusion.

3.3 Methodology

Data about financial inclusion strategies and policies and risk exposure among different income groups were obtained from the official website of the World Bank (http://worldbank.org) for 124 countries; there are three points of missing data due to unspecified income groups. Therefore, a total of 121 countries' data income groups were finally analyzed. Since the data used in this study focuses on the country level, the database provided categorical data; hence financial inclusion variables are used as independent variables while income groups are the dependent variables. The data obtained were classified into five parts: first, financial inclusion strategies, which are national financial strategy (NFS), general financial strategy (GFS), national development strategy (NDS), microfinance strategy (MFS), and financial literacy strategy (FLS); secondly, financial inclusion policy, which is the requirement policy, priority lending policy, tax incentive policy, deposit-taking institutions' policy, encouraging policy, and no policy implementation; thirdly, type of risk assessed, which are operational risk, customer risk, and other risk; fourthly, the targeted group for financial inclusion is examined among different income groups; and fifthly, the income groups that are categorized into high-income, upper-medium-income, lower-medium-income, and low- income groups.

The analysis approaches employed are descriptive statistics, one-way ANOVA, and post hoc test. Descriptive statistics provide information about frequencies and percentages of the income groups as well as mean and standard deviation (SD) of the financial inclusion dependent variable indicators. ANOVA is used to explore the differences among financial inclusion indicators across the income groups and the post hoc test identifies the income groups with a mean difference. Seamer and Melia (2015) and Mengesha et al. (2020) used ANOVA to examine the significance of the mean difference. Similarly, Nilsson (2009) used both ANOVA and the post hoc test to quantify the mean difference and specific group for the mean difference.

3.4 Empirical findings

This study provides descriptive statistics results of income groups in relation to frequency and percentage, followed by the mean and standard deviation of financial inclusion indicator variables. Similarly, a correlation matrix of financial inclusion indicator variables is examined following the ANOVA and post hoc test results. In the end, the percentage of the population living below the poverty level in selected countries and total cases of the population infected with COVID-19 across countries are presented.

Table 3.1 presents the descriptive statistics of the income groups in 121 counties in six areas namely Europe and Central Asia, East Asia and the Pacific, Latin America and the Caribbean, the Middle East and North Africa, South Asia, and Sub-Saharan Africa. As can be observed in Table 3.1, low-income earners constitute the smallest percentage, while high-income earners constitute the highest percentage. It is evident that about 67.8% are facing different issues of financial exclusion. This indicates that financial inclusion needs urgent and special attention, most especially during the current COVID-19 pandemic.

Hence, it is important to quantify the strategies and policies employed at the country level for financial inclusion. Table 3.2 presents statistical evidence of the

Table 3.1 Descriptive statistics of income groups

Income groups	*Frequency*	*Percentage*
Low-income	11	9.1%
Lower-middle income	34	28.1%
Upper-middle income	37	30.6%
High-income	39	32.2%

Source: Author's own

Table 3.2 Financial inclusion strategy

Financial inclusion strategy indicators	*Income groups*	*Mean*	*SD*
National financial strategy	Low-income	0.8162	0.4045
	Lower-middle income	0.7353	0.4478
	Upper-middle income	0.5946	0.4977
	High-income	0.1538	0.3655
General financial strategy	Low-income	0.2727	0.4671
	Lower-middle income	0.5000	0.5075
	Upper-middle income	0.4595	0.5052
	High-income	0.1795	0.3888
National development strategy	Low-income	0.2727	0.4671
	Lower-middle income	0.4118	0.4996
	Upper-middle income	0.4054	0.4977
	High-income	0.1795	0.3888
Microfinance strategy	Low-income	0.3636	0.5045
	Lower-middle income	0.4412	0.5040
	Upper-middle income	0.1622	0.3737
	High-income	0.2051	0.4091
Financial literacy strategy	Low-income	0.4545	0.5222
	Lower-middle income	0.5000	0.5075
	Upper-middle income	0.6216	0.4917
	High-income	0.6410	0.4860

Source: Author's own

financial inclusion strategies employed in 121 countries across different income groups.

In Table 3.2, the national financial strategy on financial inclusion is more in favour of the low-income group (mean = 0.8162, SD = 0.4045) than the high-income group (mean = 0.1535, SD = 0.3655). The next highest mean is for the lower-medium income group (mean = 0.7353, SD = 0.4478) followed by the upper-middle-income group (mean = 0.5946, SD = 0.4977).

However, statistical evidence shows that the national financial strategy on financial inclusion is more in favour of middle-income groups with 58.7% as both lower-middle-income (28.1%) and upper-middle-income groups (30.6%) as shown in Table 3.1. The lower-middle-income group scored the highest (mean = 0.5000, SD = 0.5075) followed by the upper-middle-income group (mean = 0.4595, SD = 0.5052).

In the same vein, statistical evidence shows that the national development strategies developed by countries are designed in favour of middle-income groups. The lower-middle-income group scored the highest (mean = 0.4118, SD = 0.4996) followed by the upper-middle-income group (mean = 0.4054, SD = 0.4977). While the high-income group (mean = 0.1795, SD = 0.3888) scored the lowest among the groups. This indicates that at the country level, both the general financial strategy and national development strategy are designed in favour of middle-income groups.

Based on statistical evidence for microfinance strategy, both low-income (mean = 0.3636, SD = 0.5045) and lower-middle-income (mean = 0.4412, SD = 0.5040) groups have a high mean score. This implies that both low-income and lower-middle-income groups are the focus of microfinance strategies.

The empirical findings on financial literacy strategy show that the high-income group (mean = 0.6410, SD = 0.4860) is more financially literate followed by the upper-middle-income group (mean = 0.6216, SD = 0.4917), while the low-income group (mean = 0.4545, SD = 0.5222) has the least financial literacy.

In addition, a summary of the financial inclusion strategy is presented in Table 3.3.

From the findings presented in Table 3.3, it can be inferred that both the national financial strategy and microfinance strategy are designed as financial inclusion strategies in favour of low-income and lower-middle-income groups. Similarly, the general financial strategy and national development strategy are in favour of middle-income groups, that is, lower-middle-income groups and upper-middle-income groups; upper-middle-income and high-income groups are financially literate.

Having grouped the financial inclusion strategy and their most focused groups, we proceeded with the financial inclusion policy, which is presented in Table 3.4.

Table 3.4 presents the report on financial inclusion policy. The mean score of the lower-middle-income group (mean = 0.5000, SD = 0.5075) is the highest followed by the upper-middle-income group (mean = 0.2162, SD = 0.4173), while the lowest-scoring group for requirement policy is the low-income group (mean =0.0909, SD = 0.3015).

Similarly, middle-income groups are the focus of priority lending. The lower-middle-income group ranked high (mean = 0.5588, SD = 0.5040) followed by the upper-middle-income (mean = 0.4054, SD = 0.4977) group while the

Table 3.3 Summary of financial inclusion strategy and their associated groups

Financial Inclusion Strategy Indicators	*Income Groups Favoured*
National financial strategy	Low-income group Lower-middle-income group
Microfinance strategy	Low-income group Lower-middle-income group
General financial strategy	Lower-middle income group Upper-middle-income group
National development strategy	Lower-middle-income group Upper-middle-income group
Financial literacy strategy	High income Upper-middle-income group

Source: Author's own

Table 3.4 Financial inclusion policy

Financial Inclusion Policy Indicators	*Income Groups*	*Mean*	*SD*
Requirement policy	Low income	0.0909	0.3015
	Lower-middle income	0.5000	0.5075
	Upper-middle income	0.2162	0.4173
	High income	0.1026	0.3074
Priority lending policy	Low income	0.2727	0.4671
	Lower-middle income	0.5588	0.5040
	Upper-middle income	0.4054	0.4977
	High income	0.2564	0.4424
Tax incentive, savings schemes policy	Low income	0.0909	0.3015
	Lower-middle income	0.1765	0.3870
	Upper-middle income	0.2432	0.4350
	High income	0.3590	0.4860
Deposit-taking Institutions Policy	Low income	0.5455	0.5222
	Lower-middle income	0.5294	0.5066
	Upper-middle income	0.4324	0.5023
	High income	0.6667	0.4776
Encouraging policy	Low income	0.5455	0.5000
	Lower-middle income	0.7647	0.4306
	Upper-middle income	0.7568	0.4350
	High income	0.5641	0.5024
None policy implementation	Low income	0.0909	0.3015
	Lower-middle income	0.0588	0.2388
	Upper-middle income	0.0811	0.2767
	High income	0.1538	0.3001

Note: SD represents Standard deviation.
Source: Author's own

high-income group scored the lowest. This shows the existence of financially excluded population in countries. However, this will not be successful in isolation and needs to be supported by access to finance strategies for low-income groups.

However, a tax incentive and saving schemes policy is in favour of high-income groups (mean = 0.3590, SD = 0.4860) followed by the upper-middle-income group (mean = 0.2432, SD = 0.4350), while the low-income group (mean = 0.0909, SD = 0.3015) is the least favoured. It is obvious that both high-income and upper-middle-income groups are at better financial capacity compared with the low-income or lower-middle-income groups.

Furthermore, on deposit-taking institutions policy, high-income groups score the highest mean (mean = 0.6667, SD = 0.4776) followed by the low-income group (mean = 0.5455, SD = 0.5222), while the upper-middle-income group (mean = 0.4324, SD = 0.5023) is the least favoured.

The encouragement policy could be inferred as favouring the middle-income group. The lower-middle-income group (mean = 0.7647, SD = 0.4306) has the highest mean followed by the upper-middle-income group (mean = 0.7568, SD = 0.4350), while the lowest mean is that of the high-income group (mean = 0.5641, SD = 0.5024). This implies that income groups above low income benefit from the encouragement policy.

For situations where a financial inclusion policy is not implemented, the high-income (mean = 0.1538, SD = 0.3001) and low-income (mean = 0.0909, SD = 0.3015) groups have the highest mean among all groups examined. This because the two groups are at the extreme ends of financial inclusion. If no financial inclusion policy is implemented, the high-income group is already financially comfortable while the low-income group has already been excluded from formal financial services. Therefore, they are not really experiencing a lack of financial inclusion policy. However, middle-income groups are the focus of financial inclusion policy, and they already understand the implication of a lack of a financial inclusion policy. Hence, the lower-middle-income (mean = 0.0588, SD = 0.2388) and upper-middle-income (mean = 0.0811, SD = 0.2767) groups are highly affected.

In summary, middle-income groups, that is, both lower- and upper-middle-income groups score high in requirement policy, priority lending policy, and encouraging policy, while the high-income group score the highest in deposit-taking institution policy and no policy implementation. This implies that the high-income group is not affected by either deposit policy or lack of financial inclusion policy while middle-income groups are.

Even if a financial inclusion strategy and financial inclusion policy were made available, access to finance is highly essential. Table 3.5 presents a statistical report on access to finance across the four income groups.

Table 3.5 reveals the access of each income group. The mean score for the lower-middle-income group (mean = 1.0294, SD = 0.7972) is the highest followed by the upper-middle-income group while the low-income group is the least quantifiable for finance in the group. This finding consistently supports the financial exclusion of the less privileged group.

To avoid a premature conclusion, we proceeded further with the identification of a targeted group for financial inclusion and the report is presented in Table 3.6. The low-income group (mean = 1.0000, SD = 0.0000) is the most targeted group for financial inclusion followed by the lower-middle-income group

Table 3.5 Access to finance

	Income Groups	*Mean*	*SD*
Access to finance	low income	0.8182	0.8739
	lower-middle income	1.0294	0.7972
	upper-middle income	1.0000	0.8498
	high income	0.8462	0.8441

Source: Author's own

Table 3.6 Specific targeted group for financial inclusion

	Income Groups	*Mean*	*SD*
Specific group target	Low income	1.0000	0.0000
	Lower-middle income	0.8000	0.4218
	Upper-middle income	0.5714	0.5136
	High income	0.3333	0.5774

Source: Author's own

(mean = 0.8000, SD = 0.4218) while the least targeted group is the high-income group (mean = 0.3333, SD = 0.5774).

Interestingly, the findings in Table 3.5 and Table 3.6 reflect the reality of financial inclusion, as the middle-income groups are the focus of access to finance while the low-income group has the least focus; financial inclusion is mainly designed for financially excluded populations, which could be a combination of low-income and lower-middle-income groups. This argument is consistently supported by OXFAM (2019) in that both low-income and lower-middle-income groups are financially excluded populations that need global attention. Therefore, how could country-level financial inclusion be effective and efficient if low-income groups are excluded from access to formal financial services mainly designed for them?

Similarly, we could not underrate the series of risks that might be associated with financial inclusion. This study examines some types of risk, such as operational risk, customer risk, other risks, and total risk, as a combination of individual risks examined. The report on risk is presented in Table 3.7.

The report in Table 3.7 indicates that the most vulnerable group to risk is the lower-middle-income group as it has the highest standard deviation for operational risk, other risks, and total risk of 0.3051, 0.3456, and 0.7184, respectively. The upper-middle-income group is in the second-highest risk position in customer risk (SD = 0.4443) and other risks (SD = 0.3078), the high-income group is in the second-highest risk position in operational risk (SD = 0.2582) and total risk (SD = 0.6217). However, the low-income group is the least vulnerable to risk as it is the second-highest risk in customer risk only.

Since this finding is novel and there is no specific benchmark for quantifying the severity of those risks found in other research studies, we therefore proceeded with examining the homogeneity of variance and the report is presented in Table 3.8. Although Sarma (2008) developed a financial inclusion index with a given range of $0 \leq w_i \leq 1$ and interpreted it as the higher the weight (w_i), the better the country in financial inclusion, this finding may not be applicable here because this study focuses on income groups and using such an index is subjective in nature due to a lack of significance test to predict how low is low and how large is large.

As observed in Table 3.8, homogeneity of variance is statistically significant for most of the indicators for financial inclusion, as examined in this study, except for financial literacy strategy, access to finance, and operational risk.

Table 3.7 Type of risk assessed

Risk Associated	*Income Groups*	*Mean*	*SD*
Operational risk	Low income	1.0000	0.0000
	Lower-middle income	0.9000	0.3051
	Upper-middle income	0.9500	0.2236
	High income	0.9333	0.2582
Consumer risk	Low income	0.7778	0.4410
	Lower-middle income	0.8667	0.3458
	Upper-middle income	0.7500	0.4443
	High income	0.9333	0.2582
Other risk	Low income	1.0000	0.0000
	Lower-middle income	0.8667	0.3456
	Upper-middle income	0.9000	0.3078
	High income	0.9333	0.2582
Total risk	Low income	2.7778	0.4410
	Lower-middle income	2.6333	0.7184
	Upper-middle income	2.8000	0.4140
	High income	2.6757	0.6217

Note: SD, standard deviation.
Source: Author's own

Table 3.8 Test of homogeneity of variance

Financial Inclusion Indicators	*Mean Coefficient*	*Significance*
National financial strategy	8.0200 [a]	0.0000
General financial strategy	14.3130 [a]	0.0000
National development strategy	10.3650 [a]	0.0000
Microfinance strategy	8.4460 [a]	0.0000
Financial literacy strategy	1.0720	0.3640
Access to finance	0.4320	0.7300
Requirement policy	16.7120 [a]	0.0000
Priority lending policy	4.6090 [b]	0.0040
Tax incentive, savings schemes policy	7.3230 [a]	0.0000
Deposit-taking institutions policy	2.2300 [c]	0.0880
Encouraging policy	5.1330 [b]	0.0020
No policy implementation	2.7280 [b]	0.0470
Specific group target	14.0100 [a]	0.0000
Operational risk	1.8190	0.1520
Consumer risk	3.6960 [b]	0.0160
Other risk	2.5410 [c]	0.0630
Total risk	2.1810 [c]	0.0980

[a] 1% significance level
[b] 5% significance level
[c] 10% significance level
Source: Author's own

We further proceed with examining the correlation between indicators for independent variables, and the result is presented in Table 3.9.

3.4.1 Correlation

Based on the correlation matrix result presented in Table 3.9, the magnitude of the relationship among the indicators is denoted by the coefficient of correlation. Most of the correlation coefficients are statistically significant, and none of the correlation coefficients is higher than the threshold correlation value. This implies that the financial inclusion indicators are within the range of low to moderate correlation. This indicates no evidence of multi-collinearity among the financial inclusion independent variable indicators. While some correlation coefficients are not statistically significant, this is consistent with the report made in the study by Nizam et al. (2020).

3.5 ANOVA result

Despite the mean differences reported in the earlier tables, the significance of the mean differences of financial inclusion is explored using ANOVA. Table 3.10 shows that there is a statistically significant difference in the mean of national financial strategy and income groups $F(3,117) = 13.990$, $p < 0.01$. There is a statistically significant difference between the mean of general financial strategy and income groups $F(3,117) = 3.632$, $p < 0.05$. Similarly, there is a statistically significant mean difference between microfinance strategy and income groups $F(3,117) = 2.947$, $p < 0.05$. This indicates that there is a statistically significant difference in the mean of national finance strategy, general finance strategy, and microfinance strategy in at least one of the income groups.

Furthermore, there is a statistically significant difference between the mean of requirement policy and income groups $F(3, 117) = 6.665$, $p < 0.01$. In addition, there is a statistically significant mean difference in priority lending policy and income groups, $F(3,117) = 2.644$, $p < 0.1$. This implies that the mean difference in requirement policy and priority lending policy is statistically significantly different in at least one of the income groups.

The ANOVA shows significant differences between some means of financial inclusion indicators. The mean difference of five financial inclusion indicators are statistically significant; three of the indicators are related to financial inclusion strategy and two indicators are related to financial inclusion policy. Moreover, we proceed with the post hoc test to identify the income groups of which the mean for financial inclusion indicators are different. The results of the post hoc test are presented in Table 3.11.

Noting that the mean differences of other financial inclusion indicators, such as access to finance, associated risks, and the rest of the financial inclusion strategies and policies, are not statistically significantly different. The implication of this is that there is no significant difference in treatment across the income groups for those financial inclusion indicators. The indication is irrespective of income

Table 3.9 Pearson's correlation matrix result

FI	*NFS*	*GFS*	*NDS*	*MFS*	*FLS*	*ATF*	*PR*	*PLP*	*TIP*	*D-TIIP*	*EP*	*NP*	*STG*	*Risk-O*	*Risk-Other*	*Risk-C*	*Risk-Total*
NFS	1																
GFS	0.2730[a]	1															
NDS	0.2150[b]	0.4640[a]	1														
MFS	0.3370[a]	0.3420[a]	0.3390[a]	1													
FLS	0.0950	0.3470[a]	0.1990[b]	0.1130	1												
ATF	0.2740[a]	0.1540[c]	0.0870	0.1910[b]	0.3290[a]	1											
PR	0.2250[a]	0.2790[a]	0.2660[b]	0.2990[b]	0.8140[b]	0.169[c]	1										
PLP	0.3030[a]	0.1360	0.2940[b]	0.2070[b]	0.1710[c]	0.257[b]	0.2960[b]	1									
TIP	0.0290	0.2000[b]	0.1850[b]	0.1710[c]	0.2980[b]	0.259[b]	0.0770	0.2960[b]	1								
D-TIP	-0.0010	0.1240	0.1370	0.2260[b]	0.0860	0.145	0.2190[b]	0.1870[b]	0.181[b]	1							
EP	0.2340[b]	0.1740[c]	0.2910[b]	0.1910[b]	0.0860	0.118	0.1570[c]	0.2660[b]	0.117	0.3150[a]	1						
NP	-0.1590[c]	-0.0570	-0.1320	0.1570[c]	-0.1550[c]	-0.150[c]	-0.2020[b]	-0.2790[b]	-0.202[b]	-0.3870[a]	-0.5080[a]	1					
STG	0.0001[a]	0.0000	0.0540	0.1470	0.1090	-0.146	0.1330	0.1290	0.032	-0.1470	-0.1330	0.0350	1				
Risk-O	0.3200[a]	-0.0890	0.1190	0.0590	-0.1250	0.115	-0.0400	0.0320	0.038	0.1730	-0.0660	0.0850	0.0001[a]	1			
Risk-Other	0.0130	0.0040	-0.0050	0.0120	0.1800	0.094	0.0290	0.1120	-0.016	0.1530	0.0770	-0.0560	0.4080[b]	0.0990	1		
Risk-C	0.0810	0.1610	-0.0690	0.0500	0.2030	0.023	0.1500	-0.0340	0.013	0.2400[b]	0.0940	-0.2360[b]	0.0550	0.1760	0.2360[b]	1	
Risk-Total	0.1840	0.0620	0.0050	0.0590	0.1550	0.105	0.0870	0.0450	0.015	0.2860[b]	0.0660	-0.1330	0.2040	0.5570[a]	0.6540[a]	0.7800[a]	1

[a]1% significance level.
[b]5% significance level.
[c]10% significance level.
NFS, national financial strategy; GFS, general financial strategy; NDS, national development strategy; MFS, microfinance strategy; FLS, financial literacy strategy; ATF, access to finance; PR, policy requirement; PLP, priority lending policy; TIP, tax incentive policy; D-TIP, deposit-taking institutions policy; EP, encouraging policy; NP, no policy implementation; STG, specific target group; Risk-O, operational risk; Risk-Other, other risk; Risk-C, customer risk; Risk-T, total risk.
Source: Author's own

Table 3.10 T-test result for Financial Inclusion Indicator

Financial Inclusion Indicators	*Sum of Squares*	*df*	*Mean Square*	*F*	*Significant level*
National financial strategy	7.9820	3	2.6610	13.990	0.0000
General financial strategy	2.3850	3	0.7950	3.6320	0.0150
National development strategy	1.3500	3	0.4500	2.1000	0.1040
Microfinance strategy	1.6860	3	0.5620	2.9470	0.0360
Financial literacy strategy	0.6000	3	0.2000	0.8090	0.4910
Access to finance	0.9110	3	0.3040	0.4350	0.7280
Requirement policy	3.2930	3	1.0980	6.6650	0.0000
Priority lending policy	1.8250	3	0.6080	2.6440	0.0520
Tax incentive, savings schemes policy	0.9270	3	0.3090	1.6700	0.1770
Deposit-taking institutions policy	1.0540	3	0.3510	1.4210	0.2400
Encouraging policy	1.1840	3	0.3950	1.8300	0.1460
No policy implementation	0.1850	3	0.0620	0.6780	0.5670
Specific group target	1.2740	3	0.4250	2.1630	0.1140
Operational risk	0.0790	3	0.0260	0.4010	0.7520
Consumer risk	0.3480	3	0.1160	0.8380	0.4780
Other risk	0.1380	3	0.0460	0.5190	0.6710
Total risk	0.4940	3	0.1650	0.4160	0.7420

df = degree of freedom
Note: between groups degree of freedom = 3, and within groups the degree of freedom = 117, therefore $F(3,117)$.
Source: Author's own

Table 3.11 Tukey post hoc test

Financial Inclusion Indicators	*Income Group*	*Income Group*	*Mean Difference*	*Significant level*
National financial strategy	Low	High	0.6643	0.0000
	Lower		0.5815	0.0000
	Upper		0.4408	0.0000
General financial strategy	Lower	High	0.3205	0.0220
	Upper		0.2800	0.0500
Microfinance strategy	Lower	Upper	0.2790	0.0400
Requirement policy	Lower	Low	0.4091	0.0220
		Upper	0.2838	0.0200
		High	0.3974	0.0000
Priority lending policy	Lower	High	0.3024	0.0410

Note that the result of the post hoc test presented in Table 3.11 is based on Tukey HSD, which is also consistent with the Bonferroni test result.
Source: Author's own

groups, and the treatment is the same. For example, the low-income group is placed on the same scale as the high-income group for access to finance, tax incentives, saving scheme policy, deposit-taking institution policy, and encouraging policy since the mean difference is not statistically significant. The statistical insignificance of financial literacy among the income groups is inconsistent with the findings by Mengesha et al. (2020).

Table 3.11 shows that those financial inclusion indicators with a statistically significant mean difference are in favour of low-income to middle-income groups, and they are within the scope of financial inclusion strategy and policy. For national financial strategy, low-income and middle-income groups have a statistically significant mean difference greater than the high-income group. The findings also show that national financial strategy is designed to favour the low-income group over the rest of the income groups. The low-income group has the highest mean difference (MD) = 0.6643, $p < 0.01$, followed by the lower-middle-income group MD = 0.5815, $p < 0.01$, and the lowest mean difference is the upper-middle-income group MD = 0.4408, $p < 0.01$.

For general financial strategy, the middle-income groups have a greater and statistically significant mean difference than that of the high-income group. This implies that the general financial strategy is designed to favour middle-income rather than low-income or high-income groups. It is found that the lower-middle-income group (MD = 0.3205, $p < 0.05$) has a greater mean difference than the upper-middle-income group (MD = 0.2800, $p \leq 0.05$).

The mean difference of microfinance strategy (MD = 0.2790, $p < 0.05$) is greater and statistically significant in favour of the lower-income group than that of the upper-middle-income group. This indicates that microfinance strategies across 121 countries were in favour of the lower-middle-income group than the upper-middle-income group. However, Chibba (2009) argued that microfinance alone is not sufficient to cater for financial inclusion as a whole.

On financial inclusion policy, a statistically significant mean difference is found in requirement policy and priority lending indicators in different income groups. There is a statistically significant greater mean difference in favour of the lower-middle-income group on requirement policy than other income groups: the low-income group scored MD = 0.4091, $p < 0.05$, the upper-middle-income group scored MD = 0.2838, $p < 0.05$) and the high-income group scored MD = 0.3970, $p < 0.01$. Similarly, the mean difference in priority lending policy (MD = 0.3024, $p < 0.05$) is significantly in favour of the lower-middle-income group than the high-income group. This finding is inconsistent with the national vision of Indonesia to achieve financial inclusion (Prasetiyani & Vikaliana, 2020).

Through these findings, an interesting inference can be made that the lower-middle-income group has the most focus of financial inclusion strategies globally followed by the upper-middle-income group, while the low-income group is the least favoured. Similarly, the lower-middle-income group is the focus of financial inclusion policy. This indicates that global financial inclusion has a greater preference for the lower-middle-income group than the upper-middle-income and low-income groups. This finding further emphasizes that financial inclusion is not designed for extremely low poverty levels and populations but rather relatively lower poverty levels and populations. Similarly, country-level financial inclusion indicators have not reduced the negative impact of urbanization and poverty by focusing mainly on the lower-middle-income group. Trivedi (2020) described financial inclusion as a pathway to normalizing the negative effect of urbanization as well as the mitigation of poverty. As claimed by Rodrigue and Roger (2020), the inequality between developed and developing countries is due to access to finance and the banking sector of the rich countries. Therefore, the mean difference in access to finance needs to be statistically significant for at least low-income and lower-middle-income groups for country-level financial inclusion indicators to be appropriate measures to eradicate poverty and support an efficient economy.

3.6 Implication of the COVID-19 pandemic on country-level financial inclusion

Country-level financial inclusion is more focused on the lower-middle-income group. However, the expectation about country-level financial inclusion is to be designed in such a way to address the poverty level of the grassroots population. Financial inclusion is to include the financially excluded population even to the bottom of the population pyramid (Prasetiyani & Vikaliana, 2020). Without that, several campaigns on SDGs may be far from achieving in the near future. This is because the COVID-19 pandemic has obstructed the economy and created more challenges to the global economy, which may increase the poverty level and even widen the inequality gap much more. Prior to the COVID-19 pandemic, several countries had committed to reducing inequality – the commitment to reducing inequality (CRI) (OXFAM, 2017). The current challenge is if the COVID-19 pandemic will prevent CRI.

Sarma (2008) states that even a certain proportion of developed countries' populations are financially excluded. Sarma (2008) further reveals that two decades ago, the policy on financial inclusion has been implemented in the USA. Still, more than 40 million people are documented as living below the poverty level, with about 18.5 million living in deep poverty (UNHCR, 2017). This finding is consistent with the OXFAM (2017) report that among wealthy economies, the USA is performing very badly on the CRI index. The aftermath of this current COVID-19 pandemic is that global poverty levels may be on the rise again, as an additional half a billion of the global population could be pushed into poverty and this could set back the fight against poverty for about three more decades, especially in Sub-Saharan Africa, the Middle East, and North Africa. This is because millions are losing their jobs globally; about half of all jobs in Africa could be lost in the aftermath of the COVID-19 pandemic (OXFAM, 2020).

3.7 Conclusion

Few of the several financial inclusion indicators examined in this study, such as national financial strategy, general financial strategy, microfinance strategy, requirement policy, and priority lending policy, are statistically significantly designed in favour of the lower-middle-income group. However, all other financial inclusion strategies and policies, such as national development strategy, financial literacy strategy, tax incentive, savings schemes policy, deposit-taking institutions policy, encouraging policy and no policy implementation, are not statistically significantly different. In addition, the mean difference in access to finance is not statistically significant across the income groups. This implies that all income groups are exposed to similar treatment on access to finance and all other indicators are not statistically different in the mean. The argument here is despite that the microfinance strategy and priority lending policy are statistically significant, as long as the mean difference on access to finance is statistically not significant, even the lower-middle-income group may need to compete with other high-income groups for finance. This will create challenges for the lower-middle-income group as well.

It is obvious that financial exclusion and the COVID-19 pandemic are pressing global issues, although their severity varies drastically across the globe. Africa has a huge proportion of a financially excluded population and is severely affected by the impact of the COVID-19 pandemic (OXFAM, 2020). Furthermore, OXFAM (2020) advised the IMF and World Bank to extend cash injections to developing countries to prevent a setback of about three decades in poverty eradication programmes. OXFAM even stressed that with about USD $82 billion donated by about 52 donor countries in December 2019 when the COVID-19 pandemic was not declared as a pandemic, still an additional USD $2.5 trillion is required on a yearly basis to make developing countries meet the sustainable development goals (SDG). In addition, Chibba (2009) references a report of the Consultative Group to Assist the Poor made in 2006 that two billion people of the three billion poor and financially excluded population live in developing countries; hence special attention is required for African regarding financial inclusion.

References

Ain, N. ul, Sabir, S., & Asghar, N. (2020). Financial inclusion and economic growth : Empirical evidence from selected developing economies. *Review of Economics and Development Studies*, *6*(1), 179–203.

Arthur, E. K., Musau, S. M., & Wanjohi, F. M. (2020). Diaspora remittances and financial inclusion in Kenya. *European Journal of Business and Management Research*, *5*(2), 110. doi: 10.24018/ejbmr.2020.5.2.289.

Brahim, W. H. B. W., & Kamalu, K. (2020). How does the Islamic banking development spur financial inclusion In OIC member countries? *Asian People Journal*, *3*(1), 170–185.

Central Intelligence Agency (CIA). (2016). *The World Factbook 2016*. Retrieved from https://www.cia.gov/library/publications/download/download-2016/index.html

Chibba, M. (2009). Financial inclusion, poverty reduction and the millennium development goals. *European Journal of Development Research*, *21*(2), 213–230. doi: 10.1057/ejdr.2008.17.

Fauzan, I. F., Firdaus, M., & Sahara, S. (2020). Regional financial inclusion and poverty: Evidence from Indonesia. *Economic Journal of Emerging Markets, 12*(1), 25–38. doi: 10.20885/ejem.vol12.iss1.art3.

Fowowe, B. (2020). The effects of financial inclusion on agricultural productivity in Nigeria. *Journal of Economics and Development, 1*, 1–19. doi: 10.1108/JED-11-2019-0059.

Ghosh, S., & Sahu, T. N. (2020). How financially inclusive the Asian's are? An empirical analysis. *Rajagiri Management Journal, 14*(1), 49–69.

Kingsley, A. F., Noordewier, T. G., & Bergh, R. G. V. (2017). Overstating and understating interaction results in international business research. *Journal of World Business, 52*(2), 286–295. doi: 10.1016/j.jwb.2016.12.010.

Melubo, K. D., & Musau, S. (2020). Digital banking and financial inclusion of women enterprises in Naro County, KENYA. *International Journal of Current Aspects in Finance, Banking and Accounting, 2*(1), 28–41. doi: 10.35942/ijcfa.v2i1.104.

Mengesha, T., Timbula, M. A., Mekonnen, Y., & Kebede, M.(2020). Financial literacy and its determinants among households in Jimma zone. *International Journal of Commerce and Finance, 6*(1), 102–112.

Nicole Pasricha (2008). Next generation access to finance: Gaining scale and reducing costs with technology and credit scoring. *Enterprise Development Microfinance, 19*(1), 59–68.

Nilsson, J. (2009). Segmenting socially responsible mutual fund investors responsibility. *International Journal of Bank Marketing, 27*(1), 5–31. doi: 10.1108/02652320910928218.

Nizam, R., Karim, Z. A., Abdul Rahman, A., & Sarmidi, T.(2020). Financial inclusiveness and economic growth : New evidence using a threshold regression analysis. *Economic Research-Ekonomska Istraživanja. 33*(1), 1465–1484. doi: 10.1080/1331677X.2020.1748508.

Omar, A., & Inaba, K. (2020). Does financial inclusion reduce poverty and income inequality in developing countries ? A panel data analysis. *Journal of Economic Structures, 9*(37), 125. doi: 10.1186/s40008-020-00214-4.

Oxford Committee for Famine Relief (OXFAM). (2017). The commitment to reducing inequality index. *Development Finance International and OXFAM Research Report*, 132.

Oxford Committee for Famine Relief (OXFAM). (2019). World Bank donor countries approve $82 billion package to fight extreme poverty: Oxfam reaction. Retrieved from https://www.oxfam.org/en/press-releases/world-bank-donor-countries-approve-82-billion-package-fight-extreme-poverty-oxfam.

Oxford Committee for Famine Relief (OXFAM). (2020). Half a billion people could be pushed into poverty by coronavirus, warns Oxfam. Retrieved from https://www.oxfam.org/en/press-releases/half-billion-people-could-be-pushed-poverty-coronavirus-warns-oxfam.

Prasetiyani, E., & Vikaliana, R. (2020). Construction of financial inclusion behaviour models in the implementation of fintech at fishermen SMEs Carita, Purwaarta. *Journal of Management and Leadership, 3*(1), 43–54.

Rodrigue, N. Y., & Roger, N. (2020). Remittances, financial inclusion and income inequality in Africa remittances, financial inclusion and income inequality in Africa. *Munich Personal RePEc Archive. 1*, 1–23.

Sarma, M. (2008). Index of financial inclusion, New Delhi: Indian council for research on international economics relations. Retrieved from https://www.icrier.org/pdf/Working_Paper_215.pdf.

Seamer, M., & Melia, A. (2015). Remunerating non-executive directors with stock options : Who is ignoring the regulator? *Accounting Research Journal*, *28*(3), 251–267. doi: 10.1108/ARJ-12-2013-0092.

Trivedi, A. S. (2020). Accessibility of the banking facilities under financial inclusion by urban women of Ahmedabad district. *International Journal of Research and Analytical Reviews (IJRAR)*, *7*(2), 203–214.

United Nations Human Rights (UNHR). (2017). Statement on visit to the USA, by Professor Philip Alston, United Nations Special Rapporteur on extreme poverty and human rights. Received from https://www.ohchr.org/EN/NewsEvents/Pages/DisplayNews.aspx?NewsID=22533.

Waghmare, S. V. (2020). An overview of financial inclusion in the Indian economic scenario routes of financial inclusion in India. *An Annual Interdisciplinary Journal of History*, *6*(6), 528–536.

4 Iran and COVID-19

An alternative crisis management system based on bottom-up Islamic social finance and faith-based civic engagement

Najmoddin Yazdi, Ali Marvi, and Ali Maleki

4.1 Introduction

The new coronavirus first emerged in late 2019 and has so far continued to hit the world. Countries, including Islamic ones, had different responses in terms of crisis management, civic engagement, societal support, social finance, etc. Iran has been a unique case since it was one of the first countries that confronted the virus, experienced two peaks, was blamed by the Western media for incapable management and least compulsory policies, for example, on home quarantine, and most importantly has been under an historically unprecedented level of economic and medical US-led sanctions. Furthermore, 'Iran's right to benefit from the [International Monetary] Fund's $50-billion Rapid Financing Instrument (RFI)' has been blocked by the United States (Mehr News Agency, 2020b; para. 1). Also, Iran has fewer physicians, hospital beds, and nurses per capita than advanced economies. For example, the number of nurses per capita of the United States, the United Kingdom, France, Spain, and Italy is about three to seven times that of Iran. They also have roughly double the physicians and up to more than five times the hospital beds of Iran (World Bank Group, 2018). The interesting point is that Iran has one of the best-performing national health systems in the region and even the world for decades, paradoxically, despite such low resources per capita. Besides combating the virus itself, Iran should have combatted the disappointing discourse propagated by the Western media's propaganda, particularly Persian-language ones (BBC World Service, 2020). Last but not least, the occurrence of the pandemic with the New Persian Year's holidays, which every year witnesses the highest peaks of travel, family gatherings, and shopping, and some regional floods worsened the situation even more.

Iran displayed successful management of the pandemic, at least in some respects, and in some phases, compared with some well-developed countries. Table 4.1 summarizes some key statistics of the current state of selected countries on the COVID-19 pandemic. It is evident from the table that in spite of sanctions and the difficulties in obtaining Personal Protective Equipment (PPE) kits, Iran's overall performance is acceptable. Iran's death per capita is the smallest, and the ratio of recovered to total cases is fairly high.

Therefore, the question should be, how has Iran's health system demonstrated a far better response in some respects than the United States, France, Italy, Spain, and the United Kingdom? This chapter sheds light on this question from the viewpoint of Islamic social finance, and also the broader picture of Islamic management of crises.

The chapter is organized in the following order: first, in Section 4.2, both governmental and civic management of the crisis are briefed, followed by the indispensable role of Islamic leadership in Section 4.3. Section 4.4 focuses on various Islamic social finance instruments that have been deployed by Iran during the COVID-19 pandemic, in which some novel approaches are presented. Section 4.5 argues that non-financial civic engagement is a necessity alongside Islamic social finance at the time of such large-scale crises when insufficient professional human resources are available. Section 4.6 discusses the examples illustrated in the two previous sections and conceptualizes them in an alternative crisis management model that is more bottom-up (i.e., based on a mobilized community), citizen-centred, and collaborative. Before concluding the chapter, the contribution to the Islamic social finance literature is discussed in Section 4.6 under the alternative crisis management system.

4.2 Governance structure

The Supreme National Security Council of Iran ordered the establishment of the 'National Headquarters of Administrating COVID-19' on 23 February 2020, which was approved by the Supreme Leader. In the first place, the President of the Islamic Republic of Iran, Hassan Rouhani, set the health minister as the chairman of the National Headquarter of Administrating COVID-19 (*Hamshahri Online*, 2020; IRIB TV2 Primetime News Slot, 2020). However, on 10 March, the president himself became the chairman by the Supreme Leader's new decree, which was a reply to the request of the parliament's chairman in making the headquarters more efficient (ISNA, 2020). The headquarters consists of several committees, including education, public relations, disciplinary-societal, scientific committees, and a spokesperson (PANA News, n.d.).

Later, two other high-level bodies were established. One was the Health Centre to Fight Corona, which was established by the Supreme Leader's order to General Staff of the Armed Forces of Iran. The other was a supporting mechanism for the decrees of the headquarters, called the Support Council for the Decisions of National Headquarters of Administrating COVID-19 (Tasnim News Agency, 2020a).

A positive point in this governance structure is that medical professionals head it. This was historically rooted in Iran's health system structure, and complemented by the structure for the national headquarters. The head of the medical university of every province, a medical doctor, is the health governor of that province and the health minister's representative. This makes medicine and health systems integrated, and scientific and practical efforts aligned. Such a system was able to help the national headquarters attain a scientific and medical orientation rather than being overly political, security-focused, or bureaucratic. The negative point was that the crisis management process in the first peak was somehow ad-hoc in that it did not pay enough attention to economic concerns and businesses.

Another point is that the armed forces (the Health Centre to Fight Corona) were able to mobilize their resources early and quickly. They dedicated 7,000 hospital beds and 32 hospitals to civil patients, disinfected cities and villages in several phases, and set up over 200 health monitoring stations at provinces' entry and exit (AJA Info Portal, 2020). The showcase was a 2,000-bed hospital set up within 48 hours in the capital (Vahdat & Krauss, 2020).

As this chapter contends, having a bottom-up crisis management system means that these formal structures are at best aiding community mobilization and citizen-centred collaboration. As conceptualized by Ghiabi (2020; para. 7),'while the inter-institutional confrontation [of Iran] escalated into mutual criticism and parallel policy interventions, the public response was driven by a diffused and granular mobilisation'. He then continues that 'this strategy ... [of] managing disorder rather than disposing order – enables the Iranian state to diffuse the task of governing turbulent phenomena, such as the pandemic' (Ghiabi, 2020; para. 10).

4.3 Leadership

> A great feat was accomplished and a glorious jihad was carried out in the country. It was a jihadi endeavor and a jihadi movement in the true sense of the word. This should be recorded in history. ... In particular, I ask Him to raise the position of those who were martyred on the path of this Jihadi movement.
>
> (Khamenei.ir, 2020; para. 3–4)

This was a recent example of the metaphors continuously in use by the Supreme Leader of Iran, Ayatollah Ali Khamenei. Iran's leadership used to depict the nation's confrontation with the new coronavirus as *Jihad*, holy defence, and martyrdom. With such a discourse, holy defence (eight-year war imposed on Iran by Iraq) has been used for the fight against the pandemic. In this view, medical staff are at the front line of the *Jihad* (holy defence), and all citizens are asked to help them at the back end. There has been no trade-off between lives and the economy in the communicated picture, but saving any single life is an Islamic value and a must. In this discourse, there has been no controversy between religion and science, but complementing roles. Deceased medical staff have been called 'martyrs of health', resembling the concepts of 'martyrs of *Haram*' and 'martyrs of *Harim*', which are well-socialized concepts in the Islamic society of Iran.

Formulating the whole confrontation as *Jihad* and the holy defence is significant in mobilizing distributed non-governmental and civic resources in a task-oriented religious society. This brought society together against the enemy, i.e., the pandemic, with high social calm and negligible riots or strikes compared with Western nations like the US. By leading such community mobilization,

Iran witnessed the emergence of a bottom-up citizen-centred crisis management system as depicted elsewhere in this chapter. It can be argued that this capacity is not merely national, but religious and international, which gets activated in crises. For example, during the 2019 flood in Golestan province, Abu Mahdi started a widespread campaign in Iraq to assist the Iranian flood victims and his close Iranian friend General Soleimani (Shariati, 2020). Such discourse and formulation of crises make them unifying situations rather than violent ones.

At the same time, the discourse was also focused on Islamic finance, including Islamic social finance. The Supreme Leader repeatedly urged all believers to help assist families in need during the pandemic, via Islamic finance, particularly *Qard Hasan*, *Khums*, *Zakat*, and *Mouwasat*, *Iftar* food in Ramadan, *Qurbani* (meat of the sacrifices), distributing votive food (*Nazr*) to the low-income families in the upcoming *Muharram*, while observing all necessary health protocols (Hawzah News, 2020d; Majlis-e-Ulama-e-Hind, 2020; Mehr News Agency, 2020c).

Interestingly, the Supreme Leader and many religious figures unceasingly asked people – before the government – to adhere to health instructions while insisting on seeing faith and religion as the most helpful components of this fight. This implicitly signalled religion along with policy and science, instead of communicating a confrontation of religion and science (policy). For example, Supreme Leader Ayatollah Ali Khamenei, on 15 March, talked about the coherence of religious, humanitarian, and *Jihadi* motives while thanking the officials and the health community (IRNA English, 2020). Another example comes from Ayatollah Abdollah Javadi Amoli, a high-ranking religious figure, who acknowledged the medical community on 21 March while advising them and society to pray for all those affected by this virus, and the medical community on the front lines (Javadi Amoli, 2020). In another instance, Ayatollah Mohsen Gharaati also called on the people of Iran to turn this threat into an opportunity by observing medical precautions, getting closer to God, and capitalizing on quality family time during the unprecedented quarantine at home (Gheraati, 2020).

In sum, the Islamic leadership of Iranian society built on Islamic discourses of *Jihad*, martyrdom, and holy defence activated the capacities of community mobilization and achieved societal cohesion, with special and detailed attention to Islamic finance instruments like *Qard Hasan*, *Zakat*, *Khums*, *Sadaqat*, and *Mouwasat*. Other religious leaders of society, from top to bottom levels, echoed this discourse. And, such a religious picture was communicated under a complementary paradigm of science (health observations).

4.4 Islamic social finance

This section illustrates some Islamic social finance measures adopted by Iranian society during the COVID-19 pandemic. These measures include *Qard Hasan* financing of those in need via family networks, *Qard Hasan* financing of the neighbourhood via mosques, dedicating *Khums* funds to victims, setting up campaigns such as rent campaigns or *Nafas* campaign, either in the private sector or in terms of public-private partnerships (PPPs), those of charities, and NGOs, and financial support by the government.

4.4.1 Family networks

Qard Hasan (also written as *Qard al-Hassan*) is 'commonly defined as an interest-free loan' or more diversely as 'a benevolent economic behaviour, an outlet for the placement of savings, an instrument of finance [or] an institution for bona fide lending' (Sadr, 2014; p. 7). A *hadith* of the Prophet Muhammad says that *Qard Hasan* has more rewards than *Infaq* (18 rewards compared to ten rewards), which indicates the importance of providing finance to those with actual needs (*HadithLib*, n.d.). *Qard Hasan* was also shown to play a role in enhancing social inclusion and financial self-sustainability (Iqbal & Shafiq, 2015; Khan et al., 2017).

Qard Hasan has, in the recent decade, been revitalized in Iran by establishing two specialized banks, i.e., Mehr Iran Qarz Al-Hasaneh Bank and Resalat *Qard al-Hassan Bank*, and 49 *Qard Hasan* funds with official permission from the Central Bank of Iran (IQNA News Agency, 2017). Of course, the number of unofficial funds is much higher such that it is approximated that Southern Khorasan, a less populated province of Iran out of 31 provinces, has about 400 *Qard Hasan* funds (Young Journalists Club, 2020). Notably, social financing used to play a role in these banks and funds, e.g. in Resalat Qard'al-Hassan Bank.

During the COVID-19 pandemic, Iran has witnessed a particular utilization of family-network *Qard Hasan* financing. Such utilization was built on a decade of a resurgence of informal funds among family networks. Some attributed this resurgence to the fact that bank loans are increasingly hard to access, have high interest rates, and ask for guarantees that are difficult to provide, at least by ordinary families (Poolnews, 2013). In family-network *Qard Hasan*, members are often committed to having a fixed payment per month. Such *Qard Hasan* loans are essentially the sum of these continuous member payments and free of interest or any extra fees. These loans are given to members in times of need or in turns, or a combination of both. Trust among the members and much less information asymmetry as regards genuine need and payment abilities are two of its pillars, which in turn yield flexibility in payments and instalments, social bonding, and financial resilience. However, some pitfalls have been observed for family-network *Qard Hasan* in Iran, which requires further analysis (Young Journalists Club, 2019).

Observation of Iran's handling of the COVID-19 pandemic suggests that this Islamic finance instrument could provide a degree of economic resilience when the government is not in an economic situation to support families and family businesses. The government's financial support was ready on 18 March 2020, one month after families were hit by the pandemic (Tasnim, 2020). The financial support was naturally insufficient due to Iran's adverse economic conditions and lack of transparent economic information about the extent to which the pandemic hit every family. In such conditions where there is a lack of reliable and timely information and an insufficient governmental capacity, *Qard Hasan* family networks can help achieve better targeting of needs.

4.4.2 *Mosques*

Mosques (*Masjed*) were another pipeline for the circulation of *Qard Hasan* funds during the coronavirus pandemic in Iran. Like family networks, mosques utilized *Qard Hasan* funds, which were voluntarily and directly collected from local residents. Again, similar to family networks, mosques have useful bottom-level information on who needs what and to what extent. But, different from a network of families which is based on blood, a mosque spans a local neighbourhood. And more importantly, this approach does not see mosques as mere receivers of societal funds, but it tries to revive the use of religious places and the role of mosques in Islamic societies (Zada & Saba, 2013). It is worthwhile mentioning that the government has recently felt these benefits of bottom-up Islamic social finance through mosques and started allocating a complementary USD$200 million budget for the *Qard Hasan* funds in mosques, for the first time in 2019. The government intends to increase it year by year (IRNA, 2020). In sum, *Qard Hasan* funding through mosques and family networks can be pictured as a system capable of carrying microfinance with more flexibility, less information asymmetry, stronger social bonds, and more trust-building in comparison with centralized governmental financing schemes.

Mosques were able to mobilize prayers, volunteers, and youths to altruistically give to people in need and were active in converting to ad-hoc factories of mask production, sewing protective gowns and gloves, and supplying food and serving beverages to both hospitals and neighbourhood residents etc. (Barron's, 2020; MSN News, 2020). This non-financial civic engagement built around mosques is discussed in Section 4.5.

4.4.3 *Charities and NGOs*

In the first two months of the pandemic outbreak, Iranian benefactors and charities donated USD$83 million to provide COVID-19 relief. Out of this, about USD$10 million was provided by non-governmental organizations (NGOs) and charities, and USD$6 million by public volunteer groups (Tehran Times, 2020b). Financial resources were used for direct payment to vulnerable families as well as distribution of disinfectants, masks, food, protective clothing, and drugs to them. The authors could not see any distinguishing feature in the role of charities in fighting the pandemic in Iran.

4.4.4 Khums *by clerics*

Several Iranian religious leaders devoted half or one-third of the *Sahm Imam* (a part of *Khums*) donations in their hands to the battle against COVID-19 due to the inability of the government to provide relief to all those in need (Baligh News, 2020; Ijtihad Net, 2020; Tabnak, 2020). *Khums* refers to 'one fifth of [surplus annual] income payable for the purpose of redeeming the rights of others' (Iqbal & Mirakhor, 2011). This dedication of *Sahm Imam* to those in need in times of crisis is, in fact, an Islamic social finance instrument complementary to the government's financial support packages. This instrument was utilized before for natural disasters in Iran like floods, including the flood in Sistan and Baluchistan province that happened at the same time as the pandemic, and earthquakes (Hamshahri Online, 2019; Hawzah News, 2020a; Mehr News Agency, 2017).

4.4.5 Rent campaigns

The country witnessed a plethora of campaigns during the pandemic, thanks to the digital age. Some of these campaigns were focused on altruistic giving to help families survive the new coronavirus. An interesting one was a nationwide campaign for shop owners not to collect rent from businesses hit by the pandemic for several months (Financial Tribune, 2020). As a more top-down approach, the Mosques Affairs Centre for Southern Khorasan, on behalf of the mosques of the province, forgave the whole or part of the rent of commercial buildings in the ownership of the mosques for some months (Hawzah News, 2020c).

Although Iran's government issued several rent policies for the first months of the pandemic, the policies did not target rent forgiveness. Specifically, the government defined a cap on the increase in rent since the country experienced considerable economic inflation due to both the US-led economic sanctions and the pandemic, thus increasing real estate prices, mortgages, and rents. In addition, a decree was issued for the postponement of rent for up to three months obligating renters to extend their contracts by another year (Iran's Ministry of Cooperatives, Labour and Social Welfare, 2020). Thus, all these supports were in the form of regulations and facilitation rather than financial support or forgiving rent. Therefore, unlike affluent countries like Germany that provided detailed and generous support plans early enough for renters, such rent campaigns could be significant in crises where countries like Iran cannot afford financing rental agreements.

4.4.6 Government's financial supports

The pandemic coincided with the Persian New Year, which not only limited celebrations and made self-quarantine policy difficult to achieve but also negatively affected family businesses. Anyone familiar with this holiday knows that most businesses wait all year for this moment due to high profits in sales. As a result, Iran's government decided to adopt various measures to help businesses and unemployment with tax levies, loans, interest discounts, and unemployment insurance, to name a few. These measures are comparable with the US in terms of scope, but not the payments (Malek Mohammadi & Solouki, 2020).

4.4.7 Private sector campaigns

Campaign *Nafas* (meaning breathe) is the nationwide corporate social responsibility (CSR) campaign set up in the early days of the pandemic. It was the first of its kind in Iran to gather the capacities and resources of the private sector and economic actors at a national scale, with the support of the commerce chambers. This campaign was able to collect about USD$40 million to support over 270 hospitals with everything from protective garments to technological equipment. While the country had seen various private sector campaigns in previous crises, Campaign *Nafas* was novel in terms of networking, collective action, resource aggregation, and agility (Sustainable Development School (of Iran), 2020).

This section showed how bottom-up Islamic social finance could provide an agile and quick-response societal crisis management system, especially when the central government is unable to provide sufficient, targeted, or timely financial supports to citizens. The next section presents a complementary pillar to this alternative understanding of crisis management, i.e., the necessity of non-financial civic engagement.

4.5 Non-financial civic engagement

The Islamic social finance activities mentioned have been complemented by non-financial civic engagement of society. Thanks to Basij's societal infrastructure, the whole country witnessed the quick mobilization of over half a million volunteers under 66,000 *Jihadi* groups (Tasnim News Agency, 2020e). In the following, some of these activities are presented. The importance of this non-financial participation goes back to the fact that in crises, official staff, facilities, and infrastructure cannot respond to society's escalated needs, for example, in terms of caregiving, case finding, health services, production and distribution, and organization and management.

4.5.1 Involvement of the society in production chains

Soon after the shortage of face masks, hand sanitizer, and disinfectants, the country saw two streams: one mobilizing ordinary citizens and households and the other mobilizing firms. The first stream was the mobilization of ordinary citizens, mostly housewives, to sew face masks and protective gowns at workshops and home for both the medical community and ordinary citizens (UNDP, 2020; Relief Web, 2020). Mosques were also converted into mask factories overnight (France 24, 2020). Refugees working in Iran also played a role in this regard. Some joined the movements mentioned above. Some teamed up with Iranian entrepreneurs, for example, switching from making high-fashion suits to producing hospital gowns and masks amid the pandemic (UNHCR Iran, 2020). This was what citizens could donate back to society, even if they could not finance these activities.

The second stream was technological innovation and localization (for the first time) of products that businesses need. For example, an Iranian technology-based firm designed and manufactured an industrial machine producing N95 face masks. This happened for the first time in the country, during the pandemic, in just ten days and nights of hard scientific work. The quality and extra features of the masks soon made it an export item to Europe and more. The Corotech2020 Exhibition was held on 13 June 2020 to host 50 knowledge-based Iranian firms that, for the first time, developed a technological product for the battle against the COVID-19 virus. These products were diverse, ranging from medical equipment and diagnostic kits to high-tech raw materials for mask production to personal protective products and disinfectants (consumables and equipment) (Iran National Innovation Fund, 2020).

Both of these streams, i.e., ordinary citizens and knowledge-based businesses, depicted involvement of the local society in the production chains of equipment and commodities urgently needed during the pandemic. Nevertheless, the governmental and para-governmental bodies were active, at least in complementing these movements. For example, the Headquarters for Execution of Imam Khomeini's Order inaugurated the opening of Asia's largest factory producing face masks in Iran with a production rate of 4 million face masks per month. This was claimed to obviate the country's need for importing medical products (Tasnim News Agency, 2020d).

4.5.2 Societal support of hospitals

Iranian society has supported the medical staff and patients combating COVID-19 by various means. For example, communities started serving 500 juice bottles per day in Tehran to the hospitals' nurses and doctors and also the patients. This reached over 4,000 bottles per day in Tehran and 2,800 bottles per day in Mashhad, just to name two of the cities, which covered over 80% of the COVID-19 hospitals there. Tons of oranges, carrots, and apples were donated daily, and all the contributors throughout the chain were volunteers (Hawzah News, 2020b; High Council for Human rights (of Iran), 2020; SNN, 2020). Serving over 2,000 warm meals for hospitals was another activity by the mobilized society (Tasnim News Agency, 2020b).

Within the first month of the outbreak, some 300,000 face masks were distributed to hospitals with the help and donations of benefactors, charitable organizations, congregations, and individual volunteers. Donating over 15,000 scrubs, 157,000 food packages, and 200,000 snacks to hospitals during the first month of the pandemic was another dimension of the community mobilization (Tehran Times, 2020a).

Furthermore, some volunteers voluntarily participated in hospital activities as '*Jihadi* accompaniment to patients and cleaning staff'. In the city of Qom, 1,000 members of the clergy registered within the first two weeks, with 150 volunteers in the waiting list. Every *Jihadi* volunteer helped about 15 patients, including giving them food and water, helping them go to the bathroom, and whatever non-medical services were needed (Mashregh News, 2020). Graduates of psychology and Islamic studies participated in setting up field hospitals, helping with fever-monitoring teams at city entrances, and provided spiritual care to patients. Telephone calls following-up suspicious cases was another kind of activity that volunteer citizens helped with (Mashregh News, 2020). This bottom-up support of hospitals and patients was broadly distributed throughout mosques, local *Basij* stations in each neighbourhood, and *Jihadi* groups (High Council for Human rights (of Iran), 2020).

4.5.3 Societal support of mortuaries

Disposal of infected dead bodies is not the only concern an Islamic society may have during a pandemic. Islamic burial preparation and bathing of the corpse is also of great concern to Islamic societies. While mortuaries were first permitted to act upon World Health Organization (WHO) protocols, including not bathing the dead, it was changed back to Islamic bathing and burial preparation, although maintaining other health, disinfection, and burial protocols were suggested by the WHO. Islamic burial preparation and bathing of dead Muslims is a collective duty (*farḍ al-kifāya*) that is imposed on the whole community of believers (*Ummah*) (Al-Dawoody & Finegan, 2020).

Here, again clergymen and clergywomen hurried to help mortuary staff throughout the country. For example, in Tehran, 130 volunteer clergies did most of the bathing and burial preparation of infected corpses (Javan Online, 2020; Tasnim News Agency, 2020c). Sixteen-year-old Zahra Keykha is the youngest volunteer *Jihadi* girl to help with the preparation of bodies infected with COVID-19 in Zahedan, a provincial centre 1,500 kilometres from the capital. Other *Jihadi* women asked her if she was afraid, and she said that she came there voluntarily, with the gentle suggestion of her father (Alef, 2020).

4.5.4 No panic buying

Iranian society created a proud image of the country with a lack of panic buying (Mehr News Agency, 2020a). Although Iran did experience a shortage of face masks and hand sanitizer, that experience was notably compared with America and Europe, which are connected to global supply chains and are not under sanctions and trade restrictions (for example, see NST Online, 2020; Rayner, 2020). Although part of it comes back to the government's ability to maintain a good supply of commodities during the pandemic, i.e., no large queues for food, washing liquids, toilet roll, disinfectants, hand sanitizer, and face masks, the role of the citizens in this regard cannot be highlighted enough.

4.6 Discussion: alternative crisis management system

Islamic social finance lies at the intersection of Islamic finance and social finance, which have similar ethical dictates and the shared goal of creating value for society via innovative financial instruments (Biancone & Radwan, 2019). The potential and drawbacks of Islamic social finance have not yet been studied regarding crises where the whole of society is engaged. The COVID-19 pandemic is a great opportunity to better understand its potential, especially in Islamic societies.

The Iranian people showed the application of a diverse array of Islamic social finance instruments in this pandemic. Some of them have been highlighted before in the literature, including the role of charities and NGOs, and dedicating *Zakat*, *Khums*, *Qard Hasan*, and *Sadaqat* to the victims of natural disasters. However, Iran's case illustrated several untapped Islamic social finance capacities which were brought to the surface during the pandemic (Section 4.4). They included (1) the circulation of *Qard Hasan* microfinance through Iranian family networks; (2) converting mosques to a *Qard Hasan* system through which volunteer citizens funded, often in the neighbourhood of that mosque, and those in need were locally identified to give financial assistance to; (3) campaigns for rent forgiveness of shops, houses, and other commercial buildings; and (4) the first nationwide private sector campaign of Iran was set up in this pandemic to support hospitals by both societal financing and non-financial supplies.

These above-mentioned socio-financial instruments would have been unable to efficiently fight the coronavirus if not accompanied by the volunteer non-financial engagement of the people. In crisis times, when the need to deploy volunteer human resources peaks, financing alone cannot get the work done. Section 4.5 showed examples of non-financial civic engagement of Iranians during the COVID-19 pandemic. They included (1) volunteer participation in the production chain of masks and other medical equipment, and converting mosques and homes into factories for sewing masks and protective clothes, cooking and serving food and beverages to medical staff, those in the neighbourhood and the elderly who could not go out to do the shopping, besides microfinancing those in need through the resources donated by the people who gather at the mosque to pray and by other local residents; (2) societal support of hospitals and other medical centres by volunteers with food, entertainment, beverages, campaigns, etc.; (3) societal protection of mortuaries and Islamic burial preparation with the aid of volunteer clergy; and (4) no panic buying of citizens, just to name a few.

Although the structure of the present chapter may imply a dichotomy between the financial and non-financial civic engagement of society, the case illustrated much synergy between them. The financial and non-financial civic engagements were underpinned by a societal infrastructure that has been developed over the decades. The institutional structures for financial and non-financial civic engagements, i.e., mainly mosques and charity NGOs, are shared. At a deeper cultural level, both share common social drivers. For example, fundraising charities, which generally mobilize financial civic engagement during crises, were further supported by volunteership of citizens. When supplying food, masks, ventilators, protective gowns, and gloves, actors get valuable information on what is needed or what is in a surplus for a particular hospital, neighborhood, or home factory. In turn, they ask for specific non-financial contribution of volunteer citizens who do not have money to give but can donate their skills, time, or commodities.

These examples can contribute to the conceptualization of an alternative crisis management system, which is based on the faith-driven engagement of citizens

(Saja et al., 2018), that is citizen-centred and collaborative governance (Cooper et al., 2006), and altruistic and Islamic financial giving. Such bottom-up crisis management systems, based on community mobilization, could be contrasted with regular systems in the following terms:

1. Bottom-up Islamic social finance benefits from intrinsic motivations during crises and pandemics, while the motivation in conventional top-down crisis management systems is often extrinsic. Financing in regular crisis management systems often goes in the form of the redistribution of centrally collected taxes.
2. Recipients of money or other kinds of help feel it as beneficence, while in regular systems this turns into a feeling of having rights against the government or the crisis management system. In such bottom-up systems, the community is an indispensable part of the management system. So, the positive feelings of belonging to the system, along with less information asymmetry at local levels, turns into stronger social bonds.
3. Although parallel work and lack of data are two major drawbacks of such bottom-up systems, as in Iran's case, preliminary observations suggest that such a capillary distribution network can compensate for these drawbacks. This was observable when government bodies tried to distribute blankets and tents to flood victims compared with civic engagement in the collection and distribution of these items.
4. An evident benefit of the alternative crisis management system is its nearly zero administrative costs. Such systems' administrative costs remain at zero, while conventional crisis management systems' administrative costs increase.
5. An attractive characteristic of bottom-up crisis management could be its fast response. The Iran case showed that governments need much time to discuss policy options, decide on and develop executive details, and operationalize them. This does not fit with a crisis and pandemic situations where timely response matters.
6. Learning in the alternative system will be more place-based, distributed, and with shorter feedback loops than the conventional top-down approaches.

The above conceptualization of Iran's crisis management system during the pandemic, along with the role envisaged for bottom-up Islamic social finance, can complement the future agenda suggested by Biancone and Radwan (2019) on Islamic social finance. They argue that *sharia* compliance is usually done through negative screening methodology, in which investment prohibitions by Islam are probed. They conceptualize a more positive approach towards Islamic social finance by giving investors an 'opportunity to affirm their belief' in their investments and pro-actively direct investment to the sectors they choose to invest in. The bottom-up Islamic social finance model suggested in the present chapter can further this issue to the point where micro-investors are micro-managers of the crisis via community mobilization and have less information asymmetry, faster responses, fewer administrative costs, and more exact targeting of those in need.

This can particularly help societies that have incapable, less-resourceful, or corrupt governments. A significant indirect impact of such citizen-centred collaborative management of crises is 'social bonding', or maybe '*Okhovat*' in Islamic terms. Finally, the significant role of social leadership (sometimes the same as religious leadership and political leadership) and trust cannot be overestimated.

4.7 Conclusion

Iran's response to the COVID-19 pandemic in some respects represents a unique case. The country's beleaguered economy – under severe US-led economic and medical sanctions – continues to combat the coronavirus under a new paradigm of crisis management. In this paradigm, the crisis management system is bottom-up and built on community mobilization, rather than conventional top-down crisis management systems. In this regard, Iran's response was built on Islamic concepts of *Jihad*, defence, and martyrdom, used Islamic institutions like *Masjed* (mosque) and *Arbaeen Mokeb* tents, and Islamic finance concepts of *Infaq*, *Qard Hasan*, and *Khums*. This is evident in the societal discourses, governmental discourse, and speeches of the Supreme Leader.

The current chapter's results are threefold. The first result is that a bottom-up crisis management model, like what Iran experienced, can benefit from its innermost incentivization, beneficence, and the resulting social bond (*Okhovat*), nearly-zero administrative costs, more targeted reach to those in need , fast response, and shorter learning loops of this crisis management system compared with a conventional top-down approach.

The second result indicates a significant role for Islamic leadership and discourse. From the first instance, the Supreme Leader of Iran started picturing the crisis as a *Jihad* and holy defence, in which medical staff are at the front line, and all citizens are helping them. There has been no trade-off between lives and the economy in the communicated picture, but saving any single life is an Islamic value and a must. In this discourse, there has been no controversy between religion and science, but complementing roles. The medical staff and others who help them on the front line or behind the scenes are all called 'health defenders'. Deceased medical staff are called 'martyrs of health', resembling the concepts of 'martyrs of *Haram*' and 'martyrs of *Harim*', which are socialized concepts in Iran.

Third, a new Islamic social finance model was practised that has been more bottom-up, citizen-centred, and collaborative. While Biancone and Radwan (2019) have called for a more positive and innovative approach to Islamic social finance instead of a mere negative screening methodology, in which investment prohibitions are investigated in Islamic *Sharia*, Iran's case illustrated that concepts of *Infaq*, *Sadaqat*, *Khums*, and *Qard Hasan* could be deployed in a more distributed, bottom-up, and collaborative manner. For example, mosques and family networks were able to act as a system circulating *Qard Hasan* funds throughout society at the bottom, where conventional governance systems as practices before could not reliably reach those in need.

From a data viewpoint, it should be clarified that the examples provided in this chapter should be approached as ad-hoc early evidence for an illustration purpose, but not stylized facts or empirical data in its strict sense.

References

AJA Info Portal. (2020). The information portal of the Army of the Islamic Republic of Iran. Retrieved from https://b2n.ir/628456.

Al-Dawoody, A., & Finegan, O. (2020). COVID-19 and Islamic burial laws: Safeguarding dignity of the dead. In: *ICRC Humanitarian Law & Policy Blog*. Retrieved from https://blogs.icrc.org/law-and-policy/2020/04/30/covid-19-islamic-burial-laws/.

Alef. (2020, July 28). Who is the smallest bathing volunteer for corpses infected with the new Coronavirus? Retrieved from http://www.alef.ir/news/3990507043.html.

Baligh News. (2020, April 28). Ayatollah Makarem Shirazi's permission to spend half of the portion of the imam for the needy. Retrieved from https://makarem.ir/news/en/News/Details/419524.

Barron's. (2020, April 6). Coronavirus: Iranians make masks and gloves at a mosque. Retrieved from https://www.barrons.com/news/coronavirus-iranians-make-masks-and-gloves-at-a-mosque-01586159105 (accessed 28 July 2020).

BBC World Service. (2020, August). Professor Marandi: 'BBC Persian is a propaganda outlet against Iran'. *BBC World News*. Retrieved from https://iranian.com/2020/08/03/professor-marandi-bbc-persian-is-a-propaganda-outlet-against-iran/.

Biancone, P. P., & Radwan, M. (2019). Social finance and financing social enterprises: An Islamic finance prospective. *European Journal of Islamic Finance*, Special Issue Islamic and Social Finance. Retrieved from http://www.ojs.unito.it/index.php/EJIF.

Cooper, T. L., Bryer, T. A., & Meek, J. W. (2006). Citizen-centered collaborative public management. *Public Administration Review*, *66*(s1), 76–88. doi: 10/c42jc8.

Financial Tribune. (2020, March 15). Iran's CB lists businesses directly affected by COVID-19. *Financial Tribune*. Retrieved from https://financialtribune.com/articles/domestic-economy/102601/irans-cb-lists-businesses-directly-affected-by-covid-19.

France 24. (2020, April 24). Mosque converted into mask factory in virus-hit Iran. Retrieved from https://www.france24.com/en/20200406-mosque-converted-into-mask-factory-in-virus-hit-iran.

Gheraati, M. (2020, March 11). Recommendations of Ayatollah Mohsen Gheraati for the coronavirus pandemic. *Supreme Council of the Cultural Revolution (of Iran)*. Retrieved from https://b2n.ir/963540.

Ghiabi, M. (2020, May 11). Managing disorder: Iran's governance amidst the COVID-19 pandemic. *Commentary, ISPI (Italian Institute for International Political Studies)*. Retrieved from https://www.ispionline.it/it/pubblicazione/managing-disorder-irans-governance-amidst-covid-19-pandemic-26080.

HadithLib. (n.d.). Superiority of rewards of Qard Hasan over Sadaqat: A hadith of the Prophet Muhammad. Retrieved from https://b2n.ir/884708.

Hamshahri Online. (2019, March 26). Believers are allowed to pay half of the Sahm Imam to the flood victims. Retrieved from https://b2n.ir/149980.

Hamshahri Online. (2020, July 14). Get familiar with Iran's national headquarter of administrating COVID-19. Available at: https://b2n.ir/884093.

Hawzah News. (2020a, January 13). Believers are allowed to pay up to one third of the Sahm Imam to the flood victims. Retrieved from https://b2n.ir/927390.

Hawzah News. (2020b, March 24). Production and daily distribution of 2800 bottles of juice for patients and medical staff of Tehran's hospitals involved with the Coronavirus. Retrieved from https://b2n.ir/273609.

Hawzah News. (2020c, March 25). Forgiving rents of commercial buildings in the ownership of the mosques in Southern Khorasan province. Retrieved from https://b2n.ir/561844.

Hawzah News. (2020d, July 23). The month of Muharram and the coronavirus disease. Retrieved from https://b2n.ir/269095.

High Council for Human rights (of Iran). (2020). Empathy to fight coronavirus with the flavor of juice. Retrieved from http://www.humanrights-iran.ir/news-77559.aspx.

Ijtihad Net. (2020, March 2). Permissions of Ayatollah Shobeiri and Makarem to use Sahm Imam for fighting COVID-19 pandemic. Retrieved from https://b2n.ir/512659.

Iqbal, Z., & Mirakhor, A. (2011). *An Introduction to Islamic Finance: Theory and Practice*. Hoboken, NJ: Wiley.

Iqbal, Z., & Shafiq, B. (2015). Islamic finance and the role of Qard-al-Hassan (benevolent loans) in enhancing inclusion: A case study of Akhuwat. *ACRN Oxford Journal of Finance and Risk Perspectives*, *4*(4): 23–40.

The International Quran News Agency (IQNA). (2017). List of Iranian Qard Hasan funds with permission from the Central Bank of Iran. Retrieved from http://iqna.ir/fa/news/3629728.

Iran National Innovation Fund. (2020). Presentation of corona achievements of 50 companies in the pavilion of knowledge-based companies. *The Corotech Exhibition of Production Leap against COVID-19*. Retrieved from https://www.inif.ir/fullcontent/-/asset_publisher/YASjeuXFqbaQ/content/id/471038.

Iran's Ministry of Cooperatives, Labour and Social Welfare. (2020, June 15). The 10th report on COVID-19, workforce and social support: Rent regulation and control system. *Tehran: Iran's Ministry of Cooperatives, Labour and Social Welfare*. Retrieved from https://b2n.ir/186247.

Islamic Republic of Iran Broadcasting (IRIB) TV2 Primetime News Slot. (2020). Letter of the parliament's president to the supreme leader regarding the change of the head of 'national headquarter of administrating COVID-19 response-, and the response. *Tehran: IRIB TV 2*. Retrieved from http://www.alef.ir/news/3981221025.html.

Islamic Republic News Agency (IRNA). (2020, February 14). Qard Hasan focal points are going to be established in mosques. Retrieved from https://b2n.ir/070758.

Iranian Students News Agency (IRNA) English. (2020, Match 15). Supreme leader thanks Iranian officials engaged in combating COVID-19. Retrieved from https://en.irna.ir/news/83715906/Supreme-Leader-thanks-Iranian-officials-engaged-in-combating.

Iranian Students News Agency (ISNA). (2020, March 10). Larijani's letter to the supreme leader to change the head of the corona headquarters. Retrieved from https://b2n.ir/034891.

Javadi Amoli, A. (2020). Ayatollah Javadi Amoli's opinion on the role of praying in repelling disasters. Retrieved from https://b2n.ir/445610.

Javan Online. (2020, April 5). Women's Jihad against coronavirus. Retrieved from https://www.Javann.ir/004BPZ.

Khamenei.ir. (2020, May 10). The Iranian nation recorded another historic jihad during the coronavirus pandemic. Retrieved from http://english.khamenei.ir/news/7546/The-Iranian-nation-recorded-another-historic-jihad-during-the.

Khan, A. A., Ishaq, M. S., Afonso, J. D. S., & Akram, S. (2017). Is it possible to provide qard hasan and achieve financial self-sustainability? The experience of Akhuwat in Pakistan. Retrieved from https://researchportal.port.ac.uk/portal/en/publications/is-it-possible-to-provide-qard-hasan-and-achieve-financial-self sustainability-the-experience-of-akhuwat-in-pakistan(e2d67742-a37f-4758-b61c-de92429890e1).html.

Majlis-e-Ulama-e-Hind. (2020, August 1). Leader: US sanctions, crime against Iranian nation. Retrieved from http://majliseulamaehind.org/MuslimWorld NewsDetails.aspx?ID=52871.

MalekMohammadi, S., & Solouki, P. (2020, March 30). Comparing Iran and the US measures in fighting with COVID-19 (the fourth report). *BehRabin Company*. Retrieved from http://behrabin.com/?p=336.

Mashregh News. (2020). Coronavirus and voluntary activities in Qom city. Retrieved from https://b2n.ir/504012.

Mehr News Agency. (2017, November 13). Permission to use one third of Sahm Imam for earthquake victims. Retrieved from https://b2n.ir/702027.

Mehr News Agency. (2020a, March 14). UK envoy highlights good supply of commodities in Iran. *Mehr News Agency*. Retrieved from https://en.mehrnews.com/news/156719/UK-envoy-highlights-good-supply-of-commodities-in-Iran.

Mehr News Agency. (2020b, April 8). US opposes IMF loan grant to Iran to battle COVID-19. Retrieved from https://en.mehrnews.com/news/157373/US-opposes-IMF-loan-grant-to-Iran-to-battle-COVID-19.

Mehr News Agency. (2020c, April 25). A different Ramadan: Bringing Iftar to the needy homes. Retrieved from https://b2n.ir/506802.

Microsoft Network News (MSN News). (2020, April 7). Mosque converted into mask factory in virus-hit Iran. Retrieved from https://www.msn.com/en-au/news/coronavirus/mosque-converted-into-mask-factory-in-virus-hit-iran/ar-BB12f43B.

New Straits Times Online (NST Online). (2020, March 22). Covid-19: Anxious Britons continue to panic-buy. Retrieved from https://www.nst.com.my/world/world/2020/03/576910/covid-19-anxious-britons-continue-panic-buy.

Pupils Association News Agency (PANA). (n.d.). PANA news on The National Headquarter for Administering COVID-19. Retrieved from https://b2n.ir/007704.

Poolnews. (2013). Iranian household banks give loans with less difficulty. Retrieved from http://www.poolnews.ir/fa/news/100295.

Rayner, J. (2020, June 21). From panic buying to food banks: How Britain fed itself in the first phase of coronavirus. *The Observer*. Retrieved from https://www.theguardian.com/food/2020/jun/21/from-panic-buying-to-food-banks-how-britain-fed-itself-in-the-first-phase-of-coronavirus.

Sadr, S. K. (2014). Qard Hasan financing in Islamic banks. *ISRA International Journal of Islamic Finance*, *6*(2): 7–20.

Saja, A. M. A., Teo, M., Goonetilleke, A., & Mohamed, Z. A. (2018). An inclusive and adaptive framework for measuring social resilience to disasters. *International Journal of Disaster Risk Reduction*, *28*: 862–873.

Shariati, G. (2020, January 6). The governor of Khuzestan narrates about Abu Mahdi's cooperation in preventing the flooding of Abadan and Khorramshahr. *IRNA*. Retrieved from https://b2n.ir/427978.

SNN (Student News Network). (2020, March 29). Daily production of 4,000 bottles of juice by congregations for the COVID-19 hospitals' patients and nurses. Retrieved from https://b2n.ir/998638.

Sustainable Development School (of Iran). (2020). Discussion webinar on the lessons learned from campaign Nafas. *Webinar Call*. Retrieved from http://sdschool.ir/post/cnafas.

Tabnak. (2020). What is Sahm Imam (a part of Khums)? Retrieved from http://www.tabnak.ir/fa/news/962856 (accessed 29 July 2020).

Tasnim. (2020, March 18). First financial support package was paid to families hit by COVID-19. Retrieved from https://b2n.ir/439603.

Tasnim News Agency. (2020a, March 14). Who attended the first meeting of the 'Support Council for the Decisions of National Headquarter of Administrating COVID-19'? Retrieved from https://b2n.ir/892462.

Tasnim News Agency. (2020b, April 4). Providing warm meals and juice for patients and medical staff for COVID-19 hospitals. Retrieved from https://b2n.ir/571036.

Tasnim News Agency. (2020c, April 9). Report on the bathing of dead bodies infected with the new coronavirus at Behesht-e Zahra cemetery. Retrieved from https://b2n.ir/906455.

Tasnim News Agency. (2020d, April 14). Iran Opens largest mask factory in Southwest Asia. *Society/Culture News*. Retrieved from /en/news/2020/04/14/2243571/iran-opens-largest-mask-factory-in-southwest-asia.

Tasnim News Agency. (2020e, June 17). Report: Over five hundred members of the construction Basij stand up against COVID-19. Retrieved from https://b2n.ir/667058.

Tehran Times. (2020a, April 13). Iranian charity organization provides food, medical items to help combat coronavirus. Retrieved from https://www.tehrantimes.com/news/446734/Iranian-charity-organization-provides-food-medical-items-to.

Tehran Times. (2020b, April 22). Iranian charities donate $83m to support COVID-19 relief. Retrieved from https://www.tehrantimes.com/news/447081/Iranian-charities-donate-83m-to-support-COVID-19-relief.

United Nations High Commissioner for Refugees (UNDP). (2020). Women in Urmia are sewing face masks and gowns to help frontline medical workers in Iran. *UNDP in Iran*. Retrieved from https://www.ir.undp.org/content/iran/en/home/presscenter/articles/2020/Women-in-Urmia-are-sewing-face-masks-and-gowns-to-help-frontline-medical-workers-in-Iran.html.

United Nations High Commissioner for Refugees (UNHCR) Iran. (2020). Afghan and Iranian entrepreneurs team up to fight Coronavirus in Iran. Retrieved from https://www.unhcr.org/ir/2020/04/29/afghan-and-iranian-entrepreneurs-team-up-to-fight-covid-in-iran/.

Relief Web. (2020). In Islamic Republic of Iran, volunteers join battle against COVID-19. Retrieved from https://reliefweb.int/report/iran-islamic-republic/islamic-republic-iran-volunteers-join-battle-against-covid-19.

Vahdat, A., & Krauss, J. (2020, March 27). Iran's army sets up hospital in capital as virus toll climbs. *US News & World Report*. Retrieved from https://www.usnews.com/news/world/articles/2020-03-27/irans-army-sets-up-hospital-in-virus-stricken-capital.

World Bank Group. (2018). The World Bank data: Physicians (per 1,000 people). Retrieved from https://data.worldbank.org/indicator/SH.MED.PHYS.ZS.

Young Journalists Club. (2019). Warning against proliferation of family-network funds with promises of zero-interest loans. Retrieved from http://www.yjc.ir/fa/news/6920968.

Young Journalists Club. (2020). Over 400 Qard Hasan funds in Iranian province of Southern Khorasan. Retrieved from https://khabarban.com/a/28656473.

Zada, N., & Saba, I. (2013). The potential use of Qard Hasan in Islamic microfinance. *ISRA International Journal of Islamic Finance*, 5(2), 153–162.

5 Impact of COVID-19 on sustainable development

A way forward

Nusrat Jafrin, Muhammad Mehedi Masud, and Abu Naser Mohammad Saif

5.1 Introduction

Almost every country in the world is currently in a state of emergency as a result of the COVID-19 pandemic, which was first identified in Wuhan, China, on 2 December 2019 (Abdi, 2020). Subsequently, this virus became widespread around the world, with the number of infected cases increasing day by day. Essentially, humans are infected through close contact with a symptomatic person exhibiting coughing and sneezing. This is because the coronavirus spreads via respiratory airborne transmission and when inhaled, the lungs are infected and they become inflamed (Kumar et al., 2020). In recognition of the gravity of this virus, the World Health Organization (WHO) declared the emergence of the novel coronavirus a 'Public Health Emergency of International Concern' on 30 January 2020 (Eurosurveillance, 2020). The COVID-19 pandemic implies great challenges for individuals, families, communities, and societies across the world. As of 25 April 2020, the total number of infected people globally was 2,719,897, with the number of deaths amounting to 187,705 (WHO, 2020). Daily activities have been altered, and economies might as well plunge into recession. The traditional, social, economic, and public health safety nets on which numerous people rely during times of hardship have been subjected to an unprecedented strain (WHO, 2020).

There is no clear forecast for the end of COVID-19 worldwide, and as a result, it is predicted that the whole world will experience great economic losses. For instance, job loss is recognized as a common phenomenon during this pandemic, regardless of the country. This is not a farfetched idea as world trade has dropped drastically, and the production of various products has ground to a halt except for the agricultural sector, which, of course, is a clear consequence of the lockdown. Besides, the economic situation is deteriorating even further for low-income and lower-middle-income countries. A large number of workers in the informal sector have become unemployed due to the closure of their workplaces. Therefore, it follows that if COVID-19 is not contained soon, temporary unemployment will transform into long-term unemployment. To make matters worse, workers in underdeveloped countries lack adequate health services and social protection. Migrant workers are severely affected during this emergency, resulting in the reduction of remittances to their country of origin.

No similar model exists for affected people around the world in terms of age group. Although senior citizens have been reported to be more vulnerable to being severely affected by the virus compared with younger people, data from other countries have revealed otherwise. In addition to the age factor, the severity of COVID-19 also depends on the patient's health history. However, nowadays, many infected patients do not exhibit any symptoms, which is quite disturbing. Global data indicate that positive cases of patients with coronavirus also vary in terms of gender. For instance, in developing countries, men tend to be more affected by the virus owing to the time they spend outside the home compared with women.

Due to the lockdown, women, children, and the elderly are now vulnerable to domestic violence more than ever. This situation takes a dangerous toll on the vulnerable in terms of their physical and mental health. As a result, many marriages have broken down during this period of the pandemic. In addition to that, unreported domestic violence cases have surged in low-income countries as no clear procedure established to ascertain the validity of claims of domestic violence. Besides, regulations on movement have also affected religious practices for all religions – people are not allowed to go to mosques, churches, pagodas, and temples to perform their religious activities – which ultimately affects the lives of human beings and their spirituality due to their lack of familiarity with this type of restriction. Therefore, this article aims to review the effects of COVID-19 on the economy, domestic violence, demographics, and religious practices with relevant information from various secondary sources.

5.2 Conceptual framework

In order to conceptualize this study, the following conceptual framework was developed based on the literature review. The framework indicates that COVID-19 has impacted three pillars of sustainable development. This certainly will impede the achievement of the Sustainable Development Goals (SDGs) by 2030. Therefore, in order to achieve the SDGs by 2030, after the COVID-19 pandemic, a new business model will be required, as shown in Figure 5.1.

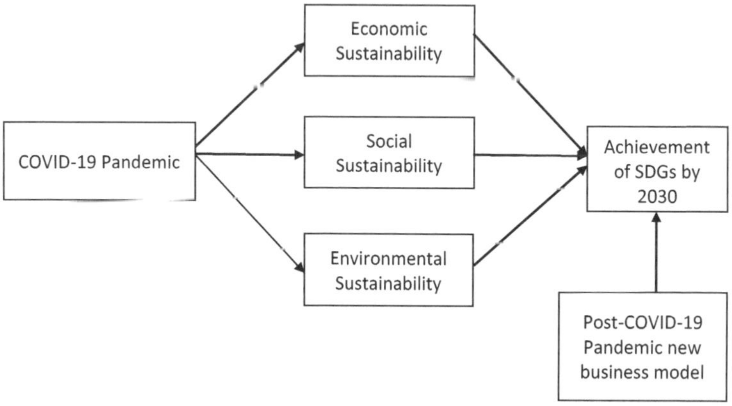

Figure 5.1 Post-COVID-19 pandemic new business model. Source: Author's own.

5.3 Findings and discussion

5.3.1 COVID-19 and its economic impact

COVID-19 is likely to have significant economic consequences since the virus is widespread on a global scale (Fornaro & Wolf, 2020). According to Duffin (2020), COVID-19 has had an alarming effect on the world economy. For instance, Singapore, which is one of the developed countries in the world with a high per capita income, is now experiencing an appalling gross domestic product contraction of 10.6% in just the first quarter of the year. Tourism, one of the main sectors in Italy, is now suffering due to the pandemic, thereby exposing the country to an unprecedented gross domestic product contraction of 5% since the commencement of the lockdown.

This economic effect could become more serious than the 2008 global financial crisis, and the Great Depression that occurred in the 1930s. The possible results of this virus are the loss of skilled and experienced workers, a reduction in the supply of labour, the loss of key personnel and activists, a slowdown in the manufacture of essential products, the disruption of the product supply chain, losses in domestic and international businesses, poor cash flow in the market, and a significant slowdown in revenue growth (Abodunrin et al., 2020; Haleem et al., 2020; Nicola et al., 2020). It is envisaged that COVID-19 will also contribute to the level of penury, as well as unemployment. For instance, the stock markets have collapsed as a result of the pandemic by a minimum of 50%, resulting in a corresponding halt in the credit market. Moreover, unemployment rates soared above 10% as well with global gross domestic product contracting at an annualised rate of 10% or more (Roubini, 2020; Abodunrin et al., 2020). COVID-19 appears to be the major factor leading to an increase in the rate of poverty and unemployment as the rate of unemployment has soared beyond the 10% mark (Abodunrin et al., 2020). All the components of aggregate demand such as consumption, capital expenditure, and exports are in an unprecedented freefall, which subsequently indicates that the contraction currently being experienced does not appear in a V-, U-, or L-shaped curve but rather an I-shaped curve, which is a vertical line representing the financial markets and the real economy in freefall (Abodunrin et al., 2020). Decision-makers, companies, and market players are trying to revise their growth expectations in the short, medium, and long term (Gormsen & Koijen, 2020).

Quite a number of sectors such as the pharmaceutical industry, solar energy sector, information and electronics industry, aviation industry, etc., are severely affected by the pandemic (Haleem et al., 2020). China is currently in a state of turmoil, and development activities cannot continue until normality is restored. Consequently, the inflation rate keeps soaring, which is currently on the 50% mark.

Undoubtedly, China is a global economic superpower with an economy linked to all other countries of the world; however, in the wake of the pandemic, its economic growth had also plummeted to 2% compared with 6% in the past. Likewise, the virus had spread all over the world including countries that have substantial business relations with China – South Korea, Iran, Japan, the United States, Thailand, Denmark, Ireland, etc. – which implies that the economic systems of these countries are also severely affected by COVID-19 (Khan & Faisal, 2020). According to some capital economists, China could lose up to USD$62 billion in the first quarter of the year, with the world losing USD$280 billion if no urgent global actions are taken to suppress the COVID-19 (Ayittey et al., 2020).

Apart from that, the tourism sector is currently one of the most affected sectors, as most of the infected countries banned air travel during the COVID-19 outbreak (Haleem et al., 2020). For instance, the World Travel and Tourism Council has warned that 50 million jobs in the global travel and tourism sector may be at risk (Nicola et al., 2020). The China Outbound Tourism Research Institute (COTRI) has estimated that about 6.3 million Chinese tourists travelled abroad during the 2019 Lunar New Year holidays, generating a travel revenue of about $73 billion. However, the numbers dropped considerably in 2020. Due to the cancellation of Chinese tours and the decline in domestic and international travellers, the tourism industry in Vietnam is expected to lose up to $7.7 billion in the first quarter of the year. With the presence of Chinese nationals in Thailand decreasing by almost 80% in the first four months of 2020, the governor of the Tourism Authority of Thailand (TAT) estimates that the country could lose $3.1 billion in income from services. In addition, the tourism industry of Indonesia, Singapore, South Korea, Malaysia, Cambodia, Hong Kong, Japan, Australia, and many other countries are expected to be affected by the pandemic (Ayittey et al., 2020). The hotel industry was also severely affected – for instance, revenue per available room in the United States fell to 11.6% as of 7 March 2020, while in China, the occupancy rates dropped to 89% in late January 2020 (Nicola et al., 2020).

In Malaysia, the unemployment rate for the year is estimated at 629,000 people, which is a 3.3% increase when compared to 2019, resulting in an estimated loss of Ringgit Malaysia (RM) 38 to 102 billion in gross domestic product when compared to the 2020 statistics. At the same time, the agricultural and services sectors in Malaysia also recorded a higher percentage of job losses (21.9% and 15.0%, respectively) when compared with other sectors (Department of Statistics, Malaysia, 2020). India's economy is also severely affected by this virus because China remains India's third-largest export partner, which could subsequently lead to a drop in the supply of organic chemicals, plastics, fishery products, cotton, minerals, etc. (Pratheeesh & Arumugasamy, 2020). The coronavirus has had a profound impact on the aviation industry; as a result of the foreclosures, airline operations have been suspended in all affected countries. According to IndiGo, the largest Indian airline recorded a 15% to 20% drop in daily bookings during the pandemic (Rani, 2020). However, the demand for medical supplies has considerably increased. There is also increased demand in the food sector, which is experiencing a surge in demand due to panic purchases and food storage (Nicola et al., 2020).

COVID-19 has had a pronounced effect on e-commerce and technology. In Malaysia, many e-commerce companies rely on China for half of its derivative products. Therefore, it is envisaged that this deadly virus will seriously affect Malaysian online businesses, especially those selling sought-after Chinese products (Hasanat et al., 2020). Despite this, for the sale of domestic products online businesses are taking off in Malaysia and other parts of the world as this is the most convenient alternative to provide selling of goods without direct physical contact.

In general, taking the loss of trade, commerce, tourism, and the main impacts on global supply chains into account, the economic impacts of the pandemic will be felt considerably in China and around the world. According to Bloomberg economists, China's gross domestic product value in the first quarter of the year 2020 could drop to 4.5% year-on-year (Ayittey et al., 2020). Model estimates in the analysis of the expected losses in different countries of the world also predict a decrease in the world's gross domestic product by 0.42% in the first quarter of the year 2020 due to the outbreak. Despite this, Bloomberg economists still believe that it is too early to gauge the full impact of the deadly disease just yet, as the infection is still yet to reach its peak (Ayittey et al., 2020).

5.4 COVID-19 and social impacts

A variety of violations committed in places of residence are regarded as domestic violence and it is also known as 'domestic abuse' or 'intimate partner violence' which is defined as 'as a pattern of behavior in any relationship that is used to gain or maintain power and control over an intimate partner' (United Nations, n.d.). Women, children, and the elderly are most prone to domestic violence. During the lockdown period, the rate of domestic violence involving physical, emotional, and sexual abuse was found to have increased alarmingly in many countries. For instance, the UN (2020) reported that since the lockdown, domestic violence has increased in France (30%), Argentina (30%), Singapore (33%), and Cyprus (30%).

The reasons for this may include the increase in the time being spent behind closed doors, thereby exposing vulnerable people to abuse, especially when it is extremely difficult for them to reach out for help. According to *The Refuge* – one of the UK's domestic abuse charities – a 25% increase in calls to its helpline was experienced during the lockdown, leading to the publication of guidelines by the UK government on the recognition and reporting of domestic violence with a list of all available services (Nicola et al., 2020).

According to Graham-Harrison et al. (2020), there is an increasing trend in domestic violence globally. For instance, violence was discovered to have increased from 40% to 50% in Brazil, while in a particular Spanish region, calls to a helpline were discovered by the government to have increased by 20% in the early days of the lockdown. In addition, when the first index case of coronavirus was detected in Cyprus, calls for help from the government increased by 30% during the same week (Bradbury-Jones & Isham, 2020). In New Zealand, the pandemic is expected to result in an even greater magnitude of domestic and sexual violence (NZFVC, n.d.). However, the incidence of domestic violence is even worse in developing countries where domestic violence abounded before the advent of the coronavirus.

The impact of COVID-19 is unique for different age categories depending on the immune system, as well as the healthy eating habits of the population of the country in question. So far, the most affected countries – including the virus' country, China – show that senior citizens of over the age of 80 are more likely to be infected with the virus compared to those in other age categories (Khan & Faisal, 2020). Apart from the elderly, people suffering from other underlying medical conditions are also susceptible to the virus and death. Also, men are more likely to be infected with the virus than women (Begley, 2020). According to the data from the director of the Institute of Epidemiology, Disease Control and Research (IEDCR, n.d.), 68% of the total coronavirus infected cases were men while women only constituted 32% of the cases in Bangladesh.

While the highest fatality rates were recorded in people aged over 85 years, it was discovered that other infected age ranges were also hospitalized and admitted to intensive care units (Statista, 2020). In the United States, hospitalization, ICU admission, and death were prominent among senior citizens rather than their counterparts in other age categories, with the highest number of infected patients in the 20–44 age group (Statista, 2020).

Young people have been identified to be the least affected by this virus because, until mid-January, no child in Wuhan – the origin of the epidemic – had contracted COVID-19 (Begley, 2020). According to the China Centre for Disease Control and Prevention, there had been no deaths in the 0–9 age bracket but a 0.2% fatality rate for those aged 10–39 years. The fatality rate further rose to 3.6% in the 60–69 age group, with an 8% fatality rate among the 70–79 age group, and a 14.8% fatality among those aged 80 years and older (McCarthy, n.d.).

However, this fact (of children being the least affected by the virus) is not firmly established, as children do not show signs of illness even when infected (Begley, 2020). The World Health Organization, therefore, warns young people to take preventive measures against COVID-19 (WHO, 2020). Generally, the risk of age-related deaths likely reflects the strength or weakness of the human body's respiratory system (Begley, 2020). However, the infected cases and fatalities in different regions were found to vary in terms of age category. A typical example is seen in South Korea and Italy, where cases of the coronavirus were higher in younger people in Korea (age 20–29), while in Italy the highest number of cases were recorded amongst the older age group (age 70–79) (Buchholz, 2020).

In Bangladesh, young men are considered most vulnerable to COVID-19, as they tend to spend most of their time outdoors. In Bangladesh, the mortality rate is also relatively high. As of 20 April 2020, according to the Institute of Epidemiology, Disease Control and Research (IEDCR), 2,948 people tested positive for COVID-19, out of which 85 patients recovered and 101 died. This implies that the mortality rate is at 3.43%. Also, between 8 March and 20 April 2020, 70% of the 15–54 age group had confirmed cases of Covid-19 and 8% of the 0–15 age group had confirmed cases of Covid-19 (WHO, 2020).

Religious practices were affected in all regions during the pandemic due to the temporary suspension of all gatherings for religious purposes by different countries; it was clear that the virus was easily spread from person to person, which could result in a serious outbreak of the disease. In Kuala Lumpur, the capital of Malaysia, several hundred Muslims attended a mosque service and became infected as well. After these incidents, the number of positive cases of the coronavirus drastically increased. Also, in Washington DC, a rector tested positive for the virus after giving communion in an Episcopalian church with worshippers numbering over 500, all of whom were subsequently asked to self-quarantine for two weeks (Robinson, 2020).

However, only a few countries were quick to adopt timely measures against gatherings for religious purposes. For example, the authority of Saudi Arabia prohibited foreign arrivals as well as visits to the cities of Mecca and Medina for the Umrah pilgrimage (Diseko, 2020). However, Saudi authorities said that these measures are only temporary, and they have not indicated any plans to disrupt the Hajj (Diseko, 2020). In Bangladesh, access to the mosques has been restricted by the government, even for Friday prayers. The Malaysian government has also banned all prayers in the mosque since the appearance of the virus.

5.5 COVID-19 and environmental impacts

Regardless of the negative consequences of the ongoing pandemic, a positive impact on the environment is still being experienced. The drastic drop in the volume of automobile traffic and mass industrial production has considerably improved air quality around the world. China and Bangladesh may be the best-cited examples in terms of countries with high levels of air pollution, as both countries have been repeatedly classified as one of the most polluted and unliveable countries in the world. Our attention has been drawn to the many pictures on social media showing wild animals in and around big cities, nature lovers enjoying the sweet songbirds, dolphins 'dancing' in the sea, different blooming flowers, etc. The pandemic was also discovered to have reduced carbon dioxide levels across many regions. According to Kienapple (2020), in this regard, in the United States, there was 40% less domestic air traffic; in the city of New York there was a 50% decrease in carbon monoxide; and in Seattle, there was a 41% decrease in peak traffic congestion. In China, the carbon emissions in the country fell by 25%.

Due to the pandemic, the operation of factories has stopped resulting in a reduction of air pollution. For instance it has been reported that the Indian citizens in Punjab state now enjoy the snow peaks of the Himalayas which before the pandemic they could not enjoy due to air pollution. In addition, New Delhi which is considered the most atmospherically polluted city in the world – being the home to the deadliest air contaminants – witnessed a whopping 60% drop in fine particulate matter during the COVID-19 outbreak (Newburger & Jeffery, 2020). The lockdown commenced on 29 March in Nepal, and within just six days of the confinement period, the Langtang range became visible in Kathmandu. A big decrease in air pollution was also observed in Kathmandu Valley, a place which consistently ranked as one of the most polluted areas in the world (Newburger & Jeffery, 2020). Moreover, global air traffic was also found to have reduced by a staggering 60% (Hamwey, 2013). As a consequence of the pandemic, this year's annual Earth Day event was observed online.

While the Earth appears to be 'healing' in some respects, the negative impact of COVID-19 on our environment is still being experienced via medical waste, wastewater generation, and electricity consumption. As such, the sudden increase in demand for plastics and plastic bottles, masks, personal protective equipment, and other medical equipment has resulted in tons and tons of medical waste. For instance, hospitals in Wuhan produced more than 200 tons of waste daily at the peak of the outbreak in Wuhan when compared to a previous average of under 50 tons (Masud, 2020). In addition to medical waste, the amount of household waste was also discovered to have increased steadily, as more people buy online and order deliveries, which comes with lots of packaging materials.

In many developing countries, however, there is a lack of proper disposal systems or recycling centres for this waste; therefore, users dispose of their waste indiscriminately, consequently polluting the fresh air and clean water. Attempts to manage, control, and prevent COVID-19 globally have resulted in a spike in wastewater generation, which is due to an increased need for sanitation and hygiene, resulting in a shortage of fresh water. The supply of electricity has also been hampered due to the pandemic (Statista, 2020). According to the World Economic Forum, the COVID-19 outbreak could result in the loss of habitat and wildlife poaching, with sales of illegally hunted animals resulting in the spread of animal-borne diseases such as zoonotic diseases. This shows a significant link between biodiversity loss and the flexibility of consistent supply chains in the global economy.

5.6 Recommendation and conclusion

Despite governments' initiatives, additional precautions should be taken to minimize the economic effects of COVID-19. First, governments should focus on minimizing the economic impact of COVID-19 instead of economic recovery. Indeed, we are completely unable to accurately estimate the economic losses due to COVID-19 at this point. The first priority should be given to saving lives. Therefore, some important and overriding factors should be addressed urgently in order to minimize not only the economic but also the social and environmental effects of COVID-19. For example, we need to increase intensive care hospital units as much as possible as well as build temporary hospitals with the help of non-governmental organizations (NGOs), and other social organizations. Second, there is an urgent need to provide sufficient resources and funds to public health sectors to disinfect affected areas and other public spaces. Most importantly, large-scale population testing is particularly important. Indeed, the identification of each case can save several lives. Third, it is high time that governments should allocate more money to detect, prevent, control, treat, and contain the virus and provide emergency assistance with food, medicine, etc. to those who need to be quarantined. Fourth, governments should promote e-business as an alternative business platform to revive businesses that have stopped in this pandemic situation. Fifth, all international and local financial institutions should provide additional financial support to developing countries like Malaysia. For example, the International Monetary Fund (IMF) provided additional funds to Guinea, Liberia, and Sierra Leone in 2014 to fight the Ebola epidemic. Last but not least, in this global health crisis, each nation's ministry of health alone is not enough to combat COVID-19; strong coordination among all government ministries is desirable.

However, post-COVID-19, government stimulus packages would be very welcome to help citizens to recover the national economy quickly. To improve the economy, governments can provide subsidies to businesses and individuals in the form of capital, wages, and salaries. The government can also provide short-term unemployment benefits to vulnerable groups to reduce unemployment and boost productivity. For example, China is accelerating the payment of unemployment insurance benefits and expanding its social safety nets. Korea is increasing jobseeker's allowances for young adults and expanding them to low-income households. Fiscal measures must be taken into account to save businesses and financial institutions from going bankrupt and to help the entire economy recover quickly once the pandemic is over. The government may also provide tax relief to the most affected individuals and businesses who cannot afford to pay tax. At the same time, it is time to announce stimulus packages to support those affected individuals and businesses, particularly for high-performing small and medium enterprises (SMEs) in Malaysia. Upcoming national budgets should be prepared in such a way where people, SMEs, and informal service sectors can be supplied with a sufficient amount of cash by which they can generate the necessary demand for products and services in the market, which will ultimately help manufacturers and producers to make the economy dynamic.

There is a strong assumption or possible explanation as to where the virus originated, and it is that it came from the habit of eating wildlife. Therefore, it is high time to ban wildlife trade around the world, especially in China. The pattern of human behaviour and our eating habits must be controlled to protect the environment. A healthy and balanced diet and cleanliness are necessary to strengthen the immune system to defeat the virus. At the same time, world leaders must realize there is a climate change crisis otherwise, this could lead to a situation as serious as the coronavirus pandemic. In order to live on this planet, human behaviour must change in such ways as to ensure the protection and preservation of nature. In the face of this pandemic, we understand that just as it is important to flatten the curve of climate change and environmental destruction, it is crucial to flatten the COVID-19 curve as well. Therefore, to protect human health, livelihoods, wildlife resilience, biodiversity, and the most vulnerable, this is the right time to frame and polish our ideas while putting plans and strategies in place to invest in new opportunities – specifically those leading to behavioural changes that are environmentally friendly.

The pandemic has also created social dilemmas and domestic violence is one issue that has increased as families are forced to be inside their houses with perpetrators 24/7 due to the lockdown measures implemented. Domestic violence affects the victim via a wide range of physical and mental health consequences. This implies that the victims require emergency support systems as well as psychological assessments. Therefore, the governments of all affected countries should focus on the provision of these emergency support systems and psychological assessments and take the necessary actions. Since no one can accurately predict the final financial damage that will be caused by COVID-19, it is essential that economic activities become more focused on electronic commerce in order to avoid the severity of long-term economic depression. Otherwise, penury and unemployment will ultimately lead to criminal activities such as theft. Global production methods must maintain a balance between environmental and economic interests. Governments, as well as other concerned bodies, should concentrate on developing a new business model that carbon-neutral and production systems that are friendly to nature.

Last but not least, to drive home the point, fighting this virus is not only the government's business but NGOs, national and international rights-based institutions, religious leaders, telecommunications companies, and the media all have an important role to play. In addition, coordination between all stakeholders are absolutely necessary to overcome the pandemic. Public figures and influencers can also educate the general public about the negative impacts of COVID-19 through various social media such as Facebook, Twitter, etc. The wealthy should also reach out to the low income families by providing food, clothing, and other basic amenities. In this critical situation, health workers, administrative agents, and police officers should be adequately protected, as these people are the frontline agents fighting this virus in all affected countries.

COVID-19 has severely affected the demographics, economics, social, religious, and environmental aspects of life in various ways around the world. As a result, each country is confronted with the major challenge of achieving the SDGs by 2030. To overcome this pandemic, the whole world must work together. In addition, individual and social efforts are essential to protect the Earth from this dangerous virus. Otherwise, human beings will continue to enhance this disaster that affects the economic and social support systems. Lockdown may not be the only measure to curtail this pandemic; therefore, the authorities concerned should implement effective measures such as maintaining social distancing in markets, surveillance of travellers, the temporary introduction of security systems, education, and online services, and more investments in the health sector to control the disease. Therefore, the bottom line is that governments, local and international financial institutions, NGOs, and other social organizations should work collectively to combat COVID-19 as well as to restore the world economy.

References

Abdi, M. (2020). Coronavirus disease 2019 (COVID-19) outbreak in Iran: Actions and problems. *Infection Control and Hospital Epidemiology, 41*(6), 754–755.

Abodunrin, O. R., Oloye, G., & Adesola, B. (2020). Coronavirus pandemic and its implication on global economy. *International Journal of Arts, Languages and Business Studies (IJALBS), 4*, 13–23.

Ayittey, F. K., Ayittey, M. K., Chiwero, N. B., Kamasah, J. S., & Dzuvor, C. (2020). Economic impacts of Wuhan 2019-nCoV on China and the world. *Journal of Medical Virology, 92*, 473–475.

Begley, S. (2020, March 3). Who is getting sick? A look at coronavirus risk by age, gender, and more. In *Stat*. Retrieved from https://www.statnews.com/2020/03/03/who-is-getting-sick-and-how-sick-a-breakdown-of-coronavirus-risk-by-demographic-factors/.

Bradbury-Jones, C., & Isham, L. (2020). The pandemic paradox: The consequences of COVID?19 on domestic violence. *Journal of Clinical Nursing, 29*(13–14), 2047–2049.

Buchholz, K. (2020). How does the coronavirus affect different age groups?. Retrieved from https://www.statista.com/chart/21134/age-distribution-coronavirus-italy-south-korea/.

Department of Statistics, Malaysia. (2020). Report of special survey on effects of covid-19 on economy and individual (round 1). Retrieved from https://www.dosm.gov.my/v1/uploads/files/covid-19/Report_of_Special_Survey_on_Effects_of_COVID-19_on_Economy_and_Individual-Round-1.pdf.

Diseko, L. (2020). Is coronavirus coming between people and their faith? Retrieved from https://www.bbc.com/news/world-51819117.

Duffin, E. (2020). Impact of the coronavirus pandemic on the global economy – Statistics and facts. Retrieved from https://www.statista.com/topics/6139/covid-19-impact-on-the-global-economy/.

Eurosurveillance. (2020). Note from the editors: World Health Organization declares novel coronavirus (2019-nCoV) sixth public health emergency of international concern. *Euro Surveil, 25(5)*, pii–20131e.

Fornaro, L., & Wolf, M. (2020). COVID-19 coronavirus and macroeconomic policy. *Macroeconomics: Monetary & Fiscal Policies EJournal*. Retrieved from https://ideas.repec.org/p/bge/wpaper/1168.html.

Gormsen, N. J., & Koijen, R. S. J. (2020). Coronavirus: Impact on stock prices and growth expectations. *Becker Friedman Institute for Economics Working Paper Series*. Retrieved from https://papers.ssrn.com/sol3/papers.cfm?abstract_id=3555917.

Graham-Harrison, E., Guiffrida, A., Smith, H., & Ford, L. (2020). Lockdowns around the world bring rise in domestic violence. *The Guardian*, Retrieved from https://www.theguardian.com/society/2020/mar/28/lockdowns-world-rise-domestic-violence.

Haleem, A., Javaid, M., & Vaishya, R. (2020). Effects of COVID-19 pandemic in daily life. *Current Medicine Research and Practice, 10*, 78–79.

Hamwey, R. (2013). Discussion forum on "why trade matters in development strategies." *United Nations Conference on Trade and Development*. Retrieved from https://unctad.org/meetings/en/Presentation/ditc_dir_2013_ppt_Hamwey.pdf.

Hasanat, M. W., Hoque, A., Shikha, F. A., Anwar, M., Hamid, A., & Tat, H. H. (2020). The impact of coronavirus (COVID-19) on E-business in Malaysia. *Asian Journal of Multidisciplinary Studies, 3*, 85–90.

IEDCR (Institute of Epidemiology, Disease Control and Research). (n.d.). Bangladesh coronavirus (COVID-19) update. *Institute of Epidemiology, Disease Control and Research*. Retrieved from https://iedcr.gov.bd/.

Khan, N. M., & Faisal, S. (2020). Epidemiology of corona virus in the world and its effects on the China economy. Retrieved from https://economics.rabobank.com/publications/2020/january/economic-implications-of-the-coronavirus/.

Kienapple, P. (2020). Coronavirus's impact on the environment [infographic]. Retrieved from https://venngage.com/blog/coronavirus-impact-on-environment-infographic/.

Kumar, D., Malviya, R., & Sharma, P. (2020). Corona virus: A review of COVID-19. *Eurasia Journal of Medicine and Oncology*, *4*(1), 8–25.

Masud, M. M. (2020, April 21). Covid-19: Will it help meet global climate targets? *Focus Malaysia*. Retrieved from https://focusmalaysia.my/opinion/covid-19-will-it-help-meet-global-climate-targets/.

McCarthy, N. (n.d.). How the fatality rate of Coronavirus changes with age. *World Economic Forum*. Retrieved from https://www.weforum.org/agenda/2020/03/coronavirus-covid19-cov2-wuhan-china-virus-disease-risks-fatality-rates.

Newburger, E., & Jeffery, A. (2020). Coronavirus: Photos show effect of air pollution drops from global lockdown. Retrieved from https://www.cnbc.com/2020/04/23/coronavirus-photos-show-effect-of-air-pollution-drops-from-global-lockdown.html.

Nicola, M., Alsafi, Z., Sohrabi, C., Kerwan, A., Al-Jabir, A., Iosifidis, C., Agha, M., & Agha, R. (2020). The socio-economic implications of the coronavirus pandemic (COVID-19): A review. *International Journal of Surgery*, *78*, 185–193.

NZFVC. (n.d.). Preventing and responding to family, whānau and sexual violence during COVID-19. *New Zealand Family Violence Clearinghouse*. Retrieved from https://nzfvc.org.nz/covid-19/preventing-responding-violence-covid-19.

Pratheeesh, J. T., & Arumugasamy, G. (2020). Impact of corona virus in Indian economy and banking sector: An overview. *Studies in Indian Place Names*, *40*(18), 2090–2101.

Rani, R. (2020). The impact of corona virus on Indian economy. *Studies in Indian Place Names*, *40*(60), 3618–3626.

Robinson, K. (2020). How are major religions responding to the coronavirus? *Council on Foreign Relations*. Retrieved from https://www.cfr.org/in-brief/how-are-major-religions-responding-coronavirus.

Roubini, N. (2020). Coronavirus pandemic has delivered the fastest, deepest economic shock in history. *The Guardian*. Retrieved from https://www.theguardian.com/business/2020/mar/25/coronavirus-pandemic-has-delivered-the-fastest-deepest-economic-shock-in-history.

United Nations. (n.d.). What is domestic abuse?. Retrieved from https://www.un.org/en/coronavirus/what-is-domestic-abuse.

WHO (World Health Organisation). (2020, April 13). WHO director-general's opening remarks at the media briefing on COVID-19. Retrieved from https://www.who.int/dg/speeches/detail/who-director-general-s-opening-remarks-at-the-media-briefing-on-covid-19--13-april-2020.

Part II

Innovation in Islamic social finance to fight against COVID-19

6 Islamic FinTech

The digital transformation bringing sustainability to Islamic finance

Mohammad Atif, M. Kabir Hassan, Mustafa Raza Rabbani, and Shahnawaz Khan

6.1 Introduction

As the Islamic finance sector is booming, from a market of just USD 200 billion in 2003 to 2.4 trillion in 2017 to 2.5 trillion in 2018, it is expected to get around 4 trillion in assets by 2030 (Reuters, 2018). Islamic finance continues to grow in different asset classes and economies through the emergence of innovative and disruptive financial technology. The present chapter is divided into five parts. It starts with the discussion of financial technology (FinTech) and sustainable Islamic finance by defining and explaining FinTech, Islamic finance, and sustainability. In the second part, a brief review of FinTech and sustainability is presented. In the third part, the importance of sustainability for a successful financial system is discussed. In the fourth part, various FinTech models like a *zakat* management system, Islamic P2P lending, and crowdfunding are discussed, and it is argued that these FinTech models can make Islamic finance more sustainable. Finally, in the conclusion, recommendation and further scope of the study is presented.

In the aftermath of the global financial crisis of 2008–2009, Islamic finance became the centre of attraction and economists, policy-makers, and other stakeholders across the globe realized that Islamic finance has the potential to offer improvements over the conventional financial system (Gheeraert & Weill, 2015). As turmoil and crisis offer a chance to push for a change, it also guarantees that tomorrow is going to be better than today. With FinTech around, there will remain little difference between the real and financial economy as FinTech ensures high-tech, automated, and seamless two-way communication (Blackstad & Allen, 2018). However, there remains a kind of cynicism among industry partners about the sustainability of the Islamic financial system. There are also concerns whether it can compete with its mighty rival, the conventional financial system, which has a stronger regulatory and policy framework along with institutional support. This chapter presents a critical discussion of Islamic FinTech and describes how FinTech can help Islamic finance emerge as a sustainable alternative. This chapter also elaborates on various FinTech models like a FinTech-based *zakat* management system, blockchain, internet of things (IoT), Islamic P2P lending, crowdfunding, artificial intelligence, and ethics. The chapter concludes by giving various examples showing that Islamic finance has already passed the stern test of sustainability and is going to stay in the long run. Moreover, Islamic finance has the capability to provide an alternative financial system, and the emergence of Islamic FinTech will only help in bringing more stability and sustainability.

Nobel Prize winner and British economist Ronald Coase wrote a paper titled 'The nature of the firm' in 1937, where he described the three types of cost to the firm. According to Coase, the three types of costs are the cost of search, coordination, and contrasting. He proposed the idea that a firm would progress if the internal cost of performing a transaction is more than the external cost of performing a transaction. The Coase theory is about the information related cost. FinTech, being a disruptive technology, disrupts several functions of the financial system, and it reduces all three costs proposed by Ronald Coase (Coase, 1937).

6.2 Islamic finance and sustainable development

One of the key factors in the development of any financial system must be sustainability. Sustainability of any system is defined as 'the situation of creating a system where it meets the demand of the current generation without compromising the future generation or providing an ability to the future generation to meet its own needs' (Sadiq & Mushtaq, 2015; p. 46). The concept of 'sustainable development' emerged in the 1960s, and is about moral values and ethics (Iqbal, 2005). The concept of sustainable development is more about environmental issues focusing on the negative effect of industrial development on the environment. The most significant route for sustainability comes from the United Nations' 2015 agenda of Sustainable Development Goals (SDGs). The SDGs are the framework to achieve enduring and sustainable development for all. The SDGs refer to the global challenges we are facing, including poverty, hunger, education, and equality, etc.

The 17 SDGs have been listed by the United Nations not to leave anyone behind and they want to achieve them by 2030. It is an ambition that requires a 'decade of delivery', starting from 2020 to be achieved by 2030. But it seems that time is running short because of the current global pandemic, the decline in healthcare, and the global recession, among many challenges. The enormity and magnitude of the challenge is gigantic, and it requires a great deal of cooperation among institutions and individuals to work in unison. It requires financial products that are innovative, disruptive, and aimed at the long-term vision of financial inclusion and development for all. A vigorous and healthy financial system such as Islamic finance is needed to unlock finance across the value chain.

Islamic finance and banking have been growing at an unprecedented pace since the inception of the first Islamic bank in Dubai in 1975. Islamic finance and banking have achieved unprecedented growth in the last decade or so and passed the test of time during the financial crisis of 2008 by being the most stable and sustainable financial system (Aliyu et al., 2017). Even during the unprecedented growth of Islamic finance, it has not deviated from its objective of social justice and sustainable and social development. In contrast with its conventional counterpart, Islamic finance and banking gives utmost importance to the social component of economic and business activities. The global financial and social community needs to discover the social objective of Islamic finance in terms of asset-backed financing, its support of the real economy, and superior financial solidity.

There are, of course, challenges to Islamic finance to provide a more stable and sustainable financial system. The challenges need to be addressed and exploited to make the most of the available prospects, and it looks auspicious for Islamic finance due to the following reasons.

6.3 Ethical finance

Ethical finance is defined as finance that considers not only current financial returns but also environmental and social factors (Gangi & Trotta, 2015). Islamic finance has already positioned itself as the sustainable financial system due to its ethical predisposition and providing financial services based on the rule and regulation prescribed by *sharia*. It is based on the profit and loss sharing (PLS) method of investing instead of guaranteed profit and interest-based financing *(riba)*. *Riba* is strictly prohibited under *sharia* law as *sharia riba* intends to exploit low-income families against the rich. Islamic finance also links its transactions to real assets to avoid any sort of ambiguity/uncertainty (*gharar*), gambling or speculation (*maysir*) is not allowed, and Islamic finance cannot invest in any unethical or *haram* business like pork, terrorism, antisocial activities, alcohol, pornography, and betting, etc. (Wahab et al., 2007). The investment options provided by Islamic finance are asset-based, i.e., it is required to acquire real assets, and it is less likely to lead to a debt crisis (Aliyu, 2015). Islamic finance offers a number of financial instruments that can be developed into an ethical finance alternative not only for micro and small entrepreneurs but also for corporations. Some instruments, like *Qardh-Al-Hasan* (capital finance), *Murabaha* (equipment finance), *Ijarah* (leased equipment), *Mudaraba* (partnership mode of financing), *and Musharaka* (project finance) are easy to manage and popular financing methods as ethical finance. The beauty of all these financing methods is the participatory, i.e., profit and loss sharing mode of financing (Rahman, 2010).

Islamic finance is ethical and sustainable as it is in alignment with the Sustainable Development Goals due to its four basic features. The four basic characteristics of Islamic finance are:

1. Asset backed. It means that Islamic finance believes in lending based on the trade rather than just money lending and borrowing. In other words, *sharia* does not permit transactions that are not based on real economic activities. Examples include *murabaha*, agency/*wakala*, etc.
2. Ethical. Islamic finance principles are based on ethical values along with Islamic values as ethical values are imbibed in Islamic values. Islamic finance aims to serve ethical finance not only to Muslims but to humanity at large. Islamic finance is based on the religious values of Islam, and it prohibits

unethical activities such as interest (*Riba*), uncertainty (*Gharar*), and gambling (*Maysir*) (Nienhaus, 2011).
3. Share risks equitably. One of the major reasons behind the global financial crises of 2008 was risk transfer in the form of an interest-based system where risk is transferred solely to one party (Kayed & Hassan, 2011). Islam prohibits interest and promotes a financing method where risk is shared rather than transferred. Various data and analyses show that due to this reason, Islamic finance handled the global financial crisis better than its conventional counterpart (Hasan, 2016).
4. Good governance. Strong governance is a critical factor for the progress of a vibrant and sound finance industry. As good governance and sustainability are directly related, Islamic finance makes sure that good governance practices are in place to safeguard the interest of all stakeholders, while also upholding the capability and sustainability of Islamic financial instructions (Kassim et al., 2018).

6.4 Fintech and sustainable development

Sustainable development is one of the basic objectives of economies around the globe. Financial institutions, governmental agencies, and social bodies around the world are considering how they can achieve sustainable development and the United Nations' Sustainable Development Goals (UN-SDGs), in addition to their financial and economic development. The regulators and financial institutions have to balance their objective of stability in terms of monetary policy, financial integrity, financial inclusion, and customer protection in addition to sustainable development (Arner et al., 2020). The role of new disruption in the field of finance in the form of FinTech, is going to be crucial and decisive in achieving the above objectives.

FinTech is the use of innovative technology-based financial services that aims to compete with traditional and conventional financial services. It is an emerging and disruptive technology, that aims to improve financial services and give the user a better experience and choice. FinTech is defined as 'The fusion of Information Technology and Finance for providing the financial services at an affordable cost with a seamless user-friendly experience' (Rabbani, 2020).

FinTech covers everything from crowdfunding to mobile payments to robo advisory services and from digital currency like cryptocurrency/Bitcoin to blockchain technology. In other words, it consists of such powerful innovations that are bound to challenge traditional financial services. Various studies have identified FinTech as the key contributor in transforming the finance sector over the next five years. Islamic finance must be ready to adapt to this challenge and transformation (Jamil & Seman, 2019).

6.5 Islamic FinTech and sustainability in Islamic finance

Islamic financial institutions have embraced FinTech with open arms as on principle, Islam adopts any innovation or technology that does not violate the basic principle of *sharia* (Haider et al., 2020). Islamic economies have already realized the importance of FinTech in sustainable development. FinTech Bay in Bahrain has recently launched a Global Islamic and Sustainable Fintech Centre (GISFC), in association with its local, regional, and international partners.

The aims of this initiative are to accelerate the growth of FinTech in the field of Islamic finance with a focus on the sustainable, social, and responsible innovation in Islamic finance. Globally, major players in Islamic finance like Iran, Saudi Arabia, Malaysia, and Bahrain are making changes to their policies and regulations in the form of regulatory 'sandboxes' to foster further innovation in the field of Islamic finance (Rabbani et al. 2020). The new innovations are aimed at capturing the untapped demand of new customers with new and attractive financial services. Islamic FinTech aims to achieve long-term growth along with sustainability as its central and strategic goal.

6.6 The proposed model of sustainable development 'IslamicFintech4SD'

The proposed model is intended to bring more transparency, user-friendliness, availability and collaboration to different sections of the Islamic financial system. If technology is combined with finance in the right way, it can bring more accuracy, accountability, and transparency to work in the best interest of society. Our proposed model 'IslamicFintech4SD' is intended to create a targeted alliance between Islamic financial institutions, multinational companies, start-ups, and new disruptive crowdfunding and P2P lending institutions along with *sharia* compliance. Based on the experience all around the world in conventional as well as Islamic finance, the present chapter proposes a five-step strategic model (IslamicFintech4SD Gearbox) to achieve sustainable development through Islamic FinTech. The first pillar is simplifying the process of opening an account and electronic 'knowing your customer' (eKYC), an anti-money-laundering (AML) process along with digital ID. The second pillar is a digital payments system, and the third pillar is the introduction of new innovative artificial intelligence (AI) and blockchain-based Islamic financial services. The fourth pillar is to use the first three pillars to deliver government services to achieve financial inclusion, and finally, the fifth and last pillar is to ensure *sharia* compliance of all four pillars of sustainable development in Islamic finance.

The five pillars of sustainable development in Islamic FinTech are elucidated below.

6.6.1 First pillar – simplified account opening and eKYC, AML, along with digital ID

Digital ID is central to achieve many important and transformational changes in developing economies. Many studies have proven that government schemes and other relief work do not reach all people due to a lack of formal identification documents like digital ID. Many developed countries like the USA, Bahrain,

Saudi Arabia, and the UK already have digital ID for its citizens and residents, but the problem is with developing countries like India, Pakistan, and African countries. In most developing countries, people have basic identification documents (Banerjee, 2016).

Since the financial crisis of 2008, the banks and financial institutions are required to follow strict regulations related to 'knowing your customer' (KYC) and AML. The crisis paved the way for institutions and regulators to make policies to safeguard the interest of customers and other stakeholders as well as increase transparency (Moyano & Ross, 2017). The evolution of digital currency like Bitcoin and other cryptocurrencies also brings the risk of money laundering and terrorist funding. An authentication check is of utmost importance to ensure the safety, security, and prompt delivery of financial services in the digital age. Electronic KYC, or eKYC, is the process of verifying the identity of the user online before providing financial services to the user. The objective behind eKYC is to ensure that the companies are regulated, and it is easy to identify any fraudulent trade practices or money laundering activities. Digital transformation has made verification and identification more challenging as it has given criminals and hackers a chance to exploit the organizations' own failure. The banks and FinTech companies have already started artificial intelligence (AI) based eKYC for account opening and other financial services. The AI-based eKYC includes image-based eKYC and video-based eKYC.

- Vid-based eKYC. The video-enabled eKYC app enables the customer to submit their KYC information through the video anywhere at their own convenience. The AI-powered FinTech automatically verifies the video information and authorizes the transaction. It improves the quality of services along with convenience and saves the cost associated with it.
- Imag-based eKYC. The user uploads the images of the required documents to the online portal of the bank's website from anywhere at their own convenience. The AI-powered FinTech matches the live photo from the available government-linked databases for safe and secure transactions.

A machine-learning-based algorithm has the potential to fight anti-money-laundering activities. Machine learning uses algorithms rather than just computer programs, and it can make decisions and modify decisions without human oversight. It is capable of making faster, more accurate, efficient, and better decisions. The banks and financial institutions can have FinTech with eKYC and AML processes as it will enable them to automatically verify the customer's records and if they have any criminal or antisocial link, the FinTech will warn them of suspicious activity. The machine-learning-based AML and eKYC FinTech has the potential to save time and money, along with making efficient and effective decisions to better serve customers.

6.6.2 Second pillar: use of digital payment system

Digital payments like bwallet, Apple Pay, BenefitPay, and Samsung Pay have been quite popular due to attractive cashback, speed, cashless transactions, comparatively higher security than credit/debit cards, and no transaction costs (Anshari et al., 2019). Digital payment is another FinTech where payments are made through digital technology. In the digital payment method, both the receiver and payer use digital technology to pay and receive money An efficient digital payment system is the central foundation of financial inclusion and the financial and sustainable development of an economy (Arner et al., 2020). The digital payment is simple, easy to use, and efficient; even the less wealthy, less educated, and SMEs can have access to this payment platform. Mobile money is one example of this.

Mobile money is the use of smartphones to pay bills, store, use, save, and receive money. It is a facility associated with the smartphone that stores money using a mobile app linked to the mobile number. It can be linked to the mobile number or the bank account number depending on the contract between the service provider and customer. Some of the popular mobile money options include PayPal and Alipay.

Mobile money can be used for online payments like PayPal, Stripe, and Payoneer; point of sale (POS) payments like Square and Bindo; mobile payments like Apple Pay and Samsung Pay. It also has some options like Alipay and WeChat pay which can be used for multiple purposes like POS payments, online payments, and mobile payments.

Mobile money is very much linked to the Sustainable Development Goals of the UN as it facilitates access to financial services for everyone. It also enables the less wealthy and the vulnerable to be resilient to financial shocks like the financial crisis, COVID-19, and other financial and environmental disasters (Jones et al., 2017). It offers tremendous scope to facilitate the ability of underdeveloped regions to financially reach out to the deprived and vulnerable sections of society at a low transaction cost, leading to financial inclusion. There are multiple benefits to mobile money. It can be used to provide financial services at lightning-fast speed efficiently with more security that can help with financial inclusion at a very low cost.

6.6.3 Third pillar: new innovative AI-, IoT-, and blockchain-based Islamic financial services

Innovation is the new normal in the field of finance. Without innovation, financial institutions would not be able to satisfy their customers' expectations and ultimately would result in a failure to compete and survive. There are several conventional financial institutions like CITI Bank, Standard Chartered Bank, and Barclays, etc. who have dedicated financial incubation and innovation centres to conduct trials and innovation using AI, big data (Khan & Kannapiran, 2019), blockchain, and IoT, etc. at different levels (Hassan, 2020). In contrast, Islamic financial institutions (IFIs) are not showing agility and dexterity in this regard, despite knowing that agility and FinTech are the future of Islamic finance (Rabbani, 2020).

Artificial intelligence is a widely accepted and proven disruptive technology, and it has already disrupted many sectors such as natural language processing (Shahnawaz, 2011; Khan et al., 2018), finance and machine translation (Shahnawaz & Mishra, 2013a; 2013b; 2015; Khan & Usman, 2019). The presence and the potential benefit of AI in the finance sector can be multifarious. According to an estimation, with AI implementation, the finance sector can save around USD$1 trillion by 2030 (The Financial Brand, 2018). AI can be implemented in IFIs in the following ways:

1. Front office. At the front office for credit score, Takaful (Insuretech) and chatbots as financial adviser, and based and in Islamic financial intuitions.
2. Middle office: With AI implantation in the middle office, tasks such as eKYC and AML can save around USD$350 billion by 2030 (The Financial Brand, 2018). It can also be used for sentiment analysis of consumers for market development.
3. Back office. Financial institutions can save around $200 billion if AI is implemented properly for the backoffice task. AI can be implemented in the back office for capital optimization, market impact analysis, customer satisfaction analysis, modelling for risk management, and asset and wealth management, etc. (Khan, 2019).
4. Regulatory Technology (Regtech). AI-based Regtech helps financial institutions with regulatory requirements. Since Islamic financial institutions have to strictly follow the rules and regulations prescribed by *sharia*, the importance of Regtech becomes immensely important (Rabbani & Khan, 2020). Islamic financial institutions will have to take the initiative and develop its own *sharia* tech that not only caters to general regulatory requirements but also helps them with *sharia* compliance.

To maintain the growth rate of the industry in the coming years, Islamic financial institutions will have to change their usage of financial resources from fully focusing on development of human resources to investment in AI-based financial services for efficient, transparent, and faster delivery of financial services.

Blockchain and IoT, along with artificial intelligence and the other fourth industrial revolution (4IR) technologies, present a great opportunity for IFIs to solidify their position in the real economy. Crowdfunding, P2P lending, and asset-backed, *sharia*-compliant cryptocurrencies like X8 currency, are certainly a step in the right direction (Peredaryenko, 2019).

6.6.4 *Fourth pillar: use of the first three pillars to deliver government services to achieve financial inclusion*

Financial inclusion is the key to achieving the objective of sustainability and balanced regional development. We argue that financial inclusion should not be seen as an end in itself; rather it is to be considered as a tool to achieving the broader objective of sustainable development including the UN-SDGs. There is a strong viewpoint from scholars and academics that FinTech-based financial services, as discussed under the first three pillars, supports financial inclusion and it is a key factor in achieving the objective of financial inclusion (Arner et al., 2020; Demirguc-Kunt et al., 2018; Gabor & Brooks, 2017). Today, governments and financial institutions are focusing on FinTech-based services to reach the maximum customers and citizens to deliver financial services. Paytm – India's largest FinTech company has almost doubled its customer base, and it has already reached more than 200 million users. The company is claiming that they are on course to achieve a 300 million user base in 2020 (Sivathanu, 2019). Another example of the use of digital finance to achieve the objective of sustainable development and financial inclusion is the 'India stack strategy'. The India stack strategy was a well planned and executed digital technology initiative supported by favourable government regulations and policy (Schuetz & Venkatesh, 2020). We argue that the first three pillars of the IslamicFintech4SD can be used to deliver government services and achieve the objective of sustainable development and financial inclusion. Here, the idea of the present study is to achieve the following three-part vision:

1. Digital infrastructure shall be the basic right of every citizen in every country. The government shall consider this as a basic utility like electricity and water.
2. There shall be on-demand delivery and governance of these services.
3. IslamicFintech4SD will empower the citizens and residents of the country.

Islamic financial technology plays an important role in fostering financial inclusion and reducing poverty by delivering valuable government schemes to those with low income because in developing countries like Malaysia, Pakistan, and Bangladesh people are dependent on government schemes (Firmansyah & Ramdani, 2018). The government must use digital payment systems and new innovative AI-, IoT-, and blockchain-based Islamic financial services to achieve financial inclusion and sustainable development.

6.6.5 Fifth pillar: sharia *compliance*

Despite the fact that Islam is a religion that is more than 1400 years old, Islamic banking came into existence only in the 1960s and 1970s (Hassan & Lewis 2014). Any advancement, disruption, or innovation is welcome in Islam as long as it does not violate the basic ethos and principles of the *Quran* (Allah's holy words) and *Sunnah* (teaching and practices of the Holy Prophet Muhammad ﷺ). Islamic finance and banking follow the *Quran* and *Sunnah* and it is brought to the common people by way of *sharia*. *Sharia* is the way of life for Muslims that they should obey, together with the rules of fasting, *salah*, *zakat*, and all other economic dealings. It is basically a guiding light that guides Muslims in every facet of life, including social, political, and economic life. (The aims of *sharia* are to the help and guide Muslims as to how they should live their life according to the will of Allah and his holy prophet Muhammad (Hassan, 2013; Haider et al., 2020).) Some of the basic principles of *sharia* are summarized as follows:

1. The community as a whole is more important than the interest of individuals.
2. All the wealth in this world belongs to Allah. We the humans are merely the trustees of the wealth. We must manage and spend our wealth according to Allah's will, which promotes social justice and equality and prohibits certain activities like illegal and *haram* activities.
3. All economic and business dealings must be respectful of other people, the environment, and Allah. The primary reason for this principle is to prohibit the accumulation of wealth by a few people, leaving others in poverty. Islam does not have a concept where a few are multi-millionaires and rest are beggars (Kayed & Hassan, 2011).
4. *Sharia* prohibits business transactions with an element of *riba*, *maysir*, or *gharar* and products and services prohibited by the law of the land and declared *haram*.

Most FinTech-based financial services are flexible enough to adapt themselves according to the needs and requirements of *sharia* (Todorof, 2018). All the FinTech-based financial services discussed above under IslamicFintech4SD like blockchain, IoT, AI, and Regtech, etc. are very much inconsistent with the principles of *sharia*. *Sharia* compliance of FinTech-based financial services is not only important from the point of view of Muslims, but *sharia* also brings a dimension like sustainability and inclusion to FinTech because Islamic principles have inbuilt characteristics like sustainability and inclusion.

6.7 Conclusion

One of the most pressing goals of the 21st century is to achieve development that is sustainable and inclusive. Disruptive technologies like FinTech allow financial institutions to do businesses by doing experiments and innovating and developing new models of business. The paper discussed and argued that FinTech-based financial services bring sustainability to the finance industry (Piliyanti, 2019). The study suggests that there is a need to build a community of experts and enthusiasts to do a critical evaluation of sustainable development through FinTech. Certain digital finance and FinTech-based financial services need to be refined and adapted as per the principles of *sharia*. The paper further argues that Islamic finance and banking have huge potential and can be the next big thing in the finance world as sustainability characteristics are built into the principles of Islamic finance (Hassan, 2013). Islamic finance, in combination with financial technology, can achieve sustainable development and financial inclusion, which has been the most critical issue of late as identified in the UN-SDGs (Arner et al., 2020).

Shari-compliant FinTech has provided another opportunity to Islamic financial institutions and banks to solve the sustainability challenge in the real economy and provide a financial model that is long-lasting and unaffected by crises such as the financial crisis and COVID-19 pandemic. To realize and overcome this challenge, the IFIs are required to develop and experiment with new innovative financial services in line with *sharia* principles. The proposed model, IslamicFintech4SD, can help Islamic financial institutions achieve the Sustainable Development Goals if implemented properly. The promise of both social and commercial reward should motivate all concerned stakeholders to put this model into practice and achieve sustainable and inclusive development.

References

Aliyu, S., Hassan, M. K., Mohd Yusof, R., & Naiimi, N. (2017). Islamic banking sustainability: A review of literature and directions for future research. *Emerging Markets Finance and Trade*, *53*(2), 440–470.

Anshari, M., Almunawar, M. N., Masri, M., & Hamdan, M. (2019). Digital marketplace and FinTech to support agriculture sustainability. *Energy Procedia*, *156*, 234–238.

Arner, D. W., Buckley, R. P., Zetzsche, D. A., & Veidt, R. (2020). Sustainability, FinTech and financial inclusion. *European Business Organization Law Review*, *21*, 7–35.

Banerjee, S. (2016). Aadhaar: Digital inclusion and public services in India. *World Development Report*, Retrieved from http://pubdocs.worldbank.org/en/655801461250682317/WDR16-BP-Aadhaar-Paper-Banerjee.pdf.

Blakstad, S. & Allen, R. (2018). FinTech revolution universal inclusion in the new financial ecosystem. SpringerLink, retrieved from https://link.springer.com/book/10.1007%2F978-3-319-76014-8.

Coase, R. H. (1937). The nature of the firm. *Economica*, *4*(16), 386–405.

Demirguc-Kunt, A., Klapper, L., Singer, D., Ansar, S., & Hess, J. (2018). The global Findex database 2017: Measuring financial inclusion and the fintech revolution. *The World Bank*. Retrieved from https://openknowledge.worldbank.org/handle/10986/29510.

Firmansyah, H. B., & Ramdani, A. L. (2018, May). The role of Islamic financial technology (FinTech) start-up in improving financial inclusion in Indonesia case: Angsur. Retrieved from https://papers.ssrn.com/sol3/papers.cfm?abstract_id=3194546.

Gabor, D., & Brooks, S. (2017). The digital revolution in financial inclusion: International development in the fintech era. *New Political Economy*, *22*(4), 423–436.

Gangi, F., & Trotta, C. (2015). The ethical finance as a response to the financial crises. An empirical survey of European SRFs performance. *Journal of Management & Governance*, *19*(2), 371–394.

Gheeraert, L., & Weill, L. (2015). Does Islamic banking development favor macroeconomic efficiency? Evidence on the Islamic finance-growth nexus. *Economic Modelling*, *47*, 32–39.

Haider, M., Khan, S., Rabbani, M. R., & Thallasinos, Y. E. (2020). An artificial intelligence and NLP based Islamic FinTech model combining zakat and Qardh-Al-Hasan for countering the adverse impact of COVID 19 on SMEs and individuals. *International Journal of Economics and Business Administration*, *8*(2), 348–361.

Hasan, Z. (2016). Risk-sharing: The sole basis of Islamic finance? Time for a serious rethink. *Journal of King Abdul-Aziz University: Islamic Economics*, *29*(2), 23–35.

Hassan, M. K., & Lewis, M. K. (Eds.). (2014). *Handbook on Islam and Economic Life*. Cheltenham: Edward Elgar Publishing.

Jamil, N. N., & Seman, J. A. (2019). The impact of fintech on the sustainability of Islamic accounting and finance education in Malaysia. *Journal of Islamic, Social, Economics and Development (JISED)*, *4*(17), 74–88.

Jones, P., Wynn, M., Hillier, D., & Comfort, D. (2017). The sustainable development goals and information and communication technologies. *Indonesian Journal of Sustainability Accounting and Management*, *1*(1), 1–15.

The Financial Brand. (2018). Artificial Intelligence and the Banking Industry's $1 Trillion Opportunity. Retrieved from https://thefinancialbrand.com/72653/artificial-intelligence-trends-banking-industry/.

Kassim, S., Hassan, R., & Kassim, S. N. (2018). Good governance and sustainability in Islamic microfinance institutions. *Journal of Islamic Finance*, *7*(2), 021–028.

Kayed, R. N., & Hassan, M. K. (2011). The global financial crisis and Islamic finance. *Thunderbird International Business Review*, *53*(5), 551–564.

Khan, N., (2019). AI applications in the Islamic finance industry. *Global Islamic Finance Report 2019*. Retrieved from https://www.researchgate.net/publication/336856090_AI_Applications_in_the_Islamic_Finance_Industry. Accessed on 26/06/2020.

Khan, S., & Kannapiran, T. (2019). Indexing issues in spatial big data management. Retrieved from https://papers.ssrn.com/sol3/papers.cfm?abstract_id=3387792.

Khan, S. N., & Usman, I. (2019). A model for English to Urdu and Hindi machine translation system using translation rules and artificial neural network. *International Arab Journal of Information Technology*, *16*(1), 125–131.

Khan, S., Mir, U., Shreem, S. S., & Alamri, S. (2018). Translation divergence patterns handling in English to Urdu machine translation. *International Journal on Artificial Intelligence Tools*, *27*(05), 1850017.

Moyano, J. P., & Ross, O. (2017). KYC optimization using distributed ledger technology. *Business & Information Systems Engineering*, *59*(6), 411–423.

Nienhaus, V. (2011). Islamic finance ethics and Shari'ah law in the aftermath of the crisis: Concept and practice of Shari'ah compliant finance. *Ethical Perspectives*, *18*(4), 591–623.

Peredaryenko, M. (2019). FinTech, blockchain, and Islamic finance: Building the future in the new Islamic digital economy. In *4IR: AI, Blockchain, FinTech, IoT Reinventing a Nation*. Retrieved from https://www.researchgate.net/publication/336318374_FinTech_Blockchain_and_Islamic_Finance_-_Building_the_Future_in_the_New:Islamic_Digital_Economy.

Piliyanti, I. (2019). Fintech achieving sustainable development: The side perspective of crowdfunding platform. *Shirkah: Journal of Economics and Business*, *3*(2), 2503–4243.

Rabbani, M. R. (2020). The competitive structure and strategic positioning of commercial banks in Saudi Arabia. *International Journal on Emerging Technologies*, *11*(3), 43–46.

Rabbani, M. R., & Khan, S. (2020). Agility and fintech is the future of Islamic finance: A study from Islamic banks in Bahrain. *International Journal of Scientific and Technology Research*, *9*(3), 6955–6957.

Rabbani, M. R., Khan, S., & Thalassinos, I. E. (2020). FinTech, blockchain and Islamic finance: An extensive literature review. *International Journal of Economics and Business Administration*, *8*(2), 65–86.

Rahman, A.R.A. (2010). Islamic microfinance: An ethical alternative to poverty alleviation. *Humanomics*, *26*(4), 284–295.

Sadiq, R., & Mushtaq, A. (2015). The role of Islamic finance in sustainable development. *Journal of Islamic Thought and Civilization*, *5*(1), 46–65.

Schuetz, S., & Venkatesh, V. (2020). Blockchain, adoption, and financial inclusion in India: Research opportunities. *International Journal of Information Management*, *52*, 101936.

Shahnawaz, M. R. (2011). ANN and rule based model for English to Urdu-Hindi machine translation system. Retrieved from https://www.researchgate.net/publication/340535366_ANN_and_rule_based_model_for_English_to_Urdu-Hindi_machine_translation_system.

Shahnawaz, & Mishra, R. B. (2013a). Rule-based approach for handling of case markers in English to Urdu/Hindi translation. *International Journal of Knowledge Engineering and Soft Data Paradigms*, *4*(2), 138–165.

Shahnawaz, & Mishra, R. B. (2013b). Statistical machine translation system for English to Urdu. *International Journal of Advanced Intelligence Paradigms*, *5*(3), 182–203.

Shahnawaz, & Mishra, R. B. (2015). An English to Urdu translation model based on CBR, ANN and translation rules. *International Journal of Advanced Intelligence Paradigms*, *7*(1), 1–23.

Sivathanu, B. (2019). Adoption of digital payment systems in the era of demonetization in India. *Journal of Science and Technology Policy Management*, *10*(1),143–171.

Thomson Reuters: Islamic Finance Development Report 2018. Retrieved from https://icd-ps.org/uploads/files/IFDI%202019%20DEF%20digital1574605094_7214.pdf.

Todorof, M. (2018, August). Shariah-compliant fintech in the banking industry. *ERA Forum 19*, 1–17. doi: 10.1007/s12027-018-0505-8.

Wahab, A. R. A., Lewis, M. K., & Hassan, M. K. (2007). Islamic takaful: Business models, Shariah concerns, and proposed solutions. *Thunderbird International Business Review*, *49*(3), 371–396.

7 Artificial intelligence and Natural language processing (NLP) based FinTech model of *Zakat* for poverty alleviation and sustainable development for Muslims in India

Mustafa Raza Rabbani, M. Kabir Hassan, Shahnawaz Khan, and Mahmood Asad Moh'd Ali

Introduction

The recent innovation in the finance world in the form of financial technology (FinTech) has changed the finance world from what it used to be a decade ago. More and more organizations are adopting FinTech as a necessary ingredient for the successful implementation of their strategies and achieving their objectives. It is the need of the hour to adopt this disruptive technology to gain a competitive advantage and not to lag behind the competition. It has not only forced financial institutions to adopt FinTech but other organizations, like *Zakat* institutions, are also finding it extremely beneficial to use this innovation (Hudaefi et al., 2019). Islamic FinTech is any FinTech catering to the needs of Islamic finance users and follows the rules and regulations laid down by *Sharia*. The present study proposes a unique FinTech model using artificial intelligence and blockchain technologies for the distribution of *Zakat* to the real deserving poor and deprived sections of society.

Zakat is one of the five pillars of Islam. *Zakat* was made compulsory for the Muslim *Ummah* since 2 Hijri/624 AD. The Holy *Qura'n* (verses from Allah) and hadith (teaching of Prophet Muhammad (SAW)) have placed so much emphasis on *Zakat* because it bridges the gap between the poor and rich in Muslim society. In modern terms, it is one of the most important tools for poverty alleviation and financial inclusion (Ahmad & Mahmood, 2009; Zaid, 2004). As Islamic finance is based on the principle of social justice and the equal distribution of wealth, *Zakat* is an important tool for promoting social justice and eradicating the unequal distribution of income. On numerous occasions, the Prophet (SAW) has emphasized on the importance of zakat. It is mentioned 32 times in the Holy *Qura'n* also.

Payment of *Zakat* in Islam is made compulsory to help people in need and those who are poor. It has a positive impact on both the giver as well as on the recipients. The recipients fulfil their financial need by accepting *Zakat* whereas the giver purifies his wealth by paying *Zakat* (Al-Faizin, 2017). If we look at the divide between the rich and poor in India, it is known fact that the number of poor in the country is significant as according to the Global Hunger Index (GHI) 2020, India is ranked 94 out of 107 countries and the level of hunger in the country is flagged as serious with a GHI score of 27.2 (Global Hunger Index, 2020).

These are just some of the highlights of the grave situation of poverty in India (Sebastian, 2009). The above statistics are related to the general population of India. If we go in detail and look at the situation of Muslims in India, we find that is even worse. Being a developing country, India is fighting poverty and Muslims in India not only have to fight religious extremism and discrimination but also have to fight to eradicate poverty and provide equal rights and resources to their poor brothers and sisters. In this case, the role of the richer section of Muslim society becomes extremely important as it is their responsibility to uplift the poor by paying *Zakat*. It is not that the rich Muslims are not paying *Zakat*, of course they must be paying it, but there is a need to utilise these payments received in an effective manner by chanelling it to the most deserved beneficiaries in a transparent manner (Taylor, 2015). Innovations such as ATMs, financial technology, mobile apps, artificial intelligence, blockchain, and big data must be used for the distribution and collection of *Zakat* in India (Muneeza & Nadwi, 2019). There is a need to introduce a comprehensive *Zakat*-based poverty threshold for the deserving beneficiaries of *Zakat*, and it must be continuously monitored, controlled, and examined by *Sharia* scholars and kept up to date with modern needs. The proposed artificial intelligence and blockchain-based FinTech *Zakat* distribution system (ZDS) will bring more transparency and accountability to the *Zakat* system and will bridge the existing gap between the rich and poor in this regard.

This research study has been organized into seven sections. The next section of the study states and defines the objective of the study. Section three discusses the *Zakat* system in India and the issues in the context of India. The following section discusses the problems and issues in the *Zakat* collection and distribution system in general. Section five proposes a FinTech *Zakat* distribution system that uses artificial intelligence, blockchain, machine learning, and natural language processes. The next section discusses the results that will occur after implementing the proposed model. The last section concludes the research study and discusses the direction of future work.

Zakat *system in India*

There is no central organization for the collection and distribution of *Zakat* in India. There are mainly private organizations/individuals that collect and distribute *Zakat* based on their own convenience and objectives. Based on a survey (Shaikh, 2019) from more than 4,500 Muslims in India, it was concluded that 70% of the respondents feel that *Zakat* is an important tool to eradicate poverty among Muslims in India. The findings have also revealed that most of the people paying *Zakat* are concerned about how their *Zakat* money is being used. It has been a practice in India that mainly private individuals and/or representatives of *Madrasa*/schools come to collect *Zakat* and use it for their own purposes. There is no transparency regarding how the funds are being used and the volume of money being collected by these individuals and representatives. There is a public view in India that Muslim underdevelopment and backwardness is a big hurdle in making India a global economic leader, and the efficient use of *Zakat* among Muslims could overcome this issue. Since India is a diverse country in terms of its social, cultural, and financial structure, this diversity is very much visible among the donors of *Zakat* also.

While developing any *Zakat* distribution model or making any principles and law/regulation, this diversity should be given due importance (Obaidullah & Manap, 2017). Basically, India's demographics are divided into rural and urban sectors. While defining poverty between the rural and urban sectors, one should also take into consideration the cost of living in these areas. It has been observed that most of the resources in terms of *Zakat* distribution go to the urban poor, and this may be due to the fact that most donors live in urban areas and they have access to these poor and vice versa (Johari et al., 2014). India is barely using information technology for the collection and distribution of Zakat. Despite everyone having access to information technology, the main medium to disseminate *Zakat* information is through word of mouth (Ahmad et al., 2015).

Problems and issues with Zakat *collection and distribution*

Zakat collection and distribution has always been changing and has seen many improvements over the years in terms of technology, infrastructure, human resources, transparency, and accountability. But still, to an extent, it has not been able to achieve the objective of *Maqasid Al-Sharia* in terms of completely eradicating poverty from the *Ummah*. No matter how good a system is, it should not leave behind the ultimate objective of *Zakat*, i.e., taking it to the needy and poor people and helping them achieve a better standard of living. There are a number of issues that need immediate attention to make *Zakat* distribution more efficient and transparent.

Zakat collection and distribution has evolved over the years, and it has improved by adopting technological advancements. In the past, people would either go to the *Zakat* houses to pay the *Zakat* or a collection agent from the *Zakat* house/charitable organization used to visit the payer to receive the Zakat. Nowadays, things have changed for good, and there are a lot of channels available through which to pay *Zakat* such as internet banking, mobile banking, card payments, and salary deduction methods, etc. Islamic finance is based on the dual objective of the equal distribution of wealth and social justice. Through the proper distribution of *Zakat*, both these objectives can be easily achieved.

There is a need for Islamic countries to come to a consensus on the need for the collection and distribution of *Zakat* to the most deserving people across the globe (Johari et al., 2015). It needs to be automated to improve efficiency in collection and distribution and also to minimize corruption. For this reason, Shirazi, Amin, and Bin (2010) conducted a study on 38 Organisation of Islamic Cooperation (OIC) countries to identify the need and total contribution received in the form of *Zakat* in the respective countries. They concluded that 50% of these countries that are receiving *Zakat* contributions are in surplus and this surplus can be used to help countries with a deficit. Shirazi et al. suggest that the surplus amount of *Zakat* must be pooled from these countries and then can be used to eradicate poverty in countries with a resource deficit. *Zakat* institutions must be assigned the responsibility of helping governments collect and distribute *Zakat* and help in the bigger objective of eradicating poverty. *Zakat* institutions should not only be responsible for the collection and distribution of *Zakat*; rather, they should uphold the spirit of Islam as the religion of humanity and compassion. *Zakat* can also be used for some other beneficiaries like creating a buffer to help the needy and poor in situations like recessions by capacity building. Problems in the collection of *Zakat* can be summarized into a few points, such as there is a lack of proper laws on the collection of Zakat, mismanagemnt of funds, and lack of coherence in governments' legal philosophies. Lack of infrastructural resources for the collection of Zakat also affects its collection. One of the biggest problems in *Zakat* collection is the differences of opinion in the different schools of thought and citing this as a reason, the states are unable to enact a uniform law for *Zakat* in the country (Abdullatif, 2012).

The collection of *Zakat* has undergone many changes and seen many technological advancements, and it is already using various financial technologies. But, the issues related to *Zakat* distribution are still the same and need to be discussed by scholars and related stakeholders (Lubis, 2011). *Zakat* payers have some serious concerns that need to be addressed. This is because *Zakat* payers are concerned about the purpose for which *Zakat* money is being used. One common factor in previous studies related to the distribution of *Zakat* is about the speedy distribution of *Zakat* money as the collection process has become advanced while distribution has not been given the due attention that it immediately needs. The distribution process can be improved with the use of technology (Ahmad et al., 2006; Yahaya & Ahamd, 2018).

The issues in *Zakat* distribution can be broadly classified into three categories, the first being the inefficiency in the distribution of Zakat. There is a need to enhance the *Zakat* management system as the money does not reach the real beneficiaries, and this may be due to a lack of publicity/advertisement from authorities or a lack of knowledge among the beneficiaries about their eligibility to receive *Zakat*. Secondly, there is no proper database for the prospective receivers and payers of *Zakat*. Finally, there is a need for capacity building as paying a sum of money in the form of *Zakat* once a year/month will eliminate poverty entierly, and it is only a short-term solution. If we keep on giving a sum of money as *Zakat*, it will not benefit the beneficiaries as they will become dependent on it and will not strive to work hard and earn their own livelihood. There is a need to undertake a capacity-building initiative by giving training or short courses to the beneficiaries or providing education for the children of beneficiaries.

Zakat disbursement must be on the basis of the income of the beneficiary, for example, a person with a low income should get more benefit than a person with a relatively higher income. Most of the beneficiaries are associated with informal or unorganized sectors labour such as 'construction workers, a labourer of small-scale industry, casual employment, the power loom workers, employees in shops and commercial establishments, sweepers and scavengers, workers in tanneries, the tribal labourer and the other unprotected labour' (Chakraborty, 2020), and governments have no actual data related to their income (Johari et al., 2013). There is a need to develop an Islamic accountability framework for *Zakat* fund management. The people responsible for the distribution of *Zakat* should feel accountable to Allah (swt), the *Zakat* payer, the *fatwa* council, and to the recipients (Saad et al., 2014). *Zakat* distribution must be based on achieving the long-term objective of providing beneficiaries with a stable economic life along with the short-term objective of supplying the necessities of life (Bakar & Ghani, 2011).

Proposed system and methodology

The previous section discussed the problems and issues in *Zakat* collection and distribution. However, from the above analysis, it is evident that the *Zakat* collection framework or process is more standardized than the distribution process. Therefore, this study focuses on *Zakat* distribution more than *Zakat* collection. This research study presents a ZDS that aims to standardize the distribution and also serves as the collection and intermediary between the payers and payees. Based on a survey of the literature, the most common problem in the *Zakat* distribution system is a lack of transparency, and there is no mechanism to check whether the intended payee has received the *Zakat* or not. Similarly, the distribution process takes a lot of time. Another major issue is the efficiency of the system, such as whether *Zakat* is reaching the right people or not; the payers and beneficiaries are not aware about their right to reveive *Zakat* and do not have a clear understanding of how the *Zakat* system works as per Islamic principles. Lack of communication has also been observed between beneficiaries and payers. At present, there is no database of the people who can pay *Zakat* and who are eligible to be the beneficiaries of it as per the guideline provided in *Quran*. The anonymity of the payers and payees is very important to the majority of the people who pay *Zakat* and the payees as well. The proposed ZDS maintains a record of all the transactions and the privacy of all the users is maintained under a username; users can only see the username when paying or receiving *Zakat*. As *Zakat* payers have to pay *Zakat* every year, the ZDS system maintains a record and sends periodic reminders to the potential payers who are identified based on their transaction history. It has also been observed that at present, there is no Islamic accountability framework that has clear responsibility for *Zakat* distribution. This is related to mismanagement or discrepancies in the distribution of *Zakat* which helps beneficiaries to build their capacity and help them so that they can also become *Zakat* payers instead of remaining beneficiaries and surviving on support from other members of society. Table 7.1 summarizes the *Zakat* distribution issues and lists the corresponding solution by the proposed *Zakat* distribution system.

The issues that have been discussed above can be solved by the proposed *Zakat* distribution system. To solve the lack of transparency in *Zakat* distribution, the proposed system introduces the use of blockchain, and if the beneficiaries do not have a linked bank account, then money cannot be transferred directly to the beneficiary. In that case, the *Zakat* money is distributed and delivered by the ZDS organization, and the *Zakat* payer gets a notification that the *Zakat* has been received by the beneficiaries. ZDS uses an artificial intelligence, machine learning, and blockchain-based model for *Zakat* distribution. The use of these innovative technologies makes the transactions fast and solves the issue related to the speed of distribution and also makes it a more transparent and secure system. The problems of efficiency in distribution, including reaching the right beneficiaries are also addressed by the proposed system. The *Zakat* distribution FinTech organization communicates regularly with the beneficiaries to record their updated financial status in the system. As per the analysis and literature review, the researchers were not able to find any central database in India; therefore, people are usually reluctant to pay *Zakat* to anyone they do not know. This also develops a lack of trust in the organization or the social worker who collects and distributes *Zakat*. ZDS maintains a central database of *Zakat* payers and all the beneficiaries after verification. It has also been observed that sometimes *Zakat* is distributed to the valid beneficiary but not to the neediest one. Some of the beneficiaries might receive *Zakat* from various sources, and some of the beneficiaries receive a very small amount while they require and deserve more. To overcome this issue, ZDS maintains an updated record of earnings of all the beneficiaries. However, ZDS does this after agreement with the beneficiary; if the beneficiary does not agree, then no record is maintained. *Zakat* distribution takes place based on the earnings of the beneficiaries. The lower the total earnings of the beneficiaries, the higher the *Zakat* they receive. ZDS also provide an automated system for calculating *Zakat*. The *Zakat* payer just has to fill in the details asked, and the ZDS provides the total amount of *Zakat* due on all kinds of assets, savings, and earnings. In India, there is no existing accountability framework as per *Sharia* law, which regulates and manages the distribution and collection of *Zakat*. This is why *Zakat* payers might have a lack of trust and confidence in the people who collect and distribute *Zakat*. ZDS maintains a record of all the transactions using a blockchain system to have transparency in all transactions. All the *Zakat* payers become the peers in the distributed blockchain.

Figure 7.1 explains the working of the proposed *Zakat* distribution system. The ZDS provides an online platform for the *Zakat* payers and beneficiaries. The *Zakat* payer can register with the ZDS platform directly by accessing the online ZDS online platform. Beneficiaries can also register online; however, the

Table 7.1 Zakat distribution issues and solution

Issues in Zakat *Distribution*	*Solutions*
Transparency	Payer gets a notification on the delivery of *Zakat* to the beneficiaries.
Speedy distribution	Most of the beneficiaries do not receive *Zakat* when they need it most. The machine learning based inference engine in the proposed system helps with fast distribution
Efficiency • In reaching the right and most well deserved beneficiaries. • Beneficiary's lack of awareness about their right to receive zakat. • Poor communication management between the distribution authority and beneficiaries.	*Zakat* payers have the option to specify the potential target payees and select the payees themselves The *Zakat* distribution system also spreads knowledge and information related to *Zakat* and other key principles of Islam The *Zakat* distribution system communicates regularly with the beneficiaries to record their updated financial status with the system
Lack of central database	The proposed system maintains a central database of the *Zakat* payers and maintains the privacy and anonymity of the payers and payees
Distribution must be based on the total earnings of the beneficiaries	The *Zakat* distribution system maintains an updated record of earnings of all the beneficiaries, with their agreement, and all the payments made to an individual beneficiary, and distributes the *Zakat* based on the earnings of the beneficiaries
Zakat on savings	The *Zakat* distribution system helps to calculate the total *Zakat* that must be paid by an individual. The proposed system also generates notifications based on past payment history
No Islamic accountability framework – distribution authority should have clear responsibility for distribution related to mismanagement or discrepancies in the distribution	The *Zakat* distribution system keeps an anonymous record of all the users (payers and payees) and uses a blockchain system for transparency in all transactions
Room for capacity building of the beneficiaries	The *Zakat* distribution system also provides an option to the payees to participate in various capacity-building projects by the *Zakat* distribution FinTech organization to further help the beneficiaries

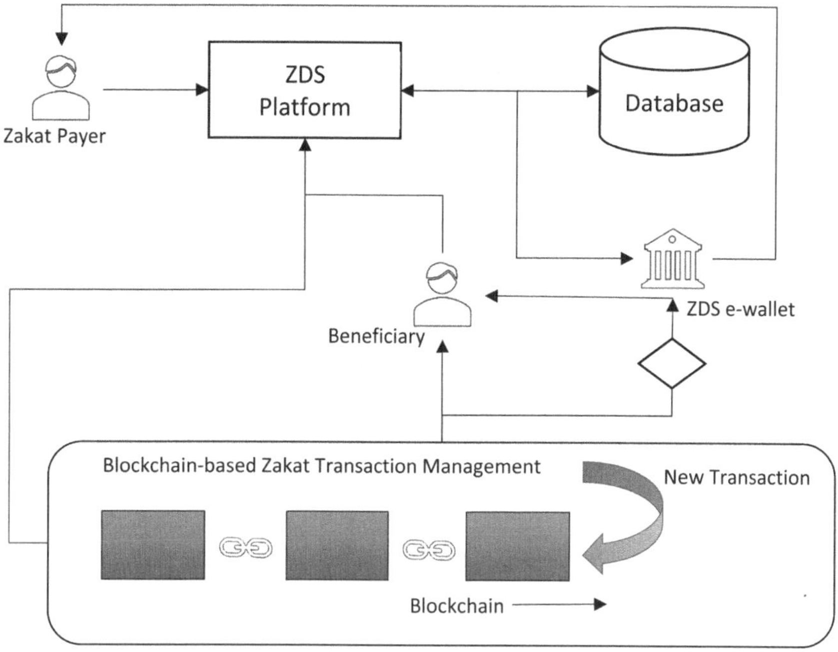

Figure 7.1 *Zakat* distribution system.

information and financial conditions of the beneficiaries must be verified before they can be eligible to receive *Zakat*. On registration, *Zakat* payers can set their preferences for choosing the potential beneficiaries for *Zakat* payments and can also calculate the exact amount of *Zakat* to be paid by an individual *Zakat* payer based on the assets they own, their savings, and earnings they receive from various categories of income resources and means.

ZDS uses artificial intelligence, machine learning techniques (Khan & Mishra, 2011), natural language processing (Khan et al., 2018), and an inference engine for recommendations. Artificial intelligence and machine learning techniques are the primary contributing technologies in predicting and forecasting, such as sentiment predictions (Shahnawaz & Astya, 2017) and machine translation (Khan & Usman, 2019; Shahnawaz & Mishra, 2015). ZDS recommends the potential beneficiaries based on the user's preferences using the inferences engine. The *Zakat* payers are presented with a list of potential beneficiaries with their financial conditions, which helps the *Zakat* payers to choose and make their decisions. The beneficiary information is displayed under a username which serves as a user account from the blockchain system. When the *Zakat* payer selects a user account for payment, the *Zakat* amount is transferred directly to the beneficiary. However, in case there is no bank account associated with the beneficiary username, the *Zakat* is transferred to the ZDS e-wallet under the *Zakat* payer's name, and when this amount is delivered to the beneficiary, a notification is sent to the *Zakat* payer. All the transactions that take place on the ZDS platform are recorded in the electronic ledger through blockchain.

Results and discussion

The current means of *Zakat* distribution and collection raise many issues such as transparency, slow and uneven distribution, lack of efficiency in reaching the right people, lack of communication management, lack of a central database and distribution authority that is accountable and responsible for mismanagement or discrepancies in the collection and proper distribution of *Zakat*. The proposed *Zakat* distribution system addresses almost all the issues in *Zakat* distribution and collection presently. ZDS uses blockchain to record transactions. Blockchain is a secure and transparent way of maintaining transaction history. The proposed *Zakat* distribution system uses machine learning and a natural language-based inference engine for beneficiary recommendations and a *Zakat* payer can send the *Zakat* amount directly to the beneficiary without any intermediary, which resolves the issues of uneven distribution and lack of efficiency in reaching right people. ZDS also serves as the central database for payers and beneficiaries and operates as the means of communication between payers and beneficiaries. Because of the immutability of the transactions in blockchain, it is almost impossible to make any changes to the transaction once it has been made, even by the ZDS itself; this feature rules out the issue of discrepancies in the collection and distribution of the *Zakat*. As has been discussed above, the proposed *Zakat* distribution system is able to address all the issues and provide a sustainable solution for *Zakat* distribution and collection.

Conclusion

The present research study discusses and identifies the major issues related to *Zakat* collection and distribution in the world and in India. The study of the existing literature reveals that at present, there are several problems and issues in *Zakat* collection and distribution in a non-Islamic country like India. This research study reviews, collects, and summarizes the issues in the context of *Zakat* distribution and collection. To address these issues, this research study has proposed a *Zakat* distribution system which uses artificial intelligence, machine learning, natural language processes, and blockchain to resolve various issues and present a solution that is reliable, transparent, and efficient and the system can be an accountable and responsible solution for the distribution of *Zakat*. The result obtained is inconsistent with the results by Syed et al. (2020). The researchers are working on improving the quality, efficiency, and effectivity of the inference engine. The authors are also looking to improve the efficiency of blockchain so that it consumes fewer resources in the consensus mechanism used in blockchain technology for new transactions.

References

Abdullatif, L. (2012). The problems faced by a state in the collection of *Zakat* (tax). In *University of Nairobi*. Retrieved from http://erepository.uonbi.ac.ke/bitstream/handle/11295/15756/The%20problems%20faced%20by%20a%20state%20in%20the%20collection%20of%20Zakat%20(Tax).pdf?sequence=3.

Ahmad, M.U., & Mahmood, A. (2009). *Zakat* fund-concept and perspective. *International Journal of Monetary Economics and Finance*, *2*(3–4), 197–205. doi: 10.1504/IJMEF.2009.029058.

Ahmad, R.A.R., Othman, A.M.A., & Salleh, M.S. (2015). Assessing the satisfaction level of *Zakat* recipients towards *Zakat* management. *Procedia Economics and Finance*, *31*, 140–151.

Ahmad, S., Wahid, H., & Mohamad, A. (2006). Penswastaan institusi *Zakat* dan kesannya terhadap pembayaran secara formal di Malaysia. *International Journal of Management Studies*, *13*(2), 175–196.

Al-Faizin, A.W., Insani, T.D., & Widiastuti, T. (2017). Zakat as an obligatory system and its implications for social psychology of society (social *Tafsīr* of *Sūrah Al-Tawbah*: 103). *International Journal of Zakat*, *2*(2), 43–53.

Bakar, M.A., & Ghani, A. (2011). Towards achieving the quality of life in the management of *Zakat* distribution to the rightful recipients (the poor and needy). *International Journal of Business and Social Research*, *2*(4), 237–245.

Chakraborty, M. (2020). Unorganised sector in India. Retrieved from https://pscnotes.in/unorganised-sector-in-india/.

Global Hunger Index. (2020). India. Retreived from https://www.globalhungerindex.org/india.html.

Hudaefi, F.A., Zaenal, M.H., Farchatunnisa, H., & Junari, U. L. (2019). How does *Zakat* institution respond to fintech ? Evidence from BAZNAS Indonesia. Pusaka Working Papers, *5*(October), 1–8.

Johari, F., Fahme Mohd Ali, A., binti Mohd Noor, Z., Ridhwan Ab Aziz, M., & Faisol Ibrahim, M. (2013). Impact of *Zakat* distribution on poor and needy recipients: An analysis in Kelantan, Malaysia. *Australian Journal of Basic and Applied Sciences Malaysia*, *7*(713), 177–182. www.ajbasweb.com.

Johari, F., Mohd Ali, A.F., Ab Aziz, M.R., & Ahmad, N. (2014). The importance of *Zakat* distribution and urban-rural poverty incidence among Muallaf (new convert). *Asian Social Science*, *10*(21), 42–53. https://doi.org/10.5539/ass.v10n21p42.

Johari, F., Ali, A.F.M., & Aziz, M.R.A. (2015). A review of literatures on current *Zakat* issues : An analysis between 2003–2013. *International Review of Research in Emerging Markets and the Global Economy (IRREM)*, *1*(2), 336–363.

Khan, S., & Mishra, R. B. (2011). Translation rules and ANN based model for English to Urdu machine translation. *Infocomp*, *10*(3), 36–47.

Khan, S. N., & Usman, I. (2019). A model for English to Urdu and Hindi machine translation system using translation rules and artificial neural network. *International Arab Journal of Information Technology*, *16*, 125 131.

Khan, S. N., Mir, U., Shreem, S. S., & Alamri, S. (2018). Translation divergence patterns handling in English to Urdu machine translation. *International Journal of Artificial Intelligence Tools*, 27, 1850017:1–1850017:19.

Lubis, M. (2011). Optimization of *Zakat* management system in Indonesia using geographic information system (GIS). In *Selected Readings in Computing and Telecommunications*. Gombak: IIUM Press.

Muneeza, A., & Nadwi, S. (2019). The potential of application of technology-based innovations for *Zakat* administration in India. *International Journal of Zakat*, *4*(2), 87–100. doi: 10.37706/ijaz.v4i2.191.

Obaidullah, M., & Manap, T. A. A. (2017). Behavioral dimensions of Islamic philanthropy: The case of Zakat. Retrieved from https://ideas.repec.org/p/ris/irtiwp/2017_002.html.

Saad, R. A. J., Aziz, N. M. A., & Sawandi, N. (2014). Islamic accountability framework in the *Zakat* funds management. *Procedia-Social and Behavioral Sciences*, *164*, 508–515.

Sebastian, A. J. (2009). Poor-rich divide in Aravind Adiga's the white tiger. *Journal of Alternative Perspectives in the Social Sciences*, *1*(2), 229–245.

Shahnawaz, & Astya, P. (2017). Sentiment analysis: Approaches and open issues. Retrieved from https://ieeexplore.ieee.org/document/8229791.

Shahnawaz, & Mishra, R. B. (2015). An English to Urdu translation model based on CBR, ANN and translation rules. *International Journal of Advanced Intelligence Paradigms*, *7*, 1–23.

Shaikh, Z. (2019, May 3). *Zakat* can transform Muslim community survey. *The Indian Express*. Retrieved from https://indianexpress.com/article/cities/mumbai/zakat-can-transform-muslim-community-survey-5707834/.

Shirazi, N. S., & Amin, M. F. Bin. (2010). Prospects of poverty elimination through potential *Zakat* collection in OIC-member countries. *Journal of Islamic Economics, Banking and Finance*, *6*(3), 55–74.

Syed, M. H., Khan, S., Rabbani, M. R., & Thalassinos, Y. (2020). An artificial intelligence and NLP based Islamic fintech model combining *Zakat* and qardh-al-hasan for countering the adverse impact of COVID 19 on SMEs and individuals. *Journal of Economics and Business Administration*, *0*(2), 351–364.

Taylor, C. B. (2015). Islamic charity in India: Ethical entrepreneurism & the ritual, revival, and reform of *Zakat* among a Muslim minority. Retrieved from https://open.bu.edu/handle/2144/13993.

Yahaya, M. H., & Ahamd, K. (2018). Financial inclusion through efficient *Zakat* distribution for poverty alleviation in Malaysia: Using fintech & mobile banking. Retrieved from http://conference.kuis.edu.my/icomm/5th/images/eproceeding2018/IC-002.pdf.

Zaid, O. (2004). Accounting systems and recording procedures in the early Islamic state. *The Accounting Historians Journal*, *31*, 149–170.

8 Online monetary donations to mitigate the impacts of the COVID-19 crisis

Evidence from Kuwait

Saeed Awadh Bin-Nashwan

8.1 Introduction

The arrival of the contagious novel coronavirus (COVID-19) has been viewed as a watershed moment in human history. In the early months of 2020, the virus rapidly spread from its origin in Wuhan, Hubei province, China, to the rest of the world, devastating lives and livelihoods (Singhal, 2020). At the time of writing in May 2020, while this highly infectious virus marches around the planet, governments, international institutions, and different organizations worldwide are compelled to tighten containment measures in many spheres of life. Yet, the propagation of the epidemic throughout the world and unprecedented restrictive efforts ordered by countries to counter the COVID-19 pandemic inevitably lead to economic and social inequalities and disruptions (Danylyshyn, 2020).

The social and economic consequences of epidemic diseases are not a new matter. For instance, in 2003, an outbreak of SARS infected some 8,000 people and killed 774 globally, disrupting the worldwide economy with an estimated loss of US$50 billion. In 2015, MERS spread in South Korea, infecting 200 people and killing 38, with an estimated cost of US$8.5 billion (Scott, 2020). However, through the spread of COVID-19 and the quarantine efforts, the pandemic has had a more catastrophic effect and more far-reaching consequences than either of its predecessors. For instance, US stocks experienced the worst loss in a week since the 2008 financial crisis; the S&P 500 index of US companies dropped 11.5 per cent in the week commencing 24 February (Scott, 2020). Oil prices also went into a steep decline, leaving the Organization of the Petroleum Exporting Countries (OPEC) confused (Ajami, 2020).

With a preventive set of measures by countries to contain the pandemic outbreak, social distancing and national or partial lockdowns are becoming a part of daily life with massive ramifications for many activities, leaving a high degree of disruption and devastating consequences for labour markets and livelihoods, as stated by the International Labour Organization (ILO) (2020a). In such an unprecedented challenge, local authorities worldwide are striving to strike a balance between preventing dangerous levels of deprivation and unemployment as well as keeping their economy going, on the one hand, and struggling to respond to dire public health imperatives and prevent the collapse of health systems and mass deaths, on the other. In a world where growing inequality has resulted in an immense number of vulnerable inhabitants, COVID-19 and measures to curtail its outbreak will inevitably affect these vulnerable groups in deadly fashion (Higgins-Desbiolles, 2020).

While labour market concerns might be raised, in the midst of this global crisis, as governments use extraordinary restrictive measures to contain the virus, many millions of workers and employees across a wide swathe of countries, business sectors, and regions are directly and seriously affected. Guy Rydesr, the Director-General of the ILO, stated that business and workers are battling catastrophe in both developing and developed economies. The lives of more than four people out of five (81 per cent) of the global workforce of 3.3 billion have been disrupted by either partial or full workplace closures (ILO, 2020a). The ILO (2020b) further highlighted that a large number of about 1.25 billion workers are employed in sectors deemed to be threatened by severe and devastating increases in layoffs or reductions in wages and working hours, leaving many in low-paid, low-skilled jobs in income loss shock.

Many regions, including the Gulf Cooperation Council (GCC) and other Middle East countries, have responded aggressively to the spread of COVD-19 through event cancellations, travel bans, and quarantines. In other regions of the world, the sharp downturn in the economy is hoped to be transitory; however, the corresponding huge decline in global oil prices points to a longer-term challenge for the economies of GCC states (Ajami, 2020). Within the framework of the GCC countries' containment effort, in Kuwait, for example, partial or full curfews and the suspension of all activities have been ordered. Many local businesses from various sectors, such as plumbing, transportation, blacksmithing, construction, trade, health, and other services, have been fully closed. As a result, since most of these sectors are heavily reliant on low-wage expatriate labour, a large number of workers are suffering from almost complete work cessation, causing a great deal of pain and these workers are finding themselves stranded, laid-off, and unemployed (ILO, 2020a; Young, 2020).

In 2018, 70 per cent of the Kuwaiti population of some 4.2 million were migrant workers (Kuwait Central Statistical Bureau, 2018). Although financial reserves allow the government to keep money flowing to its citizens, the COVID-19 crisis has had a growing and unfortunate impact not only on the national economy through significant deflation and a sharp decline in Gross Domectic Product (GDP) with fewer expatriates and lower hydrocarbon proceeds, but also on migrant workers and their families through devastating increases in layoffs and reduction in wages, leaving many in dire straits (Arezki et al., 2020; Seznec, 2020). In a rapid and strategic response to mitigate the impact of the COVID-19 pandemic, the Kuwaiti Ministry of Social Affairs and Labour (MOSAL), on Saturday, 28 March 2020, launched a fundraising campaign to deliver timely and effective support to the most affected vulnerable groups (MOSAL, 2020). More than 41 charities participated in the donation campaign via online platforms (i.e., social network sites). The fundraising reached more than US$30 million in a single day, contributing to the government's efforts to counteract the deadly

COVID-19 crisis (MOSAL, 2020). The funds raised provided logistical support for quarantine facilities and health centres and support frontline staff, as well as those affected by the epidemic. However, in this unprecedented crisis, due to uncertainty over the future and how long the danger of the COVID-19 outbreak will persist, the authorities' response to fighting the spread of the virus may be undermined as inadequate and insufficiently funded. The outpouring of charity, solidarity, and assistance sparked by this shared crisis can play an important role in fighting the epidemic until the last moment, bringing governments, charities, and donors together to coordinate and contribute to this noble battle.

The main objective of this chapter is to provide a richer understanding of people's behavioural intentions regarding online monetary donation during this time of social distancing for families and workers who are on the frontline fighting against the COVID-19 outbreak. Previous studies (e.g., Linden, 2011; Knowles et al., 2012; Smith & McSweeney, 2007; Sura et al., 2017) have examined the behavioural intention of monetary donation and applied the theory of planned behaviour (TPB) as a viable model to understand individuals' intentions and behaviour. These researchers have argued for the suitability of the TPB model in improving individuals' intentions to donate. Ajzen (1991) acknowledged that attitudes toward a certain behaviour are a very strong predictor of behavioural intentions. A robust attitude could be influenced by the relevance of the information or beliefs that could be found through some factors underlying the attitude itself (Ajzen, 1991). Given the background of an online monetary donation, previous studies, such as Treiblmaier and Pollach (2006) and Sura et al. (2017), have paid attention to extrinsic factors related to attitudes toward donating, (e.g., charitable projects and internet features) particularly on how they can predict the general donors' attitudes to donating online and strengthening intentions to make an online monetary donation. However, intrinsic factors (e.g., religious belief) that might influence attitudes have been relatively neglected in the online donation model. Therefore, the chapter sheds light on both intrinsic and extrinsic motivations that influence donors' attitudes toward donation for those affected by the COVID-19 virus, leading successively to a strong effect on behavioural intentions to donate online.

8.2 Theoretical framework

TPB is arguably the most widely recognized framework for understanding, analyzing, and explaining human intentions to engage in a given behaviour at a certain time and place (Armitage & Conner, 2001). The TPB model has its roots in the reasoned action model proposed by Fishbein and Ajzen (1975), which divided individuals' intention predictors into two fundamental determinants, i.e., attitudes and perceived norms. As an intention-based model, TPB extended the behaviour predictors by incorporating the effect of perceived behavioural control into the model (Ajzen, 1991). According to the TPB model, individuals act in accordance with their intention and perception of control over their behaviour, where attitudes (evaluation of executing a behaviour), subjective norms (perceived social pressure toward executing a given behaviour), and perceived control (perceived abilities and skills to correctly perform a behaviour) have a considerable influence on behavioural intentions (Ajzen, 1991; Armitage & Conner, 2001). An extensive stream of studies in diverse disciplines has used the TPB model as a powerful tool for predicting people's behaviours, such as education (Cheng, 2019); health (McIntyre et al., 2019); marketing (Perri et al., 2020); social entrepreneurship (Zaremohzzabieh et al., 2019); and environment (Oteng-Peprah et al., 2020).

In the charitable and donation sphere, some researchers have also employed TPB as an important framework for explaining donors' behaviours, especially in donating money. In this regard, a study by Smith and McSweeney (2007) expanded the model of TPB to investigate monetary donation; instead of examining the effect of perceived norms as a single predictor, the authors split it into prescriptive and descriptive norms. They also integrated moral norms as one of the behavioural intention determinants and found that all predictors are significantly related to monetary donation except for descriptive norms. Similarly, Linden (2011) pointed out that both prescriptive and descriptive norms that deal with the socio-psychological perspective do not have a significant relationship with monetary donation intentions. Knowles et al. (2012) also adapted the TPB-based suggestions of Smith and McSweeney (2007) to evaluate the intentions of young people in donating money to charities, revealing that behavioural intentions are considerably influenced by all constructs except subjective norms. Recently, Chen et al. (2019) extended the TPB model in explaining and predicting intentions towards donation-based crowdfunding by incorporating factors derived from social presence and norm activation aspects. The results of their research corresponded with those of Knowles et al. (2012) that perceived norms have a trivial effect. A similar circumstance is also observed in some previous research that employed perceived control to predict donation behaviours (Kashif et al., 2014; Park et al., 2009). The findings of the previous studies support TPB as the most viable behavioural model in examining the cognitive constructs of behavioural intentions. They also stated that attitudinal beliefs play a significant part in forming individuals' intentions to donate, indicating that the more favourable the attitudes regarding donation or charity behaviours, the stronger individuals' intentions are to execute the behaviour in question. Of all TPB constructs, Sura et al. (2017) have shown that an increase in a favourable attitude toward charitable donation strongly encourages behavioural intention to make monetary donations. Thus, examining and exploring the predictors that could shape attitudes toward donation behaviour are crucial to understanding donors' donation behaviours.

A growing body of research has identified that donations could be in the form of money, (Sura et al., 2017), blood (Williams & Masser, 2019), alms (Bin-Nashwan et al., 2020a), or organs (Ju et al., 2018). In order for charities to survive and thrive, financial contributions (monetary donations) are the most important form of support that aims to breathe new life into the relationship between surplus funds and funding needs (Beldad et al., 2014). Monetary donations can be made not only physically, but also in electronic form (e.g., online donation). Researchers have suggested several reasons that robustly trigger the behavioural intention of people to donate; these behaviours are shaped by their perceptions in accordance with their understanding, internal values, and attitudes (Johnson & Grimm, 2010; Sura et al., 2017; Kasri, 2013). The giving behaviour is usually motivated and triggered by two aspects, namely, extrinsic and intrinsic. The extrinsic aspect, on the one hand, is about the outside motivations that influence donors, for instance from charitable organizations (Beldad et al., 2014), charitable projects (Sura et al., 2017), location (Treiblmaier & Pollach, 2006), and technology (Li & Yu, 2020). On the other hand, the intrinsic aspect is about the extent to which people declare and hold their beliefs, values, and emotions to urge them to assist those in need, and include moral consideration (Bin-Nashwan et al., 2020b) and religiosity (Rizal & Amin, 2017).

With the advent of information technology and e-commerce as common, fast-growing practices, donations have also undergone some mainstream evolution. As traditional methods of raising monetary donations have become less productive, online donations have become an alternative, a vital and effective stream for fundraising and crowdfunding (Hoefer, 2012; Li & Yu, 2020). Internet technology has emerged as an essential platform for charity, not only to raise monetary donations but also to promote charitable activities and giving behaviour, funding grants and recruiting volunteers as well as instilling a spirit of social solidarity. To facilitate the donation process, non-profits worldwide have switched from manual donation to online donation platforms. The internet offers more efficient, rapid, and easy money transactions (Reddick & Ponomariov, 2012). Hoefer (2012) argued that non-profit organizations could sustain and gain funds using the internet based on various techniques, e.g., online donation and membership, affiliate marketing, and information products.

Intensive efforts have been devoted to examining the predictors that shape people's behavioural intentions in online donation (Treiblmaier & Pollach, 2006; Shier & Handy, 2012; Sura et al., 2017; Li & Yu, 2020). A model proposed by Treiblmaier and Pollach (2006) introduced some extrinsic determinants that shape behavioural intentions to donate online. They found that the extrinsic determinants (i.e., features of charitable projects, charities, and internet) possess a significant direct association with attitudes toward online donations, which directly influence behavioural intentions. Reddick and Ponomariov (2012) confirmed that charitable organizations play a crucial role in predicting online donations by indicating that the more closely the donor is attached to a charitable organization, the greater the likelihood of making an online donation. Apart from donors' perceptions of charitable organizations, research by Shier and Handy (2012) observed that people's perceptions of the internet exert a considerable effect on their intentions to donate online. Considering the work of Treiblmaier and Pollach (2006), Sura et al. (2017) identified extrinsic predictors (charitable project and organization, internet, and social network sites) influencing donors' general attitudes toward online giving; their attitudes directly influence their behavioural intention to donate online. They found that attitude to donating online is strongly shaped by internet technology, and behavioural intentions to donate online are positively influenced by attitudes. The general attitude toward online donations had a mediating effect on the association between features of internet technology and people's online donation intentions.

Researchers have broadly conceptualized charitable projects (Bagheri et al., 2019). Some researchers propose a project-based definition, as projects have already been created and funded through online fundraising practices (Mittelman & Rojas-Méndez, 2018; Sura et al., 2017), such as charitable crowdfunding projects via online platforms (e.g., social media). A charitable project is described as the charity event or cause that organizations support. However, in this chapter, charitable projects refer to the social causes, activities, and events promoting human welfare and supporting those in need, including poverty, disaster relief, and those affected by pandemic diseases. In the current unprecedented times, as the COVID-19 pandemic has rapidly spread, some countries have responded by launching charitable projects (e.g., fundraising campaigns) geared toward combatting the impact of COVID-19 by supporting all frontliners and the most vulnerable groups. In a community like Kuwait, regardless of the financial reserves that allow the government to keep money flowing to its citizens, two-thirds of its inhabitants are migrant workers (Kuwait Central Statistical Bureau, 2018), implying that these low-wage workers would be the most affected and suffer financially as a result of the downturn in markets, businesses, and employment. Some previous studies have demonstrated that people's feelings toward charitable projects may build their attitudes toward donation, and in turn may strengthen the donors' intention to contribute online (Sura et al., 2017; Treiblmaier & Pollach, 2006; Wong & Jusoff, 2011). How a donor feels about charitable projects could be influenced by the projects themselves (e.g., type, location, attachment, and connection to the charitable project). Thus, a donor is mostly willing to donate online to those affected by the COVID-19 outbreak if he/she feels connected and attached to the charitable projects and victims as well.

The rapid adoption of internet technologies has had a tremendous effect on daily human life. As financial institutions worldwide have rapidly shifted from branch-based banking to online-based service delivery, non-profits and charities have also integrated the internet into their charitable activities. Quinton and Fennemore (2013) argued that fundraising campaigns or donations are being democratized via social network sites by gaining the participation of mass audiences, at the same time linking them on a personal level. Internet technology has useful features for charities, including being straightforward, secure, and time-saving (Li & Yu, 2020; Shier & Handy, 2012; Sura et al., 2017; Treiblmaier & Pollach, 2006; Wong & Jusoff, 2011). The literature indicates that the features of internet technology have much to offer in forging donors' attitudes toward online donations (Shier & Handy, 2012; Sura et al., 2017; Treiblmaier & Pollach, 2006). For instance, Shier & Handy (2012) suggested that the perception of internet technology attributes as safe, trustworthy, effective, and efficient can provide a richer understanding of online donors' behaviours. Sura et al. (2017) found that general attitudes toward donation online are significantly influenced by internet technology features. However, Bandyopadhyay (2012) claimed that people are more concerned about privacy and security issues related to internet technology; this may affect donors' attitudes toward online donation either positively or negatively. It has been acknowledged that overall satisfaction with internet technologies can promote the online process of volunteering and finding satisfying opportunities. Success in grasping individuals' beliefs toward internet technology and its features could strongly encourage donors' attitudes toward online donations, especially for those affected by the COVID-19 pandemic.

Charity (charitable giving) and religion go hand in hand. Major religions, such as Islam, Christianity, Judaism, Buddhism, and Hinduism, proclaim charity as a common rule of social behaviour (Abreu et al., 2015; Ranganathan & Henley, 2008). Commands from God have always inspired religious people to give a helping hand to vulnerable groups. In Islam, for instance, an annual charitable donation called *zakah* or alms-giving is mandated upon Muslims in all areas of life (Bin-Nashwan et al., 2020c). Like Islam, the major religions of the world like Christianity and Hinduism stress the importance of generosity and giving. Religiosity is therefore considered as a crucial motive in strengthening people's inclination to donate (Reitsma et al., 2006; Abreu et al., 2015; Bin-Nashwan et al., 2020a). Abreu et al. (2015) showed unequivocally that donors with a strong religious faith are significantly related to donation behaviour. Ranganathan and Henley (2008) argued that religiosity could not be underestimated as a crucial determinant of the attitude to help others, as well as behavioural intention to donate. They showed that an individual with a high degree of religiosity possesses altruistic behaviour, and consequently would have a positive attitude toward charitable activities and positive intentions to donate. However, despite the abundance of charity behaviour research supporting the relationship between religiosity and donation practices, little is known about the influence of donors' religious beliefs on attitudes and intentions toward online donation. In a typical Muslim society like Kuwait, it can be envisaged that religious beliefs constitute a strong motive for attitudes and intentions to donate online, especially in the current situation of the widespread COVID-19 outbreak.

In this chapter, attitude signifies the degree of donors' positive feelings to contribute to a monetary donation via online platforms. The literature dedicated to behavioural intentions (Chen et al., 2019; McIntyre et al., 2019; Smith & McSweeney, 2007; Bin-Nashwan et al., 2020c), as well as the best-known model of TPB (Ajzen, 1991), has indicated that attitude is a key driver of human behavioural intentions. The burgeoning research on social capital has highlighted the important role of attitude in predicting a positive outcome of human interaction. Ranganathan and Henley (2008) indicated the role of a favourable attitude toward charitable advertisements in an effort to predict behavioural intentions of donation practices. Oosterhof et al. (2009) suggested that people's attitudes have a direct relationship with their intentions to donate to charity. Favourable attitude toward the specific charitable project, organization, and charity giving, in general, is a considerable aspect of fundraising intention (Ng et al., 2011).

Knowles et al. (2012) also revealed that donation intentions are reflected in donors' attitudes toward giving.

In connection with online donations, Treiblmaier and Pollach (2006) argued that people's beliefs and perceptions of fundraising websites strongly determine the process of donation, signifying that if positive perceptions and attitudes toward online donations are robust, individuals' intentions to donate online would be strongly shaped. Recently, an online survey of 258 participants from Asian countries was carried out by Sura et al. (2017), demonstrating that attitude contributed to informing people's behavioural intention of online donation practices. This result was reinforced by Mittelman and Rojas-Méndez (2018). In an increasingly challenging time in the midst of the COVID-19 pandemic, the lives of many people around the world are being disrupted, bringing grief and a threat to some, financial obstacles to many, and colossal changes in people's ordinary lives. As a result, people have to stand out together as pillars within their local communities, rallying support and giving a helping hand to those affected by this disease. It is expected that the more robust attitudes of donors toward online monetary donation will strengthen their behavioural intention to donate online. In addition to investigating the extrinsic and intrinsic determinants of donors' intentions to donate online, the chapter explores the mediation effect of attitudes on the relationships between intrinsic determinants (i.e., charitable projects and internet technologies features) as well as the intrinsic factor (religiosity) and behavioural intentions to donate online for those affected by the COVID-19 pandemic.

8.3 Method

Based on a cross-sectional design, this researcher launched an online survey via internet tools (e.g., e-mail and social network sites) using the snowball sampling technique. The sample employed in the study consists of online users in the collectivist culture of Kuwait. The collectivist community in Kuwait has low rates of individualism (Hofstede Insights, 2017) and long experience in donating and humanitarian contributions (Elkahlout, 2020), especially via online platforms, as officially urged by the MOSAL (2016). After discarding incomplete responses, a final set of 565 responses was retained and used for the subsequent analysis. The sample characteristics of the study showed that almost two-thirds of the participants were female (63 per cent); the largest group of respondents were aged 20–40 years (84 per cent), leaving 16 per cent of the respondents aged between 41 and above. The sample also indicated that more than half of the participants held a bachelor's degree (61 per cent), followed by holders of diploma certificate (27 per cent), master's degree (9 per cent), and doctoral degree (3 per cent). Of the 565 potential donors, 90 per cent described their economic status as average and higher than average, where the average monthly per-capita income was US$2000 (The World Bank, 2018). Generally, it seems that the sample is well diversified in terms of age, education, and income level, implying that the participants had at least the basic education level and knowledge to respond to this survey. They could also understand the importance of contributing and responding to countering the COVID-19 outbreak as well as being financially able to do so.

The design of the survey instrument was drawn from the literature. For measuring the intrinsic and extrinsic factors, a total of 25 items was ranked based on a five-point Likert scale, ranging from one = strongly disagree to five = strongly agree. Charitable projects and internet technology features were measured using five items for each variable adapted from Sura et al. (2017). Charitable projects refer to charitable endeavours to create unique and urgent responses and activities geared toward fighting the impact of COVID-19 by supporting all frontliners and those affected among the most vulnerable groups. Internet technology is about features of internet technology and information, such as security, reliability, trustworthiness, privacy, and effectiveness, that assist charitable performance. Religiosity was measured using six items adapted from Bin-Nashwan et al. (2020a), indicating the extent to which donors adhere to their religious principles, including assisting the underprivileged. Attitude is defined as the donors' feelings or assessments, whether favourable or unfavourable toward online donations for those affected by the COVID-19 epidemic. Intention to donate online refers to donors' willingness to donate online and raise funds to support all frontliners and those affected by COVID-19. Nine items were adapted from Ajzen (2002) to measure attitude (four items) and intention (five items). Regarding the data analysis technique, SmartPLS 3.2.9, popular professional software for variance-based structural modelling equation partial least squares (PLS-SEM), was used to analyze the online donation model and test the hypothesized relationships.

8.4 Discussion and findings

The reflective model assessment required inspection of the validity and reliability of the variables of interest. It is necessary to assess the criteria of convergent and discriminant validity as well as reliability for internal consistency. The results depicted in Table 8.1 show that of the 25 items used in the study, 20 loadings were greater than 0.70 and two were between 0.40 and 0.70, while three loadings were below 0.40 and thus discarded from the database. The values of Cronbach's α of all latent variables exceeded the required threshold of 0.70 (Hair et al., 2017). For the composite reliability (CR), values of all latent constructs were well above 0.70, establishing reliable latent constructs. The values of the average variance extracted (AVE) exceeded the 0.50 acceptable threshold, supporting the convergent validity of the model (Hair et al., 2017).

Another assessment for a measurement model is discriminant validity. It can be evaluated via analysis of Fornell and Larcker (1981), cross-loadings, and the heterotrait-monotrait ratio (HTMT) of correlation (Hair et al., 2017). The results of the Fornell–Larcker test, as presented in Table 8.2 for all latent variables, indicates that the square root of AVE was greater than the other square correlations in the model; therefore, no lack of discriminant validity was detected. The cross-loadings were also used to assess the discriminant validity of the model. For all

Table 8.1 Measurement model assessment

Constructs	*Items*	*Loadings*	*Cronbach's α*	*CR*	*AVE*
Charitable projects (CPR)			0.743	0.832	0.556
	CPR1	0.820			
	CPR2	0.700			
	CPR3	0.816			
	CPR4	0.630			
Internet technology features (ITF)			0.933	0.943	0.767
	ITF1	0.814			
	ITF2	0.908			
	ITF3	0.919			
	ITF4	0.879			
	ITF5	0.854			
Religiosity (REL)			0.731	0.827	0.549
	REL1	0.584			
	REL4	0.783			
	REL5	0.852			
	REL6	0.719			
Attitude (ATT)			0.864	0.908	0.713
	ATT1	0.731			
	ATT2	0.824			
	ATT3	0.916			
	ATT4	0.894			
Intention to donate online (INT)			0.922	0.942	0.764
	INT1	0.889			
	INT2	0.920			
	INT3	0.885			
	INT4	0.892			
	INT5	0.776			

Source: Author's Own

constructs, the loadings of the items on their own constructs were loaded higher than others on reflective items (Hair et al., 2017). As seen in Table 8.1, no lack of discriminant validity was confirmed. A relatively new assessment for discriminant validity is HTMT. It is an estimate of the upper boundary of the correlation between constructs. Using a value of 0.85 as the recommended threshold (Henseler et al., 2015), the chapter concluded further evidence for establishing the discriminant of all latent constructs, which have met the conventional standard. In a nutshell, a series of statistical assessments inspected the measurement model, confirming reliable and valid measurement scales used for constructs of interest, enabling testing of the structural research model.

The next step in PLS-SEM is to address and assess the structural model results. As presented in Table 8.3, the study estimated the variables' explained variance (R^2) to evaluate the predictive capability of the model. In the online donation

Table 8.2 Discriminant validity

Items	*CPR*	*ITF*	*REL*	*ATT*	*INT*
CPR1	0.820	0.202	0.131	0.336	0.247
CPR2	0.700	0.156	0.107	0.271	0.184
CPR3	0.816	0.264	0.202	0.350	0.245
CPR4	0.630	0.144	0.176	0.289	0.312
ITF1	0.169	0.814	0.123	0.290	0.140
ITF2	0.198	0.908	0.152	0.394	0.219
ITF3	0.244	0.919	0.183	0.392	0.225
ITF4	0.248	0.879	0.177	0.355	0.220
ITF5	0.272	0.854	0.167	0.425	0.286
REL1	0.134	0.095	0.584	0.116	0.080
REL4	0.174	0.128	0.783	0.219	0.180
REL5	0.173	0.202	0.852	0.239	0.171
REL6	0.129	0.091	0.719	0.128	0.094
ATT1	0.296	0.291	0.176	0.731	0.310
ATT2	0.344	0.310	0.215	0.824	0.428
ATT3	0.381	0.426	0.224	0.916	0.435
ATT4	0.390	0.408	0.233	0.894	0.450
INT1	0.315	0.251	0.191	0.468	0.889
INT2	0.274	0.204	0.183	0.405	0.920
INT3	0.297	0.199	0.175	0.385	0.885
INT4	0.291	0.235	0.178	0.442	0.892
INT5	0.264	0.216	0.103	0.410	0.776
Fornell–Larcker criterion					
CPR	0.746				
ITF	0.262	0.876			
REL	0.209	0.185	0.741		
ATT	0.421	0.429	0.253	0.845	
INT	0.331	0.255	0.191	0.485	0.874
HTMT					
CPR					
ITF	0.310				
REL	0.280	0.209			
ATT	0.526	0.470	0.296		
INT	0.405	0.268	0.214	0.538	

Source: Author's Own

Notes: ATT, attitude; CPR, charitable projects; INT, intention; ITF, internet technology features; REL, religiosity.

model, the endogenous construct of attitude possesses a high value of R^2 (0.302), indicating that the exogenous constructs (i.e., charitable projects, internet technology feature, and religiosity) can collectively explain approximately 30 per cent of the variance level of donors' attitudes toward online donation for those affected by the COVID-19 crisis. Furthermore, the R^2 value of the second endogenous

Table 8.3 Structural model assessment

Relationships	β	*t-value*	*P-value*	*Decision*	R^2	Q^2
Direct effects					0.302	0.211
CPR → ATT	0.309	7.334	0.000	Supported		
ITF → ATT	0.325	7.488	0.000	Supported		
REL → ATT	0.128	3.085	0.002	Supported		
REL → INT	0.073	1.701	0.089	Not supported		
ATT → INT	0.467	11.947	0.000	Supported		
Indirect effects					0.240	0.178
CPR → ATT → INT	0.144	5.938	0.000	Supported		
ITF → ATT → INT	0.152	6.082	0.000	Supported		
REL → ATT → INT	0.060	2.916	0.004	Supported		

Source: Author's Own
Notes: ATT, attitude; CPR, charitable projects; INT, intention; ITF, internet technology features; REL, religiosity

construct (intention) was 0.240, deducing that attitude can play a crucial role in predicting donors' intentions. For model fit assessment in PL-SEM, the researcher performed the blindfolding analysis to examine the predictive relevance (Q^2) of the research model. The results of the Q^2 test of the endogenous variables (attitude and intention) were above zero (0.211 and 0.178), exhibiting the predictive relevance of the online donation model (Hair et al., 2017).

In this chapter, the structural model assessment was tested using a procedure called 'bootstrapping with an iteration of 5,000 samples' to evaluate path relationships (path coefficients) (Hair et al., 2017). For direct relationships, the findings reveal that with one exception (for the paths: REL → INT), all direct pathways run from exogenous variables to endogenous and can be statistically accepted once the bootstrap critical t-values are ±1.96 (two-tailed). Specifically, charitable projects significantly influenced donors' attitudes to donate online ($\beta = 0.309$, $P = 0.000$); internet technology features ($\beta = 0.325$, $P = 0.000$) and religiosity ($\beta = 0.128$, $P = 0.002$) exerted significant relationships with attitudes to donate. Attitude toward donation reported a significant positive relationship with donors' intentions to donate online for those affected by COVID-19 ($\beta = 0.467$, $P = 0.000$). Contrary to expectations, the relationship between religiosity and behavioural intentions failed to reveal statistical evidence ($\beta = 0.073$, $P = 0.089$). For indirect effects, following the suggestions of Rungtusanatham et al. (2014) on the mediation (indirect) effects, the present work evaluated the mediating effects of attitudes toward donations on the association between intrinsic and extrinsic determinants and donors' intentions to donate online, as presented in Table 8.3. The results reveal that the indirect pathways from charitable projects to intention ($\beta = 0.144$, $P = 0.000$), from internet technology features to intention ($\beta = 0.152$, $P = 0.000$), and from religiosity to intention to donate online ($\beta = 0.060$, $P = 0.004$) through attitudes toward online donation were statistically significant.

To put it briefly, in reconciling the conflicting views on whether the influence of intrinsic or extrinsic factors on people's attitudes and behavioural intentions to donate online, and in response to calls by prior research (Chen et al., 2019; Sura et al., 2017; Treiblmaier & Pollach, 2006), this chapter attempts to adapt and empirically test a more elaborate model of online donation, encompassing both extrinsic, such as charitable projects and internet technologies, and intrinsic (i.e., religiosity) determinants that underline donors' attitudes toward monetary donation, consequently shaping their intentions to donate online for those affected by the COVID-19 epidemic. The results endorse the views of Chen et al. (2019) and Sura et al. (2017) that among the three constructs of the TPB model, the effect of attitude toward monetary donation on predicting online donation behaviours is the strongest and cannot be underestimated. The stability of the results in this chapter suggests that the model used could indeed capture the way in which donors' orientate toward online monetary donation; this translates ultimately into social solidarity and cohesion in encountering the various impacts of pandemics such as COVID-19.

This chapter has revealed some interesting results. Firstly, charitable projects (i.e., project type, location, welfare project) provided for those affected by the virus exerted a significant positive influence on donors' attitudes toward donation and helping others. This result is in line with research by Ahn et al. (2018), confirming this conclusion. Internet technology features (e.g., security, reliability, trustworthiness, and privacy) were significantly and positively related to attitudes toward online donations. The results correspond to those of other studies (Shier & Handy, 2012; Treiblmaier & Pollach, 2006). These external factors were also accompanied by the internal value influence of religiosity in influencing people's attitude. This is consistent with Ranganathan and Henley (2008). However, religiosity failed to report an influence on intentions to donate online, signifying the robustness of religious beliefs in predicting attitudes rather than behavioural intentions. As expected, attitude toward online donation exerted the strongest effect in the model in contributing to individuals' intentions to donate online. It is consistent with results from the literature (Chen et al., 2019; Sura et al., 2017). From a theoretical viewpoint, this evidence also conforms Ajzen's (1991) TPB model, claiming that attitudinal belief is deemed a robust positive predictor of behavioural intentions. Furthermore, the results show the mediation effect of attitudes toward online donations on the pathways from charitable projects, internet features, and religiosity to intentions to donate online for all those affected by COVID-19. Although religiosity did not directly influence behavioural intentions, it is coupled with attitudes of donors in significantly triggering their intentions of online donations.

8.5 Recommendation and conclusion

In addition to protective measures against spreading the virus through social distancing, quarantine, or isolation, individuals, communities, and charities can all do their part to help less privileged people and regions that have been affected. With the staggering number of quarantined areas and individuals, people find themselves in colossal social and financial disruption. Some countries, including Kuwait, have responded by launching fundraising campaigns to deliver timely and effective support to the frontliners and the vulnerable throughout the country. Therefore, this chapter empirically examined how the attitudes and intentions of donors toward online monetary donation for those impacted by the disease are influenced by intrinsic and extrinsic motivations. The results indicate that external factors (e.g., charitable projects and internet technologies) and religiosity as an internal factor have a direct and significant influence on attitude, as well as an indirect influence on behavioural intentions to donate online through the mediating role of attitude.

Based on the analysis outcomes, the study has important implications for theory and policy. This research significantly enriches the literature on donation and giving behaviours by extending the theoretical model for examining people's intentions toward online donation, as called for by Sura et al. (2017) in a different context and with unprecedented status. Prior research (e.g., Sura et al., 2017; Treiblmaier & Pollach, 2006) has paid little attention to donors' perceptions of online donation, whether from intrinsic or extrinsic motivation. Furthermore, there is a lack of studies emphasizing the effect of the identified intrinsic (religiosity) and extrinsic (charitable projects and internet technologies) predictors on online donations, especially amid such an unprecedented epidemic crisis. Unlike the empirical evidence of Sura et al. (2017), who failed to report a relationship between extrinsic factors and donation attitudes, the present study conclusively finds significant relationships not only between extrinsic factors and attitudes toward monetary donation but also by intrinsic motivations. The study provides further and novel insights into the mediating role of attitude toward an online monetary donation to support those affected by COVID-19 on pathways from external and internal motivations to behavioural intentions to donate online.

With the COVID-19 pandemic, governments, charities, and donors can come together and work in a challenging and changing environment. By fundraising for COVID-19 relief efforts and donating to those affected by its spread and impact, donors and contributors can all play their part and render much-needed support and aid. As part of the efforts to provide an in-depth understanding of people's attitudes and behavioural intentions towards such fundraising appeals, this chapter offers insights for governments, non-profit organizations, and individuals in formulating appropriate strategies and policies to improve the online fundraising process and to mitigate the social and economic impacts of COVID-19. It is important to understand the features of charitable projects (type, location, and human welfare) geared toward people and regions that have been affected. Governments and non-profit organizations should also be concerned about internet privacy, security, and trustworthiness, which have a considerable effect in either encouraging or discouraging online donations. The intrinsic motivation of religiosity is a crucial antecedent for predicting attitudes toward giving to charity. Religiosity directly influences people in having favourable attitudes toward online donation and indirectly influences their intentions to donate online. Authorities and non-profit organizations might engage with Islamic religious scholars, leaders, and other religious influencers in educating their followers on the significance of contributing to the fight against the virus. To this end, great attention must be paid by practitioners to trigger and strengthen people's attitudes toward online donations, as they play a strong role in mediating between both the extrinsic and intrinsic factors' relationships with intentions to donate online. This role could be fruitful by posting, sharing, and frequently updating favourable data and success stories with regards to the significance of donations using online platforms (e.g., social network sites) for those affected by the virus.

References

Abreu, M. E. De, Laureano, R. M. S., Silva, R. V. da, & Dionísio, P. (2015). Volunteerism, compassion and religiosity as drivers of donations practices. *International Journal of Nonprofit and Voluntary Sector Marketing*, *20*(3), 256–276.

Ahn, J., Sura, S., & An, J.-C. (2018). Intention to donate via social network sites (SNSs): A comparison study between Malaysian and South Korean users. *Information Technology & People*, *31*(4), 910–926.

Ajami, R. (2020). Globalization, the challenge of COVID-19 and Oil price uncertainty. *Journal of Asia-Pacific Business*, *21*(02), 1–3.

Ajzen, I. (1991). The theory of planned behavior. *Organizational Behavior and Human Decision Processes*, *50*(2), 179–211.

Ajzen, I. (2002). *Constructing a TPB Questionnaire: Conceptual and Methodological Considerations.* Retrieved from https://people.umass.edu/aizen/pdf/tpb.measurement.pdf.

Arezki, R., Fan, R. Y., & Nguyen, H. A. (2020). *Coping with COVID-19 and Oil Price Collapse in the Gulf Cooperation Council.* The World Bank. Retrieved from https://blogs.worldbank.org/ arab voices/coping-covid-19-and-oil-price-collapse-gulf-cooperation-council.

Armitage, C. J., & Conner, M. (2001). Efficacy of the theory of planned behavior: A meta-analytic review. *The British Journal of Social Psychology*, *40*(4), 471–499.

Bagheri, A., Chitsazan, H., & Ebrahimi, A. (2019). Crowdfunding motivations: A focus on donors' perspectives. *Technological Forecasting & Social Change*, *146*, 218–232.

Bandyopadhyay, S. (2012). Consumers' online privacy concerns: Causes and effects. *Innovative Marketing*, *8*(3), 32–39.

Beldad, A., Snip, B., & Hoof, J. van. (2014). Generosity the second time around: Determinants of individuals' repeat donation intention. *Nonprofit and Voluntary Sector Quarterly*, *43*(1), 144–163.

Bin-Nashwan, S. A., Abdul-Jabbar, H., Aziz, S. A., & Haladu, A. (2020a). Zakah compliance behavior among entrepreneurs: Economic factors approach. *International Journal of Ethics and Systems*, *36*(2), 285–302.

Bin-Nashwan, S. A., Abdul-Jabbar, H., Aziz, S. A., & Viswanathan, K. K. (2020b). A socio-economic model of Zakah compliance. *International Journal of Sociology and Social Policy*, *40*(3/4), 304–320.

Bin-Nashwan, S. A., Abdul-Jabbar, H., Dziegielewski, S. F., & Aziz, S. A. (2020c). Moderating effect of perceived behavioral control on Islamic tax (zakah) compliance behavior among businessmen in Yemen. *Journal of Social Service Research*, 1–11. doi: 10.1080/01488376.2020.1767260.

Chen, Y., Dai, R., Yao, J., & Li, Y. (2019). Donate time or money? The determinants of donation intention in online crowdfunding. *Sustainability, 11*(16), 4269.

Cheng, E. W. L. (2019). Choosing between the theory of planned behavior (TPB) and the technology acceptance model (TAM). *Educational Technology Research and Development, 67*(1), 21–37.

Danylyshyn, B. (2020). The peculiarities of economic crisis due to COVID-19 pandemic in a developing country: Case of Ukraine. *Problems and Perspectives in Management, 18*(2), 13–22.

Elkahlout, G. (2020). Hearts and minds: Examining the Kuwaiti humanitarian model as an emerging Arab donor. *Asian Journal of Middle Eastern and Islamic Studies, 14*(1), 141–157.

Fishbein, M., & Ajzen, I. (1975). *Belief, Attitude, Intention and Behavior: An Introduction to Theory and Research.* Reading, MA: Addison-Wesley.

Fornell, C., & Larcker, D. (1981). Evaluating structural equation models with unobservable variables and measurement error. *Journal of Marketing Research, 18*(1), 39–50.

Hair, J. F., Hult, G. T., Ringle, C. M., & Sarstedt, M. (2017). *A Primer on Partial Least Squares Structural Equation Modeling (PLS-SEM)* (2nd ed.). London: Sage.

Henseler, J., Ringle, C. M., & Sarstedt, M. (2015). A new criterion for assessing discriminant validity in variance-based structural equation modeling. *Journal of the Academy of Marketing Science, 43*(1), 115–135.

Higgins-Desbiolles, F. (2020). Socialising tourism for social and ecological justice after COVID-19. *Tourism Geographies, 22*(3), 610–623.

Hoefer, R. (2012). From web site visitor to online contributor: Three internet fundraising techniques for nonprofits. *Social Work, 57*(4), 361–365.

Hofstede Insights. (2017). *Country Comparison: Kuwait.* Retrieved from https://www.hofstede-insights.com/country-comparison/kuwait/.

ILO (International Labour Organization). (2020a). *COVID-19 Impact on Labour Market Statistics.* ILOSTAT. Retrieved from https://ilostat.ilo.org/topics/covid-19/covid-19-impact-on-labour-market-statistics/.

ILO. (2020b). *ILO: COVID-19 Causes Devastating Losses in Working Hours and Employment.* ILO Newsroom. Retrieved from https://www.ilo.org/global/about-the-ilo/newsroom/news/WCMS_740893/lang--en/index.htm.

Johnson, J. W., & Grimm, P. E. (2010). Communal and exchange relationship perceptions as separate constructs and their role in motivations to donate. *Journal of Consumer Psychology, 20*, 282–294.

Ju, M. K., Sim, M. K., & Son, S. Y. (2018). A study on nursing students' knowledge, attitude, and educational needs for brain-death organ transplantation and donation and intent to donate organs. *Transplantation Proceedings, 50*, 1187–1191.

Kashif, M., Sarifuddin, S., & Hassan, A. (2014). Charity donation: Intentions and behaviour. *Marketing Intelligence & Planning, 33*(1), 90–102.

Kasri, R. A. (2013). Giving behaviors in Indonesia: Motives and marketing implications for Islamic charities. *Journal of Islamic Marketing, 4*(3), 306–324.

Knowles, S. R., Hyde, M. K., & White, K. M. (2012). Predictors of young people's charitable intentions to donate money: An extended theory of planned behavior perspective. *Journal of Applied Social Psychology, 42*(9), 2096–2110.

Kuwait Central Statistical Bureau. (2018). *Annual Statistical Abstract in Kuwait.* Retrieved from https://www.csb.gov.kw/Pages/Statistics_en?ID=18&ParentCatID=2.

Li, Y., & Yu, L. (2020). Factors influencing social media users' continued intent to donate. *Sustainability*, *12*, 879.

Linden, S. Van Der. (2011). Charitable intent: A moral or social construct? A revised theory of planned behavior model. *Current Psychology*, *30*(4), 355–374.

McIntyre, E., Saliba, A. J., Wiener, K. K. K., & Bishop, F. L. (2019). Predicting the intention to use herbal medicines for anxiety symptoms: A model of health behaviour. *Journal of Mental Health*, *28*(6), 589–596.

Ministry of Social Affairs and Labor (MOSAL) (2016). Ministerial Decree No. 128: Fundraising Rules, MOSAL Official Gate, Kuwait.

Ministry of Social Affairs and Labor (MOSAL) (2020). Kuwaiti Donation Campaign, MOSAL Official Gate, Kuwait. Retrieved from http://pay.manpower.gov.kw/MOSAL/static/index_1.jsf.

Mittelman, R., & Rojas-Méndez, J. (2018). Why Canadians give to charity: An extended theory of planned behaviour model. *International Review on Public and Nonprofit Marketing*, *15*(2), 189–204.

Ng, J. C. Y., Lai, K. K., & Chen, Y. (2011). Individual's charity intention in Hong Kong: An empirical study on charitable behavior. In 4th International Joint Conference on Computational Sciences and Optimization, 436–440.

Oosterhof, L., Heuvelman, A., & Peters, O. (2009). Donation to disaster relief campaigns: Underlying social cognitive factors exposed. *Evaluation and Program Planning*, *32*, 148–157.

Oteng-Peprah, M., Vries, N. De, & Acheampong, M. A. (2020). Households' willingness to adopt greywater treatment technologies in a developing country: Exploring a modified theory of planned behaviour (TPB) model including personal norm. *Journal of Environmental Management*, *254*, 109807.

Park, H. S., Smith, S. W., & Yun, D. (2009). Ethnic differences in intention to enroll in a state organ donor registry and intention to talk with family about organ donation. *Health Communication*, *24*(7), 37–41.

Perri, C., Giglio, C., & Corvello, V. (2020). Smart users for smart technologies: Investigating the intention to adopt smart energy consumption behaviors. *Technological Forecasting & Social Change*, *155*, 119991. doi: 10.1016/j.techfore.2020.119991.

Quinton, S., & Fennemore, P. (2013). Missing a strategic marketing trick? The use of online social networks by UK charities. *International Journal of Nonprofit and Voluntary Sector Marketing*, *18*(1), 36–51.

Ranganathan, S., & Henley, W. (2008). Determinants of charitable donation intentions: A structural equation model. *International Journal of Nonprofit and Voluntary Sector Marketing*, *13*(March 2019), 1–11. doi: 10.1002/nvsm.

Reddick, C. G., & Ponomariov, B. (2012). The effect of individuals' organization affiliation on their internet donations. *Nonprofit and Voluntary Sector Quarterly*, *42*(6), 1197–1223.

Reitsma, J., Scheepers, P., & Grotenhuis, M. T. (2006). Dimensions of individual religiosity and charity: Cross-national effect differences in European countries? *Review of Religious Research*, *47*(4), 347–362.

Rizal, H., & Amin, H. (2017). Perceived ihsan, Islamic egalitarianism and Islamic religiosity towards charitable giving of cash waqf. *Journal of Islamic Marketing*, *8*(4), 669–685.

Rungtusanatham, M., Miller, J. W., & Boyer, K. K. (2014). Theorizing, testing, and concluding for mediation in SCM research: Tutorial and procedural recommendations. *Journal of Operations Management*, *32*(3), 99–113.

Scott, J. (2020). *The Economic, Geopolitical and Health Consequences of COVID-19.* Retrieved from https://www.weforum.org/agenda/2020/03/the-economic-geopolitical-and-health-consequences-of-covid-19/.

Seznec, J.-F. (2020). The economic outlook for MENA amid COVID-19 and the oil price drop. *Middle East Institute.* Retrieved from https://www.mei.edu/publications/economic-outlook-mena-amid-covid-19-and-oil-price-drop.

Shier, M. L., & Handy, F. (2012). Understanding online donor behavior: The role of donor characteristics, perceptions of the internet, website and program, and influence from social networks. *International Journal of Nonprofit and Voluntary Sector Marketing, 17*(3), 219–230.

Singhal, T. (2020). A review of coronavirus disease-2019 (COVID-19). *The Indian Journal of Pediatrics, 87*, 281–286.

Smith, J. R., & McSweeney, A. (2007). Charitable giving: The effectiveness of a revised theory of planned behaviour model in predicting donating intentions and behaviour. *Journal of Community & Applied Social Psychology, 17*, 363–386.

Sura, S., Ahn, J., & Lee, O. (2017). Factors influencing intention to donate via social network site (SNS): From Asian's perspective. *Telematics and Informatics, 34*(1), 164–176.

The World Bank. (2018). *World Bank Open Data: Kuwait.* Retrieved from https://data.worldbank.org/country/KW.

Treiblmaier, H., & Pollach, I. (2006). A framework for measuring people's intention to donate online. In The 10th Pacific Asia Conference on Information Systems, 808–817.

Williams, L. A., & Masser, B. (2019). Integrating self-determination theory and the theory of planned behaviour to predict intention to donate blood. *Transfusion Medicine, 29*, 59–64.

Wong, D. M. L., & Jusoff, K. (2011). Social networking in charity advocacy. *World Applied Sciences Journal, 12*, 65–72.

Young, K. (2020, April 3). How COVID-19 will change GCC labor markets. *Al-Monitor.* Retrieved from https://www.al-monitor.com/pulse/originals/2020/04/gulf-covid19-coronavirus-change-gcc-labor-markets-crisis.html.

Zaremohzzabieh, Z., Ahrari, S., Eric, S., Bin, A., Samah, A., Kwan, L., & Ariffin, Z. (2019). Predicting social entrepreneurial intention : A meta-analytic path analysis based on the theory of planned behavior. *Journal of Business Research, 96*, 264–276.

9 Adapting the Al Rajhi *waqf* model to mitigate the impact of COVID-19 on the *ummah*

A lesson to Muslim philanthropists

Umar Habibu Umar

9.1 Introduction

In January 2020, the World Health Organization (WHO) described COVID-19 as a disease that required emergency measures (Blake et al., 2020; Jackson et al., 2020). The case of COVID-19 has now spread to over 213 countries and territories (Bhandari, 2020). Nearly everybody in the world has been affected by COVID-19 (Khan & Rabbani, 2020). Hence, in March 2020, the WHO declared COVID-19 as a pandemic (Blake et al., 2020) in one form or the other. The pandemic brought about consequences that extremely deteriorated the socio-economic development of people and global economic growth and development. It exposed many countries, particularly developing ones, to economic depression. Currently, many individuals and organizations are attempting to assess or even measure the extent of the damage caused to various countries and the global economy at large. For example, UNESCAP (2020) identified the COVID-19 pandemic as the greatest test ever faced by the world since the Second World War after the establishment of the United Nations. Similarly, the economic impact of the COVID-19 pandemic crisis has exceeded earlier crises, such as the Great Depression and the global financial crisis (Hajjar, 2020; Jackson et al., 2020; Khan & Rabbani, 2020).

Moreover, according to Baker et al. (2020), the pandemic crisis produced a gargantuan uncertainty shock greater than that of the financial crisis of 2008/2009 but with an equal magnitude to the increase in uncertainty during the Great Depression of 1929–1933. It also led to a global public health and economic crisis that in turn led to the loss of USD$90 trillion in the global economy which is beyond any calamity encountered in about a century (Jackson et al., 2020). It has also worsened the enormous external debts of low- and middle-income countries (Sanchez-Duque et al., 2020). Besides, enormous capital outflows as a result of the pandemic made devaluations, debt servicing, and importing food and medical supplies more burdensome and collectively placed more pressure on the fiscal balance of developing economies, making it difficult for them to respond to the crisis (ILO, 2020c) satisfactorily.

In the beginning, the measures taken to stop the spread of the virus included travel restrictions, quarantines, and the lockdown of cities, which led to a significant decrease in aggregated demand, particularly in the service sectors, such as tourism, retail, hospitality, and civil aviation (UNESCAP, 2020). These measures also affected employment across the globe. The pandemic became a key shock to the economic and labour market, as it significantly led to unemployment and underemployment of informal workers (FAO, 2020). According to the ILO (2020b), as of 1 April 2020, it was estimated that working hours would reduce by 6.7% in the second quarter of 2020, representing 195 million full-time workers.

Given the unprecedented social and economic crises caused by the pandemic, various countries are struggling to apply possible and necessary measures to revitalize their economies for socio-economic development. In other words, poverty alleviation became a core issue if not the most important in the agenda of all the countries worldwide as a result of the pandemic. Alleviation of the extreme level of poverty and hunger has become a key challenge for the entire world in the 21st century (Olanipekun et al., 2015) even before the emergence of the COVID-19 pandemic. Similarly, poverty became a widely debated issue, being an obvious problem in both developed and developing countries (Shahimi et al., 2013). Dogarawa (2009) sees extreme poverty as the circumstances in which the struggle to find food to eat is a matter of life or death. The need to provide a long-lasting solution to the current socio-economic problems is very profound. Hence, this study seeks to show the need to adapt or replicate the Al Rajhi *waqf* model by Muslim philanthropists across the globe to provide a sustainable solution to the socio-economic problems caused by the COVID-19 pandemic.

Generally, historical evidence proved that *waqf* institutions contributed significantly to the provision of education, health, and the construction of projects that contributed adequately to the welfare of the *ummah*. Thus, *waqf* institutions are described as a powerful tool to achieve socio-economic development for eradicating poverty in Islamic society (Sadeq, 2002; Kahf, 2003; Ahmed, 2007; Hassan & Ashraf, 2010; Muhammad, 2010; Cizakca, 2014; Abu Talib et al., 2018; Umar, 2019; Umar et al., 2020). Moreover, although many Muslim entrepreneurs across the globe have established foundations for philanthropic activities, the Al Rajhi *waqf* model is found to be unique in the contemporary Muslim world. Despite the remarkable and unforgettable contributions of this foundation to Islam and socio-economic development in the Kingdom of Saudi Arabia, scholars pay little or no attention to it to the extent that its activities could be explored and spread across the globe for replication in various Islamic countries. In fact, to the best of the researcher's knowledge, no academic paper was found to have adequately presented the benefits and contributions of the Al Rajhi *waqf* model to religious and socio-economic development. This study is not only expected to contribute to the dissemination of the significance of the model but also motivate other Muslim entrepreneurs to adapt or replicate it across the globe. Certainly, the adaption or replication of the model would contribute significantly to the reduction of the extreme poverty caused by the COVID-19 pandemic to the barest minimum.

The remaining chapter is organized into five sections. Section 9.2 presents the socio-economic impact of the COVID-19 pandemic on society. Section 9.3 describes the historical and contemporary contributions of *waqf* to the socio-economic development of society. Section 9.4 describes of the Al Rajhi *waqf* model. Section 9.5 explains the essential features of the model in order to induce Muslim philanthropists to adapt or replicate it in various Islamic countries worldwide and, finally, section 9.6 provides a conclusion and recommendations.

9.2 The socio-economic impact of COVID-19 on society

Assessing the impact of the COVID-19 pandemic is essential to policymakers because the crisis has grown at extreme speed (Baker et al., 2020). The pandemic came with consequences that took people across the globe deeper into poverty. It pushed individuals and households to extreme income inequality and poverty that have already been at the borderline of poverty (UNESCAP, 2020). The economic and human costs brought by the pandemic include loss of lives, loss of jobs, derailed careers, and the permanent closure of businesses (Jackson et al., 2020). Therefore, the crisis metamorphosed into an economic and labour market shock as both the production of goods and services and demand (consumption and investment) were negatively affected (ILO, 2020d). Factors responsible for unemployment across various economic sectors during the pandemic include social distancing, self-isolation, and travel restrictions (Nicola et al., 2020). These measures were taken to stop the spread of the virus and save the lives of people although social distancing and lockdown have caused a significant fall in economic activities across the globe and have led to the current global recession (UN News, 2020). In particular, the measures have directly affected the livelihoods of about half the population in Latin America, who are largely engaged in the informal sector in services and small businesses and do not have assets or savings to support themselves during the crisis (Blofield et al., 2020). In addition, the lives people in rural areas were exposed to such problems as most of them are self-employed and wage workers; the disruption of agri-food supply chains and markets due to lockdowns and restrictions of movement had a severe effect on them (FAO, 2020). This because many poor people in the world depend on employment in the informal sector in order to earn their livelihood (Blofield et al., 2020). Similarly, due to the lockdown, businesses across the various economic sectors experienced severe losses, which become a threat to their operations and solvency, particularly among small businesses (ILO, 2020b). These consequences have collectively negatively affected the socio-economic development of society. The socio-economic consequence of the pandemic crisis on youth has been described as follows: Young people constitute major victims of social and economic consequences of the pandemic, and there is a risk that they will be scarred throughout their working life – leading to the emergence of a "lockdown generation" (ILO, 2020a, p. 2).

More so, it has been predicted that the four most vulnerable sectors of the global economy in terms of unemployment include food and accommodation

(144 million workers), retail and wholesale (482 workers million), business services and administration (157 workers million), and manufacturing (463 million workers), which collectively accounts for 37.5% of the global economy (Dutta et al., 2020). Similarly, the ILO (2020b) revealed that due to the lockdown, about 2.7 billion (81%) of the global workforce was negatively affected. This happened because 94% of the world's workers live in countries where workplaces were closed down to reduce the spread of the virus (ILO, 2020a). During the period, the demand for products exceeded their supply, leading to an increase in prices and inflation, reducing the purchasing power that eventually affected the GDP adversely (Bhandari, 2020). Consequently, in this period, people have no more options other than the disposal of their assets, securing informal loans, or child labour (FAO, 2020).

Briefly, the COVID-19 pandemic has brought nothing more than social and economic crises that exposed most economies in the world to an economic depression that has never been experienced before. Accordingly, many countries were either not known to be developing countries or just succeeded in eradicating poverty and are now poor and struggling to get out of poverty caused by the pandemic.

9.3 Historical and contemporary contributions of *waqf* to socio-economic development

Historically, it is widely known that *waqf* played a vital role in the welfare of the *ummah*, being a vehicle for socio-economic development (Muhammad, 2010). Similarly, it has been found to contribute to socio-economic development, as well as provide assistance to the poor and the underprivileged members of Islamic societies (Abu Talib et al., 2018). Since the time of Prophet Muhammad (SAW), *waqf* has been regarded as one of the pillars of the Islamic economy that greatly contributes to Muslims lives in many ways (Zakaria et al., 2013). Prophet Muhammad (SAW) was found to have commenced philanthropic *waqf* when a Jewish man known as Mukhairiq, said that when he died his seven orchards should be given to Prophet Muhammad (SAW), which were subsequently declared as *waqf* for the welfare of the *ummah* upon receipt (Kahf, n.d.). However, the real innovation of the idea of *waqf* began in the early Islamic period when the Prophet (SAW) ordered someone to purchase a well that belonged to Bayruha in Madina and provided free drinking water to the *ummah* (Kahf, 2003). This practice was followed by the dedication of land owned by Umar (the second Caliph) in Khaibar as *waqf*. Also during his reign, some companions initiated a family *waqf* with a view to giving priority to their family members before anyone else.

The early history of Islam also revealed that *waqf* institutions provided free education, scholarship, support for orphanages, free medical treatment, and inns for nomads (Khan, 2015). Similarly, *waqf* was used in the past to finance projects and activities, such as operating commuter ships, delivering water to an area, supporting retired sailors, defending a town, paying a neighbourhood's taxes, etc. (Khan, 2015). In addition, in the 11th century, every Islamic city had many *waqf* institutions that financed hospital expenses, such as surgeons, ophthalmologists, pharmacists, chemists, medicines, foods equipment, repair of buildings, etc. (Khan, 2015).

A few centuries ago, *waqf* institutions continued to contribute to the socio-economic development of society. For example, it was discovered during the reign of Muhammad Ali in Egypt that 600,000 feddan (acres) out of a total 2,500,000 feddan (acres) were primarily assigned to pay for the expenses of mosques and educational institutions (including Al-Azhar University) (Ahmed, 2007). It was established that during the Ottoman Empire, in the early 18th century, land *waqf* was approximately one-third of productive land (Khan, 2015). Cizakca (2014) also stated that substantial evidence was found that in the 18th century, the total *waqf* revenue ranged between one-third and one-half of the total revenue. Besides, when the Republic of Turkey was founded in 1923, about three-quarters of its arable land belonged to *waqf* assets, and within the same period, one-eighth of farmlands in Egypt and one-seventh of the land in Iran were *waqf* assets (Kuran, 2001). Today, many existing projects across the globe, such as the Indian Taj, the Bosnian Mostar Bridge, the Jerusalem Al-Aqsa Mosque, Al-Azhar University in Cairo, Shishli Children's Hospital in Istanbul, and Zubida's Waterway in Mecca were created with *waqf* funds (Sait & Lim, 2006). In fact, in many Islamic societies, education, health care, water resource,s and support for the poor were provided solely by *waqf* institutions without government intervention (Islamic Research and Training Institute (IRTI), 2015).

In the contemporary Muslim world, a new form of *waqf* known as cash has been introduced and formalized for socio-economic development and poverty alleviation. It is now widely accepted in many Islamic countries across the globe (Umar et al., 2020). According to Lahsasna (2010), the use of cash *waqf* has the potential to enhance the economic growth of a nation as well as perform a key role in the socio-economic development of society by enabling micro and medium sized enterprises (MMEs) to get access to financial services. Similarly, Shahimi et al. (2013) explored the potential of cash *waqf* in alleviating poverty in Malaysia by using system dynamics methodology. The model simulation results revealed the potential of cash *waqf* to alleviate poverty by up to 50%. Consequently, cash *waqf* is used in various Islamic countries, such as Malaysia, Indonesia, Bangladesh, Pakistan, etc. to support SMEs in alleviating poverty and to achieve economic growth and development.

Three key issues have clearly indicated that *waqf* has been recognized as a veritable instrument for poverty alleviation. First, many countries in the world have established ministries or departments to specifically deal with *waqf* and mandate them to manage and revitalize *waqf* assets (Shirazi, 2014). Presently, in order to enhance the efficiency and effectiveness of *waqf* institutions, independent corporate bodies were established in various countries, like the Malaysia *Waqf* Foundation (in Malaysia), the Kuwait Public Foundation (in Kuwait) and the Egyptian *Awqaf* (in Egypt) among others, to which the management and supervision of *waqf* properties were transferred from government ministries or departments (Osman,

2012). Second, even before the emergence of the COVID-19 pandemic, *waqf* was a topical issue among international organizations such as Islamic Development Bank (IsDB), International Monetary Fund (IMF), and the World Bank, scholars, and practitioners. For instance, in 2017, the Islamic Development Bank, IRTI, Jeddah, Islami Bank Bangladesh Limited, and the Centre for Zakat Management jointly organized an international research workshop to revive *waqf* for socio-economic development. The conference took place in Dhaka, Bangladesh, between 4 and 5 November 2017 and was attended by scholars and practitioners from America, Africa, Asia, and Australia. Third, during the lockdown period to stop the spread of COVID-19, many webinar lectures and training were organized by various Islamic organizations and scholars on the use of *waqf* to alleviate poverty during the pandemic. Further, many called for contributions to special issues of reputable journals, such as the *International Journal of Islamic and Middle Eastern Finance and Management* and *Jurnal Ekonomi*, in order to use Islamic finance to address the socio-economic problems caused by the pandemic. *Waqf* or generally Islamic social finance is one of the key topics of the issues.

9.4 The Al Rajhi *waqf* model

9.4.1 Background of the Sulaiman Bin Abdulaziz Al Rajhi endowment

Sulaiman Bin Abdulaziz Al Rajhi, popularly known as Al Rajhi, is a Saudi Arabian, who was one of the richest people in the Kingdom but not a member of the royal family. He was born into a low-income family and earned his wealth through hard work and tireless efforts. Now his family is one of the richest non-royals in the Kingdom (Al-Harbi, 2012; Sertin 2017). According to Forbes, Al Rajhi became the 120th richest person in the world in 2011 because his net worth was estimated at USD$7.7 billion (Al-Harbi, 2012). Al Rajhi willingly preferred becoming poor with neither the cash nor real estate he possessed earlier by sharing some portion of his entire wealth among his heirs and giving the rest to religious and philanthropic activities. The endowment has been acknowledged as one of the largest ever made in the history of Islam (Sulaiman Bin Abdulaziz AlRajhi Charitable Foundation (SACF), 2020a). Al Rajhi's lifetime donations reached USD$5.7 billion and his generosity index reached 966% (Wealth-X, 2015). But according to Islamatics (2020), the total lifetime donations made by Al Rajhi for charitable activities were equivalent to USD$16 billion (60 billion riyals) which became the highest endowment made in the Muslim world with no match yet. In any case, it is unanimously believed that his endowment and generosity are incomparable with anyone in the contemporary Islamic world. In an interview published in Arab News on why he sacrificed his entire wealth, he responded as follows:

> Yes. Now I own only my dresses. I distributed my wealth among my children and set aside a portion for the endowment to run charity projects. As far as I am concerned, this situation was not a strange one. My financial condition reached zero point two times in my life, and therefore I have had the feeling

> and understanding (about poverty) well. But now the feeling is accompanied by happiness, relaxation and the peace of mind. The zero phase in life this time is pure because of my own decision and choice (Al-Harbi, 2012).

Notable and valuable investments endowed by Al Rahji include shares in Al Rajhi Bank (19.7%), the largest poultry farm in the Middle East, and Al-Laith shrimp for organic farming in the Kingdom (Al-Harbi, 2012; Sertin, 2017; Islamatics, 2020). The most important among these investments that attracted global attention is the shares in the Islamic bank. The current equivalent value of the endowed share in the bank is the equivalent of USD$3.7 billion (Sertin, 2017). The bank was co-founded by Sulaiman Al Rajhi, together with his three brothers in 1957 (Wealth-X, 2015). It became the largest Islamic bank in the world that earned a ten-digit net worth (Islamatics, 2020).

Briefly, to ensure the perpetuity of his endowment, Al Rajhi integrated it with various profitable businesses that are going concerns with a view to ensuring the provision of adequate funds to finance the activities of the foundation. He established a holding company named Awqaf Sulaiman Bin Abdulaziz Al Rajhi Holding Company to coordinate the investments centres in order to achieve the designed charitable activities efficiently and effectively. The holding company of Al Rajhi has four centres, financial and real estate investment, food and agricultural investment, industrial investment, and educational and technological investment (ASRHC, 2020d). These centres were integrated to ensure the provision of adequate sustainable funds to discharge the foundation's activities effectively.

9.4.1.1 Financial and real estate investment

This comprises shares endowed by Al Rajhi Bank (19.7%) and the various real estate investments and projects across the country, including many international hotels located in Mecca, Medina, Riyadh, Khobar, and other cities in the Kingdom (ASRHC, 2020b).

9.4.1.2 Food and agricultural investment

This uses modern agricultural methods and technologies to provide food and poultry products that are consumed outside the Kingdom. Some of the key strengths of this investment are as follows:

- It is the biggest project for organic agriculture in the country.
- It is one of the biggest poultry farms that produces approximately 820,000 hens and a million eggs on a daily basis.
- It exports some farm products to UAE, Kuwait, Qatar, Kingdom of Bahrain, Sultanate of Oman, Yemen, China, and Vietnam.
- It has an integrated poultry project in Egypt.
- It has one of the largest poultry slaughterhouses in Egypt and the Arab world, among others (ASRHC, 2020c).

9.4.1.3 Industrial investment

This sector consists of two main divisions, an industrial production company, which is one of the largest producers of various industrial products, such as plastics, food items, paper, building materials, and caps, with two factories in Saudi Arabia and UAE and many branches in the Kingdom and other Arab countries like Bahrain, Qatar, Kuwait, and Oman; and a cement factory in Sudan, which is now among the biggest ones in Sudan and Africa with a daily capacity of 5,700 tons of cement (ASRHC, 2020e).

9.4.1.4 Educational and technological investment

This centre has three divisions as follows:

- Educational investment where the Sulaiman Alrajhi University was established in Bokayreah as a not-for-profit university with four colleges: college of medicine, college of nursing, college of applied medical sciences (radiology and medical laboratories), and Sulaiman Al Rajhi college for entrepreneurship.
- The information systems sector is a specialized information technology company that has been created with highly sophisticated systems infrastructure to serve all the members of the group.
- Training and recruitment are created as a not-for-profit entity to boost the national poultry industry through the provision of qualified and competent human resources, duly supervised experts, and professionals to meet the needs of the industry (ASRHC, 2020a).

9.4.2 Charitable activities of the Al Rajhi Foundation

The SACF has its headquarters in Riyadh, the capital city of the Kingdom of Saudi Arabia, with branches in the various regions, such as Riyadh, Madinah, Qassim, Eastern Province, Makkah, Asir, Najran, Hail, Jazan, Al Baha, Al Jouf, the Northern frontier, and Tabuk (SACF, 2020b). Opening branches in the various regions brings the foundation closer to the beneficiaries across the Kingdom. The foundation provides nine grants and five special projects (SACF, 2020d).

With these nine grants and five special projects, the foundation has been positively contributing to the welfare of the people in various forms in the Kingdom over the years. Each year, the foundation finances about 1,200 projects in 13 regions in the country, which cover no fewer than 130 cities and towns (SACF, 2020a). During 2020, the foundation recorded the following achievements:

- Implementing 138 projects: social (54), health (10), education (51), media (1), and *da'wah* (22).
- Several cities and regions (85) benefitted from the grants including Nijran (11), Al Baha (5), Madinah (11), Eastern Province (8), Tabuk (9), North frontier (6), Riyadh (18), Makkah (10), Al-Qassim (16), Asir (15) Hail (8) and Jazan (14).

- The total number of individual beneficiaries is 4,245,915 comprising social, health, education, media, and *da'wah* (SACF, 2020c).

9.5 The need to replicate the Al Rajhi *waqf* model across the Muslim world

Considering the damage caused by the COVID-19 pandemic to the socio-economic development of the *ummah*, replicating or adapting the Al Rajhi *waqf* model in Muslim countries would certainly reduce poverty to the barest minimum. There are many lessons for Muslim philanthropists in the world to learn, which could motivate them to replicate this model. However, the most essential ones are as follows.

9.5.1 The generosity of the waqf

Al Rahji could be described as the most generous person known in the contemporary Muslim world who at once sacrificed all that he earned through his hard work and dedication to the betterment of the *ummah*. He believed that wealth actually belongs to Allah, not him. This is one of the key reasons that he received the prestigious King Faisal International Prize for Service to Islam, particularly in the area of poverty alleviation through philanthropic activities (Al-Harbi, 2012). The fact is that in the contemporary Muslim world, only Al Rahji was found to have practised this kind of generosity. Nevertheless, Muslim entrepreneurs are encouraged to endow a certain proportion of their investments, say 10%, 15%, 25%, etc., as *waqf* to alleviate poverty during this pandemic.

9.5.1.1 Integration with profitable businesses

An essential requirement of *waqf* is that the endowed asset must produce perpetual income for the benefit of beneficiaries. The integration of *waqf* into an existing and profitable business (whether full or partial) provides more perpetual benefit to the beneficiaries than starting a fresh business. In this case, Al Rajhi endowed his shares or investments in various companies, such as Al Rajhi Bank, poultry farms, hotels, etc. These businesses provide the foundation with the funds to discharge its activities. Umar (2019) and Umar et al. (2020) strongly support this idea of the integration of *waqf* with businesses in order to prevent the liquidation of family-inherited businesses and also provide a sustainable source of income for the benefit of heirs, non-heirs (through a will), and other members of society.

9.5.2 Shari'ah*-compliant businesses*

All the businesses that finance the activities of the Al Rajhi charitable foundations engage in activities that conform with *Shari'ah* requirements. Therefore, income generated from businesses that involve elements of interest (*riba*), uncertainty, gambling, etc. should be used for Islamic endowments. Income generated through drug trafficking, prostitution, and other illegal businesses must not be used for *waqf* activities.

9.5.2.1 Diversification of investments

It is unwise to put all one's eggs in one basket because, as it falls to the ground, all of them could be lost. Hence, Al Rajhi diversified his *waqf* investments in different forms of business right from the beginning, such as Al Rajhi Bank, poultry farms, real estate, etc. This should serve as a signal to all philanthropists to ensure that their charitable foundations are strongly supported with sustainable incomes from businesses in different sectors.

9.5.3 Promotion of entrepreneurship and empowerment

The foundation provides support to private entities for their growth and development, which are essential for the sustainability of the private sector. It also organizes empowerment programs to enhance the skills and knowledge of people to become self-reliant or competent in the labour market. For example, the foundation, through its poultry farm called Al-Watnia Poultry, collaborated with a technical and vocational training corporation and trained people on the poultry business and activities to become qualified and trained groups needed in the poultry industry (ASAAHC, 2020d). Providing the necessary support to the private sector by capable hands like the Al Rajhi Foundation would surely, among others, contribute not only to retaining employees but also making people self-reliant during the pandemic.

9.5.4 Comprehensive welfare package

The foundation is all-encompassing to the extent that all the basic requirements and needs of life are provided, such as religious, educational, health, and other infrastructure needs. Unfortunately, the activities of many renowned world philanthropists are narrowed in one aspect, particularly health issues. Similarly, in Nigeria, the most common form of *waqf* widely practised by Muslim philanthropists is the construction of mosques (IRTI, 2015; Umar, 2019). Others donate buildings and dig wells in the country. It is hard to find a standard Islamic endowment that satisfies the requirements of generating perpetual income and continuity that supports all the basic requirements and needs of life.

9.5.5 Divisionalization

The activities of the Awqaf Sulaiman Bin Abdulaziz Al Rajhi Holding Company have been categorized into four investment centres to achieve its objectives efficiently and effectively. As mentioned earlier, they are financial and real estate, food and agricultural, industrial, and educational and technological investment centres. Divisionalization would enable each centre to discharge its duties independently and allow its performance to be assessed periodically with a view to taking necessary actions before things get out of control when deviations are found.

9.5.6 *A sufficient number of branches*

The foundation has 13 branches, which are spread across different regions to ensure that their activities are enjoyed in every town and city in the country. The foundation would not have recorded such achievements without having these branches.

9.5.6.1 *Support to other charitable and non-governmental organizations*

As mentioned earlier, the Al Rajhi Foundation designed some projects to support registered and trusted non-governmental and other charitable organizations that aim to contribute to the development of education, health, social, and religious activities in the Kingdom. These entities assist the foundation in fast-tracking and spreading the foundation's activities throughout the country.

9.5.6.2 *Special consideration to orphans and other people with no family care*

In consideration of the Islamic importance and value of taking responsibility for orphans and other people with no family care, the foundation has a special program known as *Rushd* to provide sustainable care to these people. The importance of the replication of this program in many Muslim countries is that many people are now looking for the same assistance due to the impact of COVID-19. Besides, this program would be of great help to Islamic countries that are at war as well as those exposed to various forms of terrorism and criminal activities, like Boko Haram, banditry, and kidnappings, which caused the death of the parents and guardians of many children.

So far, ten unique features of Awqaf Sulaiman Bin Abdulaziz Al Rajhi Holding Company have been discussed. The fact is that in the current situation and contemporary world, when a majority of Muslims have developed a strong desire to keep their wealth until they die with little or no care for others, it is very difficult to find Muslim philanthropists with the desire to help others However, considering the contributions of the Al Rajhi Foundation to Islam and the socio-economic development of the people in the Kingdom, it is necessary to devise a means of replicating or adapting an adequate part of the foundation in other parts of the Muslim world, for at least two reasons. First, the activities of the foundation are focused on the Kingdom of Saudi Arabia. If the Kingdom gets this kind of Islamic endowment without being listed among the poorest countries in the world, a lot of Muslim countries in Africa and Asia will need similar kinds of endowment foundations to reduce their poverty. Second, during the continuous escalation of the COVID-19 crisis, the need for Islamic endowments with all these qualities is very profound, if not necessary, particularly in African and Asian countries.

9.6 Recommendation and conclusion

The COVID-19 pandemic exposed the whole world to unprecedented socio-economic problems. Even before the pandemic emerged, many Muslim countries had been ranked among the poorest countries in the world and are now deeper the poverty as a result of the pandemic. Even developed countries and others with lower poverty rates were not spared by the crisis. Thus, this study aimed to discuss the benefits of replicating or adapting the Al Rahji *waqf* model by Muslim philanthropists in order to reduce the extreme level of poverty caused by the COVID-19 pandemic in the Muslim world. This chapter shows that the Al Rajhi Foundation has been strongly attached to diversified profitable and *Shari'ah*-compliant businesses that provide adequate funds for financing various projects for the religious and socio-economic development of the *ummah*. The foundation has essential features that make it unique and support its perpetual existence. However, its activities are limited to the Kingdom of Saudi Arabia. Hence, considering the difficulties in which Muslims are currently living across the globe as a result of the pandemic, the need to adapt or replicate the Al Rajhi *waqf* model by Muslim philanthropists is very profound. This would surely reduce the extreme poverty caused by the pandemic to the barest minimum.

References

Abu Talib, N. Y., Abdul Latiff, R., Aman, A., & Palil, M. R. (2018). An exploratory study of accounting and reporting practice for *waqf* among state Islamic religious councils in Malaysia. *International Journal of Islamic Thought*, *13*, 90–105.

Ahmed, H. (2007). Waqf-based micro finance: Realizing the social role of Islamic finance. In International seminar on integrating awqaf in the Islamic financial sector. Retrieved from https://www.findevgateway.org/paper/2007/03/waqf-based-microfinance-realizing-social-role-islamic-finance.

Al-Harbi, M. (2012, May 30). Sulaiman Al-Rajhi's life a rags to riches story. *Arab News*. Retrieved from https://www.arabnews.com/economy/sulaiman-al-rajhi%E2%80%99s-life-rags-riches-story.

ASRHC (Awqaf Sulaiman Bin Abdulaziz Al Rajhi Holding Co.). (2020a). Educational and technological investment. Retrieved from https://www.asrhc.com/educational-and-technological-investment/?lang=en.

ASRHC. (2020b). Financial and real estate investment. Retrieved from https://www.asrhc.com/financial-and-real-estate-investment/?lang=en.

ASRHC. (2020c). Food and agricultural investment. Retrieved from https://www.asrhc.com/food-and-agricultural-investment/?lang=en.

ASRHC. (2020d). Founder. Retrieved from hhttps://www.asrhc.com/founder/?lang=en (accessed 27 July 2020).

ASRHC. (2020e). Industrial investment. Retrieved from https://www.asrhc.com/industrial-investment/?lang=en.

Baker, S. R., Bloom, N., Davis, S. J., & Terry, S. J. (2020). COVID-induced economic uncertainty. National Bureau of Economic Research (NBER). Working Paper no. 26983. Retrieved from http://www.nber.org/papers/w26983.

Bhandari, R. K. (2020). Coronavirus recession a short review. *IOSR Journal of Economics and Finance*, *11*(3), 15–17. doi: 10.9790/5933-1103011517.

Blake, H., Bermingham, F., Johnson, G., & Tabner, A. (2020). Mitigating the psychological impact of COVID-19 on healthcare workers: A digital learning package. *International Journal of Environmental Research and Public Health*, *17*, 1–15. doi: 10.3390/ijerph17092997.

Blofield, M., Hoffmann, B., & Llanos, M. (2020). Assessing the political and social impact of the COVID-19 crisis in Latin America. *GIGA Focus*, *3*, 1–11.

Cizakca, M. (2014). The waqf, its basic operational structure and development. Retrieved from www.inceif.org/.../THE%20WAQF,%20ITS%20BASIC%20OPERATIONAL%20STR (accessed 20 August 2017).

Dogarawa, A. B. (2009). Poverty alleviation through zakah and waqf institutions: A case for the Muslim ummah in Ghana. *SSRN Electronic Journal*. Retrieved from https://ideas.repec.org/p/pra/mprapa/23191.html.

Dutta, J., Mitra, A., Zaman, S., and Mitra, A. (2020). Lockdown and beyond: Impact of COVID-19 pandemic on global employment sector with special reference to India. *NUJS Journal of Regulatory Studies (Special Issue)*, 6–9.

FAO (Food and Agricultural Organization). (2020). Impact of COVID-19 on informal workers. Retrieved from https://doi.org/10.4060/ca8560en.

Hajjar, B. (2020). President of the Islamic development bank group: COVID-19 and micro, small and medium enterprises, saving the global economy from the pandemic. Retrieved from https://www.isdb.org/fr/node/44432.

Hassan, M. K., & Ashraf, A. (2010). An integrated poverty alleviation model combining zakat, awqaf and micro-finance. Retrieved from https://www.researchgate.net/publication/228889744_AN_INTEGRATED_POVERTY_ALLEVIATION_MODEL_COMBINING_ZAKAT_AWQAF_AND_MICRO-FINANCE.

ILO (International Labour Organisation). (2020c). ILO monitor: COVID-19 and the world of work. Retrieved from https://www.ilo.org/global/topics/coronavirus/impacts-and-responses/WCMS_745963/lang--en/index.htm.

ILO (International Labour Organisation). (2020a). ILO monitor: COVID-19 and the world of work. Retrieved from https://www.ilo.org/wcmsp5/groups/public/---dgreports/---dcomm/documents/briefingnote/wcms_740877.pdf.

ILO (International Labour Organisation). (2020d). A policy framework for tackling the economic and social impact of the COVID-19 crisis. Retrieved from https://www.ilo.org/global/topics/coronavirus/impacts.

IRTI (Islamic Research and Training Institute). (2015). Islamic social finance report. Retrieved from https://irti.org/product/islamic-social-finance-report-2020/.

Islamatics. (2020). A Saudi man who donated "$16 Billion" in charity and kicked himself out of the billionaires club. Retrieved from https://islamtics.com/a-saudi-man-who-donated-16-billion.

Jackson, J. K., Weiss, M. A., Schwarzenberg, A. B., & Nelson, R. M. (2020). Global economic effects of COVID-19. Retrieved from https://crsreports.congress.gov.

Kahf, M. (1998). Financing the development of awqaf property. In *seminar on development of awqaf*. Retrieved from http://www.iefpedia.com/english/wp-content/uploads/2009/11/Financing-the-Development-of-Awqaf-Property.pdf.

Kahf, M. (2003). The role of *waqf* in improving the ummah welfare. Retrieved from http://monzer.kahf.com/papers/english/ROLE_OF_WAQF_IN_THE_WELFARE_OF_THE_UMMAH.pdf.

Kahf M (n.d.). *Waqf: A Quick Overview*. Retrieved from monzer.kahf.com/papers/english/WAQF_A_QUICK_OVERVIEW.pdf.
Khan, M. T. (2015). Historical role of Islamic waqf in poverty reduction in Muslim society. *The Pakistan Development Review*, *54*(4), 979–996.
Khan, S., & Rabbani, M. (2020). Financing corona virus (COVID-19) affected SMEs through Islamic finance tool *Qardh-Al-Hasan*: An artificial intelligence and NLP based Islamic Fintech model. Retrieved from https://www.researchgate.net/publication/340491799_Financing_Corona_Virus_COVID-19.
Kuran, T. (2001). The provision of public goods under Islamic Law: Origins, impact and limitations of the *waqf* System. *Law & Society Review*, *35*(4), 841–898.
Lahsasna, A. (2010). The role of cash waqf in financing micro and medium sized enterprises (MMES) a new Islamic financial approach by using cash waqf model: Testing the model on Malaysian MMES framework. In Ismail, A.G., Hassan, M.E., Ismail, N., & Shahimi, S. (Eds.), Proceedings of the 7th International Conference—The Tawhidi Epistemology: Zakat and Waqf Economy. Malaysia: Institut Islam Hadharm Universiti Kebangsaan.
Muhammad, I. N. (2010). Scholars, merchants and civil society imperative for waqf-based participatory poverty alleviation initiatives in Kano, Nigeria. *Humanomics*, *26*(2), 139–157. doi: 10.1108/08288661011074936.
Nicola, M., Alsafi, Z., Sohrabi, C., Kerwan, A., Al-Jabir, A., Losifidis, C., Agha, M. & Agha, R., (2020). The socio-economic implications of the coronavirus pandemic (COVID-19): A review. *International Journal of Surgery*. *78*, 185–193. https://doi.org/10.1016/j.ijsu.2020.04.018.
Olanipekun, W. D., Brimah, A. N., & Sanusi, H. B. (2015). The role of zakat as a poverty alleviation strategy and a tool for sustainable development: Insights from the perspectives of the Holy Prophet (PBUH). *Arabian Journal of Business and Management Review*, *5*(3), 8–17.
Osman, A. Z. (2012) *Accountability in managing waqf properties: The case of two State Religious Councils in Malaysia* [PhD thesis]. Royal Holloway University of London, UK.
SACF (Sulaiman Bin Abdulaziz AlRajhi Charitable Foundation). (2020a). About founder. Retrieved from https://www.rf.org.sa/en/main-page/541.
SACF. (2020b). Branches. Retrieved from ttps://www.rf.org.sa/en/branches.
SACF. (2020c). Charities and projects counts by Administrative regions. Retrieved from https://www.rf.org.sa/en.
SACF. (2020d). Grants. Retrieved from https://www.rf.org.sa/en/rf-grants.
Sadeq, A. M. (2002). Waqf, perpetual charity and poverty alleviation. *International Journal of Social Economics*, *29*(1/2), 135–151. doi: 10.1108/03068290210413038.
Sait, S., & Lim, H. (2006). *Land, Law and Islam: Property and Human Rights in the Muslim World*. London: Zed Books Ltd.
Sanchez-Duque, J. A., Orozco-Hernandez, J. P., Marin-Medina, D.S., Arteaga-Livias, K., Pecho-Silva, S. Rodriguez-Morales, A. J., & Dhama, K. (2020). Economy or health, constant dilemma in times of pandemic: The case of coronavirus disease 2019 (COVID-19). *Journal of Pure Applied Microbiology*, *14*(1), 717–720. doi: 10.22207/ JPAM.14.SPL1.07.
Sertin, C. (2017, April 13). These Arab billionaires made headlines with major donations and pledges. *Forbes*. Retrieved from https://www.forbesmiddleeast.com/billionaires/arab-billionaires/.

Shahimi, S., Marzuki, M. U. M., & Embong, Z. (2013). Potential of cash *waqf* for poverty alleviation in Malaysia: A system dynamics approach. *Jurnal Ekonomi Malaysia*, *47*(2), 149–163.

Shirazi, N. S. (2014). Integrating zakāt and waqf into the poverty reduction strategy of the IDB member countries. *Islamic Economic Studies*, *22*(1), 79–108.

Umar, U.H. (2019). Integrating family *waqf* into an inheritable going concern business: An instrument for the sustainable welfare of exempted heirs. In Ali, K. M., Hassan, M. K., & Ali, A. E. S. (Eds.), *Revitalization of Waqf for Socio-Economic Development Volume II* (p. 87). Cham: Palgrave Macmillan. doi: 10.1007/978-3-030-18449-0_4.

Umar, U. H., Kademi, T. S., & Haron, M. H. (2020). Integrating *wqāf* and business: Ensuring business sustainability for the welfare of heirs and non-heirs. *International Journal of Economics, Management and Accounting*, 28(1), 191–213.

UN (United Nation) News. (2020). Coronavirus: World Bank confirms ,deepest recession since World War Two. Retrieved from https://news.un.org/en/story/2020/06/1065902.

UNESCAP (United Nations Economic and Social Commission for Asia and the Pacific). (2020). The impact and policy responses for COVID-19 in Asia and the Pacific. Retrieved from www.unescap.org › files › COVID _Report_ESCAP.

Wealth-X. (2015). The most generous philanthropists in the world. Retrieved from https://www.wealthx.com/reports/2015/the-20-most-generous-philanthropists-in-the-world/ (accessed 27 July 2020).

Zakaria, A. Z. M., Abd. Samad, R. R., & Shafii, Z. (2013). Venture philanthropy waqf model: A conceptual study. *Jurnal Pengurusan*, *38*, 119–125.

10 Funding the refugee crisis in Turkey

A case for social impact *sukuk*

Ziyaad Mahomed, Ibrahim Musa Unal, and Shamsher Mohamad

10.1 Introduction

The 20th century has generated a gradually intensifying refugee crisis that has amplified into an ongoing social crisis, especially since the Cold War in 1989. Civil wars, the internal conflict of countries, mass famine, and many faltering economic, political, and social institutions (US Mission to UN, Global Humanitarian Emergency 1995) contributed to this intensification. The host countries that receive these refugees bear the cost of managing the refugees at the expense of the country's economy (Mandel, 1997). Consequently, when countries face an impossible task of efficient control and maintenance of the livelihood of these refugees on a sustainable basis, they will impose restrictions on the refugee inflow, which has recently created a global crisis.

Turkey is one good example of a country with a refugee crisis due to conflicts in Syria. By December 2019, the official number of Syrian refugees in Turkey reached 3,571,000, with an estimation of more than half a million unregistered refugees (Multeciler Dernegi, 2020). Almost every major city in Turkey is experiencing a refugee problem, and in some cities like Kilis, refugees comprise as high as 81% of the city's population. The refugee problem in Turkey is a good example of a long-standing social problem that the Turkish people have experienced at the expense of their economy and politics.

Turkey had spent as much as US$40 billion on refugees when the Syrian war started in 2011 and continued until 2019 (TRT News, 2019); it has contributed towards rising economic and political pressure as the population becomes increasingly challenged in supporting refugees within the country. The refugee crisis requires more sustainable financial solutions for Turkey (Oubdia & Raghibi, 2018). This predicament became serious when the European Union (EU) reneged on its promise to transfer €6 billion to Turkey for refugees, and thus Turkey was forced to spend its own budget on all refugee expenditure (Borsagundem News, 2019). Furthermore, concerns over political sovereignty have prevented Turkey from accepting funds from certain countries (Seker, 2006).

However, the presence of refugees contributes towards stronger economic and labour markets in host countries (Tumen, 2016). There is also a tendency for an increase in inflation in areas with predominantly refugee populations (Alix-Garcia

& Saah, 2010). There are suggestions that the inflation in migrant areas can be prevented by food aid financed by the host government or aid organizations, as this will prevent refugees from affecting local markets through their purchases. As for labour markets, many Syrian refugees are employed in low-skilled jobs, such as construction or the service sectors, as language and skills limit them from being employed in high-skilled jobs (Dincer et al., 2013). The result is a negatively affected low-skilled job market, amplified by employers hiring them unofficially for cheaper labour and avoiding paying social security taxes (Akgündüz et al., 2015).

Therefore, current efforts towards solving this refugee-based social problem are crucial, more so finding a viable financial solution to mitigate Turkey's challenge in maintaining these refugees. A *shariah*-based funding solution is suggested, consistent with the policy of the Turkish government, to prioritize Islamic finance (Karagol, 2012). This is expected to have significant spill-over advantages including controlling the excessive debt profile of the government to overcome issues with the current conventional financing of refugees and to offer a solution that is in line with the religious sensitivities of refugees and locals. For example, issuing social impact *sukuk* (SIS) to address the funding of refugee camps could be both a viable economic and political solution for the current government. This requires a well-functioning Turkish Islamic capital market to facilitate the planned funding. Besides this, resorting to charity and impermissible income accumulated in banks in the Middle East can be utilized for sustaining refugee-related projects as well.

In brief, this chapter will discuss viable alternative financial solutions for sustainable financing of refugees and suggest a potential Islamic finance solution to achieve the best possible outcomes for refugee financing in Turkey.

10.2 Alternative financial solutions

With the rising concerns of the global economic downturn, most countries have constraints on their budgets for social projects and thus are not able to effectively address these social problems (Oubdia & Raghibi, 2018). The irony is that most of these chronic social problems are in countries with majority Muslim populations. However, there is a lack of consensus-based support from wealthier Muslim majority countries and Muslim-based transnational organizations on how to seriously address these problems.

Since budgets have always been a constraint in effectively addressing these issues, cost-effective, efficient, and publicly acceptable funding for governments and institutions that have track records and strategic plans for dealing with these issues are imperative (Berndt & Wirth, 2018). An economically viable and politically feasible alternative is the pay-for-success social impact bond (SIB). The instrument uses key performance indicators (KPIs) to determine the social impact. Carter et al. (2018) showed that although SIBs are efficient in terms of collaboration, prevention, and innovation, they are basically non-tradeable bonds with high monitoring and tracking costs but have difficulty in measuring social impact. Kriesberg (2011), however, highlighted the inefficient cost management and the inefficiency of service providers that arise from increasing pressure to fulfil expectations. Since these bonds are there to achieve social impact that is reliant on human intervention and social benefits, time-specific performance measures may be too rigid, making the solution unsuitable for the desired outcome.

However, Marwan & Haneef (2019) analyzed the pilot Peterborough SIB project and acknowledged that this innovative financing tool reflected the true spirit of risk-sharing, which is fundamental to Islamic finance and has huge potential for financing social projects.

Another form of financing for social projects are socially responsible investments (SRI); they are similar to pay-for-success SIBs but without the KPIs. Bennet and Iqbal (2013) discussed the SRI as an instrument that would adequately bridge the gap of social finance between Islamic and conventional markets. SRIs create opportunities for developing a new fixed-income product that fulfils the needs of investors that are inclined both towards SRI and *shariah* requirements. Malaysia is the first country to issue social impact *sukuk* (*ihsan sukuk*) denominated in the local currency, which is Ringgit Malaysia (RM), and has led the Islamic SRI trend within global Islamic finance markets. Limited examples of social impact *sukuk* are in existence, particularly on issues such as deforestation, affordable housing, or education facilities (Securities Commission Malaysia, 2014).

Iman and Mohammad (2017), Omar and Ab. Rahman (2013), and Musari (2019) suggested the *sukuk waqf* concept in modern Islamic finance for social entrepreneurship and the development of sustainable *waqf* properties. The *waqf* development with a *sukuk waqf* facility provides the potential for development in the SRI platforms and developing social impact *sukuk* models.

Although other alternatives exist, we will focus on the most prominent: social impact bond, *waqf*, and SRI options before suggesting a comprehensive Islamic finance solution.

10.3 The social impact bond

The development of social investment or impact investing has assisted in financing programs to mitigate social problems. Contemporary social investment has evolved into SIBs that merge social responsibility with an outcomes-based capital injection. Social investment (SII) is provided only if the commissioner commits to specific KPIs built into the contract. This is called the 'pay-for-success' model and can be elaborated upon as follows: a third-party investor bears the financial risk and invests in a socially impactful project, and a service provider – often an NGO – undertakes the project. During the contract phase, mutually agreed KPIs are designated for the project to be successful, and these KPIs are tracked during the tenure of the project. If the project achieves its target, which is often solving a complex social problem, then the commissioner (often a government) accepts paying the investment amount to the third-party investor who funds the project in the initial stage, including a reasonable profit (Child et al., 2016).

SIBs become attractive for investors since the financial risk is shifted to the third-party investor such that the service provider can concentrate on the success of the project. The success of the project is tracked through designated milestones or KPIs that provide a transparent method for measuring the success of the project through establishing an outcomes metric (Oxford Go Lab – Impact Bonds Report, 2019). This measurement helps to track the project with statistical techniques for more accurate performance tracking. Also, using statistical techniques and measurements improve performance management, financialization, and analytics (Bernth & Wirth, 2018).

Thus, SIBs help to blur the distinction between the market, the state, and the third sector, and this harmony increases the efficiency of the projects. The entrepreneurial spirit is introduced to public service delivery and also instils a strong and motivated problem-solving spirit that is synergized with the application of technology to boost performance. All these efforts will facilitate the effectiveness of the social impact project through the gradual decrease in the cost and increase in operational efficiency in the long run.

Go Lab (2019) explains four main salient dimensions of SIBs: the nature of the payment outcomes, the nature of capital used to fund services, the strength of the performance management, and the social intent of the service provider. Again, they explained a core SIB with these dimensions as 100% payment on outcomes, independent and at-risk capital, a high degree of performance management, and the strong social intent of service provider.

Bernth and Wirth (2018) explain the additional benefits of SIBs by stating that they assure the investors' pre-payment and that the taxpayers will not pay for the project unless it is a success; SIBs create fiscal savings for government by improving efficiency and brings the success rate close to 100% for public expenditure, which is politically expedient.

The benefits of SIBs also include the ability to anticipate and prevent serious problems such as social issues, the transfer of financial risk from service providers and governments to third-party investors. SIBs help improve management performance culture and increase the cost and operational efficiency of public projects, they are an appropriate tool for investors to earn a return on their capital while providing a social service to society, they help service providers focus all their energy on the quality of the service, and they eliminate undercapitalization concerns.

In potential cases of social crisis that may emanate from high levels of crime, drug-abuse and other social challenges, prevention measures become a priority for government. Preventive measures through social impact projects save costs by solving a problem before it emerges. The first SIB, the Peterborough SIB, was a project based on a prevention philosophy, where the service provider prevented short-term sentenced prisoners from committing repeat offences, thus decreasing the crime rate within society.

Another salient feature of SIBs is the transfer of financial risk from service providers and governments to third-party investors. Thus, the service provider is no longer concerned with the financial portion of the project, and an increased focus can be directed toward the efficiency and success of the project. The third-party investor bears the financial risk and therefore tracks the service provider to make sure that the project is conducted in accordance with the initial agreement. This increased pressure on the service provider is often regarded as a positive impact, as it forces the service provider to be more innovative and develop creative problem-solving skills. The criticism of this close tracking is that it increases the stress levels of service providers, thereby potentially decreasing their operational efficiency.

Over the long-term, SIB approaches can be viable, help improve management performance culture and increase cost and operational efficiency if there is a proper mechanism in place to evaluate their success and these can be seen as lessons for future SIB issuances.

From the investors' perspective, an SIB is an appropriate tool for realizing a return on capital while providing a social service to society. Given the fact that payment will only be made in the case of success, an SIB ensures full commitment by investors, service providers, and other mid-level participants. Therefore, the tracking and performance evaluations not only increase efficiency and effectiveness but also increase accountability to the investor. Also, SIBs are effective tools for investors to implement public sector projects as they force the public sector to be more responsible and on par with private social projects (Pasi, 2014).

From the service provider's perspective, an SIB helps to focus all the energy on the quality of the service and eliminates undercapitalization concerns. This facilitates undertaking longer-term and outcome-based performance rather than classical short-term approaches based on input-oriented considerations. Therefore, it becomes essential to improve and adapt performance management techniques and develop new flexible and innovative strategies to complete social services (Nicholls & Tomkinson, 2013).

From the issuing country's perspective, the UK leads on SIB issuances since the Peterborough SIB. According to the Brookings Institution Global Impact Bonds Database of January 2018, it shows that Muslim countries are not major players in the SIB market internationally as 25 countries were issuers of SIB between the period of 2011 and 2018 are Argentina, Australia, Austria, Belgium, Canada, Cameroon, Congo, Colombia, Germany, Finland, France, Japan, India, Israel, the Netherlands, New Zealand, Peru, Portugal, South Africa, South Korea, Sweden, Switzerland, Uganda, the United Kingdom, and the United States. This could be because social impact investments are not well understood. Most countries seem oblivious to the salient features of SIBs, and they may very well find it not as attractive as conventional interest-based bonds. According to the Brookings Institution Global Impact Bonds Database of January 2018, more than half of the SIBs issued focus on employment (39 out of 108 issuances) and social welfare sectors (37 out of 108 issuances), globally. Sectors such as the environment (only 1 out of 108 issuances) and agriculture (only 1 out of 108 issuances) have not garnered adequate attention in the global SIB market.

10.3.1 Challenges in the existing SIB framework

First, SIBs are structured as conventional bonds and include elements of interest. When the required funding is invested in the project, the return from the government will include coupon rates that are pre-determined based on the rental of funds provided. Although the interest portion fluctuates based on the success of the milestones, the return is not based on the underlying cash flow of the project but based on the return of the funds loaned to the project. Therefore, investing in SIBs would be impermissible for investors seeking *shariah*-compliant instruments. It should be noted that the populations of most of the issuing countries are not predominantly Muslim. Therefore, issuers may not have any specific inclination towards interest-free social investments, leaving out a sizeable investment population with significant amounts of liquidity. This supports the notion that issuing social impact *sukuk* is required to meet the demand of Muslim investors.

Parties involved in SIB schemes are often groups that are eager to develop philanthropic tools with high expectations of quick results. Therefore, the main interest shifts from the organic development of the tool to the result-oriented project design for SIB structures. Beyond organic growth, there is a lack of theoretically based approaches to address the challenges and risks in designing the framework for SIB. Therefore, lack of estimation of the complexity of the issuance, resulting in legal and risk allocation in SIB, is often neglected (Pasi, 2014).

Second, discussions in the literature regarding SIBs focus on the sciences of sociology and politics. Economic studies, however, focus on the economic development of certain areas in terms of political economy and public management (Pasi, 2014). Furthermore, the economic literature is heavily focused on welfare policy implementation and the comparison of traditional models such as project financing and SIB frameworks in this context.

A bond typically has features of designated coupon rates, principal payments, secondary market transactions, and scheduled payments. Since most of these elements are often not prevalent in SIBs, categorizing SIBs as a bond is a conceptual misnomer. The SIB structure is designed for undertaking a social service or solving a social problem with the investor, a service provider, and the public sector as involved parties. Therefore, the SIB concept is much closer to project financing rather than a typical bond issue.

Further, an SIB does not just raise finance for a new project from the investors but ensures the efficient spending of the collected proceeds for the intended project, whereas a bond is mainly used to raise finance for several purposes. As the tax collecting body and being responsible for the economic and social wellbeing of its citizens, governments are expected to fulfil their duties in encouraging and undertaking more environmental and urban investment, reducing unemployment, poverty, illiteracy, crime rates, and other related social predicaments. Therefore, reformulating the definition of the SIB, it is more like a tool that increases efficiency in public investments and thus brings saving opportunities for government budgeting. It has salient features of ensuring the efficient allocation of resources and increasing the quality of service, rather than just raising capital for social projects (Pasi, 2014).

Additionally, given the needs for budgeting a return on investment, program evaluation, middle managers, and the expenses of designing complex financial and contractual mechanisms, SIBS, according to the critics, may be an expensive method of operating social programs (Pratt, 2013). According to Pratt (2013), the operational costs of SIBs are often higher than conventional bonds because their structure requires more supervision and closer monitoring. Instead of solely raising funds, a social impact measurement program is required, increasing costs with complex mechanisms and other additional costs raised from the additional mechanisms of an SIB. However, the SIB is an effective way of solving social problems. Focusing on the additional costs that arise from applying a successful tool would, perhaps, underestimate its success. Also, solving a social problem helps governments stop spending additional funds that could be much higher than the additional cost of the SIB structure.

In brief, defining an SIB is a challenging issue, as the purpose and benefits of SIBs change for each of the many parties involved. Thus, calling an SIB a multi-purpose tool could be fair. In this context, Salomon (2014, p. 1) terms SIBs a yin-yang deal that 'brings contrary forces together and they turn out to be uniquely capable of producing new life forms when taking advantage of their interdependencies'.

Another challenge related to the structure of SIBs is the liquidity and long-term investment profile. Often SIB projects are structured for five or more years, and they usually do not have any disinvestment strategies in any uncalculated case; thus it does not provide an advanced exit plan for the investors. These characteristics of SIBs restrict them to only a certain group of investors who have a strong inclination towards philanthropy and investors that are willing to experiment on a project, with perhaps the objective of improving their societal image (Pasi, 2014).

Based on the type, difficulty, and complexity of the service delivered, there are additional risks that may be raised related to the intervention as well. Such an intervention may reduce the quality of the work and distract the focus and motivation of the service provider, and could be merged with other political and financial risks and the risk of execution, or even the risks related to the intermediary's activities and reputation (Burand, 2012). All these types of risk have subcategories and are dependent on the project and parties involved. Therefore, each SIB needs to be managed and evaluated differently, making it more difficult to develop standards and frameworks on SIBs.

10.4 *Sukuk*, *waqf*, and SRI funding for sustainable financing of social projects

SIBs are an effective financing solution in supporting social programs globally, with more than 150 SIBs issued by the beginning of 2020. However, as SIBs are a type of conventional bond and contain interest, they restrict larger investment from the Middle East and investors in search of *shariah*-compliant solutions.

Islamic finance law provides numerous solutions for providing finance and financial support to social impact initiatives. The *Baitul Maal* system that survived for centuries in the Muslim world, and still exists in certain countries such as Indonesia, Saudi Arabia, Bahrain, and Kuwait, was the basis of social welfare funding for all those in need. The system relieves the pressure upon governments to provide complete funding for social welfare projects. It also tends to protect the people from government expenditure that has been channelled through to projects that benefit corrupt individuals or policies designed with objectives of self-interest.

The *waqf* instrument forms a key component in the *Baitul Maal* system and has been used in Muslim societies for centuries. It was an innovative concept proposed by the Prophet Muhammad (PBUH) in the early Islamic period when the Prophet (PBUH) migrated to Madinah. He asked if someone could buy the well of Bayruha' and declared it as free drinking water for the public. Additionally, the Prophet (PBUH) also gave advice to his companion, Umar Ibn Al Khattab, to give his most valuable land in Khaybar as *waqf* for the needy and poor.

The basic rules in *waqf* are that the property cannot be spent as the owner of it is Allah himself. Rather, it is the benefit arising from that property that is used for consumption, ensuring that the capital remains intact. *Waqf* properties are intended for support through educational institutions, medical facilities, and religious institutions that are self-sustainable. Thus, *waqf* culture helps nations have a more empowered society that is less reliant on governments, making it easier for both society and government.

Merging this with the fact that most Muslim countries lack financial resources, this necessitates the need for the reactivation of *waqf* to support social impact programs. Indeed, evidence from many countries (Turkey and Egypt in particular) has shown that the *waqf* system is an extremely effective social and financial instrument to redistribute wealth and provide adequate safety nets for the welfare of society without over-reliance on government.

Relating the *waqf* system to the SIB concept, '*cash-waqf*' could be an effective solution for funding social impact projects. In the cash-*waqf* concept, finance is raised to fund a project, where the final product of the project will be assigned as a *waqf* property, and its *usufruct* (a person or party that confers the temporary right to use and derive income or benefit from someone else's property) will be used for the designated *waqf* purpose, which is often to benefit society or a group of people.

Value creation of *waqf* property includes both economic profit and *usufruct* for society. Here it must be noted that the rental of *waqf* properties and cultivation of *waqf* land is allowed by all Islamic jurists. This means that making a profit from *waqf* property is permissible if this is for the benefit of society and supports the maintenance of the *waqf* assets (Iman et al., 2017). In basic entrepreneurship, profit generation is perceived as the interest of individuals and shareholders, but in social entrepreneurship, the economic profit is directed toward a social benefit.

In Islamic social impact projects based on *waqf*, it is both the economic profit and the social benefits that will be derived from the usage of the assets that determine effective utilization of the *waqf*. Therefore, the concept of social entrepreneurship can be perceived as very similar to *waqf* projects, where the *waqf* property is built for the purpose of social *usufruct* and if any economic profit is generated, it will be used for the designated social benefit and for the sustainability of *waqf* property.

10.5 Socially responsible investments

In 2018, the volume of SRIs reached US$8.72 trillion in the US and €20 trillion in Europe (Eurosif, 2018). Western countries have taken a considerable interest in SRI-based project developments. From an Islamic finance perspective, socially responsible investments are expected to be the priority as Islamic finance promotes socio-economic objectives, balancing profit with social responsibility. The objectives of SRI projects overlap with the main doctrines of *shariah*, which are promoting moral responsibility, ethics and justice, consideration for social well-being, and economic empowerment (Bennet & Iqbal, 2013).

SRI practices can be applied to a variety of techniques such that the investment purposes may be based on negative screening, norms-based screening, engagement and voting, environmental, social, and corporate governance (ESG) integration issues, positive screening, a theme of sustainability, and impact investing (Eurosif, 2016). Therefore, due to elements of social impact (besides the financial motive of profitability), an increasing interest in SRIs has been generated in the Islamic financial sector over the last few decades.

SRI development in Islamic finance is often associated with *shariah* compliance tools and investments (Marwan & Haneef, 2019). Traditionally, this process had not considered social and environmental concerns even though this was a core component that the system professed to follow. However, a more proactive approach of investments currently is to embrace ESG concerns and United Nations Sustainable Development Goals (UN-SDGs) criteria, probably to acquire international recognition and inclusion.

Furthermore, there is evidence that portfolios with socially responsible elements obtain significantly higher returns than conventional portfolios and that companies with good environmental performance have significantly higher returns (Statman & Glushkov, 2016). Also, SRI *sukuk* in sovereign debt management both increases returns and enables governments to have a stronger hand in solving social problems (Scholtens, 2009). For countries with majority Muslim populations or with a demand for Islamic investment tools, SRI *sukuk* could be a possible alternative for both corporate and sovereign portfolios. Increasing Islamic SRI investment, such as social impact *sukuk*, will both increase the returns on sovereign portfolios and help to develop more *waqf* assets for more improved social infrastructure.

10.6 SIS for financing the refugees budget in Turkey

The proposed *sukuk* structure is based on an investment agency with reliance on *waqf* concepts. The structure of a *sukuk waqf* does not differ from the structure of an investment *sukuk* in form, but it does in purpose (Oubdia & Raghibi, 2018). Therefore, the types of *sukuk* to be used for developing a sustainable refugee camp may vary. For our proposed model, a *sukuk Wakalah bi al-Istithmar* structure will be used as this structure can contain a flexible portfolio of investments in *sukuk* instead of a single investment. This is important because when merging different types of investors, *zakat* and charity investments shall not seek periodic returns from the *sukuk* where profit-seeking investors will. Therefore, there should be different types of investment in the same *sukuk* structure. While the proceeds from non-profit-seeking investors will be invested in the project directly, a portion of the investment from profit-seeking investors may be invested in a commodity *murabahah* portfolio so that it will provide a periodic return. Thus, the structure of a *sukuk* for developing a refugee camp is proposed in Figure 10.1.

As the *sukuk Wakalah bi al-Istithmar* structure shows, the process will begin with the appointment of the special purpose vehicle (SPV) as the *wakil* (agent) by the *sukuk* holders. The NGO will be appointed as the investment agent to invest the *sukuk* proceeds for the construction process. The NGO will use these proceeds to begin the project: building a sustainable refugee camp. The camp will be based on a sustainable *waqf* rules model, and the construction process is

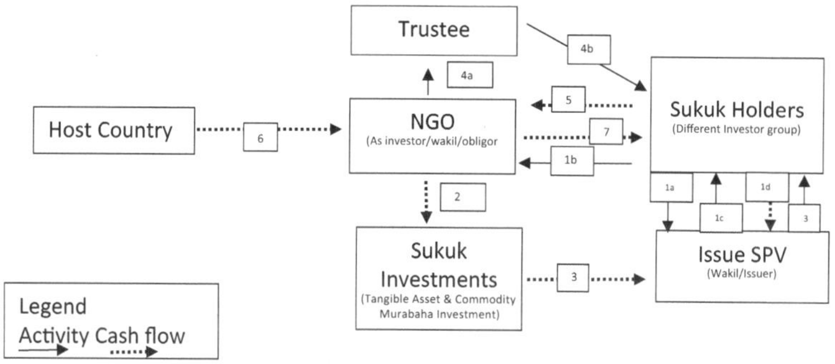

Source: Author's own

1a. Appoint SPV as Wakil (Agent)
1b. Appoint NGO as Investor Wakil to invest Sukuk proceeds
1c. Issue Sukuk
1d. Sukuk Proceeds
2. Invest into and manage Sukuk investment for refugee camps
3. Periodic Distribution
4a. Purchase undertaking (exercise price)
4b. Dissolution Distribution amount
5. NGO will purchase the facility from the Sukuk holders
6. Government will pay the facility value to NGO (If KPIs are achieved)
7. NGO will proceed the value to Sukuk holders

Figure 10.1 Social impact *sukuk* structure for refugee camp construction. Source: Author's own.

completed. This will ensure that the host country's government will not be financially burdened over the long term.

During the construction process, a portion of the proceeds will be placed in a commodity *murabaha* investment, and this will bring a periodic distribution to be transferred to profit-seeking investors. Although it may be argued that commodity *murabaha* is controversial, particularly in countries outside Malaysia due to the application of the AAOIFI (Accounting and Auditing Organization for Islamic Financial Institutions) *shariah* standards, the purpose of the project is for social benefit. In this case, the principle of overall benefit to the public, or *maslahah mursalah*, may provide further support for the use of the instrument.

In the next step, the NGO will provide a purchase undertaking to the trustees to ensure that the funding for the project is provided as the dissolution or redemption amount to be transferred to the *sukuk* holders at the end of the project. These funds will be provided by the government to the NGO to fulfil the dissolution amount. This amount will be provided only if the designated KPIs are achieved by the NGO, as the social impact *sukuk* structure requires. This means that the *sukuk* facility will be a conditional *sukuk* underwritten by the government.

10.6.1 Size of the sukuk *issuance and cost of the refugee camp*

As Vatasoiu et al. (2015) documented, US$63.5 million was spent in 2014 to build refugee camps in Jordan for Syrian refugees. This translates to approximately US$448 per refugee for the construction process. Although the required size of the camp may be uncertain due the increasing numbers of refugees, a camp for 20,000 refugees will be used for the first construction in this *sukuk* proposal. This capacity is preferred because the United Nations High Commissioner for Refugees (UNHCR) policy recommendation for the maximum size of a refugee camp is 20,000 (Lischer, 2015) for internal security, health, and the management of daily operations within the camp. With this capacity, approximately US$9 million will be required for the construction of the camp at the initial stage.

The same study (Lischer, 2015) estimates the average daily food and water needs for a refugee at US$5 per day per refugee. This cost is under Jordanian prices and translating it to the Turkish environment, based on 2020 Consumer Price Index (CPI) values (Trading Economics, 2020), it would be estimated at US$18 per day.

For a camp of 20,000 refugees, the daily cost of survival would be US$360,000 (18*20,000) under the same circumstances. This means that after the construction process is completed, the *waqf* property should have a daily income of US$360,000 to continue its operations. Since the project will become *waqf* once constructed, it is suggested that the Turkish Republic Directorate General of Foundations manages the daily operations of the camp and be a guarantor to ensure the income earned from the camp itself is sufficient to continue survival within the camp.

10.6.2 Sukuk *issuance*

For the construction process, the required funds are estimated at US$9 million. The *sukuk Wakala bi al-Istithmar* facility will be raised for this amount plus the required investment for the commodity *murabaha* investments, in the form of a single issuance. Three main investor groups may be identified for this investment: (i) *zakat* contributors, (ii) philanthropists (NGOs, foundations, and other charities), and (iii) profit-seeking investors.

For the issuance process, the NGO acting as the investment *wakil* shall invest the proceeds in the relevant investment portfolio which is proposed to comprise of *shariah*-compliant tangible assets and *shariah*-compliant commodities purchased and sold under the principle of *murabaha*. Tangible assets should be at least 33% of the *sukuk* proceeds, as the AAOIFI *shariah* standards require (COMCEC, 2018). Here tangible assets represent the required assets for the construction of the refugee camp.

The remainder of the *sukuk* proceeds will be invested in the commodity *murabaha*. The NGO as the buyer will issue a purchase order to the investment *wakil* and the *sukuk* trustee (acting on behalf of the *sukuk* holders) to purchase *shariah*-compliant commodities from the *sukuk* holders at a deferred sale price. Later, the investment *wakil* (on behalf of the *sukuk* holders) will purchase the commodities on a spot payment basis from a commodity supplier at a purchase price equivalent to the remaining balance of the *sukuk* proceeds. After the purchase of the commodities, the investment *wakil* (on behalf of the *sukuk* holders) will sell these commodities to the NGO as the buyer for a price equivalent to the *sukuk* proceeds invested in the commodity *murabaha* investment plus the aggregate profit margin to be paid on a deferred basis. The deferred sale price will be equal to the aggregate of the periodic distribution amount that will be paid to the profit-seeking investor group.

Later, the NGO as the buyer will immediately sell these commodities to a commodity buyer on spot payment basis for cash, equal to the purchase price. This structure will allow the social impact *sukuk* facility to merge several investor groups into one *sukuk* so that the possibility of having insufficient demand from investors will be reduced significantly. The tenure of the *sukuk* facility should extend to the completion of the construction of the refugee camp.

As this project will be a social impact investment, KPIs will be established for the NGO undertaking the project. As the process is primarily based on construction, the most important challenge will be time to completion and consistency with the specifications or the plan of the camp. Therefore, the KPIs could include completing the construction based on the agreed dates. This includes the requirement that the quality standards of specified are achieved for the camp units and facilities. These minimum standards should be at the level of UNHCR refugee camp standards.

The *sukuk* should be announced internationally so that different domestic and international investor groups can join the facility. Also, global impact funds such as Kohlberg Kravis Roberts (KKR) Global Impact Fund are also appropriate investors for such *sukuk* projects.

10.6.3 Political impact of the proposed model

This model mainly aims to be a self-sustainable refugee camp so that negative economic impact on the host country will be minimal. Such a social impact *sukuk* will also serve the policy of the Turkish government to prioritize Islamic finance, especially in the capital market sector, by increasing *sukuk* awareness amongst the social service providers and corporates. As an industry, Islamic finance will also benefit from such a development, enhancing its reputation through merging the humanitarian aid proposition with the potential of Islamic finance for social impact projects.

Also, such a project will be a successful example of the institutionalization of the humanitarian aid operations for Turkey. Turkey has the largest humanitarian aid operations globally, with US$8.2 billion in 2019 alone (TIKA, 2019). Capital market inclusion and close monitoring of designated KPIs for operations will increase efficiency for organizations and thus, will strengthen the global position of Turkey in the humanitarian aid sector by allowing it to create much larger projects.

The proposed model will also increase the experience and efficiency in refugee operations by pushing NGOs to use more innovation as a result of the social impact bond and the nature of *sukuk*. This will lift the experience curve for NGOs in long terms so that humanitarian operations will be done with more success.

10.6.4 Challenges

Modelling such a *sukuk* structure and camp layout should be applicable and realistic, and NGOs with experience should be prioritized to prevent any major pitfalls in construction and management. *Waqf* management after the construction phase should also be under governmental institutions so that a robust operational lifecycle will be ensured.

The key challenges in feasibility arise from *sukuk* issuance rather than the construction and management of the refugee camp, as Turkey already runs several camps with many different models since the Syrian civil war started. The *sukuk* market in Turkey is still nascent with only a few players. Therefore, raising a social impact *sukuk* in Turkey does require effective public and institutional awareness, especially for the first issuance. Cooperation with corporations and Islamic financial institutions from the Middle East to receive impermissible income (income derived from *shariah* non-compliant sources) from these organizations is an important source of funds for the success of the project.

Also, ensuring the financial inclusion of refugees both within the refugee camp employment areas and other jobs from local employers is an important part of the feasibility check for the project. Good management of production facilities and farms within the camp area will increase the efficiency and profitability of the camp.

10.7 Conclusion

In the last few decades, the frequency and intensity of social problems experienced by most developing and less developed countries have significantly increased. These social problems emanate from a combination of factors such as political instability, infrastructural issues, and economic problems, as well as the pandemic, aka COVID-19. As a result of many of these issues, the migrant crisis has strained economies and the relationship between governments and their people.

To address these social problems effectively requires proper planning and operational infrastructure, which are all dependent on adequate funding on a sustainable basis. Turkey is in dire need of finding alternative strategies to manage the refugee problem. Current funding methods for managing the refugee crisis are insufficient due to the vast volume of refugees. Several Islamic finance solutions for sustainable financing were explored before recommending a special feature social impact *sukuk* for the refugee problem, after considerations of cost-effectiveness and the current challenges of fundraising for social projects in Turkey. The choice of financing solution should also consider the effectiveness of mitigating the economic and political problem of the government in managing the refugees in Turkey.

An alternative funding solution is proposed for funding the refugee camps based on a *sukuk Wakalah bi al-Istithmar* structure. This structure can also contain a flexible portfolio of investments in *sukuk* instead of a single investment. This is important because when merging different types of investors, *zakat* and charity investments shall not seek periodic income from the *sukuk* where profit-seeking investors will. Therefore, there should be different types of investment in the same *sukuk* structure. While the proceeds from non-profit-seeking investors will be invested in the project directly, a portion of the investment from profit-seeking investors may be invested in a commodity *murabahah* portfolio so that it will bring periodic income.

This project may be a successful example of the institutionalization of the humanitarian aid operations for Turkey and will also increase the experience and efficiency in refugee operations by pushing NGOs to use more innovation as a result of the social impact bond and the nature of *sukuk*. The only challenge is that the *sukuk* market in Turkey is still nascent with only a few players, whereas raising a social impact *sukuk* in Turkey requires effective public and institutional awareness especially from corporations and Islamic financial institutions from the Middle East that have large resources of impermissible income which is incidental interest income derived primarily from regulatory fund placements. That is an important source of funds for the success of the project.

References

Akgündüz, Y., Van den Berg, M. & Hassink, W. H. (2015). The impact of refugee crises on host labor markets: The case of the Syrian refugee crisis in Turkey. Retrieved from http://repec.iza.org/dp8841.pdf.

Alix-Garcia, J., & Saah, D. (2010). The effect of refugee inflows on host communities: Evidence from Tanzania. *The World Bank Economic Review*, *24*(1), 148–170. doi: 10.1093/wber/lhp014.

Bennet, M.S., & Iqbal, Z. (2013). How socially responsible investing can help bridge the gap between Islamic and conventional financial markets. *International Journal of Islamic and Middle Eastern Finance and Management*, *6*(3), 211–225.

Berndt, C., & Wirth, M. (2018). Market, metrics, morals: The Social Impact Bond as an emerging social policy instrument. *Geoforum*, *90*, 27–35.

Borsagundem News. (2019, December 17). Cumhurbaşkanı Recep Tayyip Erdoğan, Cenevre'de Küresel Mülteci Forumu Açılış Oturumu'nda konuştu. Konuşmasında Erdoğan, Suriyeli mültecilerin durumuna dair önemli açıklamalarda bulundu. Retrieved from https://www.borsagundem.com/haber/erdogan-avrupa-birligi-sozunu-tutmadi/1457632.

Brookings Institution. (2018, January). *Global Impact Bonds Database*. Retrieved from https://www.brookings.edu/blog/education-plus-development/2019/01/02/a-global-snapshot-impact-bonds-in-2018/.

Burand, D. (2012). Globalizing social finance: How social impact bonds and social impact performance guarantees can scale development. *NYUJL & Bus.*, *9*, 447.

Carter E., FitzGerald, C., Dixon, R., Economy, C., Hameed, T., & Airoldi, M. (2018). *Building the tools for public services to secure better outcomes: Collaboration, Prevention, Innovation*. Retrieved from https://s3.eu-west-2.amazonaws.com/golab.prod/documents/BSG-GOLab-EvidenceReport-20190730.pdf.

Child, C., Gibbs, B. G., & Rowley, K. J. (2016). Paying for success: An appraisal of social impact bonds. *Global Economics and Management Review*, *21*(1–2), 36–45.

The Standing Committee for Economic and Commercial Cooperation of the Organization of the Islamic Cooperation (COMCEC). (2018). *The Role of Sukuk in Islamic Capital Markets*. Retrieved from http://ebook.comcec.org/Kutuphane/Icerik/Yayinlar/Analitik_Calismalar/Mali_Isbirligi/Toplanti10/files/assets/common/downloads/publication.pdf.

Dincer, O. B., Federici, V., Ferris, E., Karaca, S., Kirisci, K., & Carmıklı, E.O. (2013). *Turkey and Syrian Refugees: The Limits of Hospitality*. Retrieved from https://www.brookings.edu/wp-content/uploads/2016/06/Turkey-and-Syrian-Refugees_The-Limits-of-Hospitality-2014.pdf.

Economics, T. (2020). *Turkey CPI*. Retrieved from https://tradingeconomics.com/turkey/consumer-price-index-cpi#:~:text=Consumer%20Price%20Index%20CPI%20in%20Turkey%20averaged%20222.86%20points%20from,points%20in%20January%20of%202003.

Eurosif. (2016). *European SRI Study*. http://www.eurosif.org/wp-content/uploads/2016/11/SRI-study-2016-HR.pdf.

Iman, A. H. M., & Mohammad, M. T. S. H. (2017). Waqf as a framework for entrepreneurship. *Humanomics*, *33*(4), 419–440.

Karagol, E. (2012). The causality analysis of external debt service and GNP: The case of Turkey. *Central Bank Review*, *2*(1), 39–64.

Kriesberg, J. (2011). *Will Social Impact Bonds Really Improve Non-profit Performance?* Retrieved from https://www.macdc.org/content/will-social-impact-bonds-really-improve-nonprofit-performance.

Lischer, S. K. (2015). *Dangerous Sanctuaries: Refugee Camps, Civil War, and the Dilemmas of Humanitarian Aid*. Ithaca and London: Cornell University Press.

Mandel, R. (1997). Perceived security threat and the global refugee crisis. *Armed Forces & Society*, *24*(1), 77–103.

Marwan, S., & Haneef, M. (2019). Does doing good pay off? Social impact bonds and lessons for Islamic finance to serve the real economy. *Islamic Economic Studies*, *27*(1), 23–37.

Multeciler Dernegi. (2020, August 20). *Turkiye'deki Suriyeli Sayisi*. Retrieved from https://multeciler.org.tr/turkiyedeki-suriyeli-sayisi/.

Musari, K. (2019). The evolution of waqf and sukuk toward sukuk-waqf in modern Islamic economy. *International Journal of Umranic Studies*, *2*(1), 45–54.

Nicholls, A., & Tomkinson, E. (2013). *The Peterborough Pilot Social Impact Bond*. Retrieved from https://emmatomkinson.files.wordpress.com/2013/06/case-study-the-peterborough-pilot-social-impact-bond-oct-2013.pdf.

Omar, H. H., & A. Ab. Rahman. (2013). The application of sukuk in sustaining the waqf asset: Experience of selected waqf trustee. *Shariah Journal*, *21*(2), 89–116.

Oubdia, L., & Raghibi A. (2018). Sukuk-waqf: The Islamic solution for public finance deficits. *European Journal of Islamic Finance*, *9*,1–7.

Oxford Go Lab – Impact Bonds Report. (2019). Retrieved from https://golab.bsg.ox.ac.uk/.

Pasi, G. (2014). Challenges for European welfare systems. A research agenda on social impact bonds. *Review of Applied Socio-Economic Research*, *8*(2), 141–151.

Pratt, J. (2013, April 17). *Flaws in the Social Impact Bond/Pay for Success Craze*. Retrieved from http://www.nonprofitquarterly.org/policysocial-context/22149-flaws-in-the-social-impact-bond-craze.html.

Scholtens, B. (2009). Corporate social responsibility in the international banking industry. *Journal of Business Ethics*, *86*(2), 159–175.

Securities Commission Malaysia. (2014). *Sustainable and responsible Investment Sukuk Framework*. Retrieved from https://www.sc.com.my/api/documentms/download.ashx?id=84491531-2b7e-4362-bafb-83bb33b07416.

Seker, M. (2006). *Dış Borçlanmaya Teorik Bir Bakış ve Dış Borçların Ekonomik Etkileri*. Sosyoekonomi. Retrieved from https://ideas.repec.org/a/sos/sosjrn/060104.html.

Statman, M. & Glushkov, D. (2016). Classifying and measuring the performance of socially responsible mutual funds. *The Journal of Portfolio Management*, *42*(2), 140–151.

Strong Growth in Sustainable and Responsible Investment across Europe (2018). Eurosif.org. Retrieved from http://www.eurosif.org/strong-growth-in-sustainable-and-responsible-investment-across-europe/.

Turkish Cooperation and Coordination Agency (TIKA). (2019). *Turkey Keeps Breaking Records in Humanitarian Aid and Development Assistance*. Retrieved from https://www.tika.gov.tr/en/news/turkey_keeps_breaking_records_in_humanitarian_aid_and_development_assistance-49351.

TRT News. (2019, December 17). *Cumhurbaskani Erdogan: Multeci Meselesi BIrkac Ulkenin Cabasiyla Onlenemez*. Retrieved from https://www.trthaber.com/haber/gundem/cumhurbaskani-erdogan-multeci meselesi-birkac-ulkenin-cabasiyla-onlenemez-447159.html.

Tumen, S. (2016). The economic impact of Syrian refugees on host countries: Quasi-experimental evidence from Turkey. *American Economic Review*, *106*(5), 456–460.

Vatasoiu, S., Carlsen, M., & Romanski, J. (2015). *Optimizing the Size and Location of Short-Term Refugee Camps in Syria (BMCM Problem 1)*. Retrieved from http://www.dam.brown.edu/siam/2015/Syrian_Refugee_Camps.pdf.

Part III

Impact of COVID-19 on Islamic microfinance

11 COVID-19 pandemic

The Islamic social capital perspective in *Baitul Maal Wat Tamwil* institutions movement in Indonesia

Rahmawati and Fitri Rinaldi

11.1 Introduction

The financial crisis in late 1997 was caused by the unbalancing of fundamentals at a macroeconomic and microeconomic level. The financial crisis of 2007–2009 occurred by the widespread fraud in the mortgage security industry around the world. The previous financial crises are different from the pandemic crisis, which, due to health cases. The COVID-19 pandemic is, first and foremost, a health crisis (McKee & Stuckler, 2020).

The governments of countries affected by COVID-19 have imposed restrictions to reduce the spread of COVID-19 with social distancing policies and lockdown restrictions that reduced economic activities and caused interruptions to productivity and the functioning of global chains (McKibbin & Fernando, 2020). The lockdown measures had impacted financial liquidity position of small and large organizations (Ozili & Arun, 2020). As such, the respective government of affected countries are coming up with appropriate macroeconomic and microeconomic policies to overcome the fiscal constraints and stabilise the economy (McKibbin & Fernando, 2020). Financial intermediary services and institutions such as banks and cooperatives responded to COVID-19 disruptions and expected the government to rescue them from the damage of COVID-19.

Indonesia has a huge number of cooperatives operating in the country that have reached 123.048 with a total membership of 22,463,738 in 2019 of which only 1.5% are Islamic cooperatives (depkop.go.id, 2020). The number of Islamic cooperatives decreased from 2017 to 2019 because most of the cooperatives went bankrupt. The economic crisis, due to the pandemic, caused the cooperatives to go bankrupt again. To handle these issues, since 16 March 2020, the Ministry of Cooperatives has made a data collection hotline for cooperatives affected by the COVID-19 pandemic linked through a 1500-587 hotline and special message WhatsApp: 08111-450-587.

From 17 March to 13 April 2020, it was reported that there was a 56% decrease in demand for products or services in cooperatives, 3% delayed production, 22% capital problems, and difficulty in sourcing raw materials by 4% and this impeded operations as much as 15%; 1,785 cooperatives were affected by the pandemic. Through the Ministry of Cooperatives. The government provided support in the form of government assistance programs, subsidized electricity tariffs, and tax payments for six months, from April to September 2020. The Agency for Revolving Fund Management for Cooperatives and Small and Medium Enterprises of Indonesia, Lembaga Pengelola Dana Bergulir (LPDB) carried out a relaxation and restructuring of payments. With this pandemic, inevitably, cooperatives must increase their creativity by utilizing information and communication technology.

Since the COVID-19 pandemic, *Baitul Maal Wat Tamwil* institutions (BMTIs) have faced the threat of lack of liquidity due to the coronavirus outbreak and survival in the face of sudden shocks of economic downturn. The members' activities have been disrupted, their businesses temporarily closed, and so the return of loan funds to the BMTIs has stalled. Several BMTI members withdrew their savings to meet their increasing needs amid the coronavirus pandemic. PBMT Ventura states that 326 BMITs have problems with disbursement or financing, and liquidity problems due to the COVID-19 outbreak (Aldi et al., 2020). BMTIs face a financial crisis that they should survive and could be solved by strengthening all their resources and capacity.

The pandemic crisis is affecting developed and developing countries because of the lack of a cure or vaccine for this virus. The coronavirus has had an impact on the economy and finance of small and more significant institutions such as microfinance and cooperative institutions (Bartik et al., 2020). Coronavirus has affected the loan repayment ability of the members of BMTIs/Islamic cooperatives. This is due to the economic repercussions created by the pandemic due to the lockdown policies that led economic activities to be halted.

The financial crisis has created psychological issues among people too (Lindström & Giordano, 2016). As such, the psychological well-being of people needs to be addressed by financial institutions by understanding the circumstances in which people are living their life and taking actions which are appropriate to the situation to recover the debt owed by them to financial institutions. In this regard, institutions should make trust a priority and an initiative in a time of crisis because trust has remained an essential buffer against poor psychological wellness. Social capital is positively related to psychological wellness (Coleman, 1988; Putnam, 1993). During a financial crisis, a social movement will be needed more and essential to the recovery of the economy by developing social capital elements after the crisis (Aldrich, 2010). Interestingly, social capital should also concern the effects of the financial crisis on community institutions. The social interactions that occur among various individuals in these social environments and settings are also meaningful.

The Islamic social finance system is facing a crises of trust during the pandemic. A lack of proper governance mechanisms within financial institutions to minimize the social impact of debt default has significantly eroded the trust between society and financial institutions (Smolo & Mirakhor, 2010). In this respect the modes of Islamic social finance through Islamic social capital has the potential to provide an effective alternative to adequate governance mechanisms by handling customers of financial institutions who are unable to pay their debt by providing them relief through a mechanism like *zakat* (alms).

Historically, during periods of crisis, the values of cooperation, solidarity, and mutualism experience an increase in popularity. BMTIs in this regard have practically shown a social mutual cooperation governance system where one member helps the other to survive and become economically empowered to build a self-sufficient society. Members participate by supporting and using other members' products or services. To strengthen social capital in BMTI *Baitul Maal* is activated as social assistance to BMTI members.

Therefore, this study aims to investigate the ability of Islamic social capital to buffer against potential financial turmoil in BMTIs in Indonesia. This paper aims to analyze the Islamic social capital movement in the form of networking, spirituality, norms, and trust to resolve economic hardship created by pandemic in societies.

11.2 Literature review

Islamic microfinance is the ability to make a change that will eradicate poverty. The contractual framework of Islamic microfinance has been developed using Islamic principles, which are Islamic finance (profit-sharing finance) and Islamic social finance (*zakat*, *infak*, *sadaqah*, and *waqf*) (Smolo & Ismail, 2011). It proves that Islamic social finance can be used to solve the crisis (Ahmed, 2010; Smolo & Ismail, 2011; Wilson, 2007). BMTIs were established based on Islamic finance and Islamic social finance (Ascarya, 2017).

A BMTI is a microfinance institution that carries out activities based on Islamic principles that have two objectives, social and financial missions. The social mission is known as *baitul maal*, which focuses on collecting and distributing charity (e.g., *zakat*, *infak*, *sadaqah*) to the poor. *Baitul maal* is supported by donors (Nasution, 2013). BMTIs were established to help Muslim micro-entrepreneurs as a strategy for the eradication of rural poverty. *Baitul tamwil* operates based on commercial or economic activities, and collects deposits from its members tomake productive investments. BMT is a unique institution; its nature and characteristics are derived from Islamic and cooperative principles. Sometimes BMTs are also called Islamic cooperatives.

BMTIs are considered to represent a distinct type of economic and social organization, designed to serve the needs of members rather than generate profits for investors. The dual nature of Islamic cooperatives is based on two principles: Islam and cooperative principles (Adnan & Ajija, 2015; Muttaqin, 2012; Wardiwiyono, 2012). The concept of cooperation enhance the social and psychological well-being of members of the society (Valentinov, 2004).

Coronavirus (COVID-19) changes the planning and strategy used to evaluate the risk of financing sustainability programs of institutions. Coronavirus may cause major setbacks for financing sustainable development (OECD, 2020). More than ever, due to the pandemic the number of low-income and middle-income families that need financial assistance has increased as the pandemic has turned back the poverty clock. As such, financial institutions including BMTIs have a moral role to play in societies by promoting the concept of shared economic prosperity; rather than using the pandemic as an opportunity to make more profit by charging interest to those who are unable to pay their financial obligations due to loss of income created by the pandemic.

Bamidele (2019) pointed out that sustainable development needs to consider the role of all forms of capital: natural, social, financial, and cultural, and the complex ways in which they interact. Social capital is a set of shared values that enables individuals to collectively work together to efficiently achieve a common goal, and this is a concept that is normally utilized to show how members of a society are able to stick together like one family and work towards achieving prosperity.

During the crisis, social capital was proven to help communities face a crisis and recover from the COVID-19 pandemic (Pitas & Ehmer, 2020). The individuals, communities, and the governments should be strengthening social capital by bonding (networks are made of close ties, usually with family, friends and neighbours), bridging (made of weaker ties, usually among people with different backgrounds, or people engaged in different occupations or organizations) and linking (based on connections between community residents and community leaders or institutions) (University of Minnesota Extension, 2018).

Mathbor (2007) emphasizes that there are three levels to achieve social capital value, which are bonding with communities, bridging communities, and linking communities through ties to banking, health institutions, religious affairs, NGOs, and government. There are two ways to solve the COVID-19 impact, which are from external and internal BMTIs. Externally, BMTIs need financial assistance from the government to sustain their business and internally, BMTIs need to build capacity in terms of financial resources and human resources by adopting technological progress available in this era of Industry 4.0.

11.2.1 Development of Islamic social capital

Dariah (2012) observes that it is essential to enhance Islamic social capital value by creating activities related to trust, norms, spirituality, and networking. Islamic social capital strengthens the BMTIs to achieve their social and financial objectives comprehensively. Islamic social capital enhances the relationship with Allah (SWT) and humans. There are four dimensions that ought to be developed in Islamic social capital which are trust, norms, networking, and spirituality.

To increase trust and confidence of stakeholders in Islamic microfinance, the Islamic microfinance institutions ought to put in place good governance systems (Dowla, 2006). Ng et al. (2015) stated that the development of trust should relate to the principles and values of institutions by developing codes of ethics. The development of the governance of the Islamic institutions' framework should align with the institutions' principles and promote the values by making a public declaration. Chapra (1992) highlighted that there is a lack of harmony between Islamic vision and the Islamic financial system. Smolo and Ismail (2011) found that a few Islamic microfinances are aligned with Islamic principles. Besides, Rixon (2013) also points out that most cooperatives do not link their strategic initiatives to the seven cooperative principles: voluntary and open membership; democratic member control; member economic participation; autonomy and independence; education, training and information; cooperation among cooperatives; and concern for community. Novkovic (2005) points out that only 50% of members of cooperatives understand the objectives and activities of the cooperatives they belong to. This suggests that there is a gap between theory and practice in Islamic financial institutions (Azman & Ali, 2019) and Islamic cooperatives.

Ng et al. (2015) point out that the development of norms relates to social expectations that need regulation to guide activities. The regulations should align with the principles of institutions and be developed responsibly and mutually to reduce the regulatory gap. The principles-based regulatory approach will reduce the regulatory gap. Siebel and Agung (2006) showed that unsupervised Islamic cooperatives are an outright menace to their members, which risk losing their savings. Based on Bank Indonesia regulation No.15/12/PBI/2013, commercial banks should allocate 20% of their total credit at least to micro-business (Prasetyo et al., 2018). Abusharbeh (2014) found that most Islamic banks use a sales-based system (*murabahah*) rather than profit and loss sharing. Islamic banking avoids using riskier contracts such as *mudarabah* (Rahman, 2007).

Networking is significant to establish and strengthen the social structure relationship in communities (Putnam, 1993; Woolcock & Narayan, 2000). Ng et al. (2015) stated that social capital based on Islamic financial instruments (risk-sharing finance) is essential to increasing investment opportunities and infrastructure. Network intermediaries can establish a communication network to generate a mutually beneficial relationship that fulfils social and business needs, which are: equity participation by finance from the government; developing principles based on a regulatory framework to protect and spur equity crowdfunding and SME pool investment; enhancing literacy in equity crowdfunding and SME pool investment; and creating community networks comprising various stakeholders to facilitate coordination and cooperation in equity crowdfunding and pooling of SMEs (Farooqi, 2006).

There is also a connection between social capital and spirituality (Maselko et al., 2011); spirituality strengthens the social capital (Adhariani, 2017). Therefore, it is essential to combine and elaborate on the spirituality activities in the management process of institutions.

The *Quran* mentions that Muslims have an individual obligation from Allah (SW) to pay *zakat*, (Quran 2: 43; 9: 60; 103; 104; 4: 77); *infaq* and *sadaqah* (Quran 2:254, 57: 7, 51: 19, and 70: 24-25). These verses found in the *Quran* show that *zakat* is an obligation for Muslims and helping those in need financially in the community is a religious obligation as well as a communal obligation for Muslims.

11.2.2 On building Islamic social capital for a social movement

Social capital is a sociological concept that is an indispensable resource facilitating social movement and mobilization. Social capital relates to the spirit of cooperation influenced by cultures, values, and attitudes internalized by individuals in communities through socialization (Putnam, 1993). According to Bourdieu (1989), developing and improving access to social capital movement is not based on maximizing individual behaviour but on maximizing the network relationship by enhancing the connection between individuals, groups, and organizations.

The concept of Islamic social finance instruments already exists in Islam, as *zakat*, *sadaqah*, *infak*, and *waqf*, and are used to solve societal challenges (Zain & Ali, 2017). Islamic social finance instruments are valuable contributors to social development creating wealth development (Shahwan et al., 2018). The structure of BMTIs is to collect *zakat*, *sadaqah*, *infak*, and *waqf* and use them for social objectives (Cokrohadisumarto et al., 2016). It implies that to achieve social objectives, BMTIs need to develop the *Baitul Maal* system, which is supported by the BMTI movement to enhance Islamic social capital activities.

A social movement appears when there is a difference between principles and practices. A social movement challenges the implementation of principles related to the objective of the cooperative and how it works (Balkin & Siegel, 2006). Social movements are influenced by social-psychological means (i.e., changes in values, opinions, and beliefs); transformation in cultural products (e.g., literacy, books, fashion, music, visual); and transformation of the community. Currently, the COVID-19 pandemic is influencing the social-psychological means (Lindström & Giordano, 2016; Yamaguchi, 2013). It implies that knowledge is essential for movements in times of crisis (Porta & Pavan, 2017).

Based on the above explanation, this study emphasizes enhancing the BMTI movement through Islamic social finance.

11.2.2.1 Spiritual movement by setting Islamic goals

Based on *Al-Quran* and *Hadith*, Islam's goals are a guide to life with balance in both material and spiritual needs, and emphasizes brotherhood and socio-economic justice (Chapra, 1992) by ensuring social wellbeing and emphasizing increasing the development of human potential (Ahmed, 2002). *Zakat* has defined beneficiaries in the *Quran* that includes poor and needy among others and today there is a need to increase the *zakat* money given to poor (Smolo & Ismail, 2011) as poverty is widespread.

Shalat enhances the connection between Muslims. Bowen (1989) highlighted congregational prayer (*shalat jamaah*) as an Islamic ritual of worship that has received relatively little attention from anthropologists. Islamic activities include *shalat/ibadat* (either alone/congregation), rites of passage, sacrifice, recitations of the *Quran*, and the commemorations of births. It is essential to integrate the *baitul maal* and *baitul wat tamwil* with sustainable programs that enhance holistic inclusion, which integrates social inclusion, financial inclusion, and spiritual inclusion comprehensively in BMTIs in Indonesia (Ascarya, 2017).

In general, Islamic cooperative use the *shirkah mufawadah* contract, which means the business starts when two or more people contribute the same amount (*jamaah* principles). Each partner bears each other's rights and obligations, and they cannot give a different level of contribution. Islamic cooperatives use *gotong royong* (mutual help/*ta'awun ala al-birri*) and kinship principles. Members are the priority in cooperative activities (Syamsiah et al., 2019).

Cooperatives should have strategies to achieve sustainable economic development and greater social cohesion to counteract the adverse effects of neoliberal globalization (Bretos & Marcuello, 2017). To achieve sustainable economic development, cooperatives could play a leading role in the reduction of poverty by providing financial assistance to those who cannot access it from formal financial institutions like banks and the deposits placed by members of cooperatives can be invested in a productive manner to achieve shared prosperity in the community.

BMTI should enhance member participation. Member participation is influenced by factors like availability of facilities and infrastructure, motivation material, the management capability of board of cooperatives, education, and training focused on satisfying the needs of its members (Ernita & AlRozi, 2014). As such, there is a need for cooperatives to enact strategic action plans in such a way that the members would be motivated to participate actively in the cooperative's activities.

The cooperative should evaluate and monitor in a timely manner the satisfaction levels of its members about the running of the cooperatives (Bretos & Marcuello, 2017). The focus of cooperatives' management is to plan the activities of the cooperative, lead the members, monitor the implementation of cooperative goals, and identify the problem areas related to the application of cooperative management and propose appropriate recommendations to reduce problems (Lendel, 2015). It is also imperative for the governments when making policies related to cooperatives to consult the respective cooperatives and its stakeholders (Aldrich, 2010).

The BMTI movement is expected to increase Islamic social capital value. It is suggested that BMTI and other stakeholders (government, *zakat* institutions, *waqf* institutions) need to comprehensively develop the *Baitul Maal Wat Tamwil* system through a stakeholder approach and integration it to achieve sustainable development goals (Azman & Ali, 2019).

11.3 Methodology

Furthermore, to answer the research questions of this study, an interview session was conducted using a semi-structured interview with questions prepared as an interview guide to identify the views of respondents. The semi-structured interview is suitable for this study since there is a list of issues available that need to be discussed but further probing is needed to get clarification. The purpose of sampling is used to inform the selection of field research sites.

The data that informs this discussion was obtained from interviews with senior managers of BMTIs in June and July 2020, which were undertaken in Jakarta, Yogyakarta, West Java, Tangerang, and Lampung. These key informants also facilitated access to some documents containing statistical and other secondary data from the interviewee's results. In totally nine respondents participated in the interview including two regulators (R1, R2) and six senior managers of BMTIs (M1, M2, M3, M4, M5, M6), and one manager from a *zakat* institution (Z1); the medium of conducting the interview was the Indonesian language and was conducted via zoom and phone. In-depth interviews with senior managers provided insight into the development of Islamic cooperative management and how they are handling the COVID-19 pandemic.

11.4 Discussion

This section discusses the responses of the respondents regarding the way BMTI/Islamic cooperatives are handling the impact of the COVID-19 pandemic. The respondents were asked how they would solve the pandemic problem. In general, the majority of respondents strongly agreed that emphasizing the understanding of cooperative principles and Islamic principles, restructuring member payments, enhancing knowledge in Islamic and cooperative principles, integrating Islamic finance and the Islamic social finance system through Islamic social capital, and transparency on the distribution of profit and loss sharing in BMTI. This implies that regulators, BMTIs, and other stakeholders should support BMTIs as an institution that improves the Islamic social finance system that helps reduce social problems. This study builds on the insights into how the BMTI solves its crises and problems by helping their members face liquidity problems in paying their loan. Interviews with general managers of BMTIs/Islamic cooperatives, *zakat* institutions, *waqf* institutions, and regulators lead to a series of insights.

From the above information, senior managers of BMTIs found that the coronavirus pandemic poses a high risk to human health and increases the cost of living. The central government has issued large-scale social restrictions (PSBB) to reduce the spread of coronavirus, which affects the financial liquidity and social connections of BMTI members.

11.4.1 Response from the regulator

The response from the regulator of the Ministry of Cooperative and SMEs is that the government provides assistance in financing facilities to overcome the problem of liquidity for cooperatives, Islamic cooperatives, and SMEs who were affected by the pandemic. The government issued a relaxation and restructuring policy for loans or financing customers for cooperatives and Islamic cooperatives. Based on the Minister of Cooperatives and SME Decree No. 15 of 2020, has given legal guidance on restructuring of revolving loan/financing to micro-enterprises (cooperative, Islamic cooperatives, and SMEs). The policy issued in April 2020 is a relaxation policy in the form of loan/financing restructuring for cooperatives during the COVID-19 pandemic, which expects to be a fresh breath of air for cooperative members in Indonesia. Loan restructuring is essential to reducing the economic burden on the community and operational risk, especially for members of cooperatives affected by COVID-19 in 2020. The Ministry of Cooperative and SMEs also provided tax relaxation for six months for cooperatives.

However, the BMTIs that can receive financial support from the government are those that meet administrative requirements, and the BMTI must not have arrears of principal or interest. It shows that BMTIs, which have good governance and a reasonable return rate, will be assisted in these programs. While Wahyuni (2008) mentioned that the accountability of BMTIs was low, that shows that not all BMTI could apply for these programs.

11.4.1.1 Response from senior managers of BMTIs

For more clarification, this chapter's research objective is to analyze the BMTI movement with Islamic social capital in the form of networking, spirituality, norms, and trust to solve the impact of the COVID-19 pandemic. This section analyzes and discusses the responses from senior managers of BMTIs.

11.4.2 Restructuring members' payments

The pandemic crisis meant that members of BMTIs found it challenging to repay their loans. Members of BMTIs have already lost their income and become unemployed. Members of BMTIs struggle to repay their loans to BMTIs. BMTIs make a policy to reduce BMTIs' capital buffers to finance the rescheduling of loans/financing and to allow a temporary deferment of financing repayments of members affected by the economic fallout of COVID-19.

BMTIs have created a policy to extend the terms of repayment or restructure their member's loan obligations.

11.4.3 Enhancing knowledge of Islamic and cooperative principles

The senior manager of BMTI said that BMTI should realize the members' needs are aligned with the Islamic and cooperative principles.

The following statement was made by senior manager M1:

> Currently, most Indonesians have forgotten that cooperative institutions in the national economy are based on kinship (family relationship) principles that are reflected in the relationship among its members in the cooperative. The cooperative institutions should promote their members by providing for the members' needs and empowering their members. Based on Act No.25, 1992, a cooperative ought to leverage mutual financial cooperation among all of its members

Senior manager M2:

> During this pandemic, ... Islamic cooperative institutions that operate based on the principles of cooperation will survive. Without financial cooperation from its members, cooperative institutions might not survive in this pandemic and already we have started seeing some of the cooperative financial

institutions being liquidated as they do not promote the collective financial contribution practice by its members as practiced by BMTIs.

Senior manager M3:

> During this pandemic, when the members know Islamic and cooperatives principles, BMTI could encourage their members to enhance the values of cooperation, solidarity, and mutual experience. In our BMTI, new members should attend cooperative education, and after becoming a member, they should attend regular meetings with members and management. The primary aim of the cooperative education is to create awareness among the members about the cooperative philosophy and provide them with sufficient knowledge and skills about the methods and techniques of operating a cooperative institution professionally. Our Islamic cooperative contributes (2%–5% of profits) towards cooperative education.

Senior manager M4:

> We have to understand that the Islamic cooperative institution is a business and social organization formed and run by the members. It is owned and controlled by members through the democratic process. The cooperative's success depends on the quality and loyalty of the members and management (staff). In order to achieve the cooperative objective, the members' participation should be essential in cooperative operations.

Based on the above explanations, there is a possibility that if the members of BMTIs are adversely financially affected due to the pandemic, it might reduce the financial contribution made by the members of BMTIs. In line with Syamsiah et al. (2019), members prioritize BMTI activities. BMTIs need to consider the needs of its members.

Islamic cooperatives provide products and services based on the needs of their members, even though it risks providing that product or services. Senior manager M5 focused on agricultural cooperatives.

> Our Islamic cooperative considers the needs and requirements of the members in their activities as farmers. We support our members by providing education such as farm inputs, farm information, fertilizer distribution, and methods used in facilities, processing, better seeds, irrigation, communications, and consumer goods. Since it is difficult to get support from the government because of budget constraints, we connected with the Japan International Cooperation Agency (JICA) and PUM Netherlands senior experts to educate us on agriculture and business support services.

This implies that the Islamic cooperative applies Islamic principles properly in contrast with Islamic banks. According to Rahman (2007), Islamic banking avoids using risky contracts such as *mudarabah*. To enhance the understanding of the implementation of Islamic principles, BMTI further underlines the role of BMTIs in developing Islamic education. Senior manager M1 said:

> The empowerment of members should be in line with Islamic principles such as the processes of *Halal* and *Tayyib*. Most BMTIs are ignoring providing knowledge on the importance of getting *Berkah* in our life. *Berkah* relates to what our intention is and how we work with it.

M4 emphasized:

> It is important to increase spiritual activities as the spirit of BMTI. The routine *ibadah* enhances the capacity to become more active. After team management BMTI in the morning, there is a reading of *Al-Quran* (at least two verses) and reading the meaning of that verse. In the afternoon, we are closed with reading *Riyadhus Sholihin*. In two weeks, all the team management will have a lecture about Islamic knowledge.

This infers that BMTI establishment satisfies the members' needs on a collective basis. The participation of the members is key to the performance of the cooperative. Member participation is voluntary, which means BMTI depends on the participation of the members. Therefore, the strengthening of members should be primary goals in the BMTI, with programs such as education, relationships, and member empowerment. Islamic empowerment on how the members conduct their businesses is an essential issue in BMTIs. It is consistent with Ernita and AlRozi (2014) that education, training, and motivation material enhance the participation of members in BMTI activities.

11.4.4 Integrating Islamic finance and Islamic social finance through Islamic social capital

BMTIs are already involved in providing relief for their members through Islamic social finance. Islamic social finance has proved useful in delivering social services during the COVID-19 pandemic. BMTIs have provided support for their members (purchasing food for their members and employees). BMTI also receives a corporate social responsibility (CSR) fund from different companies operating in Indonesia. Senior manager M4 said, 'We received CSR funds from the company, and we are allocating that fund into 70% for the *Qard Hassan* account and 30% for the charity account'.
Senior manager M2 said:

> When people apply for finance, the bank will charge an administration fee. However, in our Islamic cooperative, there is no administration fee when applying for finance. We do not agree with BMTI, who charges an administration fee because the member is our family. As part of BMTI, the family has no need to pay anything related to this.

Senior manager M1:

> We already started integrating Islamic social finance and Islamic finance in our activities. When a new member joins with the BMTI, they pay a membership deposit which is considered as the equity of BMTIs. The members apply to get financing from the BMTI; they should follow the BMTIs requirements, which are: BMTI imposed a deduction of 2.5% of the employee's salary for *zakat* every month; BMTI receives *zakat*, *infak*, *sadaqah* and distributes the funds to low-income members and non-members; BMTI does not charge an administration fee for their members who apply for finance; BMTI is charged 1% for provision, but the provision fee is not recognized as income for BMTI. BMTI is allocated the 1% provision fee for the *Qard Hasan* account. *Qard Hasan* is used for Taawun activities (0.5%), which are for the empowerment of members and helping low-income members. The *Taawun* account cannot be used for the management of BMTI and *Takaful* (0.5%) for financing member insurance. Our BMTI already used *zakat*, *infak*, and *sadaqah* as financing tools before the COVID-19 pandemic, but we still need support from other stakeholders such as the National *Zakat* Agency. Our members are categorized as extremely poor and poor people who could not afford to pay *zakat*, *infak*, and *sadaqah*.

Senior manager M5 mentioned that their BMTI is focused on agriculture and uses *Qard Hasan* as a financing tool. I is clear from senior manager M5's response that even in the midst of the pandemic the BMTI does not face any issue in the recovery of financing facilities extended to its members. Senior manager M5 described how their BMTI created an Islamic finance scheme for their members. The views of senior manager M5 are detailed below:

> The Koperasi Pondok Pesantren (*Kopontren*) which is an Islamic cooperative institution in Indonesia like BMIT, does not have any problem with the lack of payment from members even during the crisis. Our *Kopontren* provides the requirement that has equality for both members and management of *Kopontren*. We are transparent to all our members. We believe this openness had a positive impact on our *Kopontren*. The financing procedures carried out by *Kopontren*, started when the *Kopontren* got contracts from the supermarket to provide agricultural products. The *kopontren* announced to their members the supermarket's aim to purchase vegetables in various quantities and prices. The *kopontren* asked their members to provide those vegetables at a lower price. The *kopontren* profited from the difference in price. Based on the contract, the members applied for finance to invest in their business, such as buying seeds, fertilizer, and farm tools. Then they have to pay the fund back to the *kopontren*. Members can pay back the loan without paying interest and fees.

This shows that the Islamic cooperative already uses Islamic social finance instruments to support their members. They support their members by providing demand and monitoring and evaluating their performance. This is consistent with Mansori et al. (2015), who examined how *Qard Hasan* has zero cost borrowing; 'no charge' *Qard Hasan* can be used to fight the pandemic crisis effectively.

The BMTI operate their institutions trying to use Islamic finance and Islamic social finance comprehensively. Since this pandemic started, it has challenged BMTI to integrate with technology.

Senior manager M6 states:

> Currently, we are combining Islamic finance and Islamic social finance with the technology to enhance reaching and achieving the expanded social and financial objectives comprehensively. The pandemic challenges BMTI to be more creative and innovative. We are working together with members who work in the traditional markets and built the website. This website can be used by members and non-members to order products through BMT. Please come to our website – https://warungtetanggamu.com'.

This implies that BMTI already uses Islamic finance contracts and integrates them with Islamic social finance. Since BMTI has a social objective, BMTI established and determined a social fund from the beginning. In the beginning, members were taught that the Islamic cooperative does not belong to management but belongs to its members. Members should give their contribution to support the capital and social fund of the Islamic cooperative. Since there are many members who are not eligible to pay zakat because zakat has a rule on determining who is allowed to receive *zakat*. This concept of members of BMTI contributing to pay *zakat* is supported by Jouti (2019) who believes that this would create an integrated approach for building sustainable Islamic social finance ecosystems.

Since the members of BMTI are those with low incomes, the BMTI needs to reduce their burden by decreasing the cost related to submission and administration as members.

In terms of relationships with the *zakat* institution, this study asked the *zakat* institution manager on their connection with BMTI. Only senior managers M1 and M4 have a relationship with and are supported by the *zakat* collection agency. Senior manager M2 says:

> We already applied to Indonesia's national *zakat* collection agency (BAZNAS) to allow our BMTI to get permission as an institution to receive and distribute the *zakat*. We expect that the *zakat* collection agency will give support to face the impact of the COVID-19 pandemic. We still have not received support from the *zakat* collection agency (BAZNAS).

Senior manager M3 said, '[the] *zakat* collection agency has its programs, they still do not support us yet, even during a pandemic'.

Based on the response received from the senior managers of BMTIs, it is essential to explore the views of the *zakat* institution on its relationship with BMTI. Senior manager Z1 said:

> [The] national *zakat* collection agency (BAZAS) have to manage the *zakat* fund with high expectations on accountability in particular in financial, management, and programs. BMTI should follow the legal requirements imposed on disclosure by the regulators. We found that there is low accountability in BMT on social accountability. There is a need to rearrange the accountability process in BMTI so that it is coherent and aligned with BAZNAS requirements and expectations.

The above response implies that it needs to strengthen networking with formal and informal institutions in BMTI.

11.4.5 Transparency in the distribution of profit-sharing in BMTI

BMTIs could help build the community's wealth through sharing profits. Based on the cooperative principles mentioned, members' economic participation means how members give contributions (investment) to the BMTI, benefit from the surplus, and share any financial burdens the BMTI may have in difficult times. The number of beneficiaries who would be given the financing facility will depend on the decision of all members of BMTI. The transparency of the percentage of profit-sharing BMTIs should be disclosed to the public, and then the public would be interested in joining the BMTIs.

All the respondents mentioned that their BMTIs disclose the percentage of profit-sharing in the BMTIs annual reports. Senior manager M4 points out:

> Based on yearly member meetings, it decided the percentage of profit should be divided into a 20% share for the reserved fund, 40% share for members, 10% sharing for management and the controller, 10% share for the education of members, 10% for supporting local government, and 10% for a social fund with a total of 100%.

This research concluded that BMTI still has potential that remains unrealized. BMTI has already integrated Islamic finance and Islamic social finance smoothly. To achieve full integration between Islamic finance and Islamic social finance, BMTI needs to strengthen its Islamic social capital. Islamic financial institutions need to measure social values and reports so that they can be used to evaluate programs' social impact (Azman & Ali, 2019). It implies that it is essential to develop the gradual convergence of standards, regulations, and infrastructure of BMTIs so they can expand across other countries.

11.5 Conclusion

The extent and severity of the damage caused by the COVID-19 pandemic may not be clear. This study finds that the effect of the COVID-19 pandemic causes the financial crisis of BMTIs members. Financial crises can exert a powerful influence on the shaping of Islamic social capital. The stakeholders (government, national *zakat* agency, *waqf* national agency, members, and scholars) need to support the BMTI movement through policies on increasing the function of Islamic social capital through Islamic finance and the Islamic social finance system. The BMTIs need to enhance their governance, supporting the integration process of the Islamic finance system. The integration of Islamic social finance and Islamic finance system is a useful tool to solve the financial crisis and eradicate poverty. The stakeholders expect to contribute to enhancing Islamic social values to strengthen the Islamic financial system in BMTIs comprehensively.

This study proposes a way to enhance Islamic social capital value to reduce the damage of a pandemic to society and to counter the long-term impact of the COVID-19 pandemic, which are: restructuring the members' payment; enhancing knowledge on Islamic and cooperative principles; integrating Islamic finance and the Islamic social finance system through Islamic social capital; and transparency on distribution of profit-sharing in BMTIs. The Islamic financial system should also use technology through a stakeholder approach that increases the finance and services of BMTIs. There are still limited instruments to measure the effectiveness of Islamic social finance. The government should assist in developing Islamic social finance instruments based on the needs of members and management of BMTIs. The government could influence potential members to join a BMTI by providing financial and non-financial assistance that makes it easy to make a proper blend between BMTI and other social institutions.

References

Abusharbeh, M. T. (2014). Credit risks and profitability of Islamic banks: Evidence from Indonesia. *World Review of Business Research Issue*, *4*(3), 136–147.

Adhariani, D. (2017). *Social Capital, Broken Trust, and Social Accountability: Exploring the Role of Religion in Microfinance Context.* Retrieved from https://scholar.ui.ac.id/en/publications/social-capital-broken-trust-and-social-accountability-exploring-t.

Adnan, M. A., & Ajija, S. R. (2015). The effectiveness of baitul maal wat tamwil in reducing poverty: The case of Indonesian Islamic microfinance institution. *Humanomics*, *31*(2), 160–182.

Ahmed, A. (2010). Global financial crisis: An Islamic finance perspective. *International Journal of Islamic and Middle Eastern Finance and Management*, *3*(4), 306–320.

Ahmed, H. (2002). Financing microenterprises : An analytical study of Islamic microfinance institutions. *Islamic Economic Studies*, *9*(2), 27–64.

Aldi, Andika, & Yodi. (2020). *Ancaman Krisis di Sektor Keuangan Mikro Syariah.* Retrieved from https://knks.go.id/berita/235/ancaman-krisis-di-sektor-keuangan-mikro-syariah?category=1.

Aldrich, D. P. (2010). *Fixing Recovery: Social Capital in Post-crisis Resilience.* Retrieved from https://docs.lib.purdue.edu/cgi/viewcontent.cgi?article=1002&context=pspubs.

Ascarya. (2017). *Baitul Maal Wat Tamwil (BMT): An Integrated Islamic Social and Commercial Financial Institutions in Indonesia.* ISRA-Thomson Reuters, IRTI

Islamic Commercial Law Report 2018. Retrieved from https://www.researchgate.net/publication/320827162_BAITUL_MAAL_WAT_TAMWIL_BMT_AN_INTEGRATED_ISLAMIC_SOCIAL_AND_COMMERCIAL_FINANCIAL_INSTITUTION_IN_INDONESIA.

Azman, S. M. M. S., & Ali, E. R. A. E. (2019). Islamic social finance and imperative of the imperative for social impact measurement. *Al-Shajarah: Journal of Islamic Thought and Civilization of the International Islamic University Malaysia*, Special Issue, 43–68.

Balkin, J. M., & Siegel, R. B. (2006). Principles, practices, and social movements. *University of Pennsylvania Law Review*, *154*(4), 927–950.

Bamidele, R. (2019). *Social Capital: A Tool for effective Sustainable Economic Development in Nigeria*. Retrieved from https://www.researchgate.net/publication/331113991_SOCIAL_CAPITAL_A_TOOL_FOR_EFFECTIVE_SUSTAINABLE_ECONOMIC_DEVELOPMENT_IN_NIGERIA.

Bartik, A. W., Bertrand, M., Cullen, Z. B., Glaeser, E. L., Luca, M., & Stanton, C. T. (2020). *How are small businesses adjusting to covid-19? Early evidence from a survey* (No. w26989).

Bourdieu, P. (1989). Social space and symbolic power. *Sociological Theory*, *7*(1), 14–25.

Bowen, J. (1989). Salat in Indonesia: The social meanings of an Islamic ritual. *MAN*, *24*(4), 600–619.

Bretos, I., & Marcuello, C. (2017). Revisiting globalization challenges and opportunities in the development of cooperatives. *Annals of Public and Cooperative Economics*, *88*(1), 47–73.

Chapra, M. (1992). *Islamic and Economic Challenge*. Leicester: The Islamic Foundation.

Cokrohadisumarto, W. bin M., Ismail, A. G., & Wibowo, K. A. (2016). *BMT Praktik dan Kasus* (I. R. and T. Institute, Ed., pp. 22–23, 27–38). Jakarta: Rajawali Pers.

Coleman, J. S. (1988). Social capital in the creation of human capital. *American Journal of Sociology*, *94*, 95–120.

Dariah, A. R. (2012). Improving social capital of BMT (Baitul Mal Wat Tamwil): An experience from BMT Lathifah, Sumedang Indonesia. *The International Journal of Social Sciences*, *4*(1), 64–70.

Dektop. (2020). *KEMENKOP dan UKM Rilis E-Form Pendataan KUMKM Terdampak Covid-19*. Retrieved from http://www.depkop.go.id/read/kemenkop-dan-ukm-rilis-e-form-pendataan-kumkm-terdampak-covid-19.

Dowla, A. (2006). In credit we trust: Building social capital by Grameen Bank in Bangladesh. *Journal of Socio-Economics*, *35*(1), 102–122. doi: 10.1016/j.socec.2005.12.006.

Ernita, F., & AlRozi, A. (2014). Factors affecting the members participation on cooperative in North Sumatera. *International Journal of Scientific and Technology Research*, *3*(10), 1–5.

Farooqi, A. (2006). Islamic social capital and networking. *Humanomics*, *22*(2), 113–125.

Jouti, A. T. (2019). An integrated approach for building sustainable Islamic social finance ecosystems. *ISRA International Journal of Islamic Finance*, *11*(2), 246–266.

Lendel, V. (2015). *Application of Cooperative Management in Enterprises: Management Approach, Problems and Recommendations* (Sroka, W. & Hittmár, S. Ed.). Cham: Springer.

Lindström, M., & Giordano, G. N. (2016). The 2008 financial crisis: Changes in social capital and its association with psychological wellbeing in the United Kingdom–A panel study. *Social Science & Medicine*, *153*, 71–80.

Mansori, S., Kim, C. S., & Safari, M. (2015). A Shariah perspective review on Islamic microfinance. *Asian Social Science*, *11*(9), 273–280. doi: 10.5539/ass.v11n9p273.

Maselko, J., Hughes, C., & Cheney, R. (2011). Religious social capital : Its measurement an dutility in the study of social determinants of health. *Social Science and Medicine*, *73*, 759–769.

Mathbor, G. (2007). Enhancement of community preparedness for natural disasters. *International Social Work*, *50*(3), 357–369.

McKee, M., & Stuckler, D. (2020). If the world fails to protect the economy, COVID-19 will damage health not just now but also in the future. *Nature Medicine*, *26*(5), 640–642.

McKibbin, W. J., & Fernando, R. (2020). *The global macroeconomic impacts of COVID-19.* Retrieved from https://papers.ssrn.com/sol3/papers.cfm?abstract_id=3547729.

Muttaqin, A. (2012). Model Pembiayaan Baitul Maal Wa Tamwil dan Peranannya dalam Pembinaan Kesejahteraan Usaha Kecil Menengah (UKM). *Jurnal Humanity*, *7*(2), 35–45.

Nasution, A. C. (2013). A framework to analyse the efficiency of Baitul Maal wa Tamwil (BMT) as Islamic microfinance institutions in Indonesia. *Proceeding of Sharia Economic Conference*, February, 81–86. Retrieved from http://jistecs.org/sites/default/files/proceeding/7_Atiqi%20Chollisni%20Nasution.pdf.

Ng, A., Ibrahim, H., & Mirakhor, A. (2015). On building social capital for Islamic finance. *International Journal of Islamic and Middle Eastern Finance and Management*, *8*(1), 2–19.

Novkovic, S. (2005). *Cooperative Business: What is the Role of Cooperative Principles and Values?* Retrieved from https://www.researchgate.net/publication/237577021_Cooperative_business_What_is_the_role_of_cooperative_principles_and_values.

Organisation for Economic Co-operation and Development (OECD). (2020). *The Impact of the Coronavirus (COVID-19) Crisis on Development Finance.* Retrieved from http://www.oecd.org/coronavirus/policy-responses/the-impact-of-the-coronavirus-covid-19-crisis-on-development-finance-9de00b3b/.

Ozili, P. K., & Arun, T. (2020). *Spillover of COVID-19: Impact on the Global Economy.* Retrieved from https://www.researchgate.net/publication/340236487_Spillover_of_COVID-19_impact_on_the_Global_Economy.

Pitas, N., & Ehmer, C. (2020). Social capital in the response to COVID-19. *American Journal of Health Promotion.* Retrieved from https://journals.sagepub.com/doi/full/10.1177/0890117120924531.

Porta, D., & Pavan, E. (2017). Repertoires of knowledge practices: Social movements in times of crisis. *Qualitative Research in Organizations and Management: An International Journal*, *12*(4), 297–314. doi: 10.1108/QROM-01-2017-1483.

Prasetyo, A., Effendi, J., & Nursyamsiah, T. (2018). The effectiveness of Islamic microfinance distribution on microbusiness owner's poverty alleviation (case study: BMT Bina Masyarakat Purworejo). *Jurnal AFKARUNA*, *14*(1), 1–26.

Putnam, R. (1993). The prosperous community: Social capital and public life. *American Prospect*, *13*, 35–42.

Rixon, D. (2013). Are co-operative principles reflected in performance reporting? A case study of insurance co-operatives. *International Journal of Co-Operative Management*, *6*(2), 77–91.

Shahwan, S., Shafii, Z., Mirza, A. A. I., Sapian, S., Salleh, S., Nawai, N., & Haris, A. (2018). A review on product development of Islamic social finance in tijari sector. *International Journal of Islamic Business*, *3*(2), 59–66.

Siebel, H., & Agung, D. (2006). Islamic Microfinance in Indonesia. Retrieved from https://ideas.repec.org/p/zbw/uocaef/20062.html.

Smolo, E., & Ismail, A. G. (2011). A theory and contractual framework of Islamic micro-financial institutions' operations. *Journal of Financial Services Marketing*, *15*(4), 287–295. doi: 10.1057/fsm.2010.24.

Smolo, E, & Mirakhor, A. (2010). The global financial crisis and its implications for the Islamic financial industry. *Journal of Islamic and Middle Eastern Finance and Management*, *3*(4), 372–385.

Syamsiah, N., Syahrii, A., & Susanto, I. (2019). Peran Koperasi Syariah Baitul Tamwil Muhammadiyah terhadap Pemberdayaan Usaha Kecil dan Menengah di Bandar Lampung. *Al Amin: Jurnal Kajian Ilmu Dan Budaya Islam*, *2*(1), 63–73.

University of Minnesota Extension. (2018). Strengthening Social Capital Examples. Retrieved from http://srdc.msstate.edu/fop/levelthree/trainarc/socialcapital/strengtheningnetworks.pdf.

Valentinov, V. (2004). Toward a social capital theory of cooperative organisation. *Journal of Cooperatives Studies*, *37*(3), 5–20.

Wahyuni, E. T. (2008). The accountability of Islamic microfinance institution: Evidence From Indonesia. *The Winners*, *9*(1), 22–34.

Wardiwiyono, S. (2012). Internal control system for Islamic micro financing. *International Journal of Islamic and Middle Eastern Finance and Management*, *5*(4), 340–352.

Wilson, R. (2007). Making development assistance sustainable through Islamic microfinance. *IIUM Journal of Economics and Management*, *2*(2), 197–217.

Woolcock, M., & Narayan, D. (2000). Social capital: Implications for development theory, research, and policy what is social capital? *The World Bank Research Observer*, *15*(2), 225–249.

Yamaguchi, A. (2013). Impact of social capital on the psychological well-being of adolescents. *International Journal of Psychological Studies*, *5*(2), 100.

Zain, N. R. M., & Ali, E. R. A. E. (2017). An analysis on Islamic social finance for protection and preservation of Maqāṣid Al-Sharī'ah. *Journal of Islamic Finance*, *176*(5872), 1–9.

12 Unlocking Islamic social finance to assist micro small medium enterprises in Brunei Darussalam

Khairul Hidayatullah Basir and Mohd Hairul Azrin Besar

12.1 Introduction

Many businesses around the world, particularly micro, small, medium enterprises (MSMEs) have been greatly impacted by the COVID-19 outbreak. According to the results of surveys carried out by the Organisation for Economic Co-operation and Development (OECD) on the impact of COVID-19 crisis on SMEs worldwide, more than half of SMEs face severe losses in revenue and one-third of SMEs fear they will be out of business without further support within one month and up to half within three months (OECD, 2020).

Micro-businesses are more vulnerable than SMEs due to their smaller size, lack of access to credit, and the risky nature of business. This has forced governments around the world to find ways to help fund SMEs through government relief funds, direct lending to SMEs, and providing loan guarantees to commercial banks. Generally, the expansion of funding to help MSMEs is in the form of loan schemes with lenient terms. For instance, the easing of the accessibility of loan schemes means extending the group of potential beneficiaries, simplifying and speeding up procedures to receive loans, and offering more favourable terms and reduced interest rates (OECD, 2020).

The introduction of these loan instruments may sound promising. However, even if the economy is set to recover, it would take some time for MSMEs to recover and they will take a longer time to pay off their loans. Therefore, an alternative mode of financing is required to help ease the burden of MSMEs that simultaneously promotes their growth and development.

Brunei Darussalam (herein Brunei) is not an exception in experiencing the impact of the pandemic. Shopping malls and stores see fewer patrons. Businesses and tenants are struggling to meet monthly rent payments and salaries. There are efforts by the government to help these businesses in order to stimulate the economy. Islamic finance has the potential to be a crucial tool to offer governments a strong non-traditional source of financing and has the possibility of being a game-changer, especially in Islamic economies.

12.2 Brunei's response to COVID-19

Brunei recorded its first imported COVID-19 case on 9 March 2020. Since then, Brunei has taken several preventive measures and restrictions in order to curb the spread of the pandemic such as temporary closure of several *tamu* (stalls) in Temburong, Tutong, and Belait districts; the cancellation of all *gerai* Ramadhan (Ramadhan stalls) under the provision of the Municipal Department, District Department, and Youth and Sports Department; food outlets such as restaurants, cafes, food courts, and *tamu* and its equivalent are not permitted to provide dine-in services and only permitted to provide takeaway services; the temporary closure of all sports complexes and facilities in the country, including private gyms and golf courses; temporary closure of schools and higher institutions; and closing borders which affects trade and the tourism industry. In efforts to help local businesses survive the downturn, the government provided an economic stimulus package with measures such as loan payment deferrals, wage subsidies, and social security contributions (Haji Abu Bakar, 2020).

The use of Islamic social finance tools to support MSMEs in Brunei was reflected by the Brunei Islamic Religious Council (MUIB). The MUIB, through their general administration fund, has also given financial assistance to micro-businesses and the self-employed whose income was affected due to the outbreak of COVID-19. A total of BND1.93 million was distributed among 2,154 people identified by the council's task force. This welfare assistance was also rendered to non-Muslims. The MUIB welfare aid recipients are made up of small business owners, self-employed individuals, and low-income workers officially registered under four ministries – the Ministry of Home Affairs, Ministry of Primary Resources and Tourism, Ministry of Transport and Info Communications (MTIC), and Ministry of Culture, Youth, and Sports (MCYS).

The welfare assistance funds were derived from MUIB's general administration fund, which collects money from religious services such as *halal* certification and permit fees; revenue from *syariah* courts; bank interest; shop rentals; sale and acquisition of government land, and money from *Baitul Mal* as well as unclaimed assets. The bulk of the financial aid was channelled to market vendors registered under the home affairs ministry, with BND1.72 million to be distributed among 1,910 market vendors. A total of BND72,900 was shared between 81 tour guides, while BND104,400 was handed out to 116 taxi drivers, ride-sharing DART drivers, and speedboat drivers registered with MTIC. Forty-seven small business owners received cumulative welfare assistance of BND 42,300 from the MCYS.

In addition, the country also provided financial relief for businesses considering the effect of the pandemic where people was encouraged to stay home and only go out if necessary. As a result, business slowed in tandem with the reduction in the consumption of goods and services in the economy.

12.3 Islamic social finance tools

MSMEs have always been assessed as high-risk entities by financial institutions, mainly due to the lack of assets to be collateralized and the lack of business track records and accounts (Abdul Rahman, 2007; Rahman, 2010). Considering these risks, financial institutions would normally apply stringent credit checks and rules to ensure they are protected or at least able to mitigate the respective risks (Ahmed, 2007). Acknowledging this and the importance of providing inclusive banking to all members of society, the notion of microfinancing was pushed to the mainstream with success stories such as those of the Grameen bank model, village bank model, credit union model, and self-help group model (Mobin & Ahmad 2017).

However conventional, microfinance still does not eliminate the element of interest, which is considered *riba* (Ahmed, 2007; Haneef et al., 2015; Mobin & Ahmad 2017; Rahman, 2010), where loans are still charged at a high rate of interest making it difficult for those with low incomes, in this case, MSMEs, to repay the loans. From another point of view, these institutions lack financial resources in the first place; extending interest-based loans will definitely increase their financial burden as they not only have to pay the capital but also the interest charged. Supporters of conventional microfinance would argue that the investors and depositors will require certain returns from the use of their funds considering the opportunity and cost of investing their funds in other safer, high-yielding instruments (Ahmed, 2007; Rahman, 2010).

Although these Islamic social financing instruments have been used since the emergence of Islam 1,500 years ago, its modern and contextual application remains to be explored and developed. The beauty of Islam as a way of life proved that these instruments have survived the journey of time and will always be relevant across time and space.

It is in this juncture that Islamic social financing instruments may be viable in providing a source of funding and finance for MSMEs, as the basis of these instruments is benevolent contribution, a one-sided contract without considering returns to the contributors (Ahmed, 2007; Rahman, 2010). The paper further examines three social financial contracts, namely *sadaqah*, *zakat*, and *waqf* in the Islamic sphere, which can conceptually assist MSMEs in obtaining the financial resources they need. This is also extended to the unprecedented environment of the COVID-19 pandemic, in which regulators, custodians, and the community in Brunei have leveraged these social contracts to sustain the economy at large and assist business entities (including MSMEs) and consumers (especially those with low incomes).

12.3.1 Sadaqah

The first social contract is the contract of *sadaqah*, which is a donation or voluntary charitable contribution (Zuhayli et al., 2007). The nature of the contract is an onerous one where the contributor or donor gives away his or her assets to a preferred charitable cause without expecting any return. *Sadaqah* has proven to be a flexible contract where the assets are not restricted to certain recipients or need to be preserved (Zuhayli et al., 2007). Although in its original context, *sadaqah* is used for benevolent intentions rather than economic benefit or business growth, the COVID-19 pandemic has shown that the contract can be invaluable in the sustainability of MSMEs badly hit by the pandemic. In Brunei itself, although there was no formal lockdown, the notion of social distancing and avoiding crowds has impacted many businesses, especially the service sector. Restaurants, barber, tailors, and to some extent retailers saw fewer customers subscribing to their service. In the midst of the pandemic, most business premises were ordered to close, resulting in them bearing fixed costs such as rent and employee expenses. Businesses, especially MSMEs, must find alternative and innovative business models for their survival. It was observed that MSMEs, especially in the food and beverages industry, started to open up their services to serve those on the frontline by inviting members of the public to contribute *sadaqah* in the form of food that is then cooked and delivered. This has provided a platform for the public to be involved in charitable causes while at the same time providing for MSMEs through the engagement of their service.

The potential of *sadaqah*, as a voluntary benevolent platform, can be seen in the collection of the Brunei Covid Relief Fund, which has been set up with proper governance and transparency by the government to provide financial assistance to the nation in its endeavour to combat COVID-19. As of 13 May 2020, the fund has collected BND14,128,776.79 from public contributions.

12.3.2 Zakat

The second social contract is contribution through *zakat*, or compulsory tithe, chargeable to individuals or corporations that possess the capacity and wealth in accordance with the requirement of *zakat* (Rahman, 2010). The *zakat* is to be distributed to the eight groups identified the *Quranic* verse, At Taubah 9:60. *Zakat*, unlike *sadaqah*, is mandatory in Islam on specific assets owned by individuals or entities. The eight groups are the needy (*Al-Fuqara*), the poor (*Al-Masakin*), the *zakat* administrators (*Al-Amilin*), those whose hearts are keen towards Islam (*Al-Muallaf*), those in bondage (*Ar-Riqab*), the debt-ridden (*Al-Gharimin*), those in the cause of Allah (*Fi Sabillilah*) and the wayfarer (*Ibn-Sabil*). *Zakat* can be an important component of national and NGO emergency support programs. Donors typically require that *zakat* be disbursed within one year of being given. This focus on an immediate benefit is well suited to crisis response. *Zakat* donors support both the poor and the economically insecure, an area of increased need in the pandemic. *Zakat* donors often give cash transfers, which can be especially important in emergencies.

Relevant to the extension in the definition of recipients, in Brunei, this is shown through the contribution of capital to those with low incomes to sustain them. The program named 'Program Pengupayaan Asnaf Zakat' (PROPAZ) was created to provide capital to MSMEs and provide them with training to ensure they will be able to stand on their own. Acknowledging the loss of income, especially for MSMEs, *zakat* disbursement has included entrepreneurs in the service industry such as taxi drivers, boat operators, small stall market operators, and others identified by the authorities to receive financial assistance.

Zakat agencies can adopt a structured approach to the United Nations Sustainable Development Goals (SDG) alignment and COVID-19 impact, while banks, investors, and other financers can likewise optimize their SDG impact. However, *zakat* agencies need to be more proactive in their collection and *zakat* fund management to properly serve the population. A good point to consider is the situation in Indonesia where the potential of *zakat* is valued at around 286 trillion rupiah a year, according to the national *zakat* body BAZNAS. But the actual collection is a far cry, at around only 9.5 trillion rupiah (USD$577.3 million) in 2019 (Winosa, 2020).

12.3.3 Waqf

The third contract is *waqf*, also known as charitable endowment, which is not compulsory but is highly encouraged in Islam. Brunei, since the discovery of oil in 1929, has been blessed with abundant natural resources of oil and gas that has enabled the country to finance its public spending, including generous welfare benefits (Horton, 1986). In the provision of such public amenities, the current generation is unaware of the previous benevolent contribution of the older generations who have willingly contributed assets such as land, buildings, and other public assets in the form of *waqf*. The utilization of *waqf* as a source of assistance for MSMEs has not been rigorously explored, although, in other countries such as Singapore, Malaysia, and Indonesia, it has been shown to produce competitive business entities that contribute to the economic development of the country. In addition to that, *waqf* has also been utilized in providing education to the masses, as seen in the establishment of Al-Azhar University in Egypt (Ahmed, 2007).

Most of the literature on *waqf* as instruments of microfinance provide cash *waqf* as the seed fund or initial capital outlay to be paid back to the *waqf* fund without charging any interest. The fund used for finance may be taken from the contributed fund itself or from the return of investing the capital contributed pursuant to the requirement of preserving the *waqf* asset. It is interesting to open the idea of microfinancing instruments not restricted to financial assets, which are prone to rent-seeking behaviour (El-Gamal, 2003; 2007), but extended to common assets required by MSMEs. The main burden for any businesses is the initial setup, which includes the procurement of fixed assets directly or indirectly used in the operation of the business. This normally results in sunk costs to the business, which it needs to painstakingly shoulder even before production or selling their goods or services starts. If such a cost is commonly shared or provided by an independent entity that ensures the assets are working efficiently for the users, this will help MSMEs more than financial assistance, which they will have to repay in the future.

During the COVID-19 pandemic, due to the requirements to close premises, most fixed assets were left idle. However, from a financial point of view, this incurs expenses such as rent, depreciation, maintenance, and insurance. These expenses exert financial effects on the accounts of MSMEs even though there is no active production or business activity. Fortunately, big businesses such as restaurants have also been observed willingly loaning their fixed assets for benevolent use, such as a temporary kitchen to provide food for those on the frontlines, vehicles for delivery of goods, hotel rooms for quarantine purposes, and even paying employees their full salaries so they can volunteer on the frontline. If this were translated through the provision of *waqf* assets in easing MSME operations, such as common machinery, premises, vehicles, it would save them incurring fixed expenses and ensure their sustainability in a time of hardship.

The Islamic social finance instruments have their own unique characteristics enabling them to be used in different circumstances tailored to the respective needs of the recipient. Combining the three in the quest to empower MSMEs would be interesting as there is no one definite solution to assisting MSMEs to promote their growth and sustainability.

There is much talk about microfinancing, and when people talk about Islamic social finance, it is all about *zakat*, *waqf*, and *sadaqah*. In most of the literature, each of these is studied on its own. The needs of different MSMEs might be different. Some MSMEs may need financial assistance to pay rent and wages, and some may need capital in the form of machinery and equipment for their businesses.

Previous studies have looked at individual contracts. Each contract has its own unique features and serves their purposes. In order to cater to the needs of MSMEs, a combination of contracts is recommended.

12.4 Prospects, issues, and challenges

In 2018, the total collection for *zakat fitrah* amounted to BND967,188.51, and *zakat harta* totalled BND16,588,175.08 (Mahmud, 2019). However, the use of *zakat* funds is limited to eligible recipients only. Therefore, *sadaqah* can be considered for those who are ineligible to receive *zakat* funds. This section will discuss the prospect, identifiable issues, and challenges of funding MSMEs through *sadaqah*, *waqf*, or *zakat*.

12.4.1 Sadaqah

Sadaqah is very flexible in nature. However, careful implementation is required as *sadaqah* funds will be large as it aims to help MSMEs. Funds from *sadaqah* can also be channelled to non-Muslim-owned MSMEs as long as their business operations are *shariah*-compliant. There are two factors that need to be taken into consideration, namely, transparency and custodian. As the pool of funds is from public contributions, reports on its utilization must be as transparent as possible in order to gain public trust. Proper formal and informal reporting could be done through press conferences, websites, or social media on a regular basis. Formal disclosure may include minimum information such as the sources and utilization of the fund, which can mirror the report of charitable funds for the Islamic financial institutions advocated by the Accounting and Auditing Organization for Islamic Financial

Institutions (AAOIFI). This is important to ensure that the donor is aware of the proper use of the fund, even though in its initial context, the *sadaqah* contributor may not demand such information. Nevertheless, it is still important that the custodian of this fund is transparent in their operation, taking it as their responsibility to the trustee who is accountable not only to the donor but ultimately to Allah.

While financial reporting, as usual practice, can be done on an annual basis, timely reports are also important as it provides more meaningful information to the donor. The custodian of the fund can either be a person or an entity in a formal or informal capacity, which highlights the flexibility of *sadaqah*. The COVID-19 situation has inculcated the notion of social distancing and reduced direct human contact, and technology has been leveraged as a mechanism of payment or transfer of funds. Hence, there is an increase in the use of digital platforms such as online payment, mobile payment, and virtual card transfer used by people. On the one hand, this raises the concern of digital security and safety, ensuring the fund for *sadaqah* is properly transferred for the said purpose and not misused for other activities. On the other hand, a positive side of technology is the easy access and quick processing of the *sadaqah*, which can provide financial assistance to the respective receiver without delay, as digital transactions are mostly prompt and can be executed at any time.

During this digital era, the use of technology must be secured, particularly in mobilizing the fund. Every transaction must be properly traced so that the source of the fund is known. In the Brunei context, most of the online transactions for *sadaqah* are made through online and mobile transfer platforms offered by the Islamic Bank in Brunei. In addition to that, short messaging services (SMS) have also been used as a platform for the public to donate. A major challenge for online transactions however is access to the people, especially those in need and senior citizens. In accessing the digital platform, the public need to be aware of the respective tools needed to access the service, from the availability of access points such as computer terminals and mobile devices, connectivity to the internet, the availability on online access accounts, such as emails, and in some instances security peripherals such as dongles.

On the other side, MSMEs must also be able to access this fund from the trustee. Unlike funding from formal institutions, such as a bank or any other regulatory authority, *sadaqah* can be received informally, and its distribution may not be subject to the strict financial evaluation of the receiver. This is due to the fact that the donor is not required to give back the donation or generate any returns. Once *sadaqah* is given, the donor expects the fund to be used for the specific purpose, as mentioned earlier, or general utilization such as to assist MSMEs. The restriction would centre on the utilization of the fund for *shariah* compliance purposes, which means the MSMEs and fund custodian are responsible for following through on this. The custodian as the trustee of the fund would have to evaluate, ensure, and stress to the receiver that the fund has been donated for a certain purpose, or in general that it should be used for *shariah*-compliant activities. This needs to be reported to the donor in discharging the custodian duty as trustee.

However, MSMEs needs to be transparent and act in a trustworthy capacity ensuring the fund is utilized as directed. Perhaps the major challenge for social finance through *sadaqah* is its informal and flexible nature, where the element of trust is important. If the process is done in the absence of trust, it will be subject to opportunistic and unethical behaviour, such as fraud. However, to formalize the process of *sadaqah* would discourage donors as they have to go through tedious processes that are not needed in the first place as their intention is mainly to donate to a cause.

During the COVID-19 crisis in Brunei, *sadaqah* worked effectively in sustaining and supporting MSMEs, especially those in the food and beverages sector. Faced with the difficulty of losing their sales due to restrictions imposed on businesses, the vendors had to find alternative ways to ensure they sustained their businesses. Opportunities opened up in supporting those on the frontline who were busy caring for patients and those involved in efforts containing the virus and stopping it from spreading in the community. In appreciating their effort and contribution, calls were made to provide those on the frontline with proper food and drinks so that they could concentrate on the tasks they were given. The food and beverage vendors were assigned to achieve this goal by producing food and beverages for those on the frontline; this was wholly funded through the *sadaqah* of the public. It worked efficiently, sustaining MSMEs while at the same time supporting the greater good of providing food to those on the frontlines.

The application of social media as a platform to match donors with vendors was seen as a tool fostering an environment of trust between the two, where the vendors, in their good faith, provided pictures of the food delivered to those on the frontline as proof. As a result, this attracted more donors to come forward and choose vendors to execute their *sadaqah*. The anonymity of the donors was also preserved by the vendors, which was much appreciated. This fostered a good relationship between the donor and the vendors, creating another bonus outcome of customer loyalty in the provision of the service. Although there is no formal governance structure to monitor the *sadaqah* process, it has enabled MSMEs to weather COVID-19 while at the same time gaining customer loyalty, trust, reducing waste, and importantly sustaining their businesses.

12.4.2 Waqf

Islamic Religious Councils Act and Kadis Courts Act, Chapter 77 states that the Islamic Religious Council (MUIB) is responsible for all religious matters in Brunei including *zakat*, *waqf*, *baitulmal*, *halal* certificate of pilgrimage, and mosque. The MUIB's role can be split into two categories. Firstly, as the sole trustee of all *baitulmal* property, all *waqfs*, all general vows, and all trusts of any kind MUIB can make any charitable trust to support and promote Islam in accordance with Islamic law. Secondly, as a *nazir* (manager of *waqf*) and trustee of all mosques in Brunei. In short, the MUIB is the ultimate custodian for *waqf* and *zakat* properties in the country.

Although *waqf* of wealth, which mostly constitutes land and properties, had been traditionally given by the public at large, the upkeep, maintenance, and development of the property is done by the custodian. Hence the scope of *waqf* application in Brunei is still limited and mainly focuses on mosques, schools, land, and cemeteries. According to a study done by Abu Bakar et al. (2020), the majority of Muslims in Brunei still believe that *waqf* is only limited to religious activities such as mosques and cemeteries without any element of development and investment of *waqf* property. Currently, there is an agency under the purview of the custodian, an investment body that is responsible for managing part of the properties for the purpose of expanding and developing it for the benefit of Muslims in Brunei. The commercialization or alternative utilization of *waqf* assets to spur economic activities is yet to be developed.

On the one hand, in any business, the main part of their expenses is in the procurement and maintenance of fixed assets. On the other hand, the procurement of these assets does not guarantee profit to the business entities as these assets are just tools to assist in the production of goods and the provision of services. Either way, businesses will need a large amount of funding in their initial operation to finance these fixed assets, which will eat up their working capital. These assets may be common within the industry, such as specialized machines or tools, or among businesses, such as the need for premises to serve their customers. Ironically, during the COVID-19 pandemic, it was observed that rent was still collected, even in the situation where businesses were mandated to close down their premises. In Brunei itself, the government encouraged property owners to have empathy and reduce or cancel rent during the period as a form of corporate or individual social responsibility as this will help the affected businesses to reduce their costs and ensure their survival in the absence of revenue generation.

Acknowledging this and the notion that we should, as much as possible, reduce rent-seeking behaviour, it would perhaps be appropriate to consider *waqf* as a mechanism to fund the fixed assets of businesses, especially MSMEs. The provision of *waqf* buildings for MSMEs to operate without paying rent, but ensuring they maintain the property would greatly reduce their fixed cost. This would greatly help MSMEs by providing financial relief to them as this mechanism would decrease their operational cost. Furthermore, this mechanism would also allow MSMEs to share resources between each other with the spirit of brotherhood where coworking space concepts can be practiced.

Therefore, this could solve the problems of MSMEs unable to pay rent, should there be another pandemic, such as the situation faced during COVID-19, or any other uncertainties that could happen in the future. This would also be appropriate in the provision of online-based businesses where most MSMEs do not have the capacity or capability of developing and maintaining an online platform. Similarly, as observed during the pandemic, the government, and other entities such as the Islamic banks, provided online platforms where MSMEs could market their product while at the same time providing an online payment mechanism. *Waqf* can be used in the provision of such a platform with the maintenance costs collectively borne by the MSMEs, which will greatly reduce the cost if it was to be taken up by a single business. Such a platform not only reduces the cost for the MSMEs but benefits the consumers in the form of reduced competitive price of goods and services, a win-win situation for all parties. A similar practice has been observed previously in open-source coding, as a platform for professionals to build up their programs or software by collectively contributing to the development of the code, which is also available for others to use. Such activity can be achieved through *waqf* contribution for the betterment of society at large and, in this context, MSMEs.

Aside from the above, *waqf* assets could also be used in a commercial setting, which can generate income for the *waqf*, ensuring its sustainability. If the *waqf* assets consist of funds, it can be invested in an income-generating investment or financial instruments where the returns can be used by the public or MSMEs. Any proceeds of the *waqf* properties, for instance, business profit-sharing through the *mudarabah* concept, should be invested in order to maintain the operation of physical *waqf* assets such as buildings. The potential of *waqf* in promoting MSMEs should not be overlooked. *Waqf*-based business is seen as a form of entrepreneurship that may be regarded as the disposal of wealth by a philanthropist or *nazir* for the purpose of creating wealth preferably for those in need or those with low incomes (Iman & Mohammad, 2017), which can replace the rent-seeking ideology. Hence, the business manager of *waqf* or *nazir* must be creative in managing *waqf* properties.

Although as prescribed by the act, MUIB is the sole custodian for *waqf* assets, and the authority can set up subsidiaries that can be entrusted with specific development and management of properties or assets benefiting MSMEs and ensuring the assets are productive. These subsidiaries are expected to report on the performance of the respective assets and its development to the authority for proper monitoring. The major challenge for *waqf* in funding MSMEs in Brunei is the interpretation of *waqf* assets so that it is not limited to physical properties, land, or buildings but to encompass other assets including software, financial instruments, and others.

12.4.3 Zakat

Zakat is more restricted in terms of its use. Should it be utilized in providing capital to MSMEs, only those who fall under the definition of the *asnaf* (beneficiaries of *zakat* found in the *Quran*) can benefit from it. Some may claim that this restriction may not be beneficial for MSMEs as it only caters for those with low incomes and those in need. This perception is not accurate as the poor and needy are one group defined as *asnaf*; there are other categories that can claim from the *zakat* fund. In addition, it also gives specific outlets for those in dire need, who under normal circumstances would be excluded from formal financial institutions. As such, *zakat* can cater to them directly without stringent financial assessment prior to the disbursement of funds. This is the beauty of *zakat*; in having restrictions on its distribution, it actually caters specifically for those who need funding and will never be granted from other institutions.

Prior to the COVID-19 pandemic, the MUIB has been proactive in providing capital, training, and providing business opportunities for the *asnaf* to help them be self-sufficient and later become contributors of *zakat* rather than receivers. Several successful projects were highlighted, such as the duck farm run by a single mother who used to be the receiver of *zakat*. Her success has turned her life around from being a receiver to being an employer of several workers who assist her in managing the farm. Such projects and awarding of capital however, do not turn all receivers into success stories. For instance, in the research conducted by Bashir et al. (2012), the authorities granted the recipient boats and other tools for fishing intended to sustain their livelihood. Unfortunately, the recipient had a more urgent need to pay off his debt, forcing him to sell the boat and equipment to get cash. There is also a case where the recipients of the tools cannot afford to maintain the assets given, which rendered them unusable.

During the COVID-19 pandemic, the *zakat* fund was extended to other micro-businesses, self-employed individuals, and other businesses affected by the closure of their business operations due to the pandemic. This mostly includes MSMEs in different lines of business from small traders in the public market to water taxi drivers. This is a fresh outlook from the previous recipients of *zakat* who are mostly evaluated on their individual capacity and household income rather than the business they operate. Indirectly it shows that although *zakat* is managed and distributed according to certain restrictions, it is not restrictive in nature but enables a wider inclusion of the *asnaf* in pursuing economic benefit. Hence the opportunity to fund MSMEs through the *zakat* fund is there, especially for the *asnaf*.

The main challenges that can be seen in the utilization of the *zakat* fund for MSME funding is in the interpretation of *asnaf* and how the fund can be distributed to the respective MSMEs. Basically, there is no requirement for the capital to be intact, which can be seen in *waqf*, and there is no condition attached to the disbursement of the fund to control the utilization of the fund for a specific purpose. The *asnaf* are also not required to provide financial reports or progress on the capital extended, neither on the performance of the MSMEs or whether they are making a profit or loss. It would, however, be unfair if the extension of funding to MSMEs is considered as a one-off, and they are expected to fall out of the *asnaf* categories by receiving financial assistance. Hence, an update of their progress may be needed to ensure that they receive the assistance they need, which may not be wholly financial in nature.

12.4.4 Combination of sadaqah, waqf, *and* zakat

The decision to choose which is better depends entirely on the needs of the respective business. For example, for a business in need of financial assistance only, it may opt for either *zakat* or *sadaqah*. However, if a business requires a new office, capital and financial assistance may be granted in a combination of *waqf* and *sadaqah* or *waqf* and *zakat*. It is more a contextual consideration for the MSMEs. As highlighted above, the pre-COVID-19 environment showed the rigid use of these social financial contracts, whereas during the pandemic itself, it has been used dynamically to sustain and assist MSMEs in ensuring their survival. In the long term, it is envisioned that funding MSMEs should not be restricted to one form of social financial contract but can be utilized in combination or in accordance with their needs.

For instance, *zakat* or *sadaqah* can be used in the initial setting-up of working capital for MSMEs. But ensuring their funds are not tied down to purchases of fixed assets, *waqf* can be used to provide the basic infrastructure and tools needed to produce goods and the provision of services. As the business grows, it may need further funding, depending on its needs; working capital, for example, can be raised through *sadaqah* as a voluntary contribution to assist MSMEs to grow. This may also influence MSMEs to operate differently as a social enterprise rather than a profit-seeking enterprise, which is mostly judged by the generation and growth of their bottom line and balance sheet size. Although this is a conceptual proposition that stems from the observation of the country's utilization of these social financial contracts during the COVID-19 period, it does show promise if properly implemented.

In efforts to combine the Islamic social finance contract to help MSMEs, there are several factors that need to be taken into consideration. For example, a combination of *sadaqah* and *waqf* in the Brunei context may give rise to operational challenges as these two may be under separate agencies. As mentioned earlier, *waqf*, under the current law, is solely under the custody of the MUIB, whereas *sadaqah* may be managed or entrusted to informal trustees whether individuals or entities. Regulating *sadaqah* may also defeat its purpose as donors mostly expect to retain their anonymity in donating their funds to their preferred cause.

Taking stock of the above, providing needed funding to MSMEs does not hamper efforts or the notion of utilizing social financial contracts in an integrated manner.

12.5 Conclusion and the way forward

The emergence of the pandemic has shown that the modern economic and financial system has its flaws and was unable to protect the local economy from an unprecedented crisis that forced the world to look for alternative financing that could help stimulate the economy by supporting MSMEs. This chapter aims to find ways to support and empower MSMEs during this pandemic, or other uncertainties, through the application of Islamic social finance. With Islamic social finance, profit maximization is not the prime motive. In fact, the contribution is a form of *sadaqah jariah* (a continuous and ongoing charity) whose benefit continues to flow until the *akhirat* (Judgement Day), and this more important for the donor and contributor of *sadaqah*, *waqf*, or *zakat*. It is also proposed that a combination of contracts would meet the needs of different MSMEs holistically rather than just focusing on one, and this should be further empirically explored in future studies. In the future, Islamic social finance may also be considered for the different lifecycles or the expansion and development of MSMEs. In addition, observing the potential of the social finance contract from what has been done during the pandemic, the proposition of this study can also be used as a guide and expanded to prepare for any future uncertainties faced by businesses, which might be in the form of a pandemic, economic crisis, or any other challenges. COVID-19 was unexpected and has affected the global economy. In the crisis, the utilization of the Islamic social financing contract seems to positively contribute to the sustainability and empowerment of MSMEs.

References

Abdul Rahman, A. R. (2007). Islamic microfinance: A missing component in Islamic banking. *Kyoto Bulletin of Islamic Area Studies*, *1*(2): 38–53.

Abu Bakar, M., Ahmad, S., Salleh, A. D., & Md Salleh, M. F. (2020). The SWOT analysis of waqf governance in Brunei Darussalam. *International Research of Shariah, Muamalat and Islam*, *2*(3): 1–22.

Ahmed, H. (2007). Waqf-based microfinance: realizing the social role of Islamic finance. Retrieved from https://www.findevgateway.org/sites/default/files/publications/files/mfg-en-paper-waqf-based-microfinance-realizing-the-social-role-of-islamic-finance-2007.pdf.

Bashir, M. S., Sarbini, H. N. A. H., & Abdullah, H. R. (2012). Zakat management and capital assistances programme in Brunei Darussalam. *The Journal of Muamalat and Islamic Finance Research*, 204(1167): 1–68.

El-Gamal, M. A. (2003). Interest and the paradox of contemporary Islamic law and finance. *Fordham International Law Journal*, 27, 108–149.

El-Gamal, M. A. (2007). Mutuality as an antidote to rent-seeking Shariah arbitrage in Islamic finance. *Thunderbird International Business Review*, *49*(2), 187–202.

Haji Abu Bakar, R. (2020). Over 2,100 small business owners to get $300 for three months. *The Scoop*. Retrieved from https://thescoop.co/2020/04/18/over-2100-small-business-owners-to-get-300-for-three-months/.

Haneef, M. A., Pramanik, A. H., Mohammed, M. O., Amin, M. F. B., & Muhammad, A. D. (2015). Integration of waqf-Islamic microfinance model for poverty reduction. *International Journal of Islamic and Middle Eastern Finance and Management*, 8(2),246–270.

Horton, A. V. M. (1986). British administration in Brunei 1906–1959. *Modern Asian Studies*, *20*(2), 353–374.

Iman, A. H. M., & Mohammad, M. T. S. H. (2017). Waqf as a framework for entrepreneurship. *Humanomics*, *33*(4), 419–440.

Mahmud, R. (2019, May 2). 319 Amils appointed for Zakat collection. *Borneo Bulletin*. Retrieved from https://borneobulletin.com.bn/2019/05/319-amils-appointed-for-zakat-collection/.

Mobin, M. A., & Ahmad, A. U. F. (2017). Achieving sustainable economic development through Islamic microfinance and the potential of a proposed two-tier mudarabah waqf business model. In Kabir Hassan, M. (Ed.) *Handbook of Empirical Research on Islam and Economic Life*. Cheltenham, UK: Edward Elgar Publishing.

Organisation for Economic Co-operation and Development (OECD). (2020, July 29). Coronavirus (COVID-19): SME policy responses. *OECD*. Retrieved from http://www.oecd.org/coronavirus/policy-responses/coronavirus-covid-19-sme-policy-responses-04440101/.

Rahman, A. R. A. (2010). Islamic microfinance: An ethical alternative to poverty alleviation. *Humanomics*, *26*(4), 284–295.

Wasil, W. (2020, May 29). Brunei hotel industry records over $2 million drop in revenue', *The Bruneians*. Retrieved from https://www.thebruneian.news/brunei-hotel-industry-records-over-2-million-drop-in-revenue/.

Winosa, Y. (2020, April 7). Time to mobilise zakat, retail sukuk for Indonesia's COVID-hit MSMEs—KNEKS official. *Salaam Gateway*. Available from https://www.salaamgateway.com/story/time-to-mobilise-zakat-retail-sukuk-for-indonesias-covid-hit-msmes-kneks-official.

Zuhayli, W., El-Gamal, M. A., & Eissa, M. S. (2007). *Financial Transactions in Islamic Jurisprudence* (El-Gamal, M. A., and Eissa, M. S., Trans.). Syria: Dar Al-Fikr.

13 The role of Islamic microfinance in eradicating the impact of COVID-19 on socio-economic wellbeing in Nigeria

Abdullateef Abdulqadir Maikabara, Romzie Rosman, and Habeebullah Zakariyah

13.1 Introduction

The outbreak of COVID-19 has significantly impacted every segment of social and economic life in such a way that the impediment engulfs both business operation cycles and the livelihood of the people. This constitutes a national and international concern about taking the necessary measures to energize the economy and social wellbeing during and after the pandemic. As a result of this, several approaches have been adopted, such as raising charity and relief funds to provide facilities for healthcare, giving interest-free loans in some non-Islamic-based financial institutions, and more.

Microfinance as a financial system is considered one of the tools for ensuring social wellbeing through the provision of financial services for unprivileged, low-income individuals and households. Historically, the modern evolution of microfinance is rooted in the 1970s with the establishment of the Grameen Bank in Bangladesh by Muhammad Yunus. Thus, the success of that banking system led to significant global attention from various governmental and non-governmental organizations willing to adopt the microfinance system to serve the social wellbeing (Al-Shami et al., 2013). In the context of Nigeria, as of 31 December 2019, the Central Bank of Nigeria (CBN), as part of its policies towards the facilitation of socio-economic development, has licensed 913 microfinance banks across the country, but only a small number of the MFBs are Islamic such as Tijara Microfinance, Al-Barakah Microfinance in Lagos State, 36 Kano Microfinance banks, Babura Microfinance in Jigawa State, as well as other non-governmental organizations (NGOs) like Al-Hayat relief foundation in Ogun state, south-western Nigeria, which has more than 40 branches in the southwest and north of the country (Yakubu et al., 2018).

Meanwhile, Islamic microfinance, as an alternative financial institution for the provision of financial services to the unprivileged segment of society, that are excluded from conventional microfinance that is supposed to serve their needs. However, despite having a microfinance system in Nigeria, it has not been able to serve the less advantaged and low-income groups. The report of the Vanguard Nigerian newspapers in 2011 as cited by Muhammad and Mamman (2017) indicated that that the poverty rate in northeast Nigeria accounted for 63.3% of the population while it is 62.9% in the northwest, 62.3% in north-central, while in the south, it was 51%, 42% in the southwest, and 34.3% in the southeast. This report communicated the serious problem with poverty in Nigeria even before the COVID-19 pandemic, which had a significant effect on every social and economic sector around the world. However, in this instance, Islamic microfinance as an ethical and social system has a potential role to play in fighting against the poverty epidemic as most of the studies conducted on the role of Islamic microfinance in Nigeria have shown the positive effect it has on socio-economic wellbeing (Onakoya and Onakoya, 2013; Gumel et al., 2014; Muhammad and Mamman, 2017; Maikabara, 2020).

In light of this, even though the Islamic finance industry is not exempt from the negative effects of the COVID-19 pandemic, as it has affected every single business entity and financial sector, Islamic finance will always potentially present solutions to all the calamities engulfing socio-economic stability as an Islamic system embedded with Islamic principles. This elucidates the universal attribute of Islam as a religion that implicitly or explicitly provides for human needs and wants, most especially at times of severe impediment. Therefore, this present study attempts to investigate the perception of Islamic microfinance in eradicating the effects of COVID-19 on social wellbeing.

13.2 Literature review

13.2.1 Microfinance

Technically, microfinance facilitates financial services for the less advantaged, low-income groups and individuals who are excluded from the mainstream financial system. Accordingly, conventional microfinance somehow facilitates this but with an interest-based paradigm. In contrast, Islamic microfinance aims to provide financial services based on Islamic values and principles to promote justice and wellbeing. In terms of microfinance services, Maikabara (2020) categorized the microfinance services in relation to the needs of the people with micro-credit, micro-equity, micro-savings, micro-transfer, and micro-insurance.

According to Obaidullah and Khan (2008), both conventional and Islamic microfinance have similarities in terms of their socio-development goals and financial inclusion and involvement of people with low incomes in partnership and entrepreneurship. Hence, there are also various distinctions that differentiate them in business practices and operations.

However, the concept of microfinance has been traditionally practised before the 21st century to some extent. Hence, the modern concept of microfinance can be traced back to the 1970s, starting in Bangladesh with the establishment of the Grameen Bank and the Grameen model by Professor Muhammad Yunus. The concept was later replicated by many Islamic and non-Islamic global governments across the world after critical investigation of its tremendous success in serving the wellbeing of those with low incomes (Al-Shami et al., 2013).

More so, Muhammad and Mamman (2017) observed that the operation of Islamic microfinance at that time was quite small in Latin America and South Asia as it aimed to maximize social welfare unlike in conventional banking system. Small loans were granted to millions of people without any conditions such as providing assets, collateral, or insurance. Thus, it is worth mentioning that since the 1970s, remarkable development has been seen worldwide in the sector. As of late, more than 25 million low-income individuals have been served by more than 7,000 micro-lending organizations (MLOs) around the globe (Muhammad & Hasan, 2008). However, Islamic microfinance has gained momentum due to its significant contributions to socio-economic development even though it is still small in capital and assets compared to its conventional counterpart.

13.2.2 Previous studies

Many studies conducted on the role and viability of Islamic microfinance for economic development and social wellbeing have indicated that it has a potentially significant role to achieve socio-economic development. A study by Riwajanti (2013) examined the potential of Islamic microfinance to eradicate poverty in comparison with its conventional counterpart, which has neglected moral and spiritual values. According to Riwajanti, the underlying principle of Islamic microfinance is the Islamic values to promote justice and to achieve economic development. Thus, one of the root factors behind the calamities and disasters is that special attention was not given to ethical consideration even in the Muslim world. It was concluded that improvement in regulation and social development training for microfinance employees and borrowers is necessary for the effective outcome of Islamic microfinance. The four indicators of poverty eradication that were used in this study are income levels, childhood education, healthcare, and business progress. Riwajanti used the purposive sampling method to collect data from 150 borrowers of 20 Islamic microfinance institutions in Central Java, Indonesia. The findings revealed that Islamic microfinance has a significant role in promoting three out of the four poverty eradication indicators (income level, children education and business progress) as it does not show any statistical significance with healthcare.

In Nigeria, a few studies have been conducted on Islamic microfinance as an alternative to conventional microfinance in poverty eradication. However, the Nigerian government has emphasized that Islamic microfinance is a non-interest-based institution while CBN enacted guidelines on the regulation and supervision of Islamic non-interest microfinance banks. A study conducted by Onakoya and Onakoya (2013) surveyed the viability of Islamic microfinance to eradicate poverty and its sustainability in Ogun state, Nigeria. The authors adopted descriptive analysis, ratio analysis, and percentage analysis, while questionnaires and semi-structured interviews were developed. The findings show a high level of acceptance of Islamic microfinance if implemented in the study area without any religious obstacles. It was also found that Islamic microfinance will positively contribute to poverty eradication in Nigeria if a fiscal and monetary policy framework is actively facilitated.

Gumel et al. (2014) examined the impact of Islamic microfinance products on poverty alleviation in northern Nigeria. The results indicated a significant improvement in household income, children's education, and asset acquisition. Meanwhile, Islamic loans, age, level of education, and gender were proclaimed as variables for increasing household income. In the northeast, Muhammad and Mamman (2017), in their study on northeast Nigeria, investigated the perception of Islamic microfinance on poverty eradication to examine the applicability of Islamic microfinance bank solutions to poverty reduction. Four hundred survey questionnaires were randomly distributed to respondents in six states. The criteria considered were that the respondents must fall between the ages of 18 and 61, own a small business, and have an account with one of the twelve conventional microfinance banks. The findings showed that Islamic microfinance would work as a solution to poverty alleviation and increase job creation.

Similarly, due to the limited Islamic financing schemes for many unbanked low-income individuals and low-income families running small businesses to facilitate basic amenities for the household and children's education in Kwara state situated in the north of Nigeria, Maikabara (2020) surveyed the applicability of Islamic microfinance using a questionnaire for data collection from the clients of microfinance banks in Ilorin, the capital city of the state. The findings revealed that Islamic microfinance is applicable to poverty eradication in the study area. Also, the findings indicate that Islamic microfinance has a positively strong correlation with household income, healthcare, education, and employment.

With reference to the above studies, it can be established that Islamic microfinance has an outstanding potential to solve not only socio-economic problems but rather work as a tool to tackle any unprecedented negative incidence that could endanger the socio-economic wellbeing. To support the philosophical ecosystem of Islam microfinance from being a mere hypothesis, a very few empirical studies have investigated the viability of Islamic microfinance in fighting against the unprecedented crisis. This is the gap this study aims to fill, and this study presents a genuine contribution to the field. In light of this, this study seeks to assess the role of Islamic microfinance in reducing the impact of the COVID-19 pandemic on the socio-economic wellbeing in Nigeria, adopting mixed research methods to achieve the objective of the study.

13.3 Methodology

The researchers have chosen to adopt a mixed research methodology to answer the aforementioned research objectives; the quantitative method was adopted to determine to what extent microfinance clients understand the concept of Islamic microfinance. The justification for this is to confidently mitigate any bias in measuring the respondents' understanding level on Islamic microfinance. Meanwhile, the qualitative method was used to establish meaningful interpretations of the respondents' thoughts about Islamic microfinance as a tool for eradicating the impact of COVID-19 on socio-economic wellbeing, giving an in-depth and truthful perception of a certain phenomenon.

13.3.1 Sample design

This study was conducted with the clients of the microfinance banks in Ilorin, the capital and the most populous city in Kwara state. Since the population is unknown, the non-probability sampling technique was adopted, using the convenience sampling method, which is non-probability sampling, to select a perfect sample of the population and generate effective findings. Due to unknown population, a formula recommended by many researchers was used to get a conservative sample size; as a confidence level of 95% was selected with the value of 5%, which resulted to a total number of 384 (Sekaran & Bougie, 2016). The study sample comprises clients, who fall in the age ranges of 18 to 61, and a sample of four people was chosen: two of them are experts in the field and two of them are staff at a microfinance institution. The justification for this was to investigate the role of Islamic microfinance in eradicating the impact of COVID-19 from the expert and industrial perspective. This simple sampling was chosen based on time and convenience constraints.

13.3.2 Data collection and analysis

As for the quantitative analysis, a closed-ended survey questionnaire was used to collect data from the study sample as it would effectively help to facilitate the respondents' sense of confidence and bias in articulating the understanding level. The questionnaire was adopted based on previous studies, and administered using a five-point Likert scale: 1 – strongly disagree (SD), 2 – disagree (DA), 3 – neutral (N), 4 – agree (A), and 5 – strongly agree (SA). In addition, the questionnaire was comprised of 11 items. This was examined after the presentation of the demographic profile of the respondents, which includes: gender, age, marital status, religion, region, education level, occupation, and monthly household income. More so, for the qualitative method, open-ended questions for a semi-structured interview were used for the respondents to express their views on their perception of Islamic microfinance on social wellbeing due to the COVID-19 outbreak. Meanwhile, the data collected through the questionnaire were analyzed on SPSS, version 25, using descriptive statistical analysis of frequency, percentage, mean, and standard deviation. The interviews were transcribed and interpreted using the content analysis method. The findings are presented categorically in accordance with the research questions.

13.4 Findings

13.4.1 Descriptive analysis

According to the findings shown in Table 13.1, the female respondents constitute a higher frequency of 191 (52.5%). This implies financial equality in

Table 13.1 Demographic distributions

Number of respondents		*Percentage %*
Gender	**Frequency**	
Male	176	45.8
Female	208	54.2
Total	364	100
Age		
18–30	174	45.3
31–35	74	19.3
35–40	86	22.4
45–60	45	11.7
60 and above	5	1.3
Total	364	100
Marital status		
Single	135	35.2
Married	243	63.3
Divorced	5	1.3
Widow/Widower	1	0.3
Total	364	100
Religion		
Islam	304	79.2
Christianity	76	19.8
Other religions	4	1.0
Total	364	100
Region		
Rural	40	10.4
Urban	344	89.6
Total	364	100
Educational level		
High school	28	7.3
Diploma/NCE	198	51.6
Degree	148	38.5
Master's and above	10	2.6
Total	364	100
Occupation		
Civil servant	201	52.3
Businessperson	159	41.4
Both	24	6.3
Total	364	100
Monthly household income		
Less than ₦5,000	55	14.3
₦5,000–9,999	30	7.8
₦10,000–19,999	57	14.8
₦20,000–29.999	78	20.3
₦30,000 and above	164	42.7
Total	364	100

Source: Author's Own

the study area even it is observed that most of the clients of the microfinance banks are women with small businesses that need financial support. The age level indicated that the majority are those who fall between the ages of 18 and 30, accounting for 157 (43.1%), which connotes the potential of Islamic microfinance to serve them as well as improve its sustainability to ensure socio-economic development by empowering the youth. In terms of marital status, married respondents dominated the major participation in the survey by 238 (65.5%), as one of the segments of society with a social necessity towards catering for family needs. The findings also indicated that Muslims were the majority who participated. This can be translated that the majority of the Muslim respondents are keen to patronize a microfinance system that would alternatively help them as a way to facilitate their religious practices, which prohibits engaging in interest and unlawful businesses. Meanwhile, 321 (88.2%) shown that a higher response was from the urban area compared to the rural area. This predicted a less concern given to the rural area which requires an exclusive development and social welfare for the betterment of the livelihood of the people living in the area in addition to inspirational orientation as part of the country. More so, the majority of the respondents that accounted for 180 (49.5%) were diploma or National Certificate in Education (NCE) holders having the necessity to further their educational journey to higher-level. In addition, the findings on occupation revealed that civil servants dominated the survey 202 (55.5%) compared to business people at 138 (37.9%). That is, businesspeople were not financially supported by microfinance banks as most of these people are low-income earners with no potential creditworthiness to fulfil their financial obligations. Hence, they can be supported by Islamic microfinance operations through many schemes, apart from lending, most necessarily in the current COVID-19 outbreak, such as the charity-based model using *zakat*, *waqf*, and *Qard-al-Hasaan*. Similarly, respondents with a monthly income of 30,000 Naira and above were the majority of respondents having 163 (44.8%); whereas the least were those earning 5,000–9,9999 Naira accounting for 29 (8.0%) which is slightly different from those whose monthly income was less than 5,000 at a frequency of 36 (9.9%). This means that the last two groups were not actively served by microfinance banks as it contravenes the justice of financial equality. It is imperative to note that even though the majority of the respondents were getting the higher monthly income, which could be converted to an equivalent of USD$100–150; that amount does not constitute their social wellbeing as many of them have more than seven people to cater for before the pandemic started. This necessitates a proactive measure by policy-makers to critically investigate how Islamic microfinance can be applied more effectively to eradicate poverty and alleviate the impact of COVID-19 on social wellbeing not only on economic development. Though Islamic microfinance system has been gaining momentum recently in the country, the government still needs to take the necessary measures to ensure its effectiveness.

However, the statistical analysis of the microfinance clients' level of understanding of Islamic microfinance indicates that the higher percentage of 45.3% of the respondents have an excellent understanding of Islamic micro finance (IMF). Apparently, even though it has been observed that the majority of Nigerians do not have tremendous awareness of IMF, 39.6% of the respondents shows that the majority of them agree that it is a non-interest-based financial system. However, 39.3% of them, being the higher percentage, opined that IMF is only meant for Muslims. This implies that this vital misconception is one of the pertinent challenges to the growth of Islamic finance since its birth in the country. The term 'Islamic' sounds in the minds of non-Muslims to be a strategy to Islamize a multicultural and religious country like Nigeria, whereas engaging in Islamic financial practices does not necessitate becoming a Muslim. Interestingly, the findings of questions 4, 5, and 6, revealed 53.3%, 49.5%, and 55.2% of the respondents, respectively, agreed with the statement that IMF has become a powerful tool to fight against poverty as it has a positive effect on the background of low-income individuals and families as they are given access to financial services while they are being neglected by the interest-based system. Precisely, the results of 48.9% of the micro-credit, 45.9% of the micro-equity, 46.2% of the micro-leasing, and 47.3% of the micro-insurance proved that the application of these Islamic microfinance schemes would facilitate self-employment, increase the income level of low-income groups, serving their needs and protecting them from unexpected occurrences. Interestingly, 45.6% of the respondents accepted that Islamic microfinance is better than conventional microfinance, which operates on an interest-based paradigm. However, the results of the mean (m) and standard deviation (Std. Dev.) indicated that all of the items measuring the respondents' understanding level have an overall mean value that is above 3.00 as the highest was Q4 (m = 4.22; Std. Dev. = 0.789), followed by Q5 (m = 4.13; Std. Dev. = 0.916); Q6 (m = 4.09; Std. Dev. = 0.853); Q11 (m = 4.07; Std. Dev. = 0.891); Q9 (m = 4.06; Std. Dev. = 0.864); Q7 (m = 4.00; Std. Dev. = 0.835); Q10 (m = 3.96; Std. Dev. = 0.937); Q2 (m = 3.96; Std. Dev. = 1.017); Q1 (m = 3.89; Std. Dev. = 1.136); Q8 (m = 3.84; Std. Dev. = 0.921); with Q3 (m = 3.26; Std. Dev. = 1.270) as the lowest item. Hence, these statistical analyses stipulate an outstanding understanding level among the clients of the micfrofinance institutions. That is, Islamic microfinance has a great acceptance level being a non-interest-based micro-financial system serving the needs and wants of the majority of Muslim and non-Muslim less privileged individuals. The findings are supported by various studies that surveyed the importance of Islamic microfinance in eradicating poverty and ensuring social wellbeing (Rokhman, 2013; Riwajanti, 2013; Muhammad T. and Mamman. D., 2017; Maikabara, 2020; Maikabara A.A et.al, 2020).

13.4.2 Interview

This section presents views on the role of IMF to answer research questions two, three, and four, which are to predict the viability of IMF for reducing the significant effect of COVID-19 on the social wellbeing of the people in the Nigerian context.

Table 13.2 Descriptive statistics (frequency, percentage (%), mean and standard deviation)

Items	*SD*	*D*	*N*	*A*	*SA*	*Means*	*Standard Deviation*
I would rate my understanding about Islamic microfinance as excellent	23 (6.3%)	30 (8.2%)	28 (7.7%)	165 (45.3%)	116 (32.4%)	3.89	1.136
Islamic microfinance is a non-interest based system	12 (3.3%)	20 (5.5%)	63 (17.3%)	144 (39.6%)	125 (34.3%)	3.96	1.017
Islamic microfinance is only meant for Muslim customers	50 (13.7%)	55 (15.1%)	63 (17.3%)	143 (39.3%)	53 (14.6%)	3.26	1.270
Islamic microfinance becomes a powerful tool to fight against poverty	5 (1.4%)	11 (3.0%)	19 (5.2%)	194 (53.3%)	135 (37.1%)	4.22	.789
Islamic microfinance products have a powerful impact on economic background of the poor people	8 (2.2%)	21 (5.8%)	20 (5.5%)	180 (49.5%)	135 (37.1%)	4.13	.916
Islamic microfinance provides financial help to low income families or individuals who lack access to interest-based banking services	4 (1.1%)	24 (6.6%)	22 (6.0%)	201 (55.2%)	113 (31.0%)	4.09	.853
Micro-credit of the Islamic microfinance facilitates self-employment for the poor people	2 (.5)	17 (4.7)	63 (17.3)	178 (48.9)	104 (28.6)	4.00	.835
Micro-equity of Islamic microfinance increases the income level of low income group	2 (0.5%)	35 (9.6%)	72 (19.8%)	167 (45.9%)	88 (24.2%)	3.84	.921
Micro-leasing of Islamic microfinance serves the needs of low income group	2 (0.5%)	20 (5.5%)	53 (14.6%)	168 (46.2%)	121 (33.2%)	4.06	.864
Micro-insurance (Takaful) of Islamic microfinance protects low income people from unwarranted events	2 (0.5%)	37 (10.2%)	43 (11.8%)	172 (47.3%)	110 (30.2%)	3.96	.937
Islamic microfinance is better than conventional microfinance	7 (1.9%)	12 (3.3%)	54 (14.8%)	166 (45.6%)	125 (34.3%)	4.07	.891

Source: Author's Own

13.4.2.1 The role of Islamic microfinance in eradicating poverty in Nigeria

Though the respondents ascribe several ideas to the role of Islamic microfinance, all of them agreed on certain dimensions articulating the concept of Islamic microfinance. All four respondents proclaimed the significant role of Islamic microfinance in poverty eradication in Nigeria. Meanwhile, three of them highlighted the financial inclusion aspect of Islamic microfinance, which could be considered one of the main elements that distinguish it from its conventional counterparts as Islamic microfinance to some extent does not exclude low-income groups from financial services just because they are not worthy of financial obligation. Thus, they can be served through charity-based modes of donation, *zakat*, *waqf*, and *qardul-hassan*. One of the respondents noted that Islamic microfinance has a significant role to play in business progress, income improvement, and education in Nigeria.

Respondent A1 had the following to say:

> The roles of Islamic microfinance in Nigeria in terms of reducing and alleviating poverty in Nigeria are many: it has a significant role in business progress, and I think that is so obvious to see as Islamic microfinance does assist small-scale business to stand on their feet. Likewise, there is a significant role in income improvement as well as it has a significant role in education.

Similarly, respondent A2 said:

> In my view, Islamic microfinance, being an ethical financial system embedded with Islamic principles, would surely help in eradicating the predicament of poverty through financial inclusion of many non-bankable Nigerian poor segments of society having no financial standing to access basic amenities and facilitate their small businesses, which are needed for sustenance of their livelihood and promote their children's education.

Respondent B1 said: 'Islamic microfinance has a vital role to play through financial inclusion of less privileged Muslims who are averse to conventional microfinance due to riba and other prohibited elements'.

Similarly, Respondent B2 said:

> As far I know, Islamic microfinance serves all segments of society without exclusion of the poor as Islam does not differentiate between the rich and poor in provision for their needs, so Islamic microfinance would surely serve the country in both micro and macro levels of the economy.

The foregoing discussion concludes the great potential of Islamic microfinance as an effective tool for eradicating poverty in Nigeria by elevating unprivileged people to higher levels of social and economic status through the provision of religious and ethical financing, which is based on Islamic principles and values. Thus, this positive outcome would surely ensure the social peace and economic stability of the country as a whole.

13.4.2.2 The main issues and challenges of Islamic microfinance in Nigeria

In terms of the issues and challenges faced or that could be faced by Islamic microfinance in Nigeria, it can be said that to some extent, there is a consensus in the views of the respondents on the obstacles to the growth of Islamic microfinance institutions in Nigeria. All of the respondents opined that there is a lack of awareness, misconception about the Islamification of the country, which is a multi-religious country, through the Islamic financial system. They also highlighted the issue of funding, the shortage of Islamic scholarship with industrial expertise in the field, as well as the inadequate regulatory framework governing the practice of the Islamic financial system in the country.

The following statements note the respondents' views:

> There are numerous challenges facing Islamic microfinance in Nigeria, particularly. From my own standpoint, one of the biggest challenges is mismanagement of funds, and also the issue of non-payment as some people do not return these loans after collection. Another point is inefficient finance, as most Islamic microfinance in Nigeria lacks sufficient funds to reach more and more active borrowers who need these loans. (A1)
>
> There are many issues that hinder the growth of Islamic microfinance in Nigeria which are: the Islamization of the country, shortage of expertise in the field, lack of awareness and trust, and shortage of funding, as well as inadequate regulatory framework. (A2)

Another respondent mentioned, 'Lack of funding, lack of Islamic microfinance experts, lack of awareness of Islamic microfinance, Islamophobia' (B1).

Also, respondent B2 opined that:

> The main issues that I can highlight here are: misconceptions about Islam and its practices, lack of sufficient scholarship in the field as the Islamic finance industry is still new compared to conventional finance which has been existing in the country for decades.

From the preceding discussion, the respondents seem to agree that the misconception about Islamic finance, in general, is that the non-Muslim Nigerian people see any Islamic agenda or measure to be an attempt to Islamize the country. Hence, this misconception could hinder the growth of Islamic microfinance even though the Nigerian constitution protects the freedom of religion to mitigate any religious conflicts. This issue is related to another issue that can determine the perception of people, which is a lack of public awareness about

Islamic microfinance, although the Islamic finance industry has started to gain more momentum, but is still small compared to the current conventional finance industry which dominates the market. All these translate to the crucial importance of public orientation about Islamic microfinance not just for Muslims, or as a charity tool, but rather a tool for achieving sustainable socio-economic wellbeing. This can be done through social media with cooperation between Islamic finance experts and journalists. Meanwhile, it is worth mentioning the issue of expertise which is considered one of the requirements to navigate the growth and sustainability of Islamic microfinance in enhancing socio-economic development. More so, it seems there is a consensus that a lack of funding seems to be a pertinent challenge for Islamic microfinance from a global level, but might be severe in a country like Nigeria whereby Islamic microfinance has to deal with the first three issues highlighted earlier to gain people's trust in managing their funds in a religious and effective manner, as most of its funds are from savings and charitable sources.

13.4.2.3 How Islamic microfinance can help reduce the impact of COVID-19 in Nigeria

In respect of the negative impact posed by the outbreak of COVID-19 on socio-economic wellbeing, there is a consensus in the perception of the respondents whereby they are of the view that Islamic microfinance can potentially help reduce the impact of COVID-19 through the provision of interest-free loans to small and medium enterprises (SMEs) whose business operations are likely to be affected as one the pillars of economic development. One of the respondents mentioned that Islamic microfinance could be a way to create jobs and finance agriculture in rural areas of Nigeria through interest-free loans. However, it is worth noting that there is tremendous awareness about the Islamic charity-based modes of finance such as donation, *zakat*, *waqf*, and *qardul-hassan* as all of the respondents emphasized these modes as the tools for reducing the impact of COVID-19 on social wellbeing.

For Instance, respondent A1 said:

> In my own view, there are several ways in which Islamic microfinance can come in and rescue people from the impact that COVID-19 has on them in terms of poverty. One of these ways is to create job opportunities, as many have lost their jobs to this pandemic. Islamic microfinance banks can offer some schemes that compensate borrowers and enable them to access more loans. Another way is to finance agriculture as agriculture is mostly practised in rural areas in Nigeria, and Islamic microfinance can help farmers get loans to reduce the hunger that COVID-19 has already created in our society. Agriculture helps to promote the Nigerian economy and Islamic microfinance could be a tool for enhancing this sector. Lastly, I personally think Islamic microfinance can help in social support, which is very important at this hard time as it can be helpful in controlling inflation and the unequal

> distribution of wealth, and I will recommend integrating Islamic microfinance with NGOs, *zakat*, *awqaf*, and *takaful* to fulfil a substantial social support.

Likewise, respondent A2 said that:

> Firstly, I believe that Islamic microfinance as an Islamic-based system would potentially help reduce the effect of the COVID-19 outbreak even though the outbreak has also affected the finance operations of microfinance, but through the charity element of social finance, it would relieve the social well-being of the people in the country by raising normal donations or *zakat* or *waqf* funds to provide financial assistance for the needy poor. Also, all these charity modes can be used to reenergize the operations of the affected part of the economy and facilitate micro-financing for SMEs and promote job opportunities. In the short run, SMEs can be financed through the *qardul-hassan*, which is the benevolent loan to grant respite until the financial condition improves.

Meanwhile, respondent B1 commented:

> Islamic microfinance would definitely reduce the impact of coronavirus by bailing out SMEs with interest-free loans because their business operations are greatly impacted. Also, incorporation of social finance instruments like *zakat* collection and distribution, *sadaqah*, and *waqf* would be of great help as some microfinance institutions do not have this element in their operation.

Similarly, respondent B2 said:

> Even though Islamic finance is not exempt from the negative impact of the COVID-19 outbreak, Islamic microfinance as a non-interest-based financial system can help reduce the impact through an interest-free credit facility or a religious-based donation to help the social wellbeing of small businesses and poor individuals.

The foregoing discussion thus shows the tremendous role that Islamic microfinance can have in response to the significant negative effects of the COVID-19 pandemic in the sense that several Islamic microfinance schemes can be seen to reducing such negative effects on socio-economic wellbeing. One of these is the provision of interest-free loans to SMEs with flexible repayments as well as granting respite as prescribed in Islamic commercial law. Also, it is remarkable that most of the respondents seem to agree with the role of the charity-based model of Islamic microfinance such as *qardul-hasan*, donation, *waqf*, and *zakat* to solve the crisis. It is, however, interesting to note that the charity model seems to be viable as a tool for solving a socio-economic crisis as recommended by many experts and researchers, not just as a way of raising funds to help the livelihood of the those with low incomes, but also as a financing tool to boost the economy and stabilize the social wellbeing of the country as a whole. Hence, it is suggested that the policy-makers and microfinance institutions should effectively structure and manage the denoted Islamic microfinance schemes based on the nature of financial needs for low income groups and small business to ensure sustainable socio-economic wellbeing.

13.5 Conclusion

This study attempts to assess the extent that Islamic microfinance as an alternative financial institution can contribute to the eradication of the significant negative impact posed by the outbreak of COVID-19 on the socio-economic wellbeing. However, the study captured the high level of understanding of Islamic microfinance among customers of microfinance banks. The operation of Islamic microfinance is crucial for ensuring the socio-economic wellbeing as an alternative to the predominant conventional microfinance system in Nigeria. In response to the current socio-economic crisis due to the outbreak of the COVID-19 pandemic, Islamic microfinance can actively serve the economy and society in reducing its negative effects through the provision of financing and social relief under the system of charity-based models such as *qardul-hassan*, donation, *zakat*, and *waqf*. Meanwhile, the private and public policy-makers have to proactively deal with the issues that could stand as obstacles for Islamic microfinance to effectively facilitate its roles in sustainable socio-economic development. Also, they should take exclusive measures in employing Islamic microfinance as an approach to eradicating the socio-economic crisis caused by the pandemic.

References

Al-shami, S. S. A., Majid, I., Rashid, N., & Hamid, M. (2013). Conceptual framework: The Role of microfinance on the wellbeing of poor people cases studies from Malaysia and Yemen. *Asian Social Science*, *10*, 230.

Gumel, G. B., Saad, N. M. D., & Kassim, S. H. J. (2014). Assessing the impact of Islamic microfinance on poverty alleviation in Northern Nigeria. *Journal of Islamic Economics, Banking and Finance*, *10*, 37–49.

Maikabara, A., (2020). Applicability of Islamic microfinance as an alternative tool for poverty for poverty eradication in the Kwara State of Nigeria (Unpublished Master Dissertation). International Islamic University Malaysia (IIUM).

Maikabara, A. A., Aderemi, A. M. R., & Maulida, S. (2020). Investigating the viability of the charity based model of Islamic microfinance for eradicating the impact of covid-19 on social wellbeing in Nigeria: A descriptive analysis. *Journal of Islamic Economics Perspectives*, *2*(1), 114–122.

Mohammed, A. D., & Hasan, Z. (2008). Microfinance in Nigeria and the prospects of introducing its Islamic version there in the light of selected Muslim countries' experience. MPRA Paper 8127, University Library of Munich, Germany.

Muhammad, T., & Mamman, D. (2017). Applicability of Islamic microfinance bank solution to poverty reduction in the Northeast Nigeria. *International Journal of*

Innovative Research and Development, *6*(11), 25–31. doi: 10.24940/ijird/2017/v6/i11/oct17077.

Obaidullah, M., & Khan, T. (2008). *Islamic Microfinance Development: Challenges and Initiatives.* Retrieved from https://papers.ssrn.com/sol3/papers.cfm?abstract_id=1506073.

Onakoya, A. B., & Onakoya, A. O. (2013). Islamic microfinance as a poverty alleviation tool: Expectations from Ogun State, Nigeria. *Scholarly Journal of Business Administration*, *3*(2),36–43.

Riwajanti, N. I. (2013). Islamic microfinance as an alternative for poverty alleviation: A survey. *Afro Eurasian Studies*, *2*(1&2), 254–271.

Sekaran, U., & Bougie, R. (2016). *Research Methods For Business: A Skill Building Approach.* E-book. Retrieved from https://www.wiley.com/en-kg/Research+Methods+For+Business:+A+Skill+Building+Approach,+7th+Edition-p-9781119266846.

Yakubu, S. M., Haruna, M. A., & Mohammed, A. I. (2018). Strategies for the acceptability of Islamic micro finance institutions in Nigeria. *IOSR Journal of Economics and Finance*, 9(6) (II), 71–76.

14 Islamic social finance during economic uncertainty

Special roles of *Ar-Rahnu*

Nor Fadilah Bahari, Mustafa Mohd Hanefah, and Zurina Shafii

14.1 Introduction

The pawnbroking industry in Malaysia has grown significantly, and it started prior to 1811 with the migration of Chinese citizens to Tanah Melayu (Skully, 1992). In the early years of its establishment, most pawn shops were privately owned and for-profit (Ismail & Ahmad, 1997). The majority of them were illegal and unlicenced institutions. Operated as informal credit institutions, pawnshops benefited those who were excluded from mainstream financial institutions. Similar evidence is reported by Caskey (1991) in the United States; pawnshops acts in the credit market. In developing countries, the rural economy still relies on informal financial intermediaries, including pawnbroking institutions that provide cheap financing options (Bouman & Houtman, 1988). Besides, the characteristics of pawnshops offering services without stringent procedures, easy access, and fast approval of loans provide advantages to the borrowers to meet their urgent needs. Discussions on the pawnbroking industry in the literature started in 1988 with a journal article by Bouman and Houtman (1988). They highlight pawnshops as informal institutions that act as rural banks in developing countries. At the end of 1991, an estimated 194 conventional pawnshops operated in Malaysia under the supervision of the Ministry of Local Government and Housing (Skully, 1992). However, the system of conventional pawnshops has been criticized by the Muslim community for several reasons. Hence, Islamic pawnbroking institutions, formally known as *Ar-Rahnu*, have been established in the country and provide continuous advantages to society. Therefore, this chapter highlights matters related to *Ar-Rahnu*, which are divided into four topics. These four topics are the historical development of *Ar-Rahnu* in Malaysia, the legality of *Ar-Rahnu* financing based on the *Quran* and *hadith*, the specialities of *Ar-Rahnu* compared with their conventional counterparts, and the role of *Ar-Rahnu* during economic uncertainties.

14.2 Historical development of *Ar-Rahnu* in Malaysia

In Malaysia's financial market, Islamic pawnbroking institutions are one of the Islamic financial institutions that are currently active in providing gold-based financing to their customers. The first Islamic pawnbroker was set up by the

Terengganu Islamic Religious and Malay Customs Council (MAIDAM) in 1992, known as Muassasah Gadaian Islam Terengganu (MGIT). The MGIT played vital roles in the Terengganu community, especially for women and small entrepreneurs, by providing instant cash based on Islamic principles. The establishment of MGIT was to fulfil the demand from Muslim customers and indirectly to steer Muslim customers away from conventional pawnshops and illegal money lenders. A study by Othman et al. (2013) discovered that the total number of MGIT customers from 2007 to 2011 was 190,810 at a total of nine outlets. The establishment of *Ar-Rahnu* in Terengganu influenced Permodalan Kelantan Berhad (PKB) to set up Kedai Ar-Rahnu (KAR) in March 1992. The action was taken by the Kelantan state government to help their community, especially women entrepreneurs, to obtain micro-financing based on *sharia* rules. The *Ar-Rahnu* industry continued to progress and thrive when the Ministry of Finance introduced '*Skim Ar-Rahnu*' (SAR) through the collaboration of three institutions: Bank Negara Malaysia (BNM), Malaysian Islamic Economy Development, Yayasan Pembangunan Ekonomi Islam Malaysia (YAPEIM), and Bank Kerjasama Rakyat Malaysia Berhad (Bank Rakyat) in August 1993.

YAPEIM was set up in 1976 by the federal government as a foundation under the Trustees (Incorporation) Act 1952. The objectives of its establishment was to facilitate in various types of economic activities, including pawnbroking services and real estate, and provide micro-financing to its clients, especially to lower- and middle-income groups. A part of the profit generated from the businesses was used for welfare programs. Currently, YAPEIM serves its clients nationwide, including Sabah and Sarawak, with 203 branches (YAPEIM, n.d.).

Bank Rakyat is a cooperative bank established in the country that actively provides *Ar-Rahnu* financing besides other bank products such as customer banking, commercial banking, and other investment products. In 2006, Bank Rakyat launched the *Ar-Rahnu* X'Change under the management of Rakyat Management Services Sdn. Bhd. (RMS). The establishment of RMS was to provide franchising opportunities under the *Ar-Rahnu* X'Change brand name. At present, Bank Rakyat is the largest Islamic cooperative bank in Malaysia, with 147 outlets and 183 outlets nationwide (Bank Rakyat, 2019).

The *Ar-Rahnu* industry has been operating parallel with conventional pawnshops in Malaysia's market. The number of both institutions increased over the years due to great support from society. Previous studies reveal that gold-based financing is considered to be the most popular gold-based financial product compared with gold investment (Yaacob et al., 2012). For the conventional pawnshop, business operations are supervised by the Ministry of Housing and Local Government (KPKT) and regulated under the Pawnbroking Act 1972. The introduction of this act was to ensure a healthy pawnshop industry and safeguard the interest of the customers. However, *Ar-Rahnu* is excluded from and not regulated by the Pawnbroker Act because a few sections in the act contradict *shariah* rules. In this act, the pawnbrokers are allowed to impose interest (*riba*) on the borrower, rendering this act incompatible with *Ar-Rahnu* (Nur Hayati

& Markom, 2014). The distribution of pawnshops across the states in Malaysia is uneven, and this may be due to the differences in population densities and demand from the local community (Ismail & Ahmad, 1997).

The total number of *Ar-Rahnu* operators in the country cannot be ascertained. They are regulated and supervised by different regulators and various overlapping statutes and guidelines depending on the registration of the institutions (Nur Hayati & Markom, 2014). To date, *Ar-Rahnu* operators are served by various institutions, including banking institutions and non-bank financial institutions (NBFIs). Under the banking institutions, *rahnu* financing is provided by Islamic commercial banks and cooperative banks. They are supervised under BNM. The NBFIs involve four categories of institution: government link companies (GLC), credit cooperatives, state link companies, and other private companies. They are supervised by different regulatory bodies. The Cooperative Societies Commission of Malaysia (SKM) is authorized to supervise credit cooperatives. Since its establishment, the business of *Ar-Rahnu* has been pioneered by NBFIs institutions. Several *Ar-Rahnu* operators that are currently active in serving *rahnu* financing are shown in Table 14.1.

The statistics and data on the performance of the pawnbroking industry were not collected by BNM in its statistics on total domestic credit. Nevertheless, by exploring the data provided by SKM and a few pawn shops, we can see that *Ar-Rahnu* has

Table 14.1 Ar-Rahnu operators

Commercial Banks	• Bank Islam Malaysia Berhad (BIMB) • Bank Muamalat • Agrobank • Affin Islamic Bank • RHB Islamic Bank
Cooperative Banks	• Bank Kerjasama Rakyat • Rahnu X-Change Bank Rakyat • Bank Koperasi Malaysia
Credit Cooperatives	• Koperasi MAS • Koperasi KOJUTA • Kakitangan Kementerian Pertanian Malaysia Berhad • Koperasi Milik Perbadanan Baitulmal Negeri Sabah • Koperasi Pengguna Pahang Berhad • Koperasi Angkatan Tentera
State Cooperatives	• Ar-Rahnu MAIDAM (Terengganu) • Rahnu Yayasan Bina Upaya (Perak) • Permodalan Kelantan Berhad • Rahnu Koperasi Kerajaan Negeri Kedah • Koperasi Permodalan Melayu Johor
Government Link Companies	• Yayasan Pembangunan Ekonomi Islam Malaysia • Ar-Rahnu TEKUN
Private Companies	• Ar-Rahnu Pos Malaysia • Rahnu Express (Habib Jewel)

Source: Author's own

grown tremendously in the country. In 2019, Bank Rakyat dominated 38 per cent of *Ar-Rahnu* industry in the country (Bank Rakyat, 2019). Additionally, SKM disclosed that the contribution of *Ar-Rahnu* in 2018 by credit cooperatives was about 14.30 per cent from the total income of all sectors in cooperatives (Suruhanjaya Koperasi Malaysia, n.d.). This evidence reveals that *Ar-Rahnu* is highly accepted by Malaysia's community and stimulates positive growth in the country's economy.

14.3 The legality of the *Ar-Rahnu* contract and comparisons between *Ar-Rahnu* operators and conventional pawnshops

The word '*Ar-Rahnu*' that is used to reflect Islamic pawnbroking institutions is derived from the Arabic noun '*rahana*', which means either constancy and continuity or holding and binding. Technically, *ar-rahn*, which also means pawning, mortgage, collateral, charge, lien, and pledge, refers to taking property as security against a debt, whereby the secured property can be utilized to repay the debt in the case of non-payment. The application of *ar-rahn* started during the time of the Prophet Muhammad (p.b.u.h) and its legality is mentioned in the Holy *Quran* and *hadith*: 'if you are on a journey (and then you wish to have a contract of debt with one another) and cannot find a scribe, then let a pledge taken in hand (by the one who provides the debt)' (*Al-Quran*, 2:283).

This verse indicates the alternative means of documenting the debt in the absence of a scribe, i.e., via pawning. Although it was revealed in the context of travelling, the majority of jurists, except *Mujahid* and *Zahiris*, agree that *ar-rahn* is also permissible at home, based on the *Sunnah* of the Prophet (p.b.u.h.) who permitted it without any restriction.

In addition, the permissibility of *ar-rahn* is also mentioned in the following hadith: 'A'ishah narrated that: "The Prophet (p.b.u.h.) bought some food (on credit) from a Jew, and he pawned his iron shield to him"' (Sahih Bukhari, *Hadith No.21* from Bukhari, 1966).

From the above evidence, the *ar-rahn* principle is permissible in Islam. Generally, *ar-rahn* is considered as a charitable contract as it does not require any financial obligation on the part of the creditor. However, the parties in the contract are obligated to fulfil the pillars and several conditions in the contract in order for the *ar-rahn* contract to be valid. The pillars involve the contracting parties, *sighah*, pawning object (*marhun*), and the liability or debt (*marhun bih*). Table 14.2 lists the descriptions of each pillar in the *ar-rahn* contract.

The basic structure of *ar-rahn* financing starts when the borrowers pawn their valuable asset to obtain finance from the *Ar-Rahnu* operators. Occasionally, *Ar-Rahnu* operators may take an asset like jewellery, ornaments, or any valuable item as collateral. However, currently, contemporary applications may involve a form of paper, such as property documents, vehicle papers, *sukuk*, shares, and others. The creditor or mortgage provider will provide financing according to the specific percentage from the value of the *marhun*. Practically, the margin of financing is up to 70%–80% of the value of the *marhun*. The borrowers are required to pay

Table 14.2 Pillars of *ar-rahn*

Borrower (*al-rahin*)	A party that borrows money from another party by using a valuable asset as collateral.
Creditor (*al-murtahin*)	A party that lends money to another party and is responsible for the safety of the asset pledged by the borrower. The contract should be accepted by both parties.
Pawn items (*marhun*)	Items pawned as collateral.
Financing amount	The amount of financing needed by the borrower.
Contract (*sighah*)	The agreement between the pledger and pledgee.

Source: Author's own

safekeeping fees or storage fees to the creditors as a condition precedent to enter into the contract. The imposition of storage fees is for the risk of taking care of the *marhun* (Ahmad et al., 2019). The pledged items will be taken under the custody of *Ar-Rahnu* operators until the customers settle their debt and redeem the asset. At the end of the maturity period, the borrowers are required to pay back the debt, and the pawning asset is returned to the customers. In the event of a default, the asset will be liquidated by the creditors to settle the outstanding balance. In order to safeguard the operation, *Ar-Rahnu* operators provide their own guidelines and operating procedures. For example, SKM introduced '*Garis panduan Aktiviti Pajak Gadai Islam*', GP 25, in 2013 as guidance to all credit cooperatives to conduct the business of *Ar-Rahnu* in an orderly and prudent manner.

In July 2019, BNM issued a policy document on *Ar-Rahnu* to strengthen the practice among the Islamic commercial banks to comply with the rules of *shariah* in the product and operationalization of *Ar-Rahnu*. This policy document sets out the *shariah* matters and operational requirements of *Ar-Rahnu*. For the *shariah* requirements, the silent features and optional practices of valid *shariah* contracts are highlighted in this policy. BNM, through the *Shariah* Advisory Council of BNM (SAC), in its 198th and 199th meeting in October 2019 continued to improve the current structure of *Ar-Rahnu* by introducing a ruling on *Ar-Rahnu* financing under the contract of *tawarruq*. This proposed product structure intended to replace the existing *Ar-Rahnu* product in the market.

Over the years, regulatory bodies related to the *Ar-Rahnu* industry continuously kept an eye on the current business operations in *Ar-Rahnu* and on *shariah* matters. Although *Ar-Rahnu* and conventional pawnshops provide similar services, *Ar-Rahnu* has its own standard and unique features that cater to their customers, especially in the Muslim community.

14.4 Comparisons between *Ar-Rahnu* and conventional pawnshops

In Malaysia, conventional pawnshops predate Islamic pawnbroking by a few decades. The comparisons between both systems have been extensively discussed in the literature. The existence of *shariah* was the main element that distinguished *Ar-Rahnu* from conventional pawnshops, and it is the primary factor for customers' acceptance of *Ar-Rahnu* (Razak, 2011; Hamid et al., 2014) *Ar-Rahnu* is trusted by its customers as one of the Islamic institutions that provide financing in accordance with *shariah* rules. The funds are derived from permissible sources and free from elements of *riba*. This is in contrast with the services provided by conventional pawnshops, which impose *riba* in loans and their sources of funds are controversial. The existence of *riba* elements increases the burden on customers to repay the loan, thus causing dissatisfaction among society (Ismail & Ahmed, 1997). The Muslim community gradually became aware that the conventional system was against the principles of Islam. The religious awareness and growth of Islamic finance in the country influenced Muslim customers to ask for Islamic pawnbroking institutions (Ḥanudin et al., 2007).

Besides the elements of *shariah*, *Ar-Rahnu* imposes a lower storage fee than conventional pawnshops. Studies by Appannan and Doris (2011) and Cheong and Sinnakkannu (2012) assert that lower storage charges are found to be one of the factors that influence customers to accept *Ar-Rahnu*. The service charge imposed by *Ar-Rahnu* is reasonable and much lower compared with conventional pawnshops. In conventional pawnshops, customers have been charged a minimum of 24 per cent a year for storage fees. This increases the burden on customers, primarily those in the lower-income group. In addition, in cases of default, conventional pawnshops impose extra charges on the borrower. This situation does not occur in *Ar-Rahnu* in which the storage fee (*ujrah*) imposed is reasonable and is in accordance with the rules of *shariah*. A study by Azman et al. (2016) mentions that service charges are among the main factors that influence women micro-entrepreneurs to choose *Ar-Rahnu* as their source of micro-credit.

Studies by Amin and Chong (2011), Ahmad et al. (2012), and Baharum et al. (2016) reported that management practices and quality services were the main factors for customers to prefer *Ar-Rahnu*. They claim *Ar-Rahnu* provides more ethical and better quality services. In the practice of conventional pawnshops, surplus from the auction process is not returned to the client. In some cases, pawned goods worth more than RM200 were auctioned by unethical pawnshops without notifying clients. There have been cases of pawnbrokers who do not auction goods off but takes possession of them instead. This is against Section 23(1)(b) of the Pawnbrokers Act, in which any collateral worth more than RM200 should be auctioned off by a licenced auctioneer (Razak, 2007). In contrast with the practice of *Ar-Rahnu*, if the customer is unable to pay back the loan at the maturity period, *Ar-Rahnu* provides more lenient terms by allowing customers to postpone the settlement period with lower fees. But in the event of a default, the pawned assets will be auctioned. Proceeds from the auction process will be used to pay debts, and the remaining balance from the auction will be returned to the client. *Ar-Rahnu* operators are permitted to take out only the equivalent amount of borrowed money. This action shows the practices of *Ar-Rahnu* to be transparent and accountable in providing services to the clients.

Prior studies have shown that *Ar-Rahnu* holds a special value and benefits their customers compared to its conventional counterparts. The core values of *Ar-Rahnu* are not only to make a profit but to achieve *maqasid shariah* (objectives of Islamic law). In parallel with its growth, the *Ar-Rahnu* industry has contributed significantly to Malaysia's economy.

14.5 The role of *Ar-Rahnu* during economic uncertainty

In a broader perspective, *Ar-Rahnu* has been declared as one of the Islamic microfinance institutions in the country, and it has strong performance at the community level. Primarily, microfinance institutions are recognized as a tool of economic innovation in combating poverty and serving the lower-income community. The evidence as seen in developing countries, where the rural economy still relies on informal financial intermediation like the pawnbroking system and significant instruments that minimize transaction costs (Bouman & Houtman, 1988). The existence of *Ar-Rahnu* provides an attractive alternative to the local banking system. The contribution of *Ar-Rahnu* as an Islamic pawnbroking institution in the country's economy is indisputable. At present, *Ar-Rahnu* serves two functions: as financial and social intermediation. The activities involve the provision of micro-financing, informal appraisal of borrowers and investments, collateral substitutes, streamlined loan disbursement and monitoring, and secure financing.

Traditionally, *Ar-Rahnu* operators were located in rural areas, and the majority of *Ar-Rahnu* clients were among rural communities, small-scale entrepreneurs, women, and middle-class borrowers (Razak, 2007; Ismail & Ahmad, 1997; Mokhtar & Zambahari, 2013). Furthermore, it had been used mainly by cash-strapped individuals and unbankable customers who had been excluded from mainstream financial institutions. There has been a higher demand by local societies for *Ar-Rahnu* due to its flexibility compared to formal financial providers. *Ar-Rahnu* was the best credit alternative to overcome its customers' money shortages. The flexible services, minimal credit evaluation, and fast credit approval were factors that made *Ar-Rahnu* the best choice for its customers (Skully, 1992). A customer can visit *Ar-Rahnu* to pawn their assets and leave with cash in hand within minutes without having a stringent credit assessment and enduring the waiting period required for the approval of financing. Furthermore, *Ar-Rahnu* provides means, especially during critical times (Shukor & Sabri, 2013). A study from Othman et al. (2012) found that more than 50 per cent of the respondents use *Ar-Rahnu* services to settle unexpected problems, 21 per cent for working capital requirements, and 11 per cent to set up new businesses and others. Formal financial institutions are only accessible to the most creditworthy borrowers that generally belong to middle- and high-income groups (Sanusi & Johari, 2007; Ahmad et al., 2012).

Despite the financial intermediation role, *Ar-Rahnu* plays its social obligation in serving the community by helping them to finance educational needs, medical cost, develop agricultural sectors and village industries (Nur Hayati & Markom,

2014). This is supported by Ahmad et al. (2012), who mention that about 14.2 per cent from 330 respondents pledged with *Ar-Rahnu* for education purposes. It is because of low-income salary and self-employment of some of the respondents. Moreover, the existence of small loans by pawnshops become imperatives in helping their customers to improve family wellbeing. Households with lower monthly incomes tend to visit pawnshops to cover health expenditures.

Furthermore, the minimal credit requirements and reasonable storage fees of *Ar-Rahnu* compared with the high-interest charge on loans by illegal businesses or unlicensed financial activities provide convenience to customers, especially to the rural community. In some cases, *Ar-Rahnu*, such as MAIDAM, provides financing without imposing any cost on the value of the asset pawned if it is worth less than RM2000. These elements attract more customers, mainly Muslim communities, to get financial assistance through *Ar-Rahnu* due to the application of the *sadaqah* concept and its social obligation towards the local community. The involvement of rural customers with *Ar-Rahnu* indirectly prevents them from being oppressed by illegal businesses such as loan sharks.

While the pawnshop industry is synonymous with lower-income groups, the current market segment of *Ar-Rahnu* not only serves those groups but also expands to the high-income group, especially businesses or corporations. Interviews with several *Ar-Rahnu* bank executives and gold dealers reveal that the market segment for *Ar-Rahnu* has expanded to serve high-class customers who are more educated and wealthier, especially gold buyers and business entities. For small and medium entrepreneurs, micro-financing from *Ar-Rahnu* is used to meet their liquidity purposes and sources of capital injection for their businesses (Ismail & Ahmad, 1997). Regarding this, Rafidah et al. (2017) mention that the majority from a sample of 206 customers prefer to use *Ar-Rahnu* to fulfil their needs in gold investment and business capital. *Ar-Rahnu* provides advantages to small scale entrepreneurs, primarily when they face financial difficulties in their business. Similar evidence by Zhou et al. (2016) shows that the pawnbroking industry will continue to contribute an essential role in financing SMEs in China in the foreseeable future.

14.6 Conclusion

The role of the pawnbroking industry will continue to be discussed and receive attention from society during the COVID-19 pandemic. This pandemic is not only related to a health crisis, but it is also affecting societies and the economy of the country. Recently, whole sectors worldwide, including Malaysia, were jeopardized by the crisis. The majority of sectors were unable to operate as usual due to the implementation of the movement control orders (MCO) by governments. This action increased the unemployment of Malaysia's to 3.9 per cent, which is the highest rate since June 2010 (Department of Statistics of Malaysia, 2020). Jobs were lost, and small entrepreneurs were badly affected. For some individuals, employers stopped paying their employees' salaries and did not provide any financial support to their employees. For small businesses, they were forced to stop business operations which led to declining profit. They had to find solutions to survive, and one of the actions taken was to turn to the pawnbroking system.

Several local newspapers reported long queues at pawnshops. Several customers started to visit conventional pawnshops and *Ar-Rahnu* as immediate sources of quick cash for several purposes, such as to support their daily needs, pay for medical expenses, for their festival season, and reserves for any unforeseen consequences in the future. Some customers went to the pawnshops to extend the financing period as they could not repay their debt. Besides that, some of the customers took advantage of the rising gold price in the global market. They utilized the pawnbroking services to gain profit. They started to pawn their assets, mostly jewellery, to get a higher amount of financing and invested in gold to gain profit. However, utilizing pawnshop services as tools for generating profit was not discovered much in the previous literature.

In summary, previous findings reveal that the industry of pawnbroking, including *Ar-Rahnu*, contributes an important role as a financial intermediary and has a social obligation in Malaysia's economy. They provide credit assistance even during critical times. Previous studies have proven that the pawnshop industry is an essential tool to boost economic growth and counteract the economic instability in the country. It provides ways to solve financial exclusion in Malaysia's economy. Therefore, it is crucial to ensure that the pawnbroking industry operates efficiently and is sustained in the market.

References

Ahmad, K. A., Bahari, N. F., Ahmad, N. W., & Shahar, S. S. (2019). An overview of the Shariah issues of Rahn: Based financing in Malaysia Shariah issues of Rahn-based financing. *Journal of Muwafaqat*, *2*(1), 15–29.

Ahmad, S. A. B., Mansor, N., & Nadiah, A. N. (2012). Customer acceptance on Islamic pawn broking: A Malaysian case. *Interdisciplinary Journal of Contemporary Research in Business*, *3*(10), 748–763.

Amin, H., & Chong, R. (2011). Determinants for ar-rahnu usage intentions: An empirical investigation. *African Journal of Business Management*, *5*(20), 8181–8191.

Appannan, S., & Doris, G. (2011). A study on Islamic pawn broking awareness and factors influencing the scheme in Sungai Petani. Retrieved from https://econpapers.repec.org/paper/cms2icb11/2011-271.htm.

Azman, N. H. N, Kassim, S., & Adeyemi, A. A. (2016). Role of ar-rahnu as micro-credit instrument in achieving financial self-sufficiency among women micro-entrepreneurs. *Intellectual Discourse*, *24*. Retrieved from https://journals.iium.edu.my/intdiscourse/index.php/id/article/view/925.

Baharum, N. N. B., Maamor, S., & Othman, A. (2016). Examining the factors that influence customer's intention to use ar-rahnu at post office : A case study in Kedah. Retrieved from https://platform.almanhal.com/Reader/Article/84743.

Bank Rakyat. (2019). Serving the community and nation. *Annual Report 2019*. Kuala Lumpur, Malaysia.

Bouman, F. J. A., & Houtman, R. (1988). Pawnbroking as an instrument of rural banking in the third world. *Economic Development & Cultural Change. Economic Development and Cultural Change*, *37*(1), 69–89.

Bukhari, M.I.I. (1966). *Sahih Bukhari*. Karachi: Muhammad Sarid.

Caskey, J. P. (1991). Pawnbroking in America: The economics of a forgotten credit market. *Journal of Money, Credit and Banking*, *23*(1), 85–99.

Cheong, C. W. H., & Sinnakkannu, J. (2012). Ar-rahnu: Opportunities and challenges in Malaysia. *Social Science Research Network*. Retrieved from https://papers.ssrn.com/sol3/papers.cfm?abstract_id=2112809.

Department of Statistics of Malaysia. (2020). *Key Statistics Of Labour Force In Malaysia*. Retrieved from https://www.dosm.gov.my/v1/index.php?r=column/cthemeByCat&cat=124&bul_id=Y3NVdE44azFHbzkyeFlaWGF2ZER6Zz09&menu_id=U3VPMldoYUxzVzFaYmNkWXZteGduZz09.

Hamid, M. A., Rahman, I. A., & Halim, A. N. A. (2014). Factors affecting the acceptance on ar-rahnu (Islamic based pawn broking): A case study of Islamic banking in Malaysia. *A Multidisciplinary Journal of Global Macro Trends*, *2*(4), 144–160.

Hanudin, A., Rosita, C., Hazlan, D., Rostinah, S., Amin, H., Chong, R., Dahlan, H., Supinah, R., Hanudin, A., Rosita, C., Hazlan, D., & Rostinah, S. (2007). An ar-rahnu shop acceptance model (ARSAM). *Labuan E-Journal of Muamalat and Society*, *1*, 82–94.

Ismail, A. G., & Ahmad, N. Z. (1997). Pawnshop as an instrument of microenterprise credit in Malaysia. *International Journal of Social Economics*, *24*(11), 1343–1352. doi: 10.1108/03068299710193633.

Mokhtar, I., & Zambahari, S. R. (2013). Ar rahnu: A short term financing alternative. 5th Islamic Economics System Conference (IECONS 2013), September, 863–871.

Nur Hayati, R., & Markom, R. (2014). An overview on implementation of ar-rahnu in Malaysia. *Prosiding PERKEM*, *9*, 561–570.

Othman, A., Hashim, N., & Abdullah, S. (2012). Customer satisfaction levels of service quality at ar-rahnu, Kelantan. Retrieved from https://www.semanticscholar.org/paper/CUSTOMER-SATISFACTION-LEVELS-OF-SERVICE-QUALITY-AT-Othman-Hashim/061b56a2315b4da9d51ea8c0911502bd989f5514

Othman, A., Hashim, N., Abdullah, S., & Perniagaan, K. (2013). Perkembangan Ar-Rahnu di Terengganu: Kajian Kes Terhadap Ar-Rahnu Majlis Agama Islam dan Adat Melayu Terengganu (MAIDAM). *Prosiding Perkem Viii*, 2, 951–959. Retrieved from http://www.ukm.my/fep/perkem/pdf/perkemVIII/PKEM2013_4A4.pdf.

Razak, A. A. (2007). *Malaysian Practice of Ar-Rahnu Scheme: Trends and Development*. Retrieved from http://www.assaif.org/ara/content/download/1490/16172/file/Islamic%20Pawnbroking.pdf.

Razak, A. A. (2011). *Economic and religious significance of the Islamic and conventional pawnbroking in Malaysia : Behavioural and perception analysis* [Durham E-theses, Durham University], 1–296.

Sanusi, N. A., & Johari, M. S. (2007). Permintaan Perkhidmatan Pajak Gadai: Perspektif Pengguna. *Malaysian Journal of Consumer and Family Economics*, *10*, 20–29.

Shukor, S. A., & Sabri, H. (2013). Customer satisfaction towards Islamic pawnbroking (ar-rahnu): Antecedents and consequences. *Global Journal of Commerce and Management Perspectives*, *2*(6), 29–36.

Skully, M. T. (1992). The development of the pawnshop industry in East Asia. *East Asia*, 357–374.

Suruhanjaya Koperasi Malaysia. (n.d.). *Statistik Interim Gerakan Koperasi*. Retrieved from https://www.skm.gov.my/index.php/my/mengenai-skm/gerakan-koperasi/statistik-gerakan-operasi/statistik-interim.

Yaacob, M. R., Ahmad, G., & Ibrahim, M. D. (2012). Developing a customer oriented ar-rahnu(Islamic pawn broking) model for cooperatives in microfinancing in Malaysia. Retrieved from https://pdfs.semanticscholar.org/f77b/da8ef2de9cb2b9bb42b13e3099bf4089f1df.pdf.

YAPEIM (Yayasan Pembangunan Ekonomi Islam Malaysia). (n.d.). *Yayasan Pembangunan Ekonomi Islam Malaysia (YAPEIM)*. Retrieved from https://www.yapeim.my/.

Zhou, L., Yao, S., Wang, J., & Ou, J. (2016). Global financial crisis and China's pawnbroking industry. *Journal of Chinese Economic and Business Studies, 14*(2), 151–164. doi: 10.1080/14765284.2016.1173465.

15 Profit-loss sharing principle

The strategic answer of solidarity in Islamic finance

Amira Kaddour, Badri Narayanan Gopalakrishnan, Mohamed Bechir Belaid, and Mohammad Nurunnabi

15.1 Introduction

The coronavirus pandemic has deeply affected the global economy. The adverse impact of COVID-19 on communities is expected to reverse years of progress toward development goals and tip tens of millions of people back into extreme poverty. Additionally, the unemployment rate has greatly increased in countries that were economically stable before the outbreak. These countries are Japan, Germany, UK, Canada, France, Italy, and the US (Jones & Brown, 2020). Park et al. (2020), however, estimates that the GDP reduction from the baseline may be much stronger, at between 5.7 and 8.7 trillion USD globally, or 6.7%–9.6% of global GDP, with developed countries and China facing the largest brunt of this recession, amounting to a 7%–10% reduction in GDP in many of these countries. The United Nations Conference on Trade and Development (2020) came up with an even more dire prediction that global tourism losses alone may amount to between 1.2 and 3.2 trillion USD, depending on whether a third of the year's tourism is wiped out, or a whole year is wiped out. Therefore, the total losses could be higher than these predicted losses. Numbers aside, there is an overwhelming conclusion that this is a serious global economic downturn, almost unprecedented for several decades now.

The UN imposed the sustainable development goal of eliminating poverty by 2030. Now, because of the current health and economic crisis caused by COVID-19, scholars have estimated the first increase in global poverty since 1990 (Sumner et al., 2020). A report published by UNU-WIDER, focuses on the impact of the current pandemic on people living in poverty within developing countries. This report concluded that a 5% contraction in per capita incomes would force more than 80 million people into the $1.9/day (USD) poverty line. This concentration of the newly poor would take place in the poorest places of the world (Sub-Saharan Africa and South Asia) where two-third of world's poor population is found (Sumner et al., 2020).

Additionally, it is predicted that poverty will be everlasting for the poor, in contrast to middle- and upper-income populations (World Bank, 2020). The four conditions that influence this prediction are the location of the household, work location, dependency on public services, and limited savings. In the context of developing countries, we find that poverty rates are higher in rural areas and therefore, access to public health services are limited. This is very concerning given the ongoing health crisis. Additionally, those with low incomes living in urban areas will be affected as well since they tend to be located in crowded settlements with low-quality services. This will only lead to a faster transmission rate. People on low incomes also tend to be part of the informal economy, which is the group that faces the most severe consequences. These people will be without access to any government aid. Additionally, those employed in the gig economy are the most vulnerable to slipping into poverty.

The limitations of public services will also immediately harm those with low income as most of them depend on free health services or school dinner programs. In the long term, these two factors could be devastating for future generations. Furthermore, limited savings of companies and households can be depleted and due to the pandemic it might be a challenge to replenish their depleted saving.

Many scholars and development advisors have jumped to provide solutions for the ongoing situation. The profit-loss sharing principle (PLS) of Islamic finance (IF) has been highlighted as a possible global solution. The current financial situation in many countries has left entire communities without stable incomes. The inclusion of the PLS principle of IF could improve the economic situation of these affected people.

The sudden reduction of economic flow has deeply affected welfare services in developing countries. One solution that many policymakers have been looking at has been an imposition on those with upper-income levels to share their profits with the low-income groups in this time of crisis. The United Nations Development Program (UNDP) plans to include this financial system in the economic response to the current pandemic through a range of financing tools addressing each stage. *Zakat*, an obligatory donation from individuals earning above a certain threshold for charity, could be the main resource as a short-term solution. This measure could be a solution as developing economies do not possess savings and are not in receipt of tax revenue. Individual philanthropy is expected to have a direct positive effect on the living situation of affected families. Corporate philanthropy could help companies return to business. Additionally, businesses will benefit from the expertise and experience of their new partners. Next, a medium-term solution is the alignment of the Islamic financial institutions with the UN Sustainable Development Goals (SDGs) as the coronavirus pandemic makes these goals more urgent. Finally, a long-term solution is the distribution of *sukuk*, the equivalent of bonds in the West. *Sukuk* can be the basis of long-term capital for governments and companies affected by COVID-19. IF has the potential to provide solutions required at the time of crisis as well. As such, this is an opportunity for policymakers to implement non-Western solutions globally. In the following, we will investigate the importance of and challenges faced by IF by applying PLS in such conditions.

15.2 Corporate social responsibility of financial Institutions: Islamic banks versus conventional banks

Climate change, alongside poverty, represents an important issue to be mastered in the coming years. Thinking in terms of economic growth alone is no longer enough in view of the importance of the role played by the financial institutions and its strategic role in society as a creator of wealth and employment, but also as a responsible economic agent regarding the environment. Green plans which are comprehensive environmental strategies that are intended to improve environmental quality and make rapid progress towards sustainability launched in the 1990s have highlighted the importance of the theory of negative externalities; respecting the environment and controlling the use of resources are factors of productivity and competitiveness for corporations in which all stakeholders must be involved. Several approaches for green plans have emerged, from the analysis of the lifecycles of products and services from an eco-design perspective, the analysis of the environmental impact of the company's activity to the analysis of the corporate social responsibility (CSR) performance of the entity. Socially responsible investments respond to companies' strategies and choices of engagement with these challenges in order to encourage those committed and put pressure on those less involved to get invoved in CSR.

Carroll (1979) highlights through a four-part model that CSR encompasses the economic, legal, ethical, and philanthropic expectations placed on an organization by society at a given point in time. Economic factors are related to the organization's main role as a producer of goods and services necessary for the wellbeing of society. This reflection is not contradictory with the economic objective of the organization to create profit and financial performance. At this level, Burke and Logsdon (1996) state that CSR is a strategic way for an organization to improve its public image image as well by depicting a positive brand image.

In an increasingly vulnerable economic context, the continuity of a company's activity is an economic factor with a strong societal impact that the company must protect through a legitimate profit-seeking approach. Vulnerability and economic complexity, as well as the great need for innovation, explain the ethical principles of CSR, which are of great importance and usefulness at the present time. The abusive use of resources, the digital transition with the great possibilities provided by artificial intelligence and others, emphasizes the importance of ethics in economic activity that will go beyond the legal framework defined by the law.

The principle of philanthropic responsibility is not mandatory for the company but can be framed as the responsible behaviour of the company towards society or the state. Granting donations or carrying out voluntary actions are indirectly linked to the ethical principle that heads the deontology of Caroll's pyramid.

Several debates have discussed the usefulness of CSR from different perspectives including the company's perspective as well as social and ethical perspectives. Freeman (2010) has shifted the focus of all strategic thinking in a study from shareholder satisfaction to the satisfaction of stakeholders, including shareholders, employees, the state, and society. Quairel (2004) presents CSR within the framework of the theory of legitimacy; in effect, the company communicates its CSR activity in order to respond to potential pressure to disseminate an image that can positively influence stakeholders to benefit even outside the sustainability of these actions. Lin et al. (2019) have shown that the company's role in job creation is a factor with a positive impact on the firm's financial profitability; this result is generalized across all sizes of companies and economic sectors. Cho et al. (2019) confirms that it is not only the profitability of the company which is positively affected, but the reputation of the company is also strengthened.

15.3 CSR for financial institutions

Financial institutions play a key role in financing the economy, contributing to the creation of wealth, and improving the living conditions of citizens through loans. Sustainable development and reducing poverty are great issues. Panigrahi and Sukla (2016) stipulate that 'Financial service companies acknowledge that what's beneficial to society can profit the business'. Reputation and trust are two determining factors in the banking industry, in this sense, CSR in the banking sector has another purpose.

In times of social, economic, and environmental upheavals, the banking sector finds itself at the heart of a primordial role of building the financial capacity of citizens through specific programs supervised by the government. Contributing to economic recovery after such periods is a factor related to banks' CSR (Singh & Agarwal, 2013). Wu and Shen (2013), found that CSR is positively associated with financial performance in terms of return on assets, return on equity, net interest income, and non-interest income and CSR negatively associates with non-performing loans. Hence they concluded that therefore, strategic choice is the primary motive of banks to engage in CSR (Wu & Shen, 2013).

Stanislavská et al. (2012) studied the philanthropic activity of a sample of banks during the subprime mortgage crisis period, and they highlighted the dependency between funds raised; despite this crisis period, the bank's CSR activity was not impacted. Before the subprime mortgage crisis, banks were not concerned about their social responsibility, alongside their impact on the environment, which can be quantified through the financing of projects with a large carbon footprint (Novokmet & Rogošić, 2016).

Based on Caroll's pyramid, FijbBkowska et al. (2017) classified pyramid principles with respect to the banking industry. Economic stability, contributing to the owner(s)' wealth, and mastering the bank's management are linked to the economic dimension of pyramid principles. Legal factors in the pyramid principles include the degree of satisfaction of prudential regulations and the efficient monitoring of bank risk, which will always remain a systemic risk. This dimension is crucial to establishing confidence in the banking sector after the subprime mortgage crisis. The ethical dimension remains important in the banking sector, principles of integrity, transparency, and affinity must be applied by bank employees; depositors will have faith in dealing with such employees. The philanthropic dimension has the same definition as it also has a positive impact on the reputation of the bank (Pratihari & Uzma, 2018).

15.4 CSR in Islamic banks and the reputation dimension

Opting to be a client of an Islamic bank (IBs) is done, in the first instance, based on an ideology of excellence. IBs are called upon to offer, monitor, and maintain financial services that respect a core concept of principles determined by the *shariah* (Cebeci, 2012). The *Shariah* Compliance Committee is the supervisor of good practice. In this sense, CSR within an IB has a greater dimension than in conventional banks; the core of the difference between the two is a moral difference that is manifested in all possible contracts and services and frames their exercise and functioning. In this sense, the ethical dimension is more than decisive here, based on the importance of this factor for any activity (Caroll's pyramid), the moral and ethical concepts are hence, the essential elements of customer attraction and choice.

Haniffa and Hudaib (2007) stipulate that social and ethical factors in the IBs have the same level of importance as making profit, in this sense improving general wellbeing is crucial and is the top level of the bank's preoccupations. For Dusuki (2008), this social responsibility is more important than profitability factors; CSR actions are initiated regardless of their positive or negative financial impact.

In this work we discuss the primacy of the PLS principle in the case of IBs' response to the COVID-19 crisis. Seen in the case of CSR, bearing the burden of risk with the client, is the full expression of solidarity and social responsibility (Usmani, 2002). Dusuki (2008) insists on the Islamic paradigm of CSR, which is based on moral values and this basic statement that defines the activity of the IB is not always confirmed between theory and practice (Kamla & Rammal, 2013). Several studies have attempted to quantify the good practice of CSR according to its Islamic paradigm based on published reports, and these studies have noted the existence of a difference between what is announced and what is actually done (Abbott & Monsen, 1979; Fatma et al., 2014; Ruf et al., 1998; Turker, 2009).

Zafar and Sulaiman (2019) state that moral factors have supreme value for IBs under the Shariah principles of viceregency (*khalifah*) that all humans in this world are sent by God to worship him and live in the manner prescribed by him as his vicegerent and God-consciousness where humans ought to know that God is watichig over every action done by humans in this world and once we die, there is another world (*akhirah*) where we have to be accountable for our actions. Philanthropy, charity, and promoting sustainability are also a target of IBs (Rawashdeh et al., 2017; Ullah et al., 2014). For Aziz and Mohamad (2016) IBs must conceive of services and products that reduce and curb poverty and avoid bankruptcy; this role is seen as a primary role but also tacitly as a manifestation of CSR. While conventional banks have recently been working on defining the rules for measuring good CSR practices, or defining their drivers, IBs are ahead in this domain. Williams and Zinkin (2010) and Franzoni and Allali (2018) explain the great synergy of IB ethics with global standards and the UN agenda.

This competitive advantage, which has its proponents and defendants regarding climate, environmental, and poverty challenges, is to be further nuanced since it can attract potential clients without any religious bias. It is in this sense that the opportunity afforded to IBs through CSR is illustrated, under the strict condition of remedying the reputational problem of divergence between theory and practice.

15.5 *Shariah* board role and responsibility

IBs offer only shariah compliant products and services unlike the conventional banks. The financing modes used by IBs can be divided into two main categories which are commercial and investment products.

In offering commercial products, IBs are operating in this case as intermediary traders. Currently, they are offering two major products which are *murabahah* and *ijarah*. The meaning of the word '*murabahah*' is sale contract with profit margin and there are several conditions to accepting this product such as the known cost of the goods, fixed period of reimbursement, fixed profit margin, no delay penalties, execution of two independent contracts where the first contract is made between the bank and the supplier to obtain possession of the goods and the second one is between the bank and the customer as the final owner. In the case of *ijarah* we are talking about lease contracts, and the transfer of ownership will be after the reimbursement period in a separate contract.

An example of an investment deposit product offerd by IBS are investment accounts which are equivalent to conventional banks' saving and fixed deposit accounts. These investment accounts are structured using a Shariah contract called the *mudharabah* contract.. In a *mudharabah* contract, IB is the *mudharib* who is the manager of the money deposited by the customer who is the capital provider (*rabb al-mal*) where the parties agree to do a shariah compliant business to derive profit. In this contract, it is a Shariah requirement for the partes to pre-agree to a profit shariah ration and any financal loss, except in the case of negligence, will be borne by the capital provider.

Product conformity is one of the most important ways to distinguish between these financing modes and those of conventional banks. That is why each Islamic bank must have what we call a *shariah committee* to observe and control this conformity.

15.6 *Shariah* committee

The *shariah* committee is an independent committee consisting of members qualified in both *shariah* and banking. The minimum number of members is three members, and they are assigned by the bank's board of directors. Committee decisions are mandatory for top management and all bank employees. The role of Shariah committee can be assimilated by external control or audit as they are working for a fixed period or mandate. The problem faced by this committee is a divergence in decisions due to different interpretations of the jurisdiction. This challenge is not related to Islamic banks across countries, but it can be found in the same financial market. For example, in the same country we can find one product allowed by an Islamic bank but prohibited by another. As a result, there is a misunderstanding of IF products and confusion among customers that will limit industry growth and propagation.

One of the possible solutions to this constraint is to have an apex Shariah council at the regulatory authority's level to harmonize the views among the individual Islamic financial institutions. In this case instead of a committee it is called a council to differentiate between the Shariah advisory body in individual financial institutions and that established by the regulatory authorities. For example, in Malaysia, Bank Negara Malaysia (central bank) has formed a Shariah Advisory Council pursuant to Central Bank of Malaysia Act 2009. The function of this apex Shariah Advisory Council is not only to advise the individual Islamic financial institutions operating in the market, but in case of dispute of Shariah compliance of any of the Shariah compliant products/services offered by Islamic financial institutions, it is the view of the apex Shariah Advisory Council's opinion given on the matter will prevail and this opinion will be binding not only on Islamic financial institutions; but on judges and arbitrators as well.

From a regulatory and risk perspective, this conformity is related to the reputational risk of the bank since it is affecting the image and the notoriety of Islamic banks as a whole. As a consequence, the operational risk of the bank will be highly weighted in the capital adequacy ratio. This means an adequate risk management framework must be produced to avoid a serious crisis. In the same context, we find that Islamic banks are not exempt from the financial crisis. Below, we present two case studies about a serious crisis in Islamic finance. The objective is to show that without adequate risk management, Islamic banks are also exposed to the consequences of financial and economic crisis.

15.7 Islamic finance and crisis

When financial markets are facing a financial and economic crisis, the Islamic finance industry is not exempt from the consequences of such turbulence. We will present two case studies related to this topic. The first is of an Islamic bank, and the second is linked to a capital market product, *sukuk*, or Islamic bonds.

15.7.1 The case of Ikhlas Finance Bank

Ikhlas Finance was an Islamic bank operating in the Turkish financial market. In 2001, the country was facing a serious financial crisis. The idea was that IBs would not be seriously affected by the financial crisis because of their products had risk sharing between the bank and its customers. But the reality was far from this because this bank failed in the same crisis period. This nightmare was related to several factors. One of the main reasons for its failure, which is common to all

IBs, is liquidity penury. The institution had no access to central bank resources and the deposit growth was not large enough to cover all the bank's needs. Moreover, the bank had no diversification strategy to manage risk or to prevent a crisis. For example, the deposit structure was insufficient. The investment accounts were larger than the current accounts so that the bank resources were very costly. The consequence of such mismanagement was the failure of this Islamic bank.

15.7.2 The Case of Nakheel Sukuk

The term '*sukuk*' refers to Islamic bond capital market products. Contrary to conventional products, they are considered as equity and not a debt instrument. After the 2008 subprime mortgage crisis, in 2009, the Islamic finance world faced a serious crisis with the default of *Nakheel sukuk*. *Nakheel sukuk* is a Subai based *sukuk* which was issued on *Ijarah manfaa* (leasing of asset and receiving rent) basis, where the *sukuk* holders' obtained the leasehold interest of the primary assets without transferring the title of the assets to the *sukuk* holders via SPV. In this sukuk structure, the *sukuk* holders had only the right to the stream of income generated by the assets but not on the assets themselves. It was issued on December 2006 for a period of 3 years maturing on 15 December 2009 to raise USD$3.52 billion. The proceed of the *sukuk* was used to to finance a property development project of Nahkeel Co. PJSC . In 2009, it is said that the 'entire Islamic debt market froze' (Mohammed, 2014) when it was announced that this *sukuk* need to be restructured and due to the liquidity issued faced by the originator. The reasons for this liquidity issue faced was due to huge short term borrowings of the originator, fall in oil prices, real estate price bubble burst and due to liquidity mismatch created in trying to match short term liabilities with long-term receivables from the property development project (Al Mahmoud et al., 2017; Wong, 2015). Luckily in this case, In December 2009, Abu Dhabi, also an emirate of the UAE, granted the originator a USD$10 billion loan to repay some of its debts and this loan was used to refund the *sukuk* holders their principal amount at maturity date, and the *sukuk* were redeemed (Wong, 2015).

These two case studies must be noted by the Islamic finance industry, especially in the context of this pandemic, that will probably result in a serious financial and economic recession. Appropriate risk management and diversified financing modes can be one of the ways to overcome this situation and for Islamic banks to have an important market share.

15.8 PLS is the core answer for Islamic banks to the COVID-19 crisis: risks and opportunities

Solidarity and complementarity are the core principles that govern all investment and financing contracts in Islamic finance. To avoid interest *(Riba)*, the lender shares a level of risk with the borrower that may impact the value of the profits earned. While this principle gives a great impetus for differentiating Islamic banking from conventional banking and makes it unique.

The profit sharing contracts that can be used include *musharakah* (joint venture) and *mudharabah* (profit sharing) contract partnership are the basic contracts used. In a WB study (2017), the statistics show that the use of *musharakah* and *mudharabah* contracts in Islamic banking represent 1.7% and 4.2% of total contracts used, while *murabahah* and deferred sales are about 78.5%, and leasing and hire purchase represent 10.8%. For Abdul-Rahman and Nor (2017), applying this principle is very critical for considering the problem of customers' creditworthiness, partner profile, lack of capital security, and the high level of investment risk. Mohd Nor and Ismail (2020) state that by analyzing market trends in Malaysia, Islamic bankins are using more non-PLS contracts such as *tawarruq* (monetization). Chapra (2007) presents the *musharakah* contract as the true spirit of financing in Islam, where the entrepreneur will not solely bear the loss and the common welfare of all parties participating in the contract are balanced.

The COVID-19 crisis has affected every country in the world and has had a negative impact on all sectors (other than Information and communications technology; ICT) and companies of all sizes, in this sense, contributing to economic recovery is not only an economic plan but also a plan of solidarity and shared societal responsibility, which requires greater flexibility measures. Thus, the reaction of IBs to a higher burden of risk or loss must be more apparent in order to reassure customers and prove the true ethics on which Islamic ideology is based. According to the economic outlook drawn up by the World Bank and the International Monetary Fund, underdeveloped and developing countries will be the countries most adversely affected by the COVID-19, and small- and medium-sized enterprises (SMEs) will struggle to recover based on a very short liquidity situation and limited financial equilibrium. In addition to the basic principles of *shariah* compliance, IBs must ensure their continuity through profit-generating products. This decision is totally legitimate, as refining the choice of customers helps to protect depositors.

However, in an unusual period such as the post-COVID-19 period, an unprecedented global pandemic that caused work to stop for months, banks' CSR is designed to boost economic recovery. For debt-based and leased-based financing, delaying and rescheduling of annuities is a measure that has largely been taken by conventional banks and IBs.

Trust, confidence, and transparent information exchanged between parties who are partners are crucial for PLS contracts. IBs must scale up their capabilities to assess customers' creditworthiness and profile. A new algorithm proposed by artificial intelligence opens up prospects to improve financial analysis based on a large volume of data as well as black-box models. Overcoming the limits of the assessment of applications is important, but also agreeing to boost innovative risky sectors falls within the economic responsibility of the bank.

The role of PLS is to maintain an acceptable risk level to be shared between the bank and its customers. Unfortunately, in the current pandemic crisis, some IBs did not assume their responsibilities as client partners and there was a misapplication of this principle in their transactions. Most customers are already facing serious liquidity problems due to the pandemic. The risk will not be shared but assumed by one party, which is the client. IB will have to share risk with the client as PLS principle in this context means these financial institutions must manage their liquidity risks according to Islamic finance guidelines and focus on the client as a partner not a debtor. This behaviour, if not revised, will present a reputational risk to those banks in the post-crisis period and may decelerate the growth rate of this industry.

15.9 The need for policy and regulatory support: the threat of reputational risk

The Basel Committee on Banking Supervision (BCBS), the Islamic Financial Services Board (IFSB), and the Accounting and Auditing Organization for Islamic Financial Institutions (AAOIFI) drew up a list of the risks faced by IBs. Ginena (2014) explains that the possibilities of *shariah* non-compliance are costly for the institution, in addition of financial losses and bank run. Reputational risk is at the top level of risk due to the nature of IF. If the Islamic banking principles are not applied through a choice of contracts and products to be invested, the IB will face such risk, and there will no longer be any difference between IBs and conventional banks, so the IB will lose its credibility in the face of this distinction, which is a basic element in attracting clients.

PLS contracts must be increased in the general portfolio of the banks. At this level, the CSR of IBs requires a more judicious role in these turbulent times. The COVID-19 pandemic appears to be the most serious contemporary crisis, heralding a new cycle of challenges. The prospects for the mega-trends in 2030–2050 clearly explain the challenges that humanity will face in the near future, in terms of pandemics, climate change, and the disappearance of professions due to the creation of new professions based on innovation.

To ensure *shariah* compliance, IBs are governed by a supervisory committee. As mentioned previously, this committee ensures the good practice of the Islamic spirit at the core of the bank's practice. Regarding the challenges that the IB may face, the *shariah* committee needs to boost the degree of resilience of the IB in order to ensure their role in financing SMEs and clients in times of difficulty (Rehman, 2020).

15.10 Conclusion

PLS is a core principle of Islamic banking, and its role in the COVID-19 pandemic is crucial. Therefore, the number of debt based Islamic banking products need to be minimized. Applying PLS effectively can boost social welfare, reduce unemployment and create wealth. Islamic financial institutions must review their model in order to overcome the limits of increasing their PLS contract portfolio. Applying good practice and the ideology of solidarity at the heart of Islam will attract more new customers. However, the cost of *shariah* non-compliance is considerable regarding the reputational risk that Islamic banking faces. In a period of green and digital transition, where the spirit of entrepreneurship and innovation is valued, bankers in general need to review their model in order to boost this transition and finance start-ups and SMEs, in the face of competition from new financing models linked to FinTech such as crowdfunding. The PLS principle can play a major role in financing and can contribute to a considerable increase of IF market share.

References

Abbott, W. F., & Monsen, R. (1979). On the measurement of corporate social responsibility: Self-reported disclosures as a method of measuring corporate social involvement. *Academy of Management Journal*, *22*, 501–515.

Abdul-Rahman, A., & Nor, S. M. (2017). Challenges of profit-and-loss sharing financing in Malaysian Islamic banking. *Geografia-Malaysian Journal of Society and Space*, *12*(2), 39–46.

Al Mahmoud, H., Bakhsh, M., & Aref, S. (2017). Sukuk defaults – Country wise analysis. Retrived from https://ifinanceexpert.wordpress.com/tag/nakheel-sukuk/.

Aziz, N., & Mohamad, O. Bin. (2016). Islamic social business to alleviate poverty and social inequality. *International Journal of Social Economics*, *43*(6), 573–592. https://econpapers.repec.org/RePEc:eme:ijsepp:v:43:y:2016:i:6:p:573-592.

Burke, L., & Logsdon, J. M. (1996). How corporate social responsibility pays off. *Long Range Planning*, *29*, 495–502.

Carroll, A. (1979). A Three-dimensional conceptual model of corporate performance. *Academy of Management Review*, *4*, 497–505.

Cebeci, I. (2012). Integrating the social maslaha into Islamic finance. *Accounting Research Journal*, *25*(3), 166–184. https://econpapers.repec.org/RePEc:eme:arjpps:v:25:y:2012:i:3:p:166-184.

Chapra, M. U. (2007). The case against interest: Is it compelling? *Thunderbird International Business Review*, *49*, 161–186.

Cho, S. J., Chung, C., & Young, J. (2019). Study on the relationship between CSR and financial performance. *Sustainability*, *11*, 343.

Dusuki, A. W. (2008). What does Islam say about corporate social responsibility. *Review of Islamic Economics*, *12*(1), 5–28.

Fatma, M., Rahman, Z., & Khan, I. (2014). Multi-item stakeholder based scale to measure CSR in the banking industry. *International Strategic Management Review*, *2*, 9–20

FijbBkowska, J., Zyznarska-Dworczak, B., & Garsztka, P. (2017). The relation between the CSR and the accounting information system data ? The evidence of the Polish financial institutions. *Accounting and Management Information Systems*, *16*(4), 490–521.

Franzoni, S., & Allali, A. A. (2018). Principles of Islamic finance and principles of corporate social responsibility: What convergence? *Sustainability*, *10*, 1–11.

Freeman, R. (2010). *Strategic Management: A Stakeholder Approach*. Cambridge: Cambridge University Press. doi:10.1017/CBO9781139192675.

Ginena, K. (2014). Shari'ahah risk and corporate governance of Islamic banks. *Corporate Governance*, *14*, 86–103.

Haniffa, R., & Hudaib, M. (2007). Exploring the ethical identity of Islamic banks via communication in annual reports. *Journal of Business Ethics*, *76*, 97–116.

Jones, L., & Brown, D. P. (2020). *Coronavirus: A Visual Guide to the Economic Impact*. Retrieved from https://www.bbc.com/news/business-51706225.

Kamla, R., & Rammal, H. (2013). Social reporting by Islamic banks: Does social justice matter? *Accounting, Auditing & Accountability Journal*, *26*, 911–945.

Lin, L., Hung, P. H., Chou, D. W., & Lai, C. (2019). Financial performance and corporate social responsibility: Empirical evidence from Taiwan. *Asia-Pacific Management Review*, *24*, 61–71.

Mohammed, N. (2014). Defaulting on Sukuk: Penalties, and Restructuring. Retrived from https://www.sukuk.com/education/defaulting-sukuk-penalties-restructuring-3534/#/?playlistId=0&videoId=0.

Mohd Nor, A., & Ismail, S. (2020). Profit and loss sharing (PLS) and non-PLS financing in Malaysia: Which one should be the one? *KnE Social Sciences*, *2020*, 14–25. doi: 10.18502/kss.v4i6.6585.

Novokmet, A. K., & Rogošić, A. (2016). Bank sustainability reporting within the GRI-G4 framework. *Zeszyty Teoretyczne Rachunkowości*, *88*, 109–123.

Panigrahi, C. M. A. A., & Sukla, T. N. (2016). Sustainable corporate social responsibility in financial institutions and banks in India. Retrieved from https://papers.ssrn.com/sol3/papers.cfm?abstract_id=2736814.

Park, C.-Y., Villafuerte, J., Abiad, A., Narayanan, B., Banzon, E., Samson, J., Aftab, A., & Tayag, M.C. (2020). *Updated Assessment of the Potential Economic Impact of COVID-19*. Retreived from https://www.adb.org/sites/default/files/publication/604206/adb-brief-133-updated-economic-impact-covid-19.pdf.

Pratihari, S. K., & Uzma, S. H. (2018). CSR and corporate branding effect on brand loyalty: A study on Indian banking industry. *Journal of Product & Brand Management*, *27(1)*,*57-78*..

Quairel, F. (2004). Responsable mais pas comptable: analyse de la normalisation des rapports environnementaux et sociaux. *Comptabilité Contrôle Audit*, *1*(10), 7–36.

Rawashdeh, O., Azid, T., & Qureshi, M. (2017). Philanthropy, markets, and Islamic financial institutions: A new paradigm. *Humanomics*, *33*, 563–578.

Rehman, A. A. (2020). Islamic finance takes on COVID-19. *United Nations Development Program*. Retrieved from https://www.undp.org/content/undp/en/home/blog/2020/islamic-finance-takes-on-covid-19.html.

Ruf, B. M., Muralidhar, K., & Paul, K. (1998). The development of a systematic, aggregate measure of corporate social performance. *Journal of Management*, *24*, 119–133.

Singh, R. K., & Agarwal, S. C. (2013). Does CSR orientation reflect stakeholder relationship marketing orientation? An empirical examination of Indian banks. *Marketing Intelligence & Planning*, *31*, 405–420.

Stanislavská, L. K., Margarisová, K., & Šťastná, K. (2012). Corporate social responsibility in banking sector. *Acta Universitatis Agriculturae et Silviculturae Mendelianae Brunensis*, *60*(2), 157–164.

Sumner, A., Hoy, C., & Ortiz-Juárez, E. (2020). Estimates of the impact of COVID-19 on global poverty. *United Nations University*. Retrieved from https://www.wider.unu.edu/sites/default/files/Publications/Working-paper/PDF/wp2020-43.pdf.

Turker, D. (2009). Measuring corporate social responsibility: A scale development study. *Journal of Business Ethics*, *85*, 411–427.

Ullah, S., Jamali, D., & Harwood, I. (2014). Socially responsible investment: Insights from Shari? A departments in Islamic financial institutions. *Business Ethics: A European Review*, *23*, 218–233.

United Nations Conference on Trade and Development. (2020). Covid-19 and tourism. *Economic Consequences*. Retrieved from https://unctad.org/en/PublicationsLibrary/ditcinf2020d3_en.pdf.

Usmani, M. M. T. (2002). *An Introduction to Islamic Finance*. Retrieved from https://muftitaqiusmani.com/en/books/PDF/An%20Introduction%20To%20Islamic%20Finance/An_Introduction%20_to_Islamic_Finance.pdf.

Williams, G., & Zinkin, J. (2010). Islam and CSR: A study of the compatibility between the tenets of Islam and the UN global compact. *Journal of Business Ethics*, *91*, 519–533.

World Bank. (2020). Projected poverty impacts of COVID-19 (coronavirus) . Retrieved from https://www.worldbank.org/en/topic/poverty/brief/projected-poverty-impacts-of-COVID-19.

Wong, S.N. (2015). Sukuk Bankruptcies: East Cameron and Nakheel case studies. Retrived from https://www.google.com/search?q=nakheel+sukuk+default&rlz=1C1GCEU_enLK819LK819&oq=nakheel+sukuk+default&aqs=chrome..69i57.3674j0j4&sourceid=chrome&ie=UTF-8#

Wu, M., & Shen, C. (2013). Corporate social responsibility in the banking industry: Motives and financial performance. *Journal of Banking and Finance*, *37*, 3529–3547.

Zafar, M. B., & Sulaiman, A. A. (2019). Corporate social responsibility and Islamic banks: A systematic literature review. *Management Review Quarterly*, *69*, 159–206.

Index

access to finance 41–42, 46–56
Aisya 19, 20
Allah (SW) 10, 171
Al-murtahin 218
Al-rahin 218
Al Rajhi waqf model 4, 133–135, 137–139, 141, 143–145, 147
Alzheimer's disease 24, 38
AN OVA 26, 28, 34–35, 42
anti money laundering (AML) 95
Ar-Rahnu 5, 214–224
artificial intelligence 3, 4, 12, 91, 95–98, 101–102, 104–105, 107, 109, 111–114, 146, 227, 233
asset backed 93, 98

Badan Wakaf Indonesia (BWI) 15
BaitulMaal wat Tamwil (BMT) 16, 181
BaitulMaal Wat Tamwil Institutions (BMTIS) 4, 168
Bank Negara Malaysia 17, 20, 215, 231
Bantuan Prihatin Nasional (BPN) 15
Bantuan Sara Hidup (BSH) 15
Bayruha 136, 155
Bitcoin 20, 94–96
black swan event 9
block chain 12, 18, 20–22, 91, 94–95, 97–100, 102–105, 109–112
BWallet 96

Cash Waqf 14–15, 131, 137, 146–147, 155, 189
charitable sector 10
civic engagement 3, 58–59, 63, 65, 68–69
consumer risk 35, 49, 52
conventional bank 201, 227, 229–230, 232–234
conventional microfinance 16, 187, 199–202, 206–208, 212
conventional pawnshops 214–215, 217–219, 222
Coronavirus 1–235
corporate social responsibility (CSR) 65, 177, 227
COVID-19 1–235
credit scoring 41, 56
crisis management 61, 65, 67–70
crisis management system 3, 58–61, 65, 67
crowdfunding 15, 29, 91, 94–95, 98, 102, 118–120, 129, 130, 171, 235
cryptocurrency 18, 94

deposit-taking institutions policy 42, 46, 49, 51–52, 55
digital payment system 96–97, 101, 103
donation 4, 10, 13–14, 18, 63, 66, 115–131, 138, 146, 187, 191, 208, 210–212, 226–227

Eid 11
eKYC 95–96, 98
encouraging policy 42, 46–47, 49, 51–53, 55
environmental impact 82, 227
ethical finance 93, 101

faith based 3, 58
family network 61–62
Fard-al-Kifaya 67
financial assistance 12, 68, 169–170, 173, 181, 186, 188–191, 195, 211, 221

financial capacity 2, 24–39, 46, 228
financial constraints 12
financial exploitation 24–25, 38–39
financial inclusion 40–57, 92, 95, 97–104, 114, 160, 172, 208
financial literacy strategy (FLS) 42, 208
Fintech 1, 3–4, 18, 20, 56, 91–114, 235
fiscal policies 10, 86
Freecycle Abu Dhabi and Dubai 14

general financial strategy (GFS) 42
Gharar 93, 94, 100
Global Islamic and Sustainable Fintech Center' (GISFC) 95
governance structure 59, 192
green sukuk 17–18, 20
Grocery Gift 14

Hawl 11

Ijarah 93, 230, 232
Ikhlas 231
Infaq 3, 10, 16, 62, 70, 171
interest free loan 11, 16–17, 62, 199, 210–211
International Labour Organization (ILO) 9, 115
International Monetary fund (IMF) 60, 104, 158, 226
IoT 60, 91, 97–100, 102
Islamic bank 19, 42, 55, 73, 92, 99, 101–102, 139, 171, 176, 181, 191, 193, 197, 216, 223, 229–235
Islamic Development Bank 11, 22, 138, 145
Islamic fintech 3, 91–95, 97, 99, 101, 103–104, 114, 146
IslamicFintech4SD 3, 95, 99–101
Islamic microfinance 2, 5, 16, 75, 102–103, 165, 169–170, 181, 183–184, 197–203, 205–213–220
Islamic P2P lending 91
Islamic social capital 4, 167–182
Islamic social finance 1–5, 9–11, 15–19, 21, 23, 58–59, 61, 63–65, 67, 70, 89, 138, 145, 168–169, 172, 174, 177–182, 184–187, 189, 191, 193, 195–197, 214–215, 217, 219, 221, 223
Islamic social finance tools 4, 11, 17, 19, 186
Islamic social safety nets 10, 21

joint guarantee 10

Kafala 11
KhazanahNasional Berhad 18, 21
Khums 61, 63–64, 68, 70, 74

Land Waqf 137
large scale solar (LSS) 18
leadership 3, 56–61, 70
lending facility 26–35

Maisir 93–94, 100
Malay Customs Council (MAIDAM) 215
Maqasid al Shariah 10, 19
Martyrs of Harim 60, 70
Martyrs of health 60, 70
Mazhab 19
microfinance 2, 5, 10, 16–17, 19, 41–42, 44–53, 63, 68, 75, 102–103, 165, 168–170, 181, 183–184, 189, 197–213
microfinance strategy (MFS) 42
micro small medium enterprises (MSMEs) 185
mobile applications 11
Mosques (Masjed) 63
Mouwasat 61
movement control order (MCO) 12
Muassasah Gadaian Islam Terengganu (MGIT) 235
mudharabah 11, 17, 230, 233
Mukhairiq 136
murabah 93, 157–159
musharakah 11, 233
mutual assistance 10
MySalam 15, 21

Nafas campaign 62
national development strategy (NDS) 42
national financial strategy (NFS) 42
new normal 14, 17, 97
next generation 41, 56
non-financial civic engagement 59, 63, 65, 68

operational risk 26–28, 31–35, 43, 48–49, 51–52, 174, 231
Ottoman Empire 14, 137

pandemic 1–5, 9–17, 20–21, 23–25, 36–37, 40, 43, 54–55, 58–73, 76–87, 92, 100, 115–116, 120, 122, 127
Pawnbroking Act 1972 215
Payoneer 97
PayPal, Stripe 97

POS payments (Point of Sale) 97
poverty alleviation 3, 14, 22, 103–104, 114, 134, 137, 141, 145–147, 183, 195–235
priority lending policy 41–42, 46–47, 49–53, 55
profit and loss sharing system 5, 93, 171, 174, 235

Qardhasan 11, 61–63, 68, 70–73, 75, 178–179

Ramadan 20, 23, 61, 73
rapid financing instrument (RFI) 58
Regtech 98, 100
rent campaign 62, 64
reputational risk 231, 234
requirement policy 41–42, 45–47, 49–50, 52–53, 55
riba 36, 113, 120, 207, 228, 239
risk exposure 2–3, 24, 40–45, 47, 49, 51, 53, 55, 57

Sadaqat 1, 10, 13–19, 61, 68, 70–71
Securities Commission Malaysia 17, 22, 150, 163
shariah 12–13, 18–19, 103, 149–163, 183, 190–198, 215–235
shariah board 230
shariah committee 230, 234
shariah compliance 151, 156, 226, 231, 233–234
sighah 217, 218
SINEGY and LuxTag 18
social impact 4, 22, 80, 145, 148–163, 182
social impact bond (SIB) 149
social impact Sukuk (SIS) 4, 149
social responsibility investments (SRIs) 163, 235
societal support 58, 66–68
SPV (Special purpose Vehicle) 157, 232
Square and Bindo 97
standard operating procedure (SOP) 40
Sukuk 4, 11, 15–23, 148–161, 163, 198, 217, 226, 231
Sukuk Ihsan 18, 21
Surviving Hijab 14
sustainable development 1–3, 10–11, 18, 24, 40, 55, 65, 74, 76–104, 142, 156, 169, 173, 189, 225, 226, 228

Ta'aawun 178
Tabarru 10
Takaful 10, 15–15, 103, 178, 207, 211
Takaful and Karma scheme 15
tax incentive, savings schemes policy 46, 49, 52, 55
tech-savvy youth 15
Tenaga Nasional Bhd (TNB) 32

UAE Fusion Socialites 14
Ummah 19, 67, 104, 106, 133–134, 136, 141, 144–145
United Nations Development Programme 12

value based intermediation (VBI) 37

Waqf 1, 4, 10, 14–15, 17–23, 131, 133–139, 141–147, 150, 154–158, 160, 162–163, 169, 172–174, 181, 187, 189–190, 192–197, 205, 208, 210–212
WAQF Chain & Ensany Sadaqah 19
Waqf management institution 15
Waqil (Agent) 157, 159
World Bank 10, 15, 22, 26, 28, 39–40, 42, 55–56, 58, 75, 101, 122, 129, 132, 138, 147, 161, 184, 225, 233
World Health Organization (WHO) 9, 67, 76, 133
World Zakat Forum (WZF) 12

zakat 1, 3–4, 10–14, 16, 18–23, 61, 68, 91, 99, 101, 104–114, 146–147, 157, 159, 161, 169, 171–174, 178–181, 187–190, 192, 194–197, 205, 208, 210–212, 226
zakat al fitr 11–12
zakat al maal 11
zakat management system 91, 107, 113
zakat tech 18, 20